Drew McShane was a man with a plan.

It was nearly three years since he and Kim Campion entered into their marriage of convenience to give her baby a name. Surely that was enough time to begin reconsidering their make-believe marriage.

Drew didn't regret his decision to marry Kim. He loved little Hannah with all his heart. And, despite the difference in their social status, he and Kim had always been inseparable, even as children.

So when she'd come to him, pregnant and worried, and asked him to marry her…saying no had never crossed his mind.

But now, more and more lately, Drew found himself thinking about their marriage.

He wanted more.

He wanted the real thing.

And he wanted it…with Kim.

Dear Reader,

It's the most festive time of the year! And Special Edition is celebrating with six sparkling romances for you to treasure all season long.

Those MORGAN'S MERCENARIES are back by popular demand with bestselling author Lindsay McKenna's brand-new series, MORGAN'S MERCENARIES: THE HUNTERS. Book one, *Heart of the Hunter,* features the first of four fearless brothers who are on a collision course with love—and danger. And in January, the drama and adventure continues with Lindsay's provocative Silhouette Single Title release, *Morgan's Mercenaries:Heart of the Jaguar.*

Popular author Penny Richards brings you a poignant THAT'S MY BABY! story for December. In *Their Child,* a ranching heiress and a rugged rancher are married for the sake of *their* little girl, but their platonic arrangement finally blossoms into a passionate love. Also this month, the riveting PRESCRIPTION: MARRIAGE medical miniseries continues with an unlikely romance between a mousy nurse and the man of her secret dreams in *Dr. Devastating* by Christine Rimmer. And don't miss Sherryl Woods's 40th Silhouette novel, *Natural Born Lawman,* a tale about two willful opposites attracting—the latest in her AND BABY MAKES THREE: THE NEXT GENERATION miniseries.

Just in time for the holidays, award-winning author Marie Ferrarella delivers a *Wife in the Mail*—a heartwarming story about a gruff widower who falls for his brother's jilted mail-order bride. And long-buried family secrets are finally revealed in *The Secret Daughter* by Jackie Merritt, the last book in THE BENNING LEGACY crossline miniseries.

I hope you enjoy all our romance novels this month. All of us at Silhouette Books wish you a wonderful holiday season!

Sincerely,
Karen Taylor Richman
Senior Editor

Please address questions and book requests to:
Silhouette Reader Service
U.S.: 3010 Walden Ave., P.O. Box 1325, Buffalo, NY 14269
Canadian: P.O. Box 609, Fort Erie, Ont. L2A 5X3

PENNY RICHARDS
THEIR CHILD

SPECIAL EDITION®

Published by Silhouette Books

America's Publisher of Contemporary Romance

This book is for Andrew Tyler Richards, my handsome, precious baby D. Love you.
A special thanks to Florence Moyer, whose pointed comments opened up new possibilities.

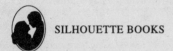 **SILHOUETTE BOOKS**

ISBN 0-373-24213-1

THEIR CHILD

Copyright © 1998 by Penny Richards

This edition published by arrangement with Harlequin Books S.A.

® and TM are trademarks of Harlequin Books S.A., used under license. Trademarks indicated with ® are registered in the United States Patent and Trademark Office, the Canadian Trade Marks Office and in other countries.

Printed in U.S.A.

Books by Penny Richards

Silhouette Special Edition

The Greatest Gift of All #921
Where Dreams Have Been #949
Sisters #1015
*The Ranger and the Schoolmarm #1136
*Wildcatter's Kid #1155
Their Child #1213

*Switched at Birth

Previously published under the pseudonym Bay Matthews

Silhouette Special Edition

Bittersweet Sacrifice #298
Roses and Regrets #347
Some Warm Hunger #391
Lessons in Loving #420
Amarillo by Morning #464
Summer's Promise #505
Laughter on the Wind #613
Sweet Lies, Satin Sighs #648
Worth Waiting For #825
Hardhearted #859

Silhouette Books

Silhouette Christmas Stories 1989
"A Christmas Carole"

PENNY RICHARDS,

of Haughton, Louisiana, describes herself as a dreamer and an incurable romantic. Married at an early age to her high school sweetheart, she claims she grew up with her three children. Now that only the youngest is at home, writing romances adds an exciting new dimension to her life.

To love one maiden only, cleave to her,
And worship her by years of noble deeds,
Until they won her; for indeed I knew
Of no more subtle master under heaven
Than is the maiden passion for a maid,
Not only to keep down the base in man,
But teach high thought, and amiable words
And courtliness, and the desire of fame,
And love of truth, and all that makes a man.

—*Idylls of the King*
Alfred, Lord Tennyson

Chapter One

Gerald Campion stood with his arms crossed over the top rail of a white board fence, watching a field of young Thoroughbred foals cavorting in the warmth of the Louisiana springtime sun. Despite some recent money problems, life was good. Still, he couldn't help worrying now and then, and lately the focus of that worry was his younger daughter, Kim.

Kim had been the proverbial mother hen since her mother died, always checking on him, making sure he was taken care of, always the dutiful daughter. And since the latest fiasco involving a high-priced stud he co-owned with the widow of an old friend, Kim had been especially troubled about the added stress he was under. He didn't like the frown that turned down the corners of her mouth so often lately, or the worry he saw in her blue-gray eyes. She'd been quieter than usual, too. Off somewhere in deep thought. Sad, almost. Of course, she probably missed Drew.

"There you are!"

Gerald turned at the sound of Kim's voice. She crossed the newly mown grass with her familiar long-legged stride. In wheat-colored jeans and a pale yellow, scoop-neck T-shirt, her long blond hair blowing in the vagrant breeze, she looked like springtime personified. Except for that anxiety in her eyes.

"All packed?" he asked.

"Yes." Her smile looked more like a grimace. "You'd think we were staying a month instead of two weeks."

He laughed. "Just like your mother."

At mention of Gwen, Kim grew serious. "Are you sure you'll be okay?"

"I'll be fine. I don't need a full-time keeper just yet, kiddo. If I didn't know better, I'd think you didn't want to go."

"It's such a long drive," Kim said, tucking back a wayward tendril of hair behind her ear.

"It'll be easier having Cindy to help you."

Kim was taking Cindy O'Connell, the younger sister of her good friend Molly Rambler. Cindy had dropped out of college for a semester to take a much-needed break and baby-sat Hannah during the mornings while Kim saw to it that Gerald's personal and social life ran smoothly.

"You and Hannah need to get yourselves to Kentucky," Gerald said. "I imagine your husband could use some of this tender-loving care you're so good at doling out."

Kim's cheeks bloomed with the red of embarrassment. It occurred to Gerald for the first time that the modern, separate life-style she and Drew lived might not be the best thing for either of them—or their marriage. They were young and needed to be together more.

"What about Amber?"

"What about her?" Gerald countered, resting one arm on the top rail of the fence. Amber, his older daughter, was the total opposite of Kim. Bold, vibrant, outgoing. She'd had him wrapped him around her little finger from the first moment she'd looked up at him from the bassinet with her big blue eyes.

"I know she called last night. What did she want?"

Gerald smiled. "What do you think she wanted?"

"Money, of course," Kim said. "What for this time?"

"She's met a clothing designer—a man—"

"Naturally," Kim interrupted.

"And she wants to help him get started by opening up a chain of shops in Los Angeles. She thinks that with her marketing skills and his talent they should be a great success."

"Good grief!" Kim said, aghast at her sister's latest scheme. "That would cost a fortune. *One* shop would cost a fortune. I hope you told her no this time."

"I did," he said with a nod. "Even though she was only asking for a hundred grand and not the whole amount."

Kim looked at Gerald sternly. "You know she won't give up."

"I know that as well as you do, honey. Stop worrying about me and get on out of here."

Kim shook her head as if to rid herself of the

whole conversation. "Okay, if you're sure you'll be all right."

"I'll be fine. Go," Gerald said. "Live it up. Have a good time for a change."

"You make it sound like I never do anything for fun."

"You don't."

Kim reached out and put her hand on his forearm that lay along the fence top. "I like taking care of you, Daddy."

"I know you do, honey, but I imagine Drew could use a little more taking care of than he gets," Gerald pointed out.

Uneasiness flitted through Kim's eyes. "You're probably right."

"Drew McShane is a good man," Gerald said. "You're lucky to have him."

The gaze that met his was steady. Gerald thought he saw her lips tremble. "Believe me, I know that."

"Is everything okay with the two of you?" he asked, feeling a sudden spurt of alarm.

"Well if it isn't, I'd better fix it, hadn't I?" she asked with forced cheerfulness.

"I'd say so. When are you leaving?"

"Right after lunch. That way I can get in several hours' driving before Hannah gets too cranky, and then finish up tomorrow." She smiled. "She doesn't sleep as much on a trip as she did when she was a baby."

"Doesn't seem like she sleeps much at all to me." He shook his head. "I can't believe she'll be two in a week."

"Me either." She sighed again. "If you're sure you'll be all right, I've got to go. I want to take

Hannah to see Cullen and Maureen before we leave. Maureen wants me to take some goodies to Drew.''

"Oatmeal cookies, no doubt," Gerald said.

"No doubt. Don't look so glum. I'm sure she made enough for you and Cullen, too.'' Kim pressed a kiss to his cheek. "I'll call when we get there.''

Gerald nodded. "Have a good time.''

She didn't answer, only waved. He watched her go, certain something was wrong between her and Drew, and praying that whatever it was could be fixed.

As his two wives had been, his two girls were as different as night and day. He'd met Melody Hartley, Amber's mother, during his senior year at Louisiana State University in Baton Rouge. They'd only dated a few weeks when she announced she was pregnant. Gerald had done what any Southern gentleman would have—he married her and sent her to Lafourche Farm, the Campion homestead, until he graduated and could join her there.

Unlike Gerald, Melody hadn't taken to married life or parenthood. Before the marriage deteriorated to the divorce stage, she was killed in a car crash—just before Amber's third birthday. The accident was even more of a scandal than a divorce would have been, since Melody had been in the car with another man. Shocked and humiliated, Gerald promised himself he'd be more selective in choosing his next wife.

He met Gwendolyn Prentiss, Kim's mother, just eight months after he buried Melody. They were married before Amber's fourth birthday, and Kim was born when Amber was five. Gerald had lost Gwen to a particularly virulent form of cancer three years ago, shortly after Amber had made the front page of a tabloid. He sighed. If it wasn't one thing with Amber, it was another. Kim was different. She'd never given him any grief. Even though Hannah had been born a little too soon after Kim and Drew married, Gerald would never condemn her for her lapse in propriety. Everyone was allowed one mistake, and having Drew McShane's child was certainly no mistake as far as Gerald was concerned.

Kim and her entourage made the trip to Kentucky without mishap. Hannah was surprisingly well behaved, even though she hated sitting in her car seat for such long periods of time. They arrived at Drew's seventy-acre Thoroughbred farm, which was situated on rolling pastureland south of Lexington, at midafternoon. While Drew was busy with the horses, Kim had tried without success to persuade Hannah to take a nap. When he had come in from the barns an hour or so later, he'd given Kim a quick hug and briefer kiss—no doubt for Cindy's benefit—shed his boots and immediately sought out Hannah, who was excited at having his undivided attention.

Now Kim fixed her pensive smoke-blue gaze on the man who'd been her husband for two and a half years. Sprawled on his stomach on the back porch of the brick Colonial-style house, Drew was busy stacking wooden blocks. Twenty-three-month-old Hannah was busy knocking them over, her blue-gray eyes alight with mischief.

Kim knew her father was right to be concerned. Things between her and Drew weren't working out the way she'd anticipated. Even though he flew to Louisiana at least once a month, and she loaded the Explorer with baby paraphernalia two or three times a year and made the long trek to Kentucky, it wasn't an ideal situation for either of them. As she'd told her father, it was up to her to set things right.

Hannah chortled in delight at something Drew had done, the sound of her joy pulling Kim's thoughts back to the present and her current dilemma. Clearly the two of them were thrilled to see each other, a fact that brought home the truth that their separate-life-style arrangement wasn't the best thing for Hannah. But that's the arrangement they had agreed to when they married, and Kim didn't see the situation getting better any time soon.

Blocks tumbled hollowly onto the painted wooden porch, the sound echoing in the empty corridors of Kim's heart. Drew gave a mock cry of dismay. Hannah giggled and flung herself across his back. "Be a horsey, Daddy."

"Again?" Horsey was one of Hannah's favorite games—and why not, since she'd been around the four-legged creatures all her life, and both her grandfathers and Drew were in the business of breeding and selling Thoroughbreds?

"Again, yeah," she said, her dark curls bobbing.

"Yes, sir," Kim corrected her automatically. Training Hannah to say her "ma'ams" and "sirs" was a constant battle.

Hannah mimed the proper response, and with a smile, Drew obliged the child by getting on his hands and knees. Hannah situated herself astride his back and knotted her small fists in the collar of his chambray shirt. For the next couple of minutes, he pranced and bucked and snorted his way around the porch.

A dull pain throbbed through Kim's heart. They looked so incredibly alike. Like Drew's, Hannah's hair was dark with a bit of curl on the end. Her eyes were blue-gray like Kim's, but there was a dimple in her right cheek, another fortuitous trait she shared with the McShanes.

"Mommy's sad."

The observation brought Kim up from the dark abyss of her thoughts. She glanced at Hannah, still perched on Drew's back, and forced a smile that didn't quite reach her eyes. "I'm fine."

"Are you?" Still on his knees, Drew looked up at her, concern in his eyes that were an unbelievable shamrock-green hue.

"A little tired, maybe."

"That's understandable," he said. "It's a long drive, even when you stop overnight."

"I don't mind."

It *was* a long trip, and traveling with a child just under two made it seem even longer, but tired or not, it was the only way Kim would consider traveling. She didn't fly. Not now. Not ever. Not since Justin Griffin, her childhood sweetheart and Hannah's biological father, had been killed in a plane crash, along with his parents.

"I mind," Drew said as he eased Hannah from his back and stood. He transferred her into the crook of his arm, and Kim stifled a wave of envy at the unconcerned way Hannah snuggled close to his broad chest. There was no doubt he loved Hannah, or that she, in turn, adored him. The problem was that Kim adored him, too, a potential disaster she hadn't given much thought to when they married.

Or had she?

The niggling worry that had plagued her the past several months surfaced again. Would she have been so eager to take up her old childhood relationship with the newly divorced Justin Griffin if he hadn't shared so many physical similarities to Drew Mc-Shane?

If her fear of becoming an old maid had prompted her to become involved with Justin again, it had been her long-buried feelings for Drew—the deep-rooted schoolgirl love and hero worship she'd felt toward him since she was a child—combined with a genuine grown-up respect that inspired her to ask him to marry her when Justin was killed. What prompted him to agree to a marriage with a woman pregnant by another man was anyone's guess.

"I worry about you when you drive so far alone."

The concern in her husband's eyes made Kim's heart skip a beat. The common sense that had guided her through most of her life cautioned her that the expression was nothing to get excited over. Like his father, Drew was a caring, thoughtful man. The tender consideration in his eyes was nothing to take personally.

"I wasn't alone, but thanks."

Drew stared at her for a moment longer, then nodded, as if he'd come to some sort of conclusion. "Definitely tired. Maybe even a case of the doldrums. What you need, lass, is a nice juicy steak, a cup of Irish coffee and an early night."

The Irish term and the twinkle in his eyes brought a grudging smile to her lips. Born in the States thirty-five years ago, and raised in America all his life, Drew's speech still held a trace of his Irish heritage, a legacy of his parents, who'd never shed their accents, even though Cullen had moved his wife, Maureen, and his two girls to the States, before Drew was even born. Kim had always found the slight Irish brogue charming...even sexy. Like the man.

"Hannah wants coffee," Hannah said.

"Not this evening, sweetie," Kim said with a shake of her head. Her father had started letting Hannah sip coffee from his cup when she was six months old. She had a cup—liberally laced with lots of milk and sugar—with Gerald every morning and Cullen every afternoon.

"Ple-e-ease."

Using a diversionary tactic, Drew smiled down at the child nestled in his arms and tickled her tummy. "Brat."

"She's not a brat," she said with a giggle, knowing it was more a compliment than an accusation. Another painful spasm squeezed Kim's heart.

"Say 'I'm not a brat,'" Kim said.

Drew smiled at her. "You're fighting a losing battle," he said, then bellowed "Cindy!" through the open screen door.

"Coming, Mr. McShane!"

The pretty twenty-one-year-old would be there in a heartbeat, Kim thought. Like every woman in town, Cindy O'Connell was smitten with her boss.

Cindy pushed through the door, looking pleased, embarrassed and a little disconcerted at having been summoned by the lord of the manor. "Sir?"

"I want you to fix Hannah's supper tonight," Drew said. "Give her a bath and see that she's in bed by eight. If possible," he tacked on, knowing from past experience that Hannah would be exhausted but wound up from the trip. "Mrs. McShane and I are going out for dinner."

A sigh of dismay fluttered from Kim's lips. She

and Drew seldom spent any time alone. Why tonight, of all nights?

"Sure, Mr. McShane," Cindy said. "No problem." She cast a knowing look at Kim.

If Drew noticed, he didn't say anything. "There's plenty to eat in the kitchen," he told Cindy. Then, in true Southern fashion, he added, "Make yourself at home."

"Great." Cindy smiled and reached for Hannah, who clung more tightly to Drew.

"Come on, wee angel," he said, prying her small fingers from his shirt. "Go with Cindy, and I'll take you riding on a real horsey in the morning."

Hannah thought about that for a moment, her eyes fixed on his. Finally, deciding she'd take a chance, she let go of his shirt and held out her arms to her baby-sitter.

Kim sighed again. What female could resist him?

"Come on, Hannah," Cindy said. "Let's go raid the refrigerator."

The screen door slammed behind them and Drew turned to Kim. "Where would you like to go for dinner?"

"You don't have to take me to dinner."

"I know I don't have to. I *want* to."

The expression in his green eyes was unreadable, but the stubbornness she'd become acquainted with through the years was evident in his voice.

"Well, then," she said, forcing a smile, "a juicy steak sounds wonderful, and a cup of Irish coffee sounds even better."

He smiled back and glanced down at the watch strapped around his brawny wrist. "Is an hour enough time for you to get ready?"

"An hour is fine."

"Great, then. I'll phone Reginald's and make reservations."

Drew McShane was a man with a plan.

He was glad Kim and Hannah had come. He was especially glad Kim had brought Cindy. Having someone to help care for Hannah would free up more time so he could talk to Kim about their future. It was nearly three years since Justin had died. Surely that was enough time for her grief to have faded, enough time that she might consider making their make-believe marriage the real thing.

Drew didn't regret his decision to marry her, but at thirty-four, he wasn't getting any younger. He loved Hannah with all his heart, but more and more lately, he found himself thinking about a child of his own. He wanted Kim to be that child's mother.

He wasn't certain when his love for Kim had changed into the love of a mature man for a woman, but he couldn't recall a time he hadn't loved her. Drew had felt those first tugs on his heartstrings when he was a boy of seven and Kim was a newborn who looked up at him from her bassinet.

Growing up, she'd been his proverbial shadow, following him over the sprawling acreage of Lafourche Farm—underfoot when he had chores to do, there when he wanted something fetched or needed an extra pair of hands to help. As he had, Kim had grown up with a deep love and respect for the delicate four-legged creatures that were the foundation of her family's wealth.

Though they were inseparable as children, it was the eight years' difference in their ages as much as

Drew's acute awareness of the distinction in their social status that became the wedge that gradually came between them. Though neither Cullen McShane nor Gerald Campion ever spoke of it, the older Drew grew, the more aware he became of the unspoken but very real distinction between the classes—a distinction that had come sharply into focus twice through the years.

The first time was when Kim's willful sister, Amber, turned eighteen and decided she wanted Drew. She'd stalked him like a cat after a mouse, following him when he went to the river to swim, showing up when he was out with his friends, leaving suggestive notes in unexpected places.

Drew's heart was never in jeopardy, but he was a healthy twenty-year-old with the usual hormonal urges and was very tempted to take what she offered.

Only his older sister, Megan, kept him from making a fool of himself, telling him that Amber Campion was out of his league, that there was no way she would ever consider him more than a passing fancy and reminding him that if Gerald found out about the liaison Drew might lose his job.

Drew had given Megan's advice a lot of thought. He liked working with his father, one of the most knowledgeable men in the industry. Drew had been saving his money to buy a mare from Gerald, one past her prime that had trouble foaling. The old mare wouldn't make many more breeding seasons, but she was a proven producer and priced fairly. Buying her was the first step in his plan to make the world sit up and take notice of Drew McShane—not for the money or the prestige, but to prove to himself, and maybe the Campions, that he could succeed against the odds.

After weighing the wisdom of a flirtation with Amber he'd turned her down, and after a scene with tearful recriminations, she'd gone on to an easier mark and put out the word that *she'd* changed her mind about *him*—after all, it would never do for her friends to know that the boss's daughter had been rejected by the farm manager's son.

The second thing that had made him intensely aware of his station in life was seeing Kim with Justin Griffin, whose family lived a few miles away. Justin had an easygoing, confident air about him that went hand in hand with being born with the proverbial silver spoon in his mouth. There were times when Drew had envied the younger man's assurance, times he wished Justin were spoiled and arrogant instead of the genuinely nice guy he really was.

Justin and Kim, both rich and privileged, had been so suited for each other it had taken Drew several years to realize his feelings about the younger man were rooted in jealousy. When Kim was nineteen and Justin dumped her for Lilith DuPree, Drew had wanted to strangle him.

Those feelings had intensified three years ago when Justin and his wife split up and he began wooing Kim again. Still, Drew hadn't yet identified his feelings for what they were until the day Justin and his parents were killed, and Kim, pregnant and alone, had come and asked Drew to marry her.

Saying no to the in-name-only marriage offer had never crossed his mind, but now he was ready to take their marriage in a new direction. He wanted more. He wanted the real thing. And he wanted it with Kim.

* * *

Gerald Campion had just finished his dinner and was settling in for a night of sitcoms when the phone rang. "Hello."

"Hello, Gerald. This is Maria Antonia."

Gerald's good friend, Lawrence Muldair, had died three years earlier, just before Gwen, and his much-younger wife, Maria Antonia, had inherited his estate, including his Thoroughbreds. Maria Antonia remarried two years ago. Gerald had never met her husband, but the general consensus was that she was too good for him. Lately when Maria called, it was with bad news. Gerald hoped against hope that tonight would be different. "Hello, Maria. How are you?"

"I could be better."

A heavy sigh escaped him. "Don't tell me there's been another one?"

"I'm afraid so."

"Who?"

"Paul Mercer from Illinois. He's threatening a lawsuit."

Gerald passed a shaking hand down his face. He and Maria Antonia co-owned a high-priced stud. Recently, they'd discovered that some mares who'd been booked to him had somehow been bred to a lesser stallion. "Dear God, when will this nightmare be over?"

"I know, I know," Maria said. "It seems never-ending, doesn't it?" She sighed. "I wish Larry were here. He'd know what to do."

Gerald thought it telling that Maria longed for the advice of her first husband instead of turning to her current husband. Prudently, he kept quiet, saying instead, "So Mercer's threatening a lawsuit?"

"Yes." Maria Antonia sighed. "It seems he

knows Talbot, and when they talked and found out both their mares had been bred to the wrong stud, they decided it couldn't have been a coincidence.''

Gerald swore. ''Are you telling me they think this was a conspiracy of some sort?''

''Evidently, they think so.''

''What we have to do is get to the bottom of this. Have you tried to find Reeves and Forester?'' Gerald asked, naming two of the men who'd held short terms as Maria Antonia's farm manager. ''And what was the other man's name?''

''Crump,'' she said. ''He's in New York. I've left word for him to call me. Forester is in Texas, and I haven't been able to locate Reeves yet.''

''Surely they ought to know how something like this could happen,'' Gerald said. ''Breeding a mare to the wrong stud might be considered an accident if it only happened once, but this is the fifth complaint we've had.''

''Believe me, I know.''

''It makes you wonder how word got out, doesn't it?'' Gerald asked, both thoughtful and perplexed. ''Drew told me he specifically asked the vet not to spread it around—not that it's the kind of problem we shouldn't get to the bottom of,'' he added.

''If the vet didn't say anything, then it may have been some of his help or a lab technician somewhere,'' Maria Antonia said. ''However it happened, every breeder who booked a mare to Flight of Dreams is checking to make sure they got a Flight of Dreams foal.''

''What about your men?'' Gerald asked. ''I know you have certain people who help with the breeding.''

"As you know, I have a lot of my fellow country-
men working for me," Maria Antonia said.

"Yes, and I think it's admirable that you want to
help them better themselves," Gerald said.

Maria Antonia laughed. "Admirable or not, sometimes I find the situation trying. When they first come
here from Mexico, they speak little or no English.
Communication can be challenging, to say the least.
I think that's one reason I've had such a hard time
keeping a foreman."

"I'm sure it's frustrating," Gerald sympathized.
"And it could be part of our problem. Someone probably misunderstood."

"Probably," Maria Antonia agreed.

"Why don't you talk to your help and see if they
can shed any light on what's happened?"

"I'll be glad to," Maria Antonia said. "But one
of these complaints goes back to last year's foals, and
you know what a high turnover I have. I'll have to
go back and check the books to see who was working
here then and see if we still employ them."

"I know it will be a pain, but I think it's going to
be necessary if we want to clear up this mess."

"You're right," Maria Antonia said. "It certainly
can't go on. But you know, other than Mercer and
Talbot and a couple of others who have wanted their
stud fees returned, everyone has been happy to accept
a free breeding to Flight of Dreams for next year."

"Thank God. We can't afford to have dissatisfied
customers, or it will affect our breeding program
from here on out. We don't want to get the reputation
of being dishonest. It would ruin us both."

"That's why I didn't hesitate offering the choice
of refunding their money or giving them a free breed-

ing,'' Maria Antonia said. ''Surely that should indicate we're trying to make amends.''

''It should,'' Gerald agreed. ''It could have happened at a better time, though. I'm pretty well strapped for cash with upgrading my foaling barn and buying those two sires.''

''I know.'' Maria Antonia was all concerned solicitation. ''I'm still dealing with some unexpected debts of David's.''

Again, Gerald kept silent. Maria Antonia's husband had been known to push a lot of money through the windows.

''Don't worry, Gerald,'' she said with a humorless little laugh. ''I can handle it.''

''I'm sure you can.'' An uncomfortable lull fell over the conversation.

''I hate to ask you, since I know you've coughed up a lot of money to repay those stud fees, and you had that tax audit, but could you send me a couple of thousand dollars to help with the attorney?''

Gerald's heart sank. At this point, even a couple of thousand dollars seemed like a lot. ''Sure,'' he told her. ''I'll get it in the mail first thing in the morning.''

''Thanks, Gerald. You're a godsend.''

Soon afterward, Maria Antonia said her goodbyes, and Gerald hung up.

He rubbed at the day's growth of stubble on his chin and pondered the situation. A few months earlier, Drew had accidentally discovered that one of his weanlings wasn't sired by Flight of Dreams, the horse Drew had paid the stud fee for. Lawrence Muldair and Gerald had bought the stallion several years earlier, but the horse stood at stud on the Muldair farm in Kentucky.

For weeks, Gerald had tried to figure out how something of this nature could have happened—not just once, but several times.

He reached for the phone again. There was nothing to do but call Drew—and Cullen, of course—and tell them of this newest development. Maybe one of them could suggest some way of dealing with the problem or have some idea how it could have happened.

Gerald dialed Drew's number in Kentucky. Of course, he'd have to stress to his son-in-law that this was to be kept secret from Kim. He didn't want her worrying about him, not when she seemed so upset herself.

Cindy answered the phone and told Gerald that Mr. and Mrs. McShane had gone out for dinner. When Gerald asked that Drew return the call when he got home, Cindy promised to relay the message.

There was nothing to do now but wait for Drew to return his call. He could tell Cullen about Maria Antonia's newest bombshell in the morning. Going against doctor's orders, Gerald poured himself a shot of whiskey. One wouldn't hurt. Then he sat down to watch television as he'd planned to do earlier. He watched the sitcoms until bedtime, but if someone had asked him what any one of them was about, he couldn't have said.

Chapter Two

Reginald's, one of the few places left where a jacket and tie are mandatory for entrance, was a Victorian mansion whose lower floor had been converted into a pricey eating establishment twenty years earlier. Even though it was situated several miles from the city proper, its out-of-the-way location had no noticeable effect on business. The parking lot was full at any given hour.

The maître d' ushered Kim and Drew to a table secluded from the other diners by two huge Boston ferns on tall, marble-topped stands of lustrous cherry wood.

When they were settled, Drew studied the wine list. Kim, wearing an off-the-shoulder peach-hued sheath, a stretchy, clingy knit dress that rose several inches above the knees, studied her husband, who was dressed in a charcoal gray suit with a pearl-tinted shirt.

He'd come a long way, she thought with undeniable pride. And he'd go a lot further, thanks to his love of his chosen field and the work ethic ingrained into him by his parents. The McShanes were fine people who loved Hannah dearly, which, Kim thought, made the lie of her marriage even harder to bear.

Cullen McShane had met the Campions' Thoroughbred trainer when Kim's grandfather had raced a particularly nice filly in a stakes race in Ireland. When the trainer offered Cullen a position as assistant trainer, he'd accepted and moved his pregnant wife and two young daughters to Louisiana. It hadn't taken Kim's grandfather long to realize what he had in Cullen, and the big, fun-loving Irishman had soon forsaken the vagaries of the racetrack for the more stable life-style of the Campion breeding farm. Cullen McShane was six years older than Kim's father, but they had always held a mutual liking and respect for each other.

Drew was born five months after their arrival and had grown up under his father's tutelage. At the age of ten, he had known as much about breeding cycles, foaling and conformation as most of his father's contemporaries. He had an uncanny memory and could recall the performance of dams and sires no matter how unsung the bloodline.

Kim knew her husband was a prime example of the American dream: a man who'd set himself a goal and attained it, not for the fame, but for the satisfaction of the climb. The McShane name might be new to the Kentucky Thoroughbred scene, but it was one to be reckoned with. And while Drew's money might not be old, there had been plenty of it the past few years, and more where that came from. Like cream, he'd risen to the top—not by cheating and scheming, but by hard work, an innate honesty and high standards for himself and those he associated with. In a time when morals and protocol seemed to have gone by the wayside, his old-fashioned mores and manners had stood him in good stead.

"Kim."

The sound of him speaking her name intruded on the bittersweet turn of her thoughts. She shifted her gaze from the arrangements of fresh gardenias and freesias to her husband's troubled green eyes. "Yes?"

"Are you sure you're all right?"

"I'm fine."

"Is everything okay with Gerald?" Drew asked, obviously determined to find out what was at the root of her silence.

"He's upset about that mix-up with Flight of Dreams and worried about Lafourche Fancy being able to service all the mares they've booked to him, but other than that, I think he's fine."

"Fancy's getting pretty old," Drew said with an understanding nod. There was an apology in his eyes. "I hated like hell to bring up the problem with Flight of Dreams, but you know I had to."

"I know."

Everyone agreed the mix-up was just that. Kim knew that Lawrence Muldair's death had changed many things at Muldair Farms. His longtime manager had gone to a better-paying job soon after Marie Antonia'd married David Perkins, and she didn't seem to be able to find anyone who was willing to stay for any length of time.

"I hope Gerald isn't still worrying about that," Drew said. "We all agreed that a free stud fee next year was fair compensation."

"I don't think that's bothering him. If you're happy with that agreement, I think he and Maria Antonia are both satisfied." Kim swirled the water in her glass. "Amber called a few days ago. That upset him a little—as usual."

Drew smiled. "Don't tell me. She has a new no-fail business venture and wants money."

Kim couldn't help smiling back. Drew knew her sister as well as anyone. "How'd you guess?"

"Amber always wants money," he said. "Or another conquest."

As it did so often lately, a feeling of jealousy pricked at Kim's heart, like a worrisome dog nipping at her heels. She infused what she hoped passed for nonchalance into her voice. "You say that like a man who knows what he's talking about."

"I do." He didn't elaborate, and since Kim wasn't sure she was up to hearing the details, she didn't press for more information. Instead, she looked away and concentrated on her salad.

After a moment he said, "She came on to me once."

"Really?" Kim asked, though she recalled that time very well. She'd been scared to death Drew would fall for her gorgeous sister, but thankfully, after a few weeks, someone new had captured Amber's attention.

"You don't remember?"

"No."

Drew's chuckle was low and warm, loaded with charm and shimmering with sex appeal. "Liar."

Kim's gaze flew to his face. He was smiling, the crinkles at the corners of his eyes and the deep crease in his cheek evidence of his amusement. "As I recollect, you were smitten with me yourself."

Hot color rushed into Kim's cheeks, and her mouth fell open in astonishment.

He held up a hand in protest. "Don't try to deny it."

Kim clamped her lips together.

He laughed again. "Come on, darlin'," he said, his Irish lilt more pronounced than usual as he spoke the unexpected endearment. "Lighten up. You take life far too seriously."

Irritated, and unsure why, Kim said, "I'm sorry I'm not the flighty, flirty woman my sister is."

"I'm not," he said. "I'm thankful." Seeing the expression she couldn't hide, he said, "Does that surprise you?"

"There aren't too many men who feel that way."

"Aren't there?" He let the observation hang between them for a moment. "I sensed a change in Amber the last time I saw her."

"Oh? When was that?"

"It must have been when Hannah was born," he said in a thoughtful voice.

"You must have been imagining things."

"Maybe," he told her. "Just in case you're wondering what happened between me and Amber back then, I—"

"I'm not!" Kim denied. "It's really none of my business."

"You're my wife."

Even though he spoke as if she had a right to know and he wanted to tell her, Kim didn't think she could face the truth. To her knowledge, there had never been a man her sister wanted who hadn't succumbed to her wiles, if only temporarily.

"There's no use digging up ancient history."

He gave her a long, considering look. "Maybe you're right."

The waiter came, and after ordering for them and accepting the bottle of wine, Drew said, "So what's she up to now?"

"She's met a man, a clothing designer she claims is very talented. She wants to open up a chain of boutiques featuring his designs."

Shaking his head, Drew laughed. "Does she actually think Gerald would finance something so risky after her health spa fiasco?"

Kim picked up her wineglass. "He says he won't, but you know as well as I do that when push comes to shove, he seldom denies her anything for long."

"He'll never learn, will he?"

"Apparently not."

"So how are Mom and Dad?" Drew asked, thankfully finished with the topic of Amber.

"They're fine. Maureen sent you a basket of cookies and things. Megan came for a visit last week. Bonnie is coming for Easter weekend."

Their steaks arrived, and they spent the remainder of the meal, including coffee and dessert, in easy conversation about Drew's family, the syndication of his latest stud and what was happening at Lafourche Farm. It had been a long time since they'd spent any considerable time together, and Kim had forgotten how easy Drew was to talk to, how intelligent he was, how funny he could be…how much he enjoyed life, all things that made him the exceptional man she knew him to be.

All too soon, Drew had paid for the meal and they were heading back to the farm. Alone with him in the intimacy of the car, Kim ran out of words. So, apparently, had he. They drove in silence, and once again, she felt crushed by a feeling of impending doom. Did he sense it? She cast him a sideways glance.

Why did he have to be so handsome? His profile was strong, classic, from the broadness of his forehead to the boldness of his nose and the firmness of his chin. Kim ached to feel the slight rasp of his freshly shaven cheek against her palm, to trail impressionable fingertips over his strong nose and the sweep of his eyelashes…to trace them along the shape of his mouth. She clenched her hands and felt the bite of her nails into her palm. She shouldn't be thinking of Drew this way. Couldn't. During the rest of the drive she stared out the windshield and forced her mind to a numbing emptiness.

"We're here."

She blinked and saw that they had indeed arrived at the farm. Drew turned off the car and cut the lights. He was silhouetted in the soft glow of the porch light Cindy had left on for them. Without speaking, he got out of the car and started around the hood. Kim opened her own door and hurried up the steps before he could play the gentleman and do it for her.

The length of his stride enabled him to reach the front door at the same time she did. He leaned past her for the doorknob, his chest brushing against her shoulder. Kim sucked in a sharp breath.

"We should do that more often."

The words were spoken so close to her ear that she felt the heat of his breath, smelled the minty scent of an after-dinner candy and the woodsy aroma of his cologne. "What?" she asked, her own voice sounding breathless.

"Go out. Have a date." She heard the smile in his voice. "That's what Megan calls it when she and Bruce get a night away from the kids."

"Oh." Feeling as if she needed to contribute more than a monosyllable, she glanced over her shoulder. "I enjoyed it. Thank you." Though she meant them, the words came out with a schoolgirl's politeness. She wondered if she imagined disappointment in his sigh.

"I'm glad."

He opened the door, and she bolted inside.

"See you in the morning," he called after her.

She turned on the bottom step and faced him. "See you then." She forced a smile, then sped up the stairs and into the sanctuary of her room. As she had so often in the past, Kim felt a strong urge to cry. But she wouldn't give in to that need. Amber was the one who used tears to get what she wanted, not Kim.

Two hours later, Kim was no closer to finding the forgetfulness of sleep than she had been when she'd raced up the stairs away from her husband. Instead, her mind churned with memories of the evening they'd spent together, recalling everything they'd said, reliving every smile he'd smiled, every gesture of his long-fingered, tender hands.

She had intimate knowledge of that tenderness. She'd observed it often as he probed the legs of a limping horse, searching out imperceptible soreness. She'd seen it as he moved his sensitive palms over a pregnant mare's gravid belly. Witnessed it in the way he brushed Hannah's hair away from her face.

Kim rolled to her back and stared dry-eyed at the ceiling, arms tense at her sides, her nails digging a row of half-moons into her palms. How could she have let herself fall in love with him when she knew there was no possible way he could ever love her? Not plain little Kim Campion.

Even Justin, whom everyone expected her to marry, had chosen pretty Lilith DuPree, instead. Never mind that the marriage had ended in shambles in less than four years, or that Justin had come crawling back to Kim asking for her forgiveness and begging for a second chance.

Her parents, who'd always had a soft spot for Justin, seemed thrilled when he'd come back into her life. Gerald, who had made the same mistake as Justin in his own youth, had predicted from the start that Justin's marriage would fail. The Griffins, longtime friends of Gerald and Gwen, had known and loved Kim all her life. They, too, were pleased when Justin "came to his senses." While their relationship with their former daughter-in-law had been tolerable, they had never considered her background quite good enough for their son and heir.

Kim's own bloodline was impeccable. Like their close neighbors, the Ramblers, the Campions were one of the oldest families to settle along Bayou Lafourche. Kim's mother's family had made its money in Texas oil. Gwen could trace her roots back to Sam Houston, something Amber's mother couldn't do. But the lack of what Thoroughbred people called "black type" lineage on her mother's side had never bothered Amber. She was a Campion, and she had vowed to make her own destiny, ignoring the old, unspoken social taboos and setting her sights on Drew. Though the McShanes were well thought of, there were those in the Campions' exalted social circle who—had they known what she was up to— would have shunned Amber for fraternizing with the hired help's son.

It wasn't those unspoken social restrictions that kept Kim from pursuing Drew herself. It was the eight years' difference in their ages, and the fact that he'd always been her good friend, the equivalent of a big brother.

Yet, even though Drew had moved to Kentucky when Kim was sixteen and their lives had gone separate ways, he was the first person she'd thought to turn to when she realized she was carrying Justin's baby. At twenty-four, she should have been able to deal with the mess she'd made of her life, but all she could think of was that she'd let her father down.

In retrospect, Kim knew she hadn't been thinking clearly when she'd made her fatal proposal to Drew. The summer had been one straight from hell. Her mother had been diagnosed with a rare form of cancer in May. In mid-July, Amber had made the front page of the tabloids. She'd been arrested for being drunk and disorderly in a posh L.A. restaurant with a famous movie star who was very married, and whose wife was very pregnant.

Gerald had suffered a heart attack just hours after seeing the story. Thankfully, there was little damage to his heart. Gwen seemed to give up after the tabloid fiasco. They buried her two weeks later. Kim, who

wanted to strangle her sister for her irresponsible behavior, would always believe it was the added stress
that had hurried her mother's demise and brought on
her father's heart attack.

Justin had been a rock throughout the ordeal.
Though he'd been trying to no avail to win Kim back
for several weeks, it was during this period when her
resistance was low that she'd finally allowed him
back into her life. Feeling more alone than she ever
had, needing someone to lean on, someone to vent
her fury to, someone to hold her and tell her it would
all come out all right, she gave him access to her
body the same night she buried her mother.

A lifetime of habit had first sent Kim in search of
Drew, who'd flown in for her mother's funeral. She'd
found him in the office with Amber, who'd flown in
for the afternoon. Disappointed, and not wanting to
disturb their earnest conversation, Kim had then
sought out Justin, who was only too glad to comfort
her.

They'd been back together five weeks when Justin
and his parents were killed in a small-plane crash
coming home from Florida. On the day of the triple
funeral, she sat rigidly in her pew, dry-eyed and pale,
sick with the certainty provided by an in-home pregnancy test.

It hadn't seemed fair that she should be caught by
that one night, the first night they were together, but
Kim had learned long before that railing against fate
solved nothing. What she had to do was deal with
the situation.

The most important thing was not to cause her father any more undue worry. The loss of his two close
friends so soon after her mother's death and the hu-

miliation of Amber's fiasco was enough. Kim couldn't add to his burdens. She'd known better than to do something so irresponsible, so *stupid;* after all, she was the good daughter, the one who always did what was right.

As she'd lain awake, wondering what to do, she realized she should ask Drew's advice. In a show of respect, he'd once again flown back to Louisiana for the Griffin family interment, which was more than Amber had done. Kim knew Drew would be staying at his father's small house on the far side of the farm, but she also knew he liked to play poker with the other hands when he came to town. There was a chance she'd find him in the tack room.

She'd pulled on a pair of shorts, let herself out of the house and followed the swath of yellow light across the wide lawn to the barn, her heart in her throat, her courage in her trembling hand....

When she reached the tack room, the door was ajar and the light was on. Drew was alone, playing solitaire. His head was propped in one hand, which also held a cheroot whose smoke spiraled up toward the single bare lightbulb. The other hand flipped over cards with a lazy insouciance.

She must have made a sound, because he raised his head with the suddenness of an animal that senses something or someone is nearby. Seeing her in the doorway, he frowned.

"What are you doing up so late?"

She shrugged. "I couldn't sleep. Too many things on my mind, I guess."

Drew swept the cards up into a pile and pushed out a chair with his foot. "Sit." As Kim crossed the room to do his bidding, he asked, "Do you want something to drink? I saw some cream sodas in the fridge."

Surprised that he remembered that cream sodas were her favorite, she smiled. "No, thanks."

Never taking his piercing gaze from hers, he picked up the half-empty bottle of beer sitting in front of him and took a healthy swallow. "Are you going to be okay?"

"I'll survive," she said, aware of the bitterness in her voice.

He smiled. "Oh, there's no doubt about that. You're a survivor if ever there was one, Kimberly Anne." He took another sip from the bottle and favored her with a wry smile. "This is one of those awkward moments in life. You know, like trying to ignore an elephant in the room. Do I not say anything about Justin to try to spare you any more pain, or do I offer you sympathy and make you uncomfortable?"

"How about offering me some advice?" The words rushed from her in a breathless tumble.

He flicked ash into a battered metal ashtray. "Sure. If I can."

"What advice would you give to a woman who got herself in trouble?"

A fierce frown drew his dark eyebrows together. "What kind of trouble?"

She raised her chin in an age-old gesture of defiance. "Now, what kind of trouble do you think I'm talking about?" she asked softly, daring him to make something of it.

His keen gaze probed the dullness of hers for seconds that seemed like an eternity. "I thought you had more sense than that," he said at last. "Hell, I thought Justin had more sense than that."

She heaved a deep sigh and began to pick at a speck of paint on the table. Dejection caused her shoulders to slump, but there was a hint of fire in her voice. "It doesn't change things to say that I'd just buried my mother and I was under a lot of stress and needed a little comforting because of her illness and Daddy's heart attack—not to mention Amber's little escapade. And it certainly makes no difference that we were only careless once, but there it is."

"You're right. It doesn't make a bit of difference," he agreed.

She raised her tormented gaze to his. "I'd gone looking for you, but you were in the office with Amber."

His eyes closed, as if to block out something too painful to deal with. When he opened them, they held a terrible sorrow. "So you went to Justin."

"Yeah. I went to Justin." She exhaled another harsh, angry breath. "I can't imagine what I was thinking. Maybe that's the problem. Maybe I wasn't."

Instead of replying, he picked up the beer bottle, took a long pull and put it back on the table.

She shook her head. "I don't want Daddy to know what a stupid, irresponsible thing I've done."

"Everyone's entitled to do at least one stupid, irresponsible thing in life."

"Not me."

Drew's mouth twisted into a sardonic smile. "That's right. I forgot I was talking to Saint Kim."

"Is that how you see me?" she asked, her voice tinged with surprise. "Holier-than-thou?"

"No," he told her, shaking his head. "I see you as a devoted daughter who's done her best to make up for all her sister's wrongs."

"It seemed the least I could do considering the hell she put my parents through. That's why I can't have a baby out of wedlock. I'm afraid of what it might do to Daddy."

"He has been through a lot lately."

"Yeah." Her laughter held no real mirth. She offered him a reckless smile. "So what are you doing tomorrow?"

"Nothing. Why?"

"I don't suppose you'd want to drive over to Texas and get married, would you?"

To this day, Kim had no idea where the question had come from. When she'd gone looking for Drew, she certainly hadn't planned on proposing. But the question had just...popped out, and to her never-ending amazement, he'd said yes. Even now, she could only guess that it was his concern for her father's health and loyalty to her family that prompted him to accept her ridiculous offer.

They'd done as she teasingly suggested and eloped to Texas, telling her father and Drew's parents that they'd realized the extent of their feelings for each other when Drew came back for Gwen's funeral. If anyone thought it strange when Kim explained she was staying in Louisiana the next few months to help her father, no one said a word. When her pregnancy became obvious, everyone expressed their excitement, and when Hannah was born seven and a half months after their marriage, no one said what must have been on all their minds.

Now, here they were, less than three years later, Hannah's second birthday approaching, and stuck in a relationship that was going nowhere. It was bad enough that Kim was in love with Drew, but what bothered her most was that he was stuck in a loveless relationship when he could have a real marriage with someone he loved.

When Kim proposed to him, she'd given little thought to the possibility of his falling in love with someone else, but she'd recently run across a magazine snapshot of Maria Antonia and Drew at a select yearling sale. The picture validated that likelihood. Maria Antonia was petite, whipcord lean and lithe from years in the saddle. She was naturally dark-skinned, with huge brown eyes and a glorious mane of black hair that hung almost to her waist.

Looking at the picture made Kim, who was several inches taller and who'd never dropped ten of the twenty pounds she'd gained during her pregnancy, feel like a big, ungainly cow. It didn't matter that the added weight gave her figure a much-needed softness or that Maria Antonia had remarried and was older than Drew by at least eight years. It still made Kim take a hard look at her marriage and her feelings for Drew.

When she finally realized the emotion gnawing at her insides was jealousy, she'd gone around shrouded in a haze of stunned disbelief. Jealousy implied that her feelings for Drew went deeper than the hero-worship-good-buddy kind of love she'd always felt for him. Jealousy implied a grown-up kind of love. The love of a woman for a man and everything that went with it.

Unfortunately, Drew had shown no sign of returning those feelings during their marriage. He was kind, gentle, attentive. Nothing more. That understanding, coupled with the snapshot, and Drew's mother's statement a few weeks earlier that he wanted another child, made her acutely aware of how unfair their marriage was.

She'd entered into the marriage certain that she'd never love anyone with the fervency of her youthful feelings for Justin—even though his coming back into her life hadn't been the earth-shattering event she'd once imagined it would be. She'd never considered the possibility that even though there was no one in Drew's life at the time of their marriage, he might find someone. After weeks of soul-searching, she'd decided she should do the decent thing and give him his freedom, even though her own feelings for him had changed.

Restless and troubled by her memories, she flung back the sheet and went to stand at the window overlooking the back garden. The quarter moon was a lopsided, Cheshire cat's grin in the Cimmerian sky. The pinpricks of starlight seemed echoed by the dark garden, where white flowers—just beginning to poke up through the warming earth—twinkled in the gloom. Though the garden wasn't in full bloom, Kim was familiar with the subtle harmony created by the pureness and simplicity of the all-white flowers. She could find reassurance and hope among the sweet fragrance of iris and paper whites and contentment in the sound of the water splashing over the fountain's rocks. Without stopping to pull on a robe, she let herself out of the room, needing the promise of peace offered by the garden and the anonymity of the darkness.

Her laughter was strained with embarrassment at her brashness. "You're kidding, aren't you?"

"Not if you're not," he said.

"Why?"

He knew she was asking why he was willing to give up his bachelor's life-style to take on a woman he didn't love and a baby that wasn't his. Drew, who had no trouble finding willing, eligible women to date, had no answer for that, so he replied simply, "Why not?"

"You aren't kidding, are you?"

"No."

She laughed again, rubbing her temple and shaking her head in disbelief. "This is crazy. I can't believe I just asked you to marry me, and I really can't believe you agreed."

"What's so hard to believe?" he asked. "We've helped each other a lot through the years. Now you need a husband and father for your baby because you don't want to cause your dad any more pain. I'm willing to do this for you. For him. God knows he's done plenty for the McShanes."

"I can't marry you and go off to Kentucky if we do this. He's too fragile right now. Physically and emotionally." She shoved her hair back and laughed again, a high-pitched, strained sound that caught on what sounded like a sob. "Good grief! I can't believe we're having this conversation."

"It isn't exactly what I had in mind for a proposal, either," Drew said. "But life is seldom the way we plan it, is it?"

"What did you have in mind?" she asked, the too-serious expression he'd grown so familiar with drawing her fair eyebrows together.

He rubbed the side of his nose and slanted her a wry grin. "The old moonlight-and-roses routine, I guess. Me doing the asking."

"Yeah, me too," she confessed with another sigh. "So. If we actually do this, what will we tell everyone? They're going to know I'm pregnant soon enough."

"Did your dad know you were sleeping with Justin?"

Her face flamed with the bluntness of the question. "I don't think so. He knew I was reluctant to let Justin back into my life. I don't think I acted any differently when I...did."

"So I'm the one who takes the blame?"

If possible, she grew even more pale. "It sounds so selfish of me when you put it that way." She threw back her head and looked up at the ceiling. "Damn you, Justin!" she said in a low, harsh voice. "Why did you have to go and get killed and leave me in this mess?"

When Drew kept his silence, she got up from the table and began to pace the length of the small room. "I can't *believe* I was so stupid. I mean, it isn't like we were sex-crazed teenagers. Why did I get caught when I was only careless one time?"

"Life isn't always fair," Drew said. "Stop beating yourself up for making one mistake. Whatever the reason, it happened. Granted, it didn't happen at a good time, but you'll get through it. I'll help you."

A reluctant, halfhearted smile made a brief appearance. "Look, McShane, I don't want rationalization and I don't want your infernal optimism or your—" she hesitated, searching for the right word "—tenderness."

"What do you want?"

He saw the bewilderment creep into her eyes, saw the last of her anger ebb. When she answered him, she sounded like a child again. "I don't know."

"Maybe we can figure it out together." She didn't answer. "By the way, you don't have to go back to Kentucky with me."

"But what will people say?" she asked, her surprise a clear indication that that possibility had never occurred to her.

"How we live our lives is no one's business, but if you feel like you have to explain, tell everyone Gerald needs you here—at least for a while. I'll fly back every month or so, and you can fly out to Kentucky a few times a year. That should keep the tongues from wagging too much."

Kim hugged herself and rubbed her hands up and down her arms as if she were fighting off a chill. "I won't be flying anywhere," she replied, her tone flat and final. "Not ever again. And I wish you wouldn't, either."

"If I don't fly, I'll soon be out of business."

She closed her eyes briefly and turned toward the window.

Understanding the turmoil she must be feeling, Drew rose and turned her around to face him. The muscles in her upper arms were tight with a tension that made her back ramrod straight. The smile in his eyes was gentle, designed to let her know he understood her fear. "If I didn't know better, I'd think you were afraid something might happen to me," he teased.

Worry lurked in the smoke-hued eyes that roved

over his features uneasily. "That's exactly what I'm afraid of."

His hands moved up and down her arms the way her own had just moments before. "Lightning never strikes twice in the same place."

"That's an old wives' tale," she countered, unconvinced.

"You can't go through the rest of your life being afraid of something that will probably never happen again."

"That's easy for you to say."

"Maybe it is." He lifted both hands and smoothed the hair away from her flushed cheeks. "Look at you," he chided. "You're a wreck."

She grimaced. "Thank you very much."

He smiled and tucked the hair behind her ears, his fingertips trailing down her throat to her shoulders. "And so prickly," he murmured. "You didn't used to be so prickly. What's happened to you since I went away, Kim?"

"I grew up," she said. "Unlike my sister, I became a responsible adult."

His hands kneaded the taut muscles of her shoulders. "And you resent her for it, don't you?"

"Yes," she said, "I do."

"You have a right to be angry with Amber, and a right to be angry about the things that have happened to you. You've dealt with more the past few months than some people have in a lifetime. You're worn out from taking care of your parents, you're angry at Amber for contributing to your father's stress, you're grieving over Justin, and you're feeling trapped by this pregnancy. But I haven't seen you shed a tear for any of it."

"I don't have time for tears, and even if I did, they don't change a thing." She broke free and brushed past him.

He grabbed her wrist, forcing her to turn and face him. Her pulse raced beneath his fingertips. "You're wrong. Tears ease the pressure that builds up inside us. And they cleanse."

"I'm fine."

He shook his head. "I don't think so."

"I won't explode."

"I hope not."

"It's just been a few hellacious months."

His thumb caressed the delicate bones of her wrist. "Yes, it has."

They stood there staring into each other's eyes for long moments. Drew wanted her to know he would support her, that he was *with* her no matter what. But he didn't say it, because he knew she didn't want to hear it. She wanted the world to think she was tough enough to make it by the sheer dint of her will. He was surprised she'd come to him at all and realized that if it hadn't been for Gerald, she probably wouldn't have.

"So," he said at last, "it's been a bad few months, but all that is over with."

"It is?"

"Yes. You and I are expecting a baby. That's generally perceived as good news, isn't it?"

"Usually."

"Then cheer up, sweetness," he told her, making a vee with his fingers and pushing up the corners of her mouth, "or we'll never make the world believe ours is a match made in heaven."

* * *

A match made in heaven. Not bloody likely, Drew thought, rolling to the side of the bed and swinging his feet to the floor. From long habit, he reached for the cheroots that usually lay on the nightstand, only to realize he'd given up smoking two weeks earlier. As usual when he was worried, the longing for tobacco was a sharp hunger. As sharp as his growing hunger for Kim.

He rubbed his face in frustration and leaned forward to rest his elbows on his knees. Like Kim, he had been surprised at how well his family and her father had taken the news of their marriage. Gerald even went so far as to say he understood now why she'd been so reluctant to forgive Justin.

It had taken Drew all of thirty seconds to realize that he'd been so eager to take her up on her offer because he figured it would be his only chance. He had the reputation of knowing a good thing when he saw it, and he couldn't help feeling that this ridiculous proposal of hers was a good thing.

The time had been right. He'd sown his share of wild oats, and he'd scrimped and saved and planned and gambled his way up through the elite ranks of Thoroughbred breeders. He wasn't just the Irish farm manager's kid anymore. He was respected, well liked and wealthy. In all the ways that mattered, he was finally Kim Campion's equal, which had been the goal that motivated him all along. He wanted her family and the world to consider him worthy of her because, as corny as it sounded, he'd loved her for longer than he could remember.

She probably wouldn't believe it, but he'd been faithful to the wedding vows they'd taken. Even when the need for a woman became an unbearable ache, the hectic pace of his life-style and the fact that he came into contact with few eligible women he found even remotely interesting made staying faithful easy. No, that wasn't true. What made it easy was that it wasn't just any woman he wanted. It was his wife.

They'd never discussed the possibility of their marriage being anything other than one in-name-only. Kim had been grieving for Justin, carrying his baby. Once, she'd gone so far as to tell Drew that if he ever met anyone and wanted to call the whole thing off, she'd give him an annulment, no questions asked. They certainly hadn't talked about the rules changing if they did grow to love each other.

Drew hadn't told her that an annulment was the last thing he would ever want. He'd hoped that if he could help her through her bad time, if he could be a good husband and a good father to her baby, maybe—once she got over losing Justin—she might consider making their marriage a real one.

Which is why he'd planned to wine and dine her at Reginald's. He'd hoped a quiet, romantic dinner would lead to something more—a glass of wine or two when they got home, a walk in the garden, and finally the suggestion that it was time they took their marriage in a new direction.

Preparation and planning with the occasional well-researched gamble was his road game. Maybe that's where he'd made his mistake. Maybe he should have risked everything by grabbing her and kissing her right there in the car before she bolted like a green-broke filly.

The thought of kissing her full lips sent a rush of desire through him, a jolt of longing that sent him surging to his feet and to the window, which he'd opened to let in the cool nighttime breeze.

Then, as if his thoughts had conjured her up, he saw her moving wraithlike along the stone path winding through the dark blanket of the yard. She stopped and reached down to pick a flower, and her long gown ballooned around her. Straightening, she carried the small white blossom to her nose and moved on to the gazebo, which was all but hidden by a thatch of rhododendrons.

She couldn't sleep, either. Why? Without stopping to consider the wisdom of his actions, Drew dragged on a pair of clean jeans and grabbed the shirt he'd worn earlier from the back of a nearby chair, shrugging into it on his way out the door.

The night was balmy, with just a hint of coolness. Spring had definitely arrived. When Drew reached the gazebo, he found Kim sitting on the built-in bench that ran along the perimeter, turned so that her bare forearms rested on the rail. She was staring off into the darkness, and even though he couldn't see her face, there was something in the slump of her shoulders that reinforced his earlier feeling. Something was bothering her.

"Are you all right?" His voice sounded loud against the backdrop of singing frogs and the chuckling of the waterfall.

She turned with a startled gasp and crossed her arms over her breasts in an involuntary gesture. The modest reaction was both sweet and sad. She was more covered in the gown than she would be in a swim suit.

"What are you doing out here?"

"I couldn't sleep," he confessed. "Too much coffee, I guess. What about you?"

"Overly tired from the trip, I think."

"Last chance," he told her.

"For what?"

The disembodied question floated on a darkness so absolute, Drew couldn't see the expression on her face. "To tell me what's bothering you."

"I've just been—" she paused, as if she were choosing her words with care "—thinking about a lot of things lately."

"Me, too."

"Time has a way of slipping by unnoticed."

"*I* noticed," he said, his voice holding a droll note.

She sighed. "It's hard to believe Hannah will be two next week, or that Mom and Justin have been gone almost three years."

"It still bothers you?"

"What?" she asked. "Mom's death?"

"Justin's."

"I think about him sometimes. Often, in fact."

Drew didn't expect the painful stab of jealousy her admission brought. "That's to be expected."

She rubbed her palms up and down her arms in a familiar gesture. "Sometimes I'm sorry Hannah will never know him. He was a good man, and he'd have made a good father."

The fist squeezing Drew's heart tightened. "Yes, he was, and you're right. He would have made a good father."

"Not that you aren't!" she said, a note of panic in her voice. "You're excellent with Hannah, and she's crazy about you."

How about you, Kim? How do you feel about me?

"I'm crazy about her, too," Drew said. "I can't remember what it was like without her in my life, and I wouldn't ever want her not to be a part of it."

"Too bad you had to take the mom to get the child," she quipped.

"No," he said. "It's too bad the mom had to lose the man she loved and settle for second best."

Abruptly, Kim stopped massaging her upper arms. "No one could ever consider you second best, Drew."

The softly spoken words were the sweetest he'd heard from her in years, but he knew better than to read too much into them. "What I meant was I know losing Justin was painful."

There was a slight pause before she replied. "I'm not still grieving for him, if that's what you're getting at."

Drew embraced a tentative hope. "I'm glad."

"I've learned that life goes on. Sometimes we have to make hard decisions, take action we hadn't planned on. Sometimes it works. Sometimes it doesn't. And if it doesn't, we have to figure out another way."

Drew assumed she was talking about her pregnancy, Justin's death and their resulting marriage. Encouraged, he added, "And sometimes all that's needed to make something work is a little fine tuning."

"True."

A cool breeze riffled the tender new leaves. She shivered. "You're chilly," he stated.

"A little," she admitted. "But it feels good, too. It helps make me think more clearly."

Drew didn't reply, but he knew what she meant.

He had often contemplated how the darkness, while somehow making situations seem more grave, also provided a certain anonymity that made weighing problems and evaluating circumstances easier. It was as if night absorbed the problems, the worries, and gave you back solutions and second chances with the dawning of a new day.

"We could go in and have some of Mom's oatmeal cookies and milk."

Before Kim could reply, they heard the back door slam and a child's wail from the porch. Almost simultaneously, Cindy called, "Mrs. McShane, are you out there? Hannah's had a bad dream."

"I'm coming!" Kim shouted back. She brushed past Drew, who followed more slowly. The child's timing couldn't have been worse. When he got to the house, he found Hannah in Kim's arms, her legs around her mother's waist, her arms around her neck.

"Hey, sweetness," he said, reaching out and trailing his knuckle along her cheek, "are you okay?"

Hannah raised her head from Kim's shoulder and regarded him with tear-drenched eyes. Unclasping her arms from around her mother's neck, she strained toward him. "Daddy!" she said, her voice catching on a sob. "I want Daddy."

Drew's heart turned over with a powerful surge of love. Knowing she wanted him, trusted him in this moment of extreme fright was potent stuff. Heady and sobering at the same time. Still, when Kim relinquished Hannah to him—reluctantly, it seemed—he knew it had to be a blow for him to be chosen over her.

He'd have to say something to Kim about that later, but for the moment, he cradled the warmth of

Hannah's chubby body close and pressed a kiss to her damp cheek. "Come on. Let Daddy take you back upstairs."

"No!" she cried, leaning back in his arms and looking up at him with tear-drenched eyes.

"She's scared!" Kim replied.

"Of what?" he asked.

"Mon'ser unner the bed."

"Why do you think there's a monster under your bed?" Drew asked.

"She saw it," Cindy said.

"You were dreaming, sweetness," he told her. "It was all just a bad dream, and now that you've told me and Mommy about it, you won't dream it anymore. But," he said, rubbing her nose with his, "if it will make you feel better, I'll go in and make sure there are no monsters under your bed. And if there are, I'll say the magic word and make them go away. Okay?"

"What's magic word?" Hannah asked.

"It's something that makes bad things disappear—go away."

"Oh," she said.

That problem settled to Hannah's satisfaction, Drew carried her up the stairs. Kim and Cindy followed. At the door of the room Hannah and Kim shared, Drew handed her back to Kim. Then he went inside, got down on his knees and looked under the bed. "No monsters," he pronounced solemnly. "Not even a dust bunny."

"I wanna see." Hannah squirmed to be free, and Kim set her bare feet on the floor. She knelt beside Drew and peered beneath the dust ruffle. "All gone," she said.

"All gone." Drew stood and swung Hannah up onto the bed. "That means you can go back to sleep and have sweet dreams. Tomorrow we'll go somewhere and buy a dream catcher to hang over your bed."

"What's a dream catcher?" she asked, sinking against the pillow.

Drew pulled the sheet and light blanket up to her chin. "Indians make them. It's a round hoop with feathers and cord that looks sort of like a spiderweb. There's a hole in the middle. The good dreams go through the hole and the web catches the bad dreams to keep them from getting through."

"Oh."

Down the hallway, the phone rang. "I'll get it," Cindy said.

"Do you want me to stay with you until you go to sleep?" Drew asked.

Hannah nodded. "Tell me three bears."

"Okay." He glanced at Kim, who stood silently in the doorway, watching them. "Can Mommy listen?"

Hannah nodded again and Kim approached the bed. Cindy appeared in the doorway. "It's for you, Mr. McShane. Mr. Campion." She turned red to the roots of her hair. "He called earlier, and I forgot to tell you. I'm sorry."

"No problem," Drew said, assuring the young baby-sitter with a smile that deepened the rose staining her cheeks.

"I wonder what he wants?" Kim asked.

Drew shrugged and turned to Hannah. "I have to go talk to Grandpa on the telephone. Is it okay if Mommy tells the story?"

Hannah sighed. "Yes, sir."

His gaze found Kim's. "Fill in for me, will you? I'll be back as soon as I can."

"Sure," Kim said.

Drew bent and kissed Hannah on the forehead. Then he tweaked her nose. "I'll be back in a shake."

"What's a shake?"

"Fast. I'll be back fast."

He went to the doorway and blew her a kiss. Then he took the cordless phone from Cindy and started down the hallway to his room. Behind the privacy of the closed door, he punched the mute button and said, "Hi, Gerald. What's up?"

"Maria Antonia called tonight," Gerald said.

"Don't tell me there's been another one?"

"I'm afraid so. Paul Mercer. It seems he knows Denny Talbot."

"Talbot's mare was bred to the wrong stud, too, wasn't she?" Drew asked.

"Yes," Gerald said heavily. "The two of them started talking and decided that two mistakes can't be a coincidence. Mercer's threatening a lawsuit."

Drew shoved a hand through his hair and swore.

"Exactly."

Gerald told Drew everything he and Maria Antonia had discussed, including the fact that she said she'd look back on her records and see who had been working for her and that she was trying to locate the last of her former farm managers.

"She has her attorneys standing by. She's a little short of cash and needs me to send her a couple of thousand dollars for a retainer." Drew heard the embarrassment in his father-in-law's voice. "I couldn't tell her no. Not since I own half the stallion."

"How can she be short of cash?" Drew asked. "I thought Lawrence left her well-fixed."

"She'd never admit it, but I hear David has a gambling problem."

"I don't doubt it. I've only met him a couple of times, but I can't say he impressed me as an upstanding sort of guy," Drew said, his mind seething with skepticism. Ugly questions had been roiling around in his head lately. He didn't like them, and he didn't think Gerald would, either, so he didn't say anything. "Don't worry about the money. I'll take care of it."

"That isn't why I called," Gerald said stiffly.

"I know it isn't, but I don't want you worrying about this."

Gerald expelled a harsh sigh. "The tables have certainly turned, haven't they? I never thought you'd be helping me out of a financial bind."

"It's just a temporary thing. Besides, what's family for?" Drew said, deliberately injecting a light note into his voice. He knew it galled Gerald to be beholden to him in any way. Like a lot of so-called wealthy people, Gerald had more assets than actual cash. With the improvements to the breeding facility and the purchase of the new stallions, and some recent trouble with the IRS, he was overextended, at least for the near future.

"I appreciate it, Drew," Gerald said. "More than you know."

"I do know."

"Give the girls a kiss for me."

"I'll be glad to," Drew said. "Talk to you soon. Good night."

He turned off the phone. Unlike Gerald and Maria Antonia, Drew wasn't so sure the whole mix-up was a coincidence. But if it wasn't an honest mistake—five honest mistakes so far—it implied that something far more sinister was going on.

The question was, who was behind the scheme and why had they done it? The why was easy. It cost a small fortune to breed to Flight of Dreams, so the more mares that could be booked to him, the better-off Maria Antonia and Gerald would be. But the stallion could only service a certain amount of mares during breeding season. It would be so easy to take the money and use another horse. Too easy. So who was behind it?

The farm managers? No. Maria Antonia had changed them like she changed her socks since Lawrence died. The help couldn't be held responsible. They only did what they were told, and besides, they couldn't get their hands on the money unless they were in league with someone else. Drew had known Gerald Campion long enough to be certain that he was genuinely shocked and sickened by what was happening. Besides, the man was—had always been—the personification of integrity.

Which left Maria Antonia. By her own admission to Gerald, money was tight. Was it the beautiful Maria Antonia who had concocted the scheme because she needed the money to keep her husband happy?

Drew didn't know, but he did know one thing. He was darn well going to find out, no matter what happened. He'd known Maria for years, and he liked her, but the Campions meant too much to him for him to sit back and watch them be destroyed. Tomorrow he would start asking some questions, start looking into things himself, but right now, he had a daughter to tell a story to.

* * *

Kim told the story of the three bears and sang "Froggie Went a Courtin'," but all the while, her mind was filled with thoughts of her husband. Seeing the love Hannah felt for him made her heart ache. Even though it hurt that Hannah had wanted Drew instead of her when she was frightened, Kim was also pleased that there was such trust between father and daughter. It didn't make her situation any easier, though. She loved him, and while it was obvious that he was fond of her, fondness wasn't love. She had to tell Drew that she wanted to end their marriage. It was the best thing for them all. Wasn't it?

She had just finished the song and was tiptoeing from the room when Drew stepped through the doorway. "Gone, is she?"

"Yes," Kim whispered.

"Just let me give her a good-night kiss." He crossed the carpeted room and got down on his knees beside the bed. For long moments, he just looked at Hannah, as if watching her sleep gave him enormous pleasure. Kim felt her throat tighten with emotion. He wasn't making this easy.

She watched him brush the hair away from Hannah's face and press a kiss to her cheek. There wasn't a hint of embarrassment on his face as he got to his feet and joined Kim at the door. Instead, he smiled at her.

"She's so bonnie," he said, his voice a soft masculine rumble, the phrase Kim heard so often from Cullen now spilling from his son's lips as naturally as the smile that curved them. "Like her mother."

Kim didn't know if it was the look in his eyes or the compliment that set her heart to racing and drove away the words she'd intended to say. Fighting the impulse to flee, she licked lips that had gone bone-dry.

To her surprise, Drew gave a little groan. Before she could do more than register the sound and wonder what it meant, he dipped his head and touched his mouth to hers. Surprise left her unable to think or move. Other than a quick brush of his mouth to hers for the sake of the family, he'd never kissed her. Not like this. Not since the wedding ceremony.

His lips were firm, warm and electrifying. She heard another groan and realized with overwhelming dismay that it had come from her. Drew took the sound for acquiescence, permission, even. What began as a simple touching of one mouth to the other segued quickly into something with more promise. His arms went around her and he deepened the kiss.

He tasted of the hard peppermints he ate by the dozen since he'd given up smoking. He smelled of a manly soap and an intoxicating woodsy cologne. The sensations rode roughshod over her determination and overwhelmed her senses, making her feel hot and cold at once, as if she were burning up with fever and shaking with a chill—but euphoric, somehow. Trembling and weak-kneed. Desperate for air. Needing a pacemaker to regulate the erratic beating of her heart.

His body was hard and warm against hers.

While she tried to find the strength to end the kiss, he urged her lips apart and drew the fullness of her bottom lip into his mouth with a gentle sucking action. She felt the tugging all the way to the nucleus of her womanhood, a sweet, sharp pleasure, closely akin to pain. What did it mean? she wondered as her fingers dug into the firm flesh of his waist. What did *he* mean by doing this now, when she was ready to end it, ready to offer him the freedom he deserved?

Dredging up every bit of strength she could muster, Kim pushed free of him. To her surprise and reluctant dismay, he let her go. They stood in the doorway of Hannah's room, searching each other's eyes. His gaze was hooded, revealing nothing. Disconcerted and breathing heavily, she asked, "Why did you do that?"

He shrugged. "Gerald said to give his girls a kiss. I was just passing it on."

She was about to tell him she didn't think that was what her father had in mind, when Hannah rolled over and cried out, "Mommy!"

Kim reacted automatically, turning and rushing to the bed where Hannah thrashed her head back and forth. It only took a moment to quiet her, but when she glanced back at the doorway, Drew was gone.

Chapter Four

Weary from the late-night flight from California to Louisiana, Amber Campion tossed the morning paper onto the table's glass top next to her orange juice. The local newspaper had picked up the story of the breeding fraud from the Associated Press. She reached for her cigarettes. What lousy, rotten timing! Why couldn't Paul Mercer have waited a few more days before deciding to have her father's breeding operations investigated? In a few days—a week, tops—she'd have had her check in hand and be back on her way to sunny California, her problems all solved. Temporarily, anyway. Now she'd have to be very careful how she approached her dad. The last thing she wanted was to cause him to have another heart attack. She didn't think she could take that.

"Top o' the mornin', Amber. I thought that might be you I saw pullin' in late last night."

Amber looked up at the sound of the familiar voice, a pleased smile on her face. "Good morning, Cullen," she said to the aging farm manager. "Yep, it's me. The bad penny turning up again when you least expect it." She tapped the newspaper with a plum-tinted fingernail. "And not a good time, it seems. How are you?"

"I'm fine, lass. And you?"

"Great. You're looking well. How's the family?"

His green eyes, so like his son's, crinkled at the corners. "All fine. Grandkids are making an old man of me."

"Ah, Cullen!" Amber said with a genuine laugh. "You're like Daddy. You'll never get old. You're too full of vim and vinegar."

"If only it were true," he said with another smile. "But I fear you've kissed the Blarney stone." He looked her over from the top of her shining blond head with its stylish cut to the tips of her pedicured toes. "Speaking of looking well, you certainly are, even though you look a wee bit weary."

"Now who's feeding blarney to whom? I'm the one who's getting old, Cullen." As she said the words, she realized just how true they were and how sad it made her to realize it.

His eyes twinkled. "Ah, lass, there's nothing wrong with getting older, if you do it with grace and style. You've got the style down, just fine, but it's the grace that needs some workin' on."

Amber felt she should be offended, but the friendly expression in his eyes forbade annoyance.

He smiled again. "Has your father seen the morning paper?"

"Yes."

"How's he taking it?"

"He didn't say much to me."

"Well, I'll just go and have a word with him," Cullen said, crossing the veranda. When he reached the door, he turned. "It's good to have you here, lass. You always did make me smile. And," he added, "I wouldn't call you a bad penny. A tad tarnished, maybe, but precious metals shine up real good with just a little care."

A curious, inexplicable sorrow filled Amber as she watched Drew's father enter the house. What was it about Cullen that he always said nice things to her, but somehow still made her feel as if she were lacking in some way? And why was it that even when she knew he was pointing out her faults with his pithy wisdom, she could never find it in her heart to be angry with him?

On the morning following Drew's kiss, Kim deliberately waited until he was gone for the day before she ventured downstairs for breakfast. The problem she'd had resting before he kissed her was nothing compared to her inability to sleep afterward. Thankfully, there was no sign of Hannah or Cindy, Kim thought as she took a coffee mug down from the cabinet.

She was about to fill it when she saw the note propped against the coffeemaker.

Kim,
Hope you slept well. I have an appointment for lunch, but I should be in by three or so. Forgive me for last night. We need to talk.
                                        Drew

There was no closing other than the bold scrawl of his name. She put the note into the pocket of her robe. He thought they should talk. Well, so did she, and the sooner the better. She had no idea what had prompted him to kiss her—a kiss he now wanted forgiveness for—but she imagined it had a lot to do with his being a typical man with typical male impulses and urges. For her, the kiss only underscored her growing certainty that he was missing out on things he deserved: a wife who'd share his bed. Someone to love him.

She'd be more than happy to do both if he'd only ask.

Maybe that's what the kiss was all about. Maybe he was making a move toward a change in their relationship.

A mocking smile curved her lips. As if there were a chance that she and Drew could have a real marriage! Real marriages—marriages that hoped to last—were based on mutual love and respect. Liking each other. Not unexpected, unplanned pregnancies and vows spoken spur-of-the-moment.

Kim poured her coffee and took it out onto the back porch. The morning was chilly, but it would soon warm up into a gorgeous spring day. She went around to the front of the house, picked up the morning paper and carried it to the back. Settled into a wicker chair, her coffee on a matching table, she opened up the newspaper. The headline involved national politics, but lower down the word *horse* caught her attention.

Local Horse Breeder Accused!

"Local Thoroughbred breeder Maria Antonia Perkins has been accused of taking stud fees for one stallion and breeding to another." Stunned by the accusation, Kim continued to read. The allegation had been made by Paul Mercer. The article was blessedly brief, giving an overview of Mercer's position and stating that the same thing had happened to a friend, who remained anonymous. The Lexington police as well as the Kentucky Breeder's Association were looking into the charges. The last line of the column stated that the stallion's co-owner, Gerald Campion of Louisiana, could not be reached at press time.

Kim read the article twice, as if by doing so she might be able to make more sense of it. The thing that made the strongest impact on her was that her father didn't need the pressure of a police investigation. She was reading the allegations a third time when the phone rang. Muttering at the interruption, she tossed down the paper and rushed inside before the ringing woke Cindy and Hannah.

"Hello."

"Kim?"

Kim recognized Cullen McShane's soft brogue. "Cullen? Have you heard the news?"

"I have," he said heavily. "The newshounds were ringing the doorbell before daylight."

"What does Dad say? Is he okay?"

"He's not saying much, and he's holding up just fine. I just came from talking with him," Cullen told her, but Kim had the feeling he was holding something back.

"What is it?" she asked.

"Amber came home last night."

Kim's mind raced. There could be only one reason Amber had decided to visit their father.

"She looks tired," Cullen said thoughtfully.

"Too many nights carousing, I imagine," Kim said. It would take more than bags under Amber's eyes to elicit any sympathy from Kim.

"Come now, lass," Cullen said in a teasing voice. "Where's your Christian charity?"

"Don't tell me she's got you wrapped around her little finger, too," Kim said. "I thought you got her number years ago."

"There's nothing wrong with your sister that a firm hand couldn't have corrected. You can't blame her for the spoiling your father gave her."

"I suppose not, but she isn't a child anymore, Cullen."

"I can't argue with that." Cullen gave her his love and told her to have Drew give him a call. Kim hung up feeling more depressed than she had on waking. The fact that Amber had decided to visit their father said that she didn't plan on taking no for an answer to her latest request. The fact that her visit corresponded with Kim's own absence from Louisiana was no coincidence.

Kim knew she had to go back.

You just got here. You're supposed to have Hannah's birthday with Drew in a few days.

Drew would just have to understand. He knew how much she worried about her father. Hannah wouldn't be upset if Drew wasn't at her birthday party. She was too young to realize just what it was all about, and Drew was an adult; he'd survive.

What about the reason you came? What about telling him you want to end your marriage?

Kim didn't want to think about that just yet, not with the recollection of their kiss still a tantalizing memory and a tempting prelude to the possibility of something more.

No. Drew wasn't the shy type. If he wanted more from her than what he was getting, he'd have no problem telling her so. Disgusted by her own weakness, she dumped her coffee into the sink. She had to leave before she made a complete fool of herself. She'd been abandoned once; she wouldn't make the mistake of putting her heart on the line again. Not with a man like Drew McShane, who could have any woman he wanted.

Kim took the stairs two at a time. She had to wake Hannah and Cindy and get on the road. Thank goodness they hadn't unpacked everything yet. It would be a grueling trip, and they would all be exhausted, but if Cindy helped her drive, they could be home late tonight.

Where was Kim's car? Drew wondered as he pulled into the driveway that afternoon. After he'd read the newspaper article and fielded several calls about his father-in-law's possible connection to the fraud, he'd tried several times to call Kim to see if she'd heard the news and, if so, how she was taking it. But the phone had rung and rung and no one answered. He considered the possibility that she'd taken Cindy sightseeing. It was her first time in Kentucky.

As Drew slammed the Bronco's door and headed for the house, an inexplicable feeling of foreboding gathered inside him. He hurried up the porch steps, his boots thudding hollowly on the oak planks. He thrust open the back door, calling her name. His only greeting was the ticking of the grandfather clock in the foyer and the hum of the refrigerator. Surely she'd left him a note, he thought, going to the pad on the countertop near the wall phone.

There was nothing there.

Fighting a growing apprehension, he headed for the bedroom, taking the stairs two at a time. After a perfunctory knock on Kim's door—which he didn't wait for her to answer—he turned the knob and pushed into the room. Like the kitchen, the bedroom showed no signs of recent habitation. The bed didn't look as if it had been slept in. There was no evidence of the suitcases he'd carried up the evening before. Not one stitch of clothing tossed across a piece of furniture. No shoes scattered here and there, as if she'd just stepped out of them—a habit he found amusing in a person who was generally neat.

There was no sign that she'd even arrived yesterday. No sign that she'd ever been there. Drew's stomach gave a sickening plunge. Turning on his heel, he made his way to Cindy's room, finding the same abandoned air in it.

He cursed and stalked toward his own room, stripping off his dirty shirt as he went. Where had she gone? he asked himself as he yanked open the door and tossed the shirt onto the bed.

The answer was simple. She'd gone back to Louisiana. But why?

Because you couldn't keep your hands to yourself. Because you had to go and kiss her. He sank onto the edge of the bed and pulled off his boots—something he usually did at the back door. So he'd kissed her! She was his wife, darn it!

But that wasn't in your agreement, was it, McShane?

Actually, he didn't recall their having an agree-

ment other than that he'd marry her to give her baby
a name and that they'd live in separate states. He'd
been too busy being the gentleman, too concerned
about her getting over Justin's death to tell her how
he felt and try to make her fall in love with him.
Now he'd botched whatever chance he might have
had with her if he'd taken things slow and easy.

But slow and easy hadn't been uppermost on his
mind as he'd stood staring down at her, seeing the
confusion and something that looked like anticipation
in her eyes. He'd been too keenly aware of the delicate floral scent wafting from the warmth of her
body, of the smooth flawlessness of her creamy
shoulders and the soft rise and fall of her breasts,
barely concealed by the tiny tucks and embroidered
flowers on the bodice of her gown. Too acutely at-
tuned to the fact that there was probably nothing beneath the satiny, opaque fabric but satiny flesh.

The need to feel her firm curves pressed against
him, to experience the feel of her in his arms—the
way a man holds a woman, not the way a friend holds
a friend—had overcome his usual good sense and
caused him to react to her nearness like a green
schoolboy with howling hormones.

*The one time in your life you lose control and look
what happened.*

Even now, at the memory of how she felt in his
arms, of the taste of her mouth, he felt the typical
response of a healthy male body. Muttering, he
dragged his jeans and undershorts down his legs and
headed naked toward the bathroom. What he needed
was a cold shower to clear his head, bring him to his
senses. Then he'd figure out just what to do about
her leaving.

He found the note taped to the mirror above the lavatory, where there was no chance he could overlook it. Bracing his hands on the edge of the sink top, he leaned over to read.

Dear Drew,
I suppose you saw the paper. You know as well as I do that there's no way my father could do the things insinuated in that article. Cullen says Dad is doing pretty well, but I really think I need to be there right now. He also said that Amber came home last night. I guess you've figured out that we've gone back to Louisiana. Maybe it's for the best.

   You said you sensed there was something wrong with me, and you were right. I was just having a hard time finding a way to tell you what needs to be said. The truth is, I made the trip not only so Hannah could have her birthday with you, but to tell you that while I appreciate all you've done for me the past few years, things between us aren't working out the way I imagined they would. I've realized this marriage isn't fair for either of us and that a divorce would be in the best interest for us both. I know this may come as a shock, and that telling you in a note is the coward's way out, but I truly believe that once you think things through, you'll see that I'm right.

Kim

With a snarl of rage, Drew ripped the piece of pink stationery from the mirror and tossed it into the trash can. His desire had vanished in the face of a sudden, irrational anger. He turned on the shower, automatically testing the temperature of the water before stepping into the small cubicle. He didn't need a cold shower now. He needed it hot, because he was madder than hell.

Cursing, he pressed his palms against the cool tile walls, dropped his head forward and let the steaming water pound him with its needlelike spray. The stinging heat couldn't begin to compete with the sharp, stabbing pain that seemed rooted in his soul and spread throughout his body with every agonized beat of his bruised and bleeding heart.

Divorce! So that's what had been bothering her. All the time she was telling him she was fine, Gerald was fine, everything was just hunky-dory, she was working up her courage to tell him she wanted a divorce.

Drew lathered his head while bits and pieces of what she'd said in the note flitted through his mind.

Appreciate all you've done... Things aren't working out...

Well, they hadn't worked out the way he'd thought they would, either, or they wouldn't be in this unholy mess.

This marriage isn't fair for either of us...divorce would be in the best interest for us both....

He ducked his soapy head beneath the spray. What was she trying to pull, anyway, implying that they were both miserable? It was obvious that she was the one who was feeling the pinch of her wedding ring, crystal clear that the kiss they'd shared hadn't meant anything to her. Because if it had meant half as much to her as it had to him, she wouldn't have mentioned ending their marriage. She'd have given herself time to think about the kiss and consider what it meant in the scheme of things. The fact that she hadn't could only mean one thing: she'd met someone else.

Drew swore again. He finished showering in record time, then pulled on a pair of briefs, hauled his suitcase from the closet and began dumping clothes into it. If his precious bride thought she could just write him off like a bad debt, she had another think coming. He wasn't about to let her break up their marriage without some serious dialogue, not only about what she thought was right, but about his wants and needs—Hannah's, too. He swore again. How dare Kim think she could take his daughter away from him! And whether she liked it or not, Hannah *was* his, in all the ways that counted.

Drew made up his mind. If Kim wanted a divorce, she'd have to ask him for it face-to-face, not by leaving him some blasted note. He slammed the suitcase shut. Hell, he thought, heading down the stairs to the Bronco, a divorce was out of the question. How could they get a divorce when they'd never consummated their marriage?

The trip back to Louisiana was much as Kim expected it to be. Other than expressing a concern for Gerald, Cindy had made no protest about cutting their trip short. Hannah was another matter. When she wasn't sleeping, she was fussing. Kim couldn't blame her. The only good thing about the child's demands was that they kept Kim from dwelling on Drew's reaction to her note.

Various scenarios played through her mind during the trip, but for the life of her, she couldn't decide which was most likely to be his true reaction. Though

Drew had a memorable temper, he kept it carefully under control. Most likely, he'd be relieved that she'd finally taken steps to end their sham marriage, since she was the one who'd proposed. Drew—ever the gentleman—might have been waiting for her to offer him back his life and the freedom to pursue love and happiness again. It wasn't that she thought he'd been miserable the past few years, but there was a vast difference between contentment with the status quo and true happiness.

There was the possibility the he'd be irritated that she'd taken the coward's way out. He was a man who believed in confronting things head-on. Still, he was a reasonable man, and once he got past the initial surprise, no doubt he'd be happy to work things out. The important thing was his relationship with Hannah. Kim planned to be fair about visitation rights. It would be hard to let Drew take Hannah to Kentucky for visits, but Kim knew she'd survive. Other mothers did. And it would be criminal to keep the two of them apart.

Of course, the fantasy that most appealed to her was the one where Drew read the letter, realized he loved her, followed her to Louisiana and told her he wanted to make their marriage a real one.

"When pigs fly," she muttered under her breath.

"I'm sorry, Mrs. McShane," Cindy said, looking up from the romance novel she was reading. "What did you say?"

Kim offered her young friend a rueful smile. "Nothing important, Cindy. I was just thinking out loud."

Miles passed, measured by mile markers, signs telling how far it was to the next town, and the ne-

cessity of finding a new radio station as they drove
out of range. Hours passed, gauged by pit stops, pe-
riodic naps for Hannah and the lowering of the sun
on the horizon.

They pulled over for dinner just after dark. Kim
hoped that once Hannah was fed and darkness fell,
she would succumb to sleep. Thankfully, she did.

It was almost midnight when Kim arrived at Lafourche Farm. She was surprised to see a light on in
her father's study. A frisson of irritation raced
through her. Gerald needed his rest if he didn't want
to suffer another heart attack. She parked in her regular place in the garage—once the carriage house—
and turned off the engine with a sigh of relief.

Home. She'd put Hannah to bed, tell her father
they'd arrived and fall into her own bed. The sleep-
lessness of the night before was catching up with her.

Drew sat in Gerald Campion's study, flicking a Bic
on and off and staring longingly at the unlighted cig-
arillo lying on the desktop. His father-in-law had
been surprised but glad to seen him when he'd shown
up earlier in the evening after catching the first available flight out. Gerald was happier still to know Kim
was on her way back. If Gerald wondered why Drew
hadn't driven back with his wife, he was too polite
to ask.

They'd spent the evening talking about the investigation and the possibility of a lawsuit, and finally,
after a late supper Drew had sent his father-in-law up
to bed, assuring him he'd wait up for Kim.

As he watched the headlights slicing through the
darkness and heard the Explorer pull into the garage,
Drew felt his anger coming back full force. Kim

would be surprised to see him. But that was okay.
He had a couple of surprises for her, too.

Kim turned off the ignition and faced Cindy in the
darkness. "Thanks, Cindy. You've been a great
help."

Cindy covered a huge yawn and smiled. "No problem, Mrs. McShane, but I am glad to finally be here."

"Yeah," Kim said, "me, too."

Without warning, the light in the garage came on.
Kim squeezed her eyes shut against the sudden pain,
then blinked several times to let her pupils adjust to
the unexpected brightness. She turned to check on
Hannah, praying the light hadn't awakened her.
Thankfully, she was still sound asleep.

"Mr. McShane! What are you doing here?"

The sound of Cindy's shocked voice and the fact
that Drew was there—had followed them—sent
Kim's heart plummeting to her toes and her head
swiveling toward the door of the breezeway leading
to the house. To her surprise, her husband was stepping through the doorway.

Drew smiled at Cindy. "I agreed with Kim that
we should all be here for Mr. Campion," he explained with consummate smoothness. "There are
some things that needed to be taken care of face-to-
face."

The answer was for Cindy, but he was looking
directly at Kim. She didn't like what she saw in his
eyes. Something that looked like unbridled rage,
something she'd never associated with him before.
Irritation she halfway expected, but not true anger.

Her knees shook as she opened the door and got
out of the Explorer. She was reaching for the handle

of the rear door when Drew's hand closed over hers. She turned with a gasp and found herself trapped between him and the car. She hadn't expected him to move so fast.

"Hello, love."

His palms were pressed against the top of the vehicle. He was so close she could feel the heat radiating from his body. So close she could feel emotion pulsing off him in huge waves. And that emotion was definitely anger, she thought, looking up into his eyes. The longing to close her own eyes and block out the sight of his ire was overwhelming. In all the years she'd known him, she'd seldom seen him angry, and never at her.

"Are we going to unload the car tonight?" Cindy asked, shattering the growing tension.

"No," Drew said, sparing her a smile. "It's late. Go on to bed. We'll bring Hannah up."

Cindy smiled her appreciation and covered another yawn. "Great! See you in the morning, then."

"Right," Drew said. "Good night, Cindy."

Kim added her good-night, and Cindy left her alone with her husband. Overpowered by his nearness, Kim could only look up at him and wonder what his next move would be. When he continued to stare down at her, she blurted the first thing that came to mind.

"You didn't have to come. Cullen told me Dad is handling things pretty well, and I can deal with Amber."

"I'm sure you can. You can deal with everything but your own personal problems." Without giving her an opportunity to reply, he said, "I can't believe you wrote me a damned note telling me you want a divorce. The least you could have done was tell me in person. God knows I gave you plenty of opportunities."

Bitterness laced his voice. Feeling like the lowest form of life, Kim whispered, "I'm sorry." She gave a helpless shrug. "I couldn't seem to find the right words."

"You didn't seem to have any trouble finding the right words in the letter. Dear Drew," he quipped. "I have to go home. My daddy needs me, and, oh, by the way, I want a divorce."

Misquoted as it was, she got the point. Okay, so she hadn't approached it the right way, but she still couldn't imagine him being so upset. He was supposed to be relieved. Maybe even happy to get his freedom.

"Surely you know we can't go on the way we have been."

"Maybe not," he conceded, "but the least we could have done was sit down like two reasonable adults and talk about the alternatives."

"You're right," she said. "I'm sorry."

"You should be."

"I can't believe you're so angry."

"Wouldn't you be if the tables were turned?"

Kim thought about that. Would she be angry if Drew wanted to end their marriage? No. Not angry. Devastated.

From the back seat, Hannah whimpered.

"Look," Kim said, pushing the hair away from her face in a weary gesture. "It's late. We're both tired. Can't we talk about this later?"

He took a backward step and let his hands fall to his sides. "Oh, we're definitely going to talk about it. But you're right. There's plenty of time, and I'm going to be here a while.''

The something in his voice that sounded like a threat matched the look in his eyes. A tickle of apprehension made her heart start beating faster. *Get a grip, Kim. This is Drew. You've never been afraid of him before.*

Maybe *afraid* was too strong a word. But whatever the feeling was and however strange it felt didn't change the fact that the man she'd been talking to was a stranger, one she didn't know at all. For the first time, she was aware of how time, distance and circumstance could change someone.

''Don't you have things to do in Kentucky?''

''I've got plenty of things to do in Kentucky. But they can wait. Family comes first, right?'' The undisguised sarcasm hinted that he was talking about the two of them and not her father's problems.

''Right,'' she told him, unable to think of anything else to say. ''I'll just...take Hannah up.''

''Go on to bed,'' he told her, his voice sounding suddenly weary. ''I'll take care of Hannah.''

''She may wake up.''

''I can handle it.''

The expression in his eyes said he wouldn't be swayed. Kim was left with no alternatives, nothing else to say. ''All right, then. Thanks.''

''My pleasure,'' he said, but he didn't sound pleased at all.

''Good night.''

Instead of answering, Drew took another step back and made a sweeping gesture toward the door. Kim scooted between the narrow place between him and the car and ran into the house as if she were afraid he'd pounce on her.

"Sweet dreams."

The words followed her as she stumbled through the breezeway door that led to the kitchen. They stayed with her while she shucked out of her clothes and fell into her solitary bed. Even though her mind was filled with questions and doubts, she slept, her misgivings an unworthy foe of her exhaustion.

Surprisingly, she did dream.

Dreamed of Drew kissing her...stripping off her clothes and making love to her. She dreamed he told her he loved her, that he didn't want to end their marriage.

When she awakened the next morning, she was as tired as when she'd gone to bed.

"Sweet dreams." The memory of his words drifted through her weary mind. Oh, she'd had dreams, all right. But they were more bitter than sweet.

Chapter Five

Spring was much further along in Louisiana than it was in Kentucky, Drew thought the next morning. A warm sun peeked through tender emerald leaves and newly born foals gamboled around on flimsy stick legs in the greening fields beyond the century-old, wrought-iron fence that separated the yard from the pasture.

He hadn't slept much. Finally giving up on the endeavor near dawn, he got up, showered and joined Gerald on the back *galerie* of the old plantation house Gerald Campion, his father and his father before him had called home. They were indulging in a rarity for Gerald since his heart attack—a traditional breakfast of eggs, ham, biscuits and grits.

"I appreciate your coming, but you didn't have to, you know," Gerald said.

"I know I didn't have to," Drew told his father-in-law for the second time.

There was no point telling Gerald his reasons had more to do with Kim's note than concern for the scandal connected to the possible breeding fraud.

"Well, you shouldn't have left your own business to come and hold my hand. I'm a big boy. And Kim shouldn't have cut her visit short, either. Good grief! She'd just arrived."

"I know," Drew concurred. "But you know your daughter. She worries about you, and when she makes up her mind to do something, she does it."

But not this time. She won't get her darned divorce and take Hannah away from me without a fight.

"Besides," he added, "I wanted to be with Hannah for her birthday."

Gerald sighed. "I can't believe she's going to be two already." He slanted Drew a sideways look and a crafty smile. "The two of you should start thinking of giving her a brother or sister soon, or the age gap will be too great for them to be close."

"I've been thinking about it," Drew said truthfully. He busied himself with pouring another cup of coffee to keep from meeting Gerald's shrewd gaze. "Talking Kim into it might take some doing, though." That, too, was the truth.

"Is she okay?"

"What do you mean?" Drew asked as he spooned sugar into his cup.

Gerald shook his head. "I'm not sure, but she's been acting strangely lately. She's always been the type to keep her thoughts and feelings to herself, but there's something on her mind. I was hoping a visit to Kentucky would snap her out of the doldrums, but she wasn't there long enough to unpack, much less have time to unburden herself to you.''

Oh, she unburdened herself. Never fear about that.

''I'll talk to her,'' Drew promised. He reached for the cream pitcher. ''See if I can't get it all straightened out.''

Gerald smiled. ''She's been a rock since her mother died, but I've always believed her tough act is just that—a facade to cover up how she really feels.''

Drew, who had also been worried about Kim's unwillingness to shed any tears when her mother and Justin died, was surprised by Gerald's observation. In the past, he had seemed to accept Kim's commitment to her family and her willingness to hold things together as a natural course of action. Was he finally beginning to see that his younger daughter had devoted the majority of her life to trying to make up for her sister's sins?

''She does need to stop trying to hold the world together single-handedly,'' Drew observed, raising his coffee cup to his lips.

''The two of you need to spend more time together, too,'' Gerald said. ''In fact, as much as I'd miss her and Hannah, they should move to Kentucky to be with you.''

Drew set his cup in his saucer without saying anything. Well, now was certainly a fine time for Gerald to realize it.

''I know she stayed here in the beginning because I'd just lost her mother and had the heart attack, and she felt I needed her, but it's been almost three years, and I can't depend on her the rest of my life. It isn't fair to her or you.''

Drew had no argument for that. In the beginning, the arrangement hadn't been a problem. He'd known that—tears or no tears—Kim was grieving for Justin, and since there was no question of their marriage being a normal one, their living in separate states had been no problem. But since he'd started fantasizing about changing their relationship to a more personal one, he'd begun to view Kim's selfless dedication to her father as a possible handicap. It was reassuring for Drew to know that Gerald saw the situation in the same way he did.

"Don't worry about it," Drew told Gerald. "We'll work it out. You have enough on your plate."

"Yes," Gerald said heavily. "It's a mess, isn't it?"

"It is that," Drew said, wishing he could call back the words. Gerald seemed to have aged in the span of seconds. While they couldn't put off talking about the breeding mix-up indefinitely, Drew wished he'd postponed it, at least for a while.

"Have you heard anything else?" he asked.

"No. Maria Antonia called early this morning to tell me the police spent all day yesterday going over the books and breeding records for the past three years. They haven't even scratched the surface. They want to talk to her past farm managers, too, and see if they can remember anything to help clear things up."

"That's smart."

"I thought so. One of them might know something."

"Daddy!"

Hannah's cheerful greeting thankfully ended the conversation. Bright eyed and ready to go after her long ordeal in the car, she ran through the French doors. Smothering a yawn, Cindy followed close behind. Hannah launched herself at Drew, who scooted back his chair and reached out to scoop her into a close embrace.

Smiling with pure happiness, she patted his cheeks with both plump hands and then, with a gesture of complete trust and contentment, wrapped her arms around his neck and laid her head on his shoulder.

"Hi, Cindy," Drew said, rubbing Hannah's back. "Is Kim still sleeping?"

"She was when I got Hannah out of the bathtub," Cindy said, taking a chair between Drew and Gerald. She shook her finger at Hannah. "With the noise that one was making, she may be awake by now."

"Ah," Gerald said. "The resiliency of youth."

"Yeah, well, I'm young," Cindy said. "And I'm not bouncing back very well."

Drew and Gerald laughed.

Hannah leaned back in Drew's embrace and smiled. "Daddy's funny."

"Do you think so?" Drew asked, tickling her tummy. "Well, I think Hannah is funny."

"She's not funny," Hannah said. "She's hungry."

"*I'm* not funny," Drew corrected her. "*I'm* hungry."

She giggled. "Uh-uh!" she said, shaking her head. "Daddy's funny. *Hannah's* hungry."

Her innocent commentary brought another round of laughter.

"What's so hilarious?"

Amber stood poised in the doorway, her short bleach-blond hair fluffed and moussed into artful disarray, her pouty peach-tinted lips curved in a sexy smile. The skimpy white shorts she wore did great things for her long, tanned legs.

It crossed his mind that Amber was a good-looking woman, but then, that was something he'd always known. He thanked his lucky stars that he hadn't given in to his hormones when he was younger. A woman like Amber Campion could tie a man in knots.

"Hi, honey," Gerald said to his older daughter. "You're up early."

"I couldn't sleep," she said, crossing over to give him a kiss on the cheek. "Must be the fresh air and early nights."

"There's a lot to be said for clean living," Drew said dryly.

"And who is this big girl?" Amber asked. Though Hannah's face was buried against Drew's neck, she had sneaked a curious look at her aunt. Amber's smile widened and she bent over to look at Hannah. "Don't tell me it's Hannah, because if it is, I have a surprise for her. All the way from California."

The promise of a present captured Hannah's attention. She drew back to look at Drew. "Who's that, Daddy?"

"That's your aunt Amber, sweetness. Mommy's sister. It's been almost a year since she's seen you. Can you tell her hi?"

Shyly, Hannah turned to face Amber. "Hi."

Amber's gaze found Drew's. "Lord, she looks just like you."

"Thanks," he said, his mouth curving in a pleased smile. "That'll thrill Kim." As he knew it would, the comment went over Amber's head.

"Can I have my 'prise?"

"*May* I have my surprise," Cindy corrected her.

"You don't have a 'prise, Cindy. I do," Hannah said with a pout that brought another round of laughter.

"You certainly may have it," Amber said. "I'll just run upstairs and get it." She cast another look at Drew. "She's priceless."

His hold on Hannah tightened the slightest bit. "Yes," he replied, "she is. And why don't you save her present for her birthday?"

"Because I have another present for her birthday. This is just a little 'It's good to see you again' kind of present."

"You'll spoil her."

"So?" Amber said, arching her delicately shaped eyebrows and raising her shoulders in an innocent shrug. "Isn't that what grandparents and aunts and uncles are for?"

"I suppose so," Drew agreed reluctantly.

"Good." Amber smiled at Hannah and touched a finger to the tip of her snub nose. "I'll be back in a jiffy. Don't go away."

"I won't," Hannah promised.

Drew watched her go, thinking how amazing it was that a child could make such a change in a person's attitude.

Kim heard Hannah and Cindy in the bathroom, but she was too weary to pry open her eyes, much less face whatever the day might bring. Kim smiled at Cindy's attempts to keep Hannah quiet. When they finally left to go down to breakfast, she pushed aside the sheet, stumbled into the bathroom and turned on the shower.

While she waited for the hot water to make its way up through the old pipes to the second floor, she regarded her reflection in the mirror. The dark circles beneath her eyes were mute testimony to her sleepless night. She'd lain awake for hours thinking about Drew's reaction to her note and wondering how she could have misjudged him so badly. Why was he so upset about her request?

No doubt she'd find out soon enough, she thought, stripping off her nightshirt and testing the water. Drew wasn't one to let things slide. If he had a bone to pick with her, he'd do it at the first opportunity. She wasn't looking forward to the confrontation, but she wouldn't back down from it, either.

As distressing as it had been, she'd made her decision. Now it was up to her to make him see the wisdom of it. Loving him and not having that love returned was too painful to bear. And as painful as it might be, dissolving their marriage was the only thanks she could give him for what he'd done for her.

She had her resolve in a firm grasp when she went downstairs ten minutes later. She hadn't expected to see Drew, but there he was, sitting on the porch with her father, Cindy, Hannah and Amber. Larger than life and handsome as sin in a pair of wash-softened jeans and a green-plaid knit shirt.

To keep from staring, Kim focused her attention on her sister, who was kneeling beside Hannah. As usual, Amber looked as if she'd just spent the afternoon with José at the Beverly Center. Kim wished she'd taken time to blow her hair dry and put on at least the minimum of makeup.

She sighed in frustration as Amber, her every

movement one of exaggerated animation, helped
Hannah conquer the unwrapping of a gift box tied
with sunshine yellow ribbon. As Kim paused in the
doorway, Hannah giggled at something her aunt did.
Kim was unprepared for the sharp pang of jealousy
that stabbed at her heart. She was marginally aware
that Hannah pulled a frilly-frocked baby doll from
the box.

"Look, Daddy!" she cried, her pleasure obvious
as she held the doll up for everyone to see. "A baby.
And a passie!"

"I see," Drew said. "She's really nice. What do
you say to Aunt Amber?"

Completely won over, Hannah reached out her
chubby arms toward her aunt, who gathered her in a
close hug. "Thank you, Aunt Ammer."

"You're very welcome, Hannah Banana."

A spurt of anger carried Kim through the doorway.
Wasn't it enough that Amber use her wiles on every
man she came into contact with? Did she have to
charm her daughter, too?

"Good morning, honey," Gerald said.

"Good morning." Kim gave her dad a kiss on the
cheek. As she passed by Drew to go to Hannah, he
caught her hand, stopping her next to his chair. She
looked down at him questioningly, and he tugged
gently, urging her to lean over, at the same time
reaching up and cupping her cheek. Her eyes widened as she realized he meant to kiss her, which he
did—a fleeting brush of flesh against flesh that siz-
zled through her body like a jolt of low-voltage elec-
tricity.

"Hi," he said when she straightened. "Sleep
well?"

Kim saw the mockery in his eyes and knew the tenderness in his voice was only for the benefit of the onlookers, just as the kiss had been. She'd rather die than let him know their short confrontation in the garage had kept her awake most of the night. "Passably."

"I'm sorry I didn't wait up for you," Gerald said. "I was bushed. You didn't have to cut your trip short because of all this breeding brouhaha." His apology snapped the tautness stretching between Kim and Drew.

"I imagine she decided to cut it short when she found out I was here." Amber made the comment as she disengaged herself from Hannah's embrace and stood to face Kim. "Isn't that right, sis?"

Fighting the urge to snap at her sister, Kim turned to Cindy instead. "Will you take Hannah inside and give her a bowl of cornflakes, Cindy? She's not much on eggs."

"Sure thing, Mrs. McShane," Cindy said, scooting back her chair. "Come on, Hannah. Let's go give your baby some breakfast and see if we can find her a place to take a nap."

"Okay!" Hannah said eagerly, hopping down from her chair and following Cindy into the house.

With her daughter gone, Kim allowed her gaze to meet Amber's. "I came because I was worried about Daddy." She consoled herself with the fact that it wasn't a complete lie.

"No need. I've been taking good care of him, haven't I, Dad?" Amber said.

"I have no complaints," Gerald said with an uncomfortable smile, unable to ignore the unmistakable undercurrent of hostility between his two daughters.

Of course he had no complaints, Kim thought, sitting down between her husband and her father. Amber was his favorite, his darling. Anything she said or did would be viewed as sacrosanct. Kim knew this, had always known it, so why did she let Amber get to her this way? She drew a deep breath and summoned what she hoped passed for a smile. "It's wonderful that you were here, then, Amber."

Amber's return smile mimicked Kim's. "I aim to please."

Was it Kim's imagination or did her sister's lips hold a bitter twist? From far away, Kim heard the front doorbell ring. She longed to excuse herself to go get it but was certain the housekeeper would answer the summons.

"Now, let's not dwell on all these negative things," Gerald said in a teasing tone. "It'll make us wrinkled and sour. We're going to have a birthday party for our little sweetheart in three days, and I want it to be the best darn party in the parish." He looked from one daughter to the other. "You two girls see to it, for me, all right?"

"Sure, Daddy," Amber said, flashing a devilish grin at Kim. "I'd love to help. What did you have in mind?"

"I hear there's rain in the forecast, so I want to rent a big tent and maybe some clowns," he said. "Kim, you call all Hannah's friends. Don't forget the Rambler and Robichaux kids."

Kim's heart had taken a nosedive when her father asked Amber to help. It plummeted to her stomach when she heard the word *tent*. She wasn't in the mood to play ringmaster to a bunch of kids and their

parents, even though many of them, like Shiloh Robichaux and Molly Rambler, were good friends.

"Why don't we keep it simple, Daddy?" Kim
said. "Just the family and maybe a couple of close
friends. It's awfully short notice to put together a big
affair, and Hannah's too little to care one way or the
other. As long as she has a cake and some presents,
that will be just fine."

"Don't be ridiculous. A little girl doesn't turn two
every day. It may be short notice, but you just tell
your friends you had a change of plans and the party
will be here. They're all good people. They'll come."

"Excuse me, Mr. Campion." Cindy stood in the
doorway. Hannah, who was examining her new doll's
open-and-shut eyes, was planted securely on her hip.

"Yes, Cindy?" Gerald said.

"There are a couple of people from the newspaper
here to see you."

"Please, tell them I'm not available."

Almost simultaneously, Kim heard a series of
clicks. She, along with Gerald, Drew and Amber,
turned to see a young man standing a few feet from
the porch rail, snapping away at what had started out
as a family breakfast. An older, red-haired woman
stood next to him, her pen and pad in hand, a look
of supreme glee on her sharp features.

"Mr. Campion," the woman said imperiously.
"What do you have to say about the fact that people
paid good money—lots of it—to breed their high-
bred mares to your stallion only to find out they were
serviced by another stud?" She gave him a malicious
smile. "Sort of like paying for a call girl and getting
a street hooker, isn't it?"

Gerald swore and started to his feet, but Drew was

faster. He was out of his chair, down the steps and had the woman by the arm before Kim fully realized his intentions. The young man with the camera ske-daddled around the side of the house.

"What the hell do you think you're doing?" Drew asked the woman in a low voice.

"Getting a story."

"I believe you were asked to wait in the front until Mr. Campion agreed to see you."

"A good reporter makes her moments, Mr., uh...McShane, isn't it?" she said, placing him al-most as quickly as he'd negotiated the steps. "Mr. Campion's involvement with the breeding scandal in Kentucky is news. The people in the parish are cu-rious."

"Just because Mr. Campion owns half the stallion doesn't make him guilty of any wrongdoing—assum-ing, of course, anything wrong has actually been done. I'm sure that a person in your position has a at least a rudimentary knowledge of basic American rights, even if you don't have a clue to good man-ners."

"What are you talking about?"

"The fact that in this country a person is innocent until proved guilty in a court of law." He released his hold on her arm, and she stumbled back a bit, automatically straightening the jacket of her teal pantsuit.

"Now, I suggest you go back to your editor and tell him there'd better not be a word of anything re-motely sounding like libel against my father-in-law, or you'll be slapped with the biggest lawsuit you've ever seen. Do you understand?"

"Clearly." Subdued but not beaten, the woman

followed the path her colleague had taken moments before.

"By the way," Drew said, "what's your name?"

"Mavis Davenport," she said with a haughty lift of her chin.

"Have a nice day, Ms. Davenport," Drew said, showing her his teeth in what passed for a smile.

The woman rounded the corner of the house in a huff.

"Very impressive," Amber said when Drew returned to the porch.

"Some media people are like vultures," he said, taking his seat.

"I knew there'd be trouble when I saw her," Cindy said, anxiety shadowing her blue eyes. "That's why I told them to wait at the front door. She wrote all kinds of lies about Molly and Garrett a few years ago."

"It's okay, Cindy," Gerald said.

"You did just fine, Cindy," Kim assured her with a wry smile. "People like that Davenport woman are out of control."

Relief washed over Cindy's expressive features. "Hannah ate her cereal. Is it okay if I take her to see Grandma Maureen now?"

"Sure," Kim said, smiling her approval. Hannah adored Drew's parents, and if Kim had searched the world over, she couldn't have found any two people who'd love a child more than Maureen and Cullen McShane. "Just don't let her get in Maureen's way if she's busy."

"I won't."

When the two had disappeared into the house, Amber, who'd taken the seat Hannah had vacated earlier, drained her orange juice glass and rose. "If you'll excuse me, I'll go start making some phone calls."

"You don't have to do that," Kim protested. "I can."

"Don't be silly," Amber said. "You're exhausted. You need to rest. I've arranged some pretty big bashes when I worked in that art gallery in L.A. I assure you I can handle a child's birthday party."

"I didn't mean to imply you couldn't," Kim said.

"Good." Amber pointed a finger at Drew. "Make sure she gets some rest."

"Don't worry," Drew said. "I plan to."

Amber rounded the table and kissed her father on the forehead. "Be good," she said. Then, with a wave of her hand, she left Kim with her husband and father.

"She seems different, doesn't she?" Gerald said, a thoughtful—or was that hopeful?—expression in his eyes.

"It's hard to say," Kim evaded. The very idea of Amber changing was beyond comprehension.

"Well, she's willing to help with the party," Drew said. "That's a plus. She's never seemed interested in doing anything with the family before."

Kim didn't comment. She still wished they could keep the party small and simple but knew it would be futile to try to buck her father on this. He spoiled Hannah, the same way he had Amber.

"Are you going to eat?" Drew asked, dragging her wandering attention back to him.

She looked over at the silver-covered chafing dishes sitting on a damask-covered table. "I don't think so."

"Walk with me down to the office, then," he said.

"I need to talk to Dad, and I know he'll want to say hi."

Kim shot him a look that would have made a lesser man tremble in his boots. But not Drew McShane. He sat there smiling at her with an innocence that would do a saint proud, knowing there was no way she could refuse his request without Gerald thinking something was wrong between them, which was the last thing she wanted.

"Maybe later," she said with a falsely apologetic smile. "If Dad wants this party put together for Friday, I'd better get with it."

The look in Drew's eyes said he knew he was being put off, but that it was okay. What he had to say would wait. "In that case, I'll leave you to it. I imagine Mom is wondering why I haven't made an appearance yet."

He scooted back his chair and, leaning over, brushed Kim's cheek with a kiss. A wave of longing washed over her before he straightened and smiled down at her. "See you later."

She forced a reciprocal smile. "Yeah."

"Don't work too hard."

"I won't."

Kim made a list of the friends and neighbors who had children near Hannah's age, or children Hannah was familiar with. Drew's sister was called, as well as a couple of high school friends Kim still kept in touch with. She invited Cal Simmons, the recently elected sheriff, who often fished with Drew when he was in town, asking him to bring his nephew and niece, whom he was raising since his brother died and his sister-in-law had left for parts unknown. She also phoned Shiloh Robichaux, formerly Shiloh Rambler, who lived down the road at Magnolia Manor, a plantation house she and her husband, Cade, had restored.

Shiloh and her sister-in-law, Molly Rambler, were both older than Kim, but good friends nonetheless. Kim didn't get to see as much of them as she'd like, because the three of them, as with most wives and mothers, led busy lives. Molly used part of Rambler's Rest, the former plantation house she and her husband, Garrett, owned, as a bed-and-breakfast, and she also hosted occasional dinners for local groups. Shiloh had opened up her own restaurant a couple of years earlier, and even though she left the day-to-day running of the lucrative business to a very competent manager, she was the kind of woman who wanted to keep her hand in as much as possible.

Regardless of their lack of time to actually get together, the three kept in touch frequently via Ma Bell. Occasionally, Kim and Molly, who owned a stable of quarter horses, got together to ride along the bayou for an hour or so. Both friends were thrilled that Hannah's birthday would be celebrated in Louisiana instead of Kentucky and promised to be there with their respective offspring—and husbands, since both men were self-employed and could work their schedules to include an afternoon with friends.

"I can't believe Hannah will be two on Saturday," Molly told Kim.

"I know. Time flies, doesn't it?"

"Is that a wistful note I hear in your voice?" Molly asked.

"Wistful. Depressed. I'm not sure."

"Do you want to talk about it? Is it Drew?"

"Yes."

Molly laughed. "Which question is that the answer to?"

"It's Drew, but I don't think I can talk about it." By mutual consent, Kim and Drew hadn't told anyone he wasn't Hannah's biological father.

"Do you want my two cents' worth?"

"I have a feeling I'm going to get it whether I do or not," Kim said.

"Yeah," Molly said, "you are. You know as well as I do that there are bound to be problems that come up between a couple when they spend as much time apart as you and Drew do."

"I know."

"So why don't you pack up and move to Kentucky?"

"He's never asked me to."

A lengthy silence stretched over the phone lines. "He's never asked you to," Molly finally said. "You're his wife. He's your husband. Why do you need a formal invitation?"

Hearing Molly's take on the situation made Kim realize she'd said the wrong thing. Good grief! What must her friend think?

"Dad needs me."

"I know he was pretty shaky when you and Drew first got married, but your dad is a grown man who can take care of himself," Molly told her. "Your first obligation is to Drew, Hannah and your marriage."

"That's easy for you to say."

"I know, I know, you're going to tell me I can't know where you're coming from, because I haven't walked a mile in your shoes. But in a way, I have, remember? I've done the superwoman routine."

Kim knew Molly was referring to the time before she married Garrett, when she single-handedly tried to hold back the ravages of time from the plantation house that meant so much to her.

"I'm going to ask you the same question Shiloh once asked me. Don't you get tired of being the strong one? Don't you ever want to let go and let someone else do it for a while?"

Kim was surprised that Molly had homed in on part of her problem so easily. As much as she loved her dad, she was tired of trying to be all things to all people—his caring daughter and social secretary, Drew's part-time, pretend wife and Hannah's mother. The problem was that she didn't know how to break the chain without causing a major upheaval. "Yeah, but who? Amber isn't going to suddenly become Dad's caregiver."

"Why does anyone have to be Gerald's caregiver? He isn't sick or senile."

"But his heart—"

"Is obviously okay," Molly broke in. "He hasn't had another moment's trouble in over three years."

"I know, but with all the stress he's under he might."

"And you might get hit by a car going to the grocery store. Or worse, Drew might, and then you'd feel guilty for not giving him the love and attention *he* needs."

As it did every time she knew he got on a plane, the thought of something happening to Drew sent a bone-deep chill through Kim.

"I don't know how to be any other way," Kim confessed. "For as long as I can remember, Amber has been the flighty one, and I've been the one who's tried to keep things on an even keel.''

"All I'm saying, Kim, is that this isn't a dress rehearsal for life. This is it. You'd better make the best of it. You and Drew should be living together, not apart. He's a handsome man. There are a lot of women out hunting for someone like him, and they don't give a darn if the man they want is wearing a wedding ring or not...."

"I know."

"Look, Kim," Molly said. "If you want things to be different, it's up to you to make them different. Uh-oh! Gotta go. I hear the school bus."

"Okay," Kim said. "See you on Friday."

"We'll be there with bells on," Molly said. "Bye."

Kim hung up and stared unseeingly out the library window. Her friend's advice was solid. The problem was that she'd burned her bridges when she left the note for Drew.

No matter what she really wanted, the die was cast.

Chapter Six

Kim finally slept that night, mostly, she suspected, because she was physically exhausted. She awakened on her second morning home with a feeling of dread. Would Drew be at breakfast, the way he had been the day before? Would Amber be there looking like a million bucks? Would she be weilding that sexy smile at Drew and enticing Hannah with gifts?

Kim shook her head and thrust the image away. She didn't like the jealous possessiveness she felt toward Drew lately, especially when, in her own mind, she came up short when compared to other women, lacking in some fundamental way that men found necessary. *The same way you felt when you were young and all the girls flirted with Justin and all the guys swarmed Amber.*

She sighed. That was a long time ago. She wasn't a girl anymore, and Justin had been nothing like

Drew. Kim glanced over at the other twin bed and saw that Hannah was still sleeping soundly, just as she knew Cindy would be in the room across the hall. Careful not to wake her daughter, Kim got up and eased to the door that connected Hannah's room to the one where she herself usually slept. When Drew came to Louisiana—never more than a few days at a time—Kim moved to the twin bed in Hannah's room. She always made sure the bed was made up neatly and that there were sufficient articles of her clothing left scattered among Drew's to keep down speculation as to the state of her marriage.

Thankfully, Drew was gone, and she found her room neat with the bed made. The morning ritual was a holdover from his youth, a time before he was able to afford someone to clean his house. Kim took a quiet pleasure in the fact that he hadn't forgotten his roots or lost respect for the ways of the family that raised him.

She went into the bathroom, took a quick shower and slathered her body with some floral-scented lotion. She donned shorts and a T-shirt, and, unlike the previous morning, she took time to blow her hair dry and put on her makeup. When she regarded the efforts some twenty minutes later, she was satisfied with the results. She wasn't sure why, but to her, putting on makeup was the equivalent of a soldier readying himself for battle. She spritzed herself with a perfume whose scent complemented the lotion and set out to join her family for breakfast, ready to face the world—including her sister and her husband.

Before heading down the stairs, she checked the bedroom and saw that Hannah was still sleeping. Resisting an impulse to go over to the bed and kiss her daughter's rosy cheek, Kim went downstairs. When she stepped through the French doors onto the *galerie,* she saw her father, Drew and Amber at the table, engrossed in conversation. Her heart sank.

With trying to find a party company with clowns available on such short notice, Kim had kept busy enough to stay out of Drew's way until dinner the previous evening. She'd hoped to evade being alone with him another day.

"Good morning," Kim said, summoning a smile and stepping through the doorway and into the fray.

"Good morning." The automatic response came from all three adults at the table. Kim's father's face wore its usual smile, and Amber's wore a tentative one. Drew wasn't smiling at all, and there was something in his eyes as his gaze moved from her head to her toe that gave her a breathless, uncomfortable feeling.

She wasn't sure how to deal with this unexpected anger of his, and she didn't know what to think of his resistance to her offer to set him free. At least she wasn't as exhausted as she had been the day before. If he did insist on talking about her note, maybe she could come up with answers that would satisfy him and still keep her pride intact when he asked her those hard questions.

She kissed her father on the cheek and did the same for Drew, so there would be no repeat of the kiss he'd forced on her the day before. As she straightened, her eyes met his, and she saw the hint of mockery hiding there.

"Did you sleep okay?" Gerald asked.

"Yes, finally, thanks."

"That's good. Amber says the party is shaping up nicely."

"It is," Kim said. She glanced at her sister who was tapping ash from her cigarette. "I almost never found any clowns."

"It is short notice," Gerald said, speaking for the first time. "Did you reach everyone you wanted to invite?"

Kim nodded. "The Rambler and Robichaux kids will be here. Moms and dads, too, I think."

"That's great!" Gerald said. "I like it when the parents tag along. All of us adults are so busy, it's hard to find a time to get everyone together."

"It will be good to see them," Kim agreed, reaching for a napkin.

"I don't suppose you've seen the paper," Amber said as Kim helped herself to a variety of fresh fruit.

"No." She glanced at her father and saw the flicker of irritation in his eyes. "Don't tell me Mavis Davenport printed something, after all."

"'Fraid so," Amber said. She crushed out her cigarette and handed the folded paper to Kim.

There on the front page of the small daily paper was a snapshot of them as they'd been the morning before when the reporter and her cohort had barged into the middle of their family gathering.

The piece beneath the photo was titled "Campion's Champions?" It recapped the information from the Associated Press article the day before and explained that all Gerald's children and his son-in-law had come to be with him during this difficult time.

As might have been expected from her past performances in situation-twisting and manipulation,

Mavis Davenport had put her own inimitable slant to the facts, telling of Gerald's longtime friendship with Lawrence Muldair and reminding the readers of his recent skirmish with the IRS.

What she didn't say was that the problems with the tax people had been satisfied or that they could be laid squarely at the feet of the accountant he'd employed for fourteen years who'd developed an insatiable need to gamble with the coming of the riverboats. Not only had he embezzled huge sums of money, but he had neglected to take care of the many and varied taxes that went with running an operation as large as Lafourche Farm.

The barely veiled implication was simple and infuriating. Gerald was in a financial bind, ergo, he and Maria Muldair Perkins had concocted the elaborate breeding scheme to amass money, not caring what the implications might be to the racing industry.

"That woman is poison," Kim said, refolding the paper and laying it beside her plate. "Someone needs to slap a lawsuit on her and the paper."

"Remember that liberty we have called freedom of speech?" Gerald said.

"Yes, but there's also something called libel."

"Read it again," Drew said. "She never actually accused Gerald of anything. She just laid all her information out in a way that the reader has no choice but to draw the conclusion she wants them to."

"It still isn't right."

"No, it isn't," Drew agreed. He laid his napkin next to his plate and scooted back his chair. "I hate to leave so soon after you've come down," he said to Kim, "but I need to go see Dad. He's good at keeping up with who's working where. I'm going to see if he has any idea where Bud Reeves may be."

"Good thinking, Drew," Gerald said. "Thanks."

Drew smiled. "Sure."

Resting his hands on the arms of her chair, he bent and brushed Kim's lips with his, enveloping her with a woodsy, masculine scent and the potency of his nearness, which made the sturdy *galerie* take a sudden dip.

He drew back and looked into her eyes. Then, as if he were drawn by a feeling he couldn't deny, he helped himself to another kiss. As brief and light as it was—a couple of seconds at best—this one concentrated the ache inside Kim to a place that left no doubt about what her need was. Desire. Pure and simple and devastating.

A subtle panic had begun to unfurl inside her when he straightened—reluctantly?—and smiled. "See you later. Give the brat a kiss for me."

Kim nodded and watched, bemused as he strode down the steps and across the lawn with that loosely elegant stride of his. She glanced at her father, whose face wore an indulgent smile. Contrarily, Amber's eyes held an undeniable sorrow.

"I'm going to run into town," Amber said, rising suddenly. "Do you need me to pick up anything for the party, or are the caterers handling all the decorations and things?"

Kim's startled gaze met her sister's. The unexpected offer caught her off guard. It wasn't like Amber to be so helpful. What was going on with her, anyway?

"Thanks," she said, hoping the word didn't sound

as grudging as she thought it did. "But I think we're pretty well set."

"Okay. The tent people will be here around noon day after tomorrow to set up things."

"That sounds good."

"Well, I'll see you later," Amber said. She had disappeared through the double doors when the cordless phone lying beside Gerald's plate rang.

"Hello." He frowned. "Yes, she's here. Just a moment." He pushed the mute button. "Amber!" he shouted. "A phone call for you."

Amber came back onto the porch, a frown puckering her forehead. "For me?"

Gerald nodded and handed her the phone. If Kim didn't know her sister better, she might have thought the expression in her eyes was worry and that she took the receiver reluctantly. She brushed aside the notion as ridiculous. Most likely Amber was upset that one of her friends had tracked her down. She'd certainly never been the worrying kind.

"Hello, sweet cheeks."

The sound of the masculine voice sent a shudder of apprehension skittering down Amber's spine. So much for hiding out for a while and buying herself some time.

"You!"

"Who else? You didn't tell me you were going out of town, Amber. Imagine my surprise when I called your apartment in L.A. for several days running and you weren't there."

"I didn't know I was supposed to tell you every time I left to go to the grocery store."

The masculine laughter held a mocking coldness.

"I'd say a prolonged trip to Louisiana is more than a trip to the store, wouldn't you? I thought you were trying to skip out on me."

Amber ignored the question. "How did you find me?"

"I saw the picture of you and your loving family in the paper. This breeding scandal is big enough for all the newspapers in horse country to pick it up."

Amber murmured a curse. She could gladly strangle the life from the meddling biddy, Mavis Davenport.

"Do you have my money?"

She tapped a cigarette from the pack. "I'm working on it."

"Well, you need to work faster."

Amber snatched the unlit cigarette from her mouth. Irritation lent an edge to her voice. "If you saw the papers, then you know my father is in a wee little financial bind right now. I'll have to find the right time, the right way to ask him. Causing him to have a heart attack won't help either of us."

The voice on the other end of the line laughed, a menacing, mocking sound. "Well, you're certainly right about your father being in a financial bind. I just hope he doesn't do anything desperate."

Amber stiffened, wondering if she was imagining the threat she felt. Desperate to assuage him and buy herself more time, she said, "Look, they're having a big birthday party for my niece on Friday afternoon. If I upset my dad before that, my sister will kill me. Once that's out of the way, I'll ask him, I promise."

She heard a deep sigh, as if the man had lost all patience with her. "Well, see that you figure something out soon—real soon—or you know what the consequences will be.''

The sound of Gerald and Kim laughing drifted in through the French doors. Amber squeezed her eyes shut. ''Yeah,'' she said. ''I know the consequences.''

That evening, as they ate roast beef on the *galerie,* making the most of the chance to enjoy the outdoors before the Louisiana weather got so humid even breathing was a chore, Kim decided that Cullen was right. Something was wrong with Amber. When she'd returned from her shopping trip, she'd gone straight to her room, pleading a headache. Kim had never known her sister to have headaches before, but there was no disguising her paleness. Beneath the perfection of her makeup, her washed-out complexion had become a colorless palette for the bold slash of coral lipstick and complementary blush.

Amber was also unusually quiet during dinner, speaking only when spoken to. Usually, she was a vital and involved part of all dinner conversations. There was definitely something wrong, Kim decided, and in spite of herself, she couldn't help feeling a twinge of concern for her sister.

They were having coffee and dessert when Drew turned to Kim and said, ''I need to go see my parents for a few minutes. Why don't you come with me?''

Kim hoped her discomfiture didn't show. She'd managed to steer clear of Drew for two days, and even though she knew a confrontation was inevitable sooner or later, she'd been hoping for later.

''Sure,'' she said, scooting her chair back and favoring him with what she hoped was an agreeable smile. "I've been so busy with the party preparations, I haven't been to see your mother."

"She mentioned that."

"We won't be long, Daddy," Kim said, standing and going to the steps where Drew waited for her.

"Don't worry about me, honey," Gerald said. "The two of you deserve a little time together. Especially since your Kentucky trip got cut short. Amber can keep me company."

"Yeah," Amber said, urging a halfhearted smile to her shapely mouth. "I'll whip him in gin rummy or something."

Kim's smile felt as forced as her sister's looked. What was behind this sudden push for her and Drew to be together? First Drew himself had suggested they have more "dates," and now her father was insisting they spend more time together.

With a wave, Kim matched her stride to Drew's. A few steps past the porch, he threw a casual arm across her shoulders. She stiffened in surprise, but he only drew her closer.

"Relax," he said, his breath warm against her ear. "I'm not going to bite."

She cast him a sideways look. "No?" The question came out soft and breathless.

"No."

Until two nights ago, she'd have believed him, but his uncharacteristic anger when he'd confronted her in the garage had thrown her lifelong perception of him all out of kilter. That Drew wasn't the person she'd grown up with. She wasn't sure she knew him at all anymore and had no idea what motivated him. More important, she was growing more and more confused about her own actions and behavior the past week. Just when she thought she had their future mapped out, he'd kissed her and thrown all her plans into turmoil—not to mention her emotions.

"How do you think your dad is taking everything?" he asked, interrupting her thoughts as they made their way toward the lane that led to the breeding barn.

"He seems fine," she said, amazing herself as she said it. "He's actually in good spirits."

"That's what I thought. Maybe it's good that Amber came home."

Despite her recent softened feelings for her sister, Kim slanted a disbelieving look up at him. "Surely you jest."

"Actually, I'm not. Look, Kim, Amber is your sister, and you're both adults. It's time to get past your petty jealousy."

Shock brought Kim's footsteps to a halt. She pivoted to face him. "Is that what you think I am?" she asked. "Jealous? Drew, the woman has never grown up. She's never taken responsibility for her actions. She's caused my parents untold misery. How dare you suggest that what I feel toward her is jealousy!"

Drew held up his hands, palms out. "Okay. I'm sorry. I know you're right about the things she's done, and maybe she was—is—Gerald's favorite. Well, get over it, love, because you can't change that, and I can't, either. But Gerald's kind of love is the kind that cripples. You said it yourself. Amber has to grow up, and she can't do that if someone keeps bailing her out. On the other hand, did you ever stop to think that just maybe if you tempered your advice with a little love, she might react to it differently?"

"So you've bought into the new-and-improved

Amber?'' Kim asked, sarcasm throbbing through each word.

''I do see a change in her. Everyone does but you. I don't know if it's real, or if it will last, but I believe we should give her the benefit of the doubt. Sometimes we have to take things and people at face value until we're proved wrong.''

''She's thirty-two years old. She won't change.''

''You say that with such authority,'' he said, shaking his head in disbelief. ''It makes me curious about what you'll do if she does make some drastic change in her life.''

''What do you mean?''

''I mean that you've used Amber as a convenient reason to set yourself up as Saint Kim, martyr *extraordinaire*.'' He crossed his arms over his chest and regarded her with a considering gleam in his green eyes. ''But I really think the martyrdom is just a cover-up for your real problem.''

''What real problem?'' The question was a whisper.

''Your feelings of inferiority,'' he told her with brutal bluntness. ''That you aren't pretty enough or charming enough or witty enough to deserve your father's love.''

Kim felt as if he'd slapped her. ''Why are you doing this?''

''Doing what?''

''Attacking me.''

''I'm not attacking you. I'm stating the truth as I see it.''

''Truth? Is that what you call it?'' she said, her voice low and filled with anger. ''Admit it, Drew, you're ticked off—maybe your pride is even hurt a little—because I left you that note.''

He grabbed her shoulder and spun her around to face him. The shadows of evening were settling in, laying long tree-shaped stripes across the yard and arranging the lines and angles of Drew's face into a mask of light and shadows. A capricious breeze that had quickened with the setting of the sun riffled his dark hair. The longing to reach up and smooth it back in place was so strong Kim shoved her hands into the pockets of her shorts.

"I'd say finding a note from my wife asking for a divorce is reason enough to be ticked off," he said.

"I'm not your wife." She turned and headed toward the barn, Drew hard on her heels.

"Really? I happen to have legal papers to the contrary."

"You know what I mean!" she said, her own irritation rising. "We don't have a real marriage. Think about it. Your life will be much simpler if you don't have to make these monthly trips back and forth."

"I don't mind the trips. I usually have business here. Besides, it's important for me to spend as much time as possible with Hannah. Have you thought about her reaction if I suddenly drop out of her life?"

"I don't expect you to drop out of her life." She tossed him the crumb over her shoulder. "I know you love her, and she loves you. I don't want that to change. Your parents live here. It isn't as if you'll never see her."

"What about your dad? Don't you think your timing is a bit off?"

She pulled up short and turned to face him. He was right. With Amber campaigning for more money and with the investigation hanging over his head, her father didn't need the added worry of his daughter's divorce preying on his mind.

"I've been thinking about that the past couple of days," Kim admitted. "You have a point. We should wait until his name is cleared before we do anything."

Drew shrugged and shook his head. "How can I argue with someone who seems to have all the answers?"

"I don't pretend to have all the answers."

"What is this, then? Why the sudden need to change the status quo? If you're so unhappy, the least you could have done was talk things over with me. Or is it that I've served my purpose, and it's time for you to move on?"

"No!" She lifted her hands in a helpless gesture. "It's just that there should be...more."

"More?"

"More," she reiterated. "There should be love."

A series of emotions crossed Drew's features. "You know I care about you, or I'd never have married you."

"I know. And maybe that's partly why I asked you," she said, knowing the time had come to be honest with him. Or at least as honest as she could be without letting him know her true feelings. "But it isn't enough, and it isn't fair—to either of us."

"There's someone else."

That statement surprised her as much as his anger. Afraid he'd see the truth in her eyes, she looked past him to the grazing horses silhouetted against the evening sky. "There's no one else." She turned and started toward the barn.

"Then why disrupt everyone's lives if we're both happy with the way things are?"

"Are you?" she countered, pulling up short just outside the barn's double doors. "Are you really happy with the way things are?"

Drew took her upper arm and propelled her toward the doorway. He ushered her inside where the shadows were diffused by the occasional overhead fixture. "Happy? Not exactly. Let's say I'm content. Mostly. At least for now."

She waffled between relief and frustration. Relief that maybe he wasn't eager to find someone else, and frustration because he couldn't see the wisdom of her offer. Contentment wasn't enough. Not for her, and not for him, either.

"I don't understand why you're being so hard-headed about this," she said. "It isn't like this is a real marriage. I mean—"

"I know what you mean," Drew said. He reached out and let the tips of his fingers trace the shell of her ear. "That's something that can be changed."

The look in his eyes set her heart to beating faster. Memories of the kiss they'd shared in Kentucky seeped into her mind. Whatever he'd just said—and she knew it was important—had vanished beneath a sudden light-headed, weak-kneed dizziness. Wanting to move away from his touch and unable to find the strength to do so, she murmured, "What did you say?"

"I'm an accommodating kind of guy. If it's sex you want—or need—I'm willing to oblige."

Kim felt her face flame. How could she tell Drew that sex—or the lack of it—was only a small part of the problem? How could she tell him she didn't just want the occasional use of his body to satisfy her physical urges. She wanted his love and his heart. His soul.

She pulled free, as much because his nearness made clear thinking a near impossibility as because his attitude rankled her. She lifted her chin and plunged before her determination deserted her.

"It isn't. A divorce is what I want."

"What *you* want?" he demanded. The horses in the stalls shuffled uneasily at the sound of his rising voice. He ushered her into the office and closed the door behind them. "What about what *I* want?" he asked, gripping her shoulders and pinning her to the door. "What about what's best for Hannah?"

Kim didn't know what to make of the reckless gleam in his eyes. She licked her lips. "What's best for Hannah is what's best for us," she said, trying to ignore the way his gaze followed the movement of her tongue. "I just think it would be easier if we split up."

His green eyes had darkened with some emotion she couldn't define. He lifted his hand from her shoulder and dragged his thumb over the moisture clinging to her bottom lip.

Kim froze. She wasn't even sure she was breathing.

"What does easy have to do with anything?" he asked in a slow, slurred voice that sounded as if he'd been drinking. His thumb moved to her top lip. "Nothing in my life has been easy. I don't know why this marriage should be."

He dipped his head, and she knew he was going to kiss her. She was right. His mouth crashed down on hers. Though she still didn't understand the reason

for it, she felt the anger in the way his fingers dug
into the fleshy part of her upper arm. She struggled
against him...tried to pull free, but he only dragged
her closer and shifted her until her body was pressed
fully against his.

When she wrenched her mouth from his, he began
to string moist, openmouthed kisses along her jaw-
line, down the side of her neck and back to her ear.
The touch of his lips kindled feelings she hadn't experienced in years...since before Justin died.

But Justin's touch had never made her feel the way
she was feeling now. Her body responded with an
unaccustomed wantonness to Drew's every touch...
to the way his taut thighs moved against hers. The
way his hands molded themselves to her shoulders,
her back and the roundness of her bottom. The way
his mouth coaxed a response from her she didn't
want to give.

Nerve endings that had languished from lack of
attention for three long years seemed to have sprung
suddenly to life, from the bare flesh of her back—
when had he pulled her shirt free?—to her mouth,
sensitive to the subtle change in his kisses, kisses that
had transmuted from angry and demanding to soft
and coaxing.

Even as her mind told her to stop him, that giving
in to the heady drunkenness of his kisses and the
persuasiveness of his nimble, clever hands was a
foolishness she couldn't afford, she slid her hands up
his chest and twined her arms around his neck, holding him close, the way Hannah did. Deep down inside her, in a place she wasn't willing to examine too
closely, she knew her actions were far from wise.

She pushed the thought aside. She'd deal with the

regrets later. For now, all she wanted was to revel in the way Drew's hands moved over her bare back, how his tongue delved deeply into her mouth, how his lips sipped and nipped and tugged at hers, drawing the desire she felt for him to the surface as surely as cream rises. It occurred to her that she'd never felt this way with Justin—brazen and boldly, vibrantly woman.

He half lifted her until their bodies were joined as closely as two fully clad bodies could be. As their kisses grew wilder, she pressed against him. His hardness was heady, as intoxicating as the finest brandy. Needing to be closer, to feel the warmth of his flesh against hers, she began to work his buttons free, tugging at his shirt with grasping, impatient hands, aware that Drew was helping while his mouth continued to plunder hers.

She parted his shirt and put her hands against the crisp hair covering his chest. Delighting in the feel of him, she slid her fingertips eagerly over his wide, smooth shoulders, over sharply defined pectorals, and down over the hard flatness of his abdomen. And all the while he kissed her, and kissed her....

With her head spinning wildly, when she thought she would die from lack of oxygen, his mouth released hers, but she realized that oxygen wasn't what she needed, after all. What she needed was more of his kisses. Eyes tightly shut, she captured his whisker-rough cheeks between her palms and sought his lips blindly. He didn't disappoint her. His mouth fastened on hers again, and she felt the warmth of his hands against her. She heard a whimper and realized with a start of mortification that the needy, hungry sound had come from her....

Drew raised his head and looked at her. Whatever he saw in her eyes, he took as capitulation and swung her up into his arms. In seconds, she felt the hardness of her father's desk against the backs of her legs as Drew seated her on the edge.

She rested her hands on his shoulders and closed her eyes to block out the intensity in his. Waited. But not for long. His arms circled her again. She felt his breath, soft and hot against her ear. Felt his thumbs moving over her flesh in small, slow circles. Felt the dampness of his skin beneath her fingers. Suddenly she realized how painful it would be to let him go if they finished what he'd started.

Tears stung her eyes as she recognized her fate. She raised her lips to his. There was no doubt that they would finish it....

The first thing Kim heard when she came back to reality was the ticking of the utilitarian clock hanging over the door and the harsh sound of their breathing in the quietness of the room. She wasn't on the desk anymore; she was on the ancient leather sofa. She had a vague memory of Drew carrying her there, her legs wrapped tightly around him, their lips fused in a kiss.

Now his body rested heavily on her, and his head rested against her breasts. His hair was damp with the perspiration that sheened both their bodies.

He'd taken her once with a near-rough, deep-rooted hunger that had ignited a similar hunger in her. Then, as they lay quietly, letting their hearts slow to a sedate pace and before she thought it was possible, he'd begun to work his magic over her again.

This time, he made love to her slowly, sweetly. The end result was no less devastating.

Now, with tears drying on her eyelashes and feeling a strange and poignant elation, Kim succumbed to the impulse to tangle her fingers through his dark hair. He raised his head and looked at her. She searched his eyes, trying to see past the dark green into his soul…his heart. The expression she saw there was unreadable. She didn't know what to say, wasn't sure what to expect from him.

Slowly, wordlessly, he pulled away from her and began to dress. The growing silence gave her a vulnerable and somehow desolate feeling. Why didn't he say something? she wondered, as she began to pull on her own clothes. Maybe, she reasoned, he didn't know what to say. There was no doubt that what had happened had changed things between them, but just what those changes would be, she couldn't be sure.

Drew sat to pull on his boots, then stood and began to stuff his shirt into his Wranglers. He dragged the zipper upward and smoothed the placket with his palm.

"You can have your divorce now," he said, his voice as empty as his eyes. "If you still want it."

Chapter Seven

Shock robbed Kim of logical thought, much less speech. She stared at Drew, trying to decide if she'd heard him correctly, if he'd really made the cruel remark. Had he just made love to her—not once, but twice—and then calmly put on his clothes and told her to go ahead and get the divorce? Surely he was joking. But he didn't look as if he were joking. He looked dead serious.

She finished pulling on her clothes. She was searching her mind for some comeback that sounded even semi-intelligent when he said, "I want to warn you that if you do go through with it, you'll have a custody battle on your hands."

The threat of losing Hannah broke through the numbness initiated by his announcement. Panic and no small anger welled up inside her. How dare he threaten to try to take her daughter away from her?

She wasn't aware she'd spoken the words aloud until she heard him say, "Oh, believe me, Kim, I dare."

"I can't believe you're this upset when she isn't really your child."

"That's funny," he said. His smile held more grimness than humor as he added, "You said we didn't have a real marriage—and maybe we didn't until we consummated it—even though I had papers that said we were. Now you tell me Hannah isn't really my daughter, but if I remember correctly, it was my name they put on the birth certificate."

"Why?" she asked him, her voice a bare thread of sound.

"Why, what?" he countered, his voice low and filled with fury. "Why am I upset about Hannah, or why did I make love to you?"

She shrugged. "Why are you so upset about Hannah?"

"Why? You tell me you're going to take my daughter away from me and then wonder why I'm so upset? Dear God, the thought of her not being part of my life…it makes my heart hurt as if it's been torn into shreds. But who am I to say that that's anywhere near the kind of pain Justin might have felt if he were in my shoes? After all, he's her *real* father."

Kim knew he was right, knew she'd been wrong to underestimate the pain he must be feeling, but somehow—maybe because they lived apart—she'd never expected him to take losing Hannah so hard.

"Why did you make love to me?" she asked, needing to know the answer to that question as well.

"Because it's something I've wanted to do for a long time."

The knowledge that he wanted her—had wanted her for a long time—almost expelled the shock of his threat. Almost. The questions in her mind tumbled and roiled, finding no answers, adding to her growing confusion about this man she'd known all her life. Or thought she'd known.

"Why now, then?" she asked.

His mouth curved in a sardonic smile. "I was trying to be the gentleman everyone expects me to be. I was waiting for you to get over losing Justin. My mistake. What's that they say about nice guys? Oh, yeah, they finish last. So when you decided you wanted a divorce, I decided there'd be no more Mr. Nice Guy."

Frowning, Kim mulled that over, trying in her state of shock to make sense of it.

"Damn you, Kim," he said, his voice throbbing with anger. "We could have sat down and discussed this like two rational adults."

"You're threatening to take Hannah away from me if I go ahead with the divorce because we didn't talk it over?" she asked, her voice mirroring her disbelief.

"I'm not threatening," Drew said, ignoring part of her question. "I'm stating a fact."

Her blood ran cold. The uncompromising expression on his face—the angry eyes, flared nostrils, the hard set of his jaw—told her he meant everything he said. "You'd take me to court and fight for custody of Hannah?" she asked. "Why? To get back at me?"

His eyes never wavered from hers. "I'm not interested in one-upmanship, Kim. I want Hannah in my life because I love her. I may not have donated the sperm, but she *is* my daughter. And I'm willing to fight for her—for everything I want—because, unlike you, I'm not willing to concede defeat at the first sign of trouble, and I'm not willing to set aside my own wants because I'm afraid of hurting someone else. I've learned the hard way that if you want something, you've got to be willing to fight for it.''

Kim wondered how the conversation had gone from the reasons he'd made love to her and the reason he was willing to engage in a custody battle for Hannah to some weakness he saw in her character.

''What's that supposed to mean?''

''It means that not all of us are as perfect as you, Kim. The rest of us make mistakes and do things that may be wrong. But most of us ask for each other's forgiveness and most of us grant it and go on instead of holding on to the hostility and disappointment. It means that you've played the role of the perfect daughter, the perfect person for so long, that you've sacrificed your own life for your parents. I love my parents, too, but I haven't made every decision in my life using their happiness as a guideline the way you have.''

''I haven't!''

''Of course you have. You married a man you didn't love because you didn't want to hurt your father. Even though you want a divorce now, you're willing to stay with me indefinitely for the same reasons. Why? Because you don't want to rock the boat, don't want to make any waves.''

Her eyes stung with unshed tears. She didn't like the picture Drew painted of her. A person with no backbone, a person who let life do what it would with her. It was funny how a perspective changed depending on where a person stood. She'd seen her actions as good. Drew saw them as bad.

"I was trying to be considerate," she said, in defense of her behavior.

"And you were. You are. And that's commendable. But you have to draw the line somewhere, love," he told her, the heat leaving his voice. "What about what Kim wants? What about what makes her happy? Don't you ever want to just forget the rules, forget what's the acceptable, polite thing to do and just go for it? Just once in your perfect life wouldn't you like to be like your sister and just let go and see what happens?"

"No!" she said. "I'd never want to be like Amber."

Even as she said it, Kim knew it was a lie. How often had she wished she had her sister's easygoing ways, her fearless way of looking at life, her ability to let things roll off her like water off a duck's back.

She crossed her arms over her breasts and laughed, a harsh, unhappy sound that was more like a sob. "I thought I was doing exactly what you said when I told you I wanted a divorce."

"Touché. But it doesn't fly, somehow. I keep asking myself why you want the divorce. It doesn't fit your MO as they say in all the cop shows. And when you think about what just happened between us, it makes even less sense." He swept his arm wide. "How do you explain what just happened here, Kim?"

Uncomfortable with the fact that he wouldn't just let it lie, she raised her chin and tried for a bravado she didn't feel. "Maybe I was just doing what you said I should—going for what I wanted."

Something glittered in his eyes. "So you wanted me, too."

Surprise stole her breath. She had the sudden feeling of having been led skilfully into a trap. Thank goodness he'd phrased it as a statement, not a question. She was afraid that if she admitted wanting him, she'd be admitting to far more.

When she didn't answer, he said, "It doesn't make sense. On one hand, you say you want a divorce. On the other, we engage in some pretty fantastic lovemaking. So tell me what's going on in that pretty head of yours."

Again, she could come up with no explanation that would exonerate her or her actions without committing herself to feelings she wasn't ready to admit to.

"I think the answer is fairly cut-and-dried, myself," he told her. "Or maybe it's just wishful thinking on my part."

"What do you mean?" she asked, frowning.

To her amazement, he pulled her to her feet and kissed her. Thoroughly. Roughly. She pressed her hands against his chest to push him away, but he wouldn't budge and, in spite of her anger and confusion, Kim felt her senses weakening, giving over to another heady rush of passion. Her fingers curled around fistfuls of his shirt. She gave a little moan and traded kiss for drugging kiss.

When her legs threatened to buckle, he lifted his head and smiled down at her, almost sadly, it seemed. "You're a smart woman. If you think about it, maybe you can figure it out."

Without another word, he turned and left her standing in the middle of Gerald's office, her hair a wild tangle, her lips swollen and bruised from his kisses, and a stunned look in her blue eyes.

* * *

The hot water of the shower beat down on Drew's head and shoulders. Curses bounced off the walls of the tile shower stall.

You're a damned fool, McShane, and that's a fact.

Lord, what had gotten into him? Though he'd wanted to force the issue between them, to talk to Kim sensibly and rationally, maybe even feel her out about things and let her know he was willing to work at their unusual marriage, he hadn't expected to make love to her in her father's office. Why, after all this time, had he lost control? And why had he thrown that cruel remark about getting the divorce at her?

Because he was still angry with her for having the audacity to want to end their marriage, that's why. Because then he'd be another statistic, one of failure. He understood that there were marriages that just didn't work, and in those cases, divorce might be the only recourse, but he and Kim didn't know if a "real" marriage—as she insisted on calling it—between them would work or not. Having struggled against the odds to get where and what he wanted, the idea of giving her and Hannah up without a fight was unthinkable.

Be honest. Fear of failure has nothing to do with why you made love to her.

No. He'd forced things to try to make her see that there could be something more between them. She hadn't objected. If anything, she'd seemed as hot for him as he'd been for her. Just thinking about the soft smoothness of her body, the way she made those little whimpering sounds deep in her throat and the way her hands moved over him with a feverish intensity brought another rush of desire.

He cranked the cold water higher. He suspected he'd done a very foolish thing.

When Maria Antonia came home from shopping late that evening, she found David Perkins sprawled on the rose damask sofa reading the paper, drinking brandy and smoking.

She closed her eyes and counted to ten, praying she wouldn't say anything to start a full-scale battle. She liked a good yelling match every now and then. There was something liberating about it, as if getting out all the anger and frustration inside helped clear the air. She and Larry had had vocal sparring matches on a regular basis and out-and-out verbal free-for-alls on several memorable occasions.

She and David had gone a round or two from time to time, and she'd learned that, unlike her dead husband, he could be vicious when he was on the defensive. On the other hand, there was the making up, but lately she'd found herself uninterested in either sport. She was tired, and having someone going over her books and snooping into every aspect of her business was making her edgy. If Larry were still alive, she'd have vented her feelings to him, but David wasn't Larry. He wasn't even close.

She realized suddenly that she missed her dead husband, and acknowledged the fact that she'd taken up with David so soon after Larry's death because she was lonely and hungry for masculine attention and he'd caught her in a moment of weakness. A sad commentary on her life, perhaps, but there it was.

"What's the matter, Ree Ree?" he asked, calling her by the nickname she hated. "Are your nerves a little shot?"

"It's been a long day," she said, pouring herself a splash of brandy and swirling the liquid round and round the snifter.

"How does a little time by yourself sound?"

She glanced at him sharply. "What do you mean?"

"I'm going away for a few days," he said, folding the paper and dropping it on the floor at his feet. "Business."

His eyes held a gleam that looked like cunning in the dim light of the room. "What kind of business?"

"Just business."

The fact that he was being deliberately obtuse didn't escape her. She wondered again just what it was he did for money besides gamble, but she wasn't foolish enough to ask.

"That's wonderful," she said, raising her glass in a mock salute. "I wish you success."

"I'm sure you do." Still wearing that sardonic smile that she'd once found so fascinating, David set his glass on the table and stood. "I think I'll go on up and get my things together."

He left the newspaper on the floor and the brandy snifter on the table along with the ashtray bearing the smelly remains of his cigar. Disgust—for herself and him—rose inside her on a giant wave of remorse. He was at the foot of the stairs when she called his name.

"Yeah?" he said, turning.

"While you're packing for your trip, pack all your things." When his eyes narrowed, she added, "I don't want you back here."

"No woman tells me when it's over," he said. "I decide when it's over."

The lethal expression in his eyes made the glass in

her hand tremble, but she stood firm. "Consider this a first, then," she said, and turned her back on him.

Surprisingly, Drew found Amber alone at the table the next morning. Kim was either still sleeping or hiding out until he left for the day. Neither scenario pleased him. He wanted to see her in morning's light, wanted to see if there were any visible signs of their lovemaking prowling behind the shuttered glances she was so good at using to hide her true feelings.

"Who put the burr under your saddle?" Amber asked.

"I beg your pardon?" he said, going to the buffet and heaping eggs, biscuits and Virginia ham on his plate.

"You look like you could bite nails," Amber said, a lazy smile curving her lips.

"Where's Gerald?" Drew asked, hoping to divert the conversation to something besides his own foul mood. He put down his plate and drew out a chair.

"He hasn't come down yet." Amber tapped the ash of her cigarette into a crystal ashtray. "Maybe he's like the rest of us and can't get to sleep until the wee hours."

"Is that why you're down so early every morning?" Drew asked. "Because you can't sleep?"

Amber looked as if she wished she'd kept her mouth shut. She ground out the half-smoked cigarette. "Yeah. All this noise is driving me nuts."

"Noise? There's no noise here at night but the frogs and owls."

She smiled drolly. "Exactly. I'm more used to traffic and the wail of sirens."

Drew smiled. "I can see how country life could be a hardship for a woman like you."

"A woman like me, huh?" she said, pushing back her plate and propping her elbows on the table. "And what kind of woman is that?"

Drew popped a bite of ham into his mouth and chewed it while pretending to give her question some hard thought. "One who likes the fast life," he said finally. "Excitement. Things happening."

"Yeah, well, the fast life can get to you after a while," she said, a contemplative gleam in her eyes. "To tell the truth, I'm actually enjoying my visit." Then, as if she realized what she'd just owned up to, she said, "I can't believe I said that, much less meant it."

"Did you?"

"Yeah," she said, looking as if this admission, too, surprised her. "I don't see nearly enough of Dad, and Hannah is growing up way too fast."

"Yes, she is." Drew wondered at the regret in Amber's voice. Was it possible that he was right, that she was finally beginning to grow up?

"Your bad mood couldn't have anything to do with the fact that you and Kim left together after dinner but came back separately, could it?" Amber asked after a couple minutes of silence.

Drew picked up his coffee cup. "Don't be so nosy."

"I prefer to think of it as curiosity," Amber said, her smile still firmly in place. "Or better yet, let's call it concern. It has a better connotation."

"I still don't want to discuss it with you. Now, can we drop it?"

"Hmm," Amber said with a nod of understanding.

"You and my little sister had a fight. Well, I'd be the first to admit she's hard to get along with. Or maybe it's just that my insecurities put me on guard with her."

"You have insecurities?" Drew asked, feigning surprise.

She favored him with another strange smile. "It surprised me when I realized it, too," she said. "Sometimes I think I feel so inferior next to Kim because her standards are so high, I know I can never attain them."

"You aren't Kim, Amber."

"Don't I know it?" she said with a bitter twist of her lips. "You're talking opposite ends of the spectrum here. Good and evil. Smart and dumb. Abbott and Costello."

Drew smiled at her comparisons. "I didn't mean that in a negative way. I just meant that we can't all be the same, thank God. And for the record, you are neither evil nor dumb. You are, however, funny sometimes."

"I am? Thanks." She reached for her cigarettes. "That's interesting."

"You smoke too much."

Amber gave him a mind-your-own-business look. "I know."

For the next few minutes she smoked and Drew finished his breakfast, surprised by—yet content with—the companionable silence developing between them.

"You're a nice guy," she said, finally breaking the silence. "My sister's a lucky girl."

Drew's mouth was full of coffee. He choked on

surprise, almost spewing the chicory-flavored drink all over the pristine white tablecloth.

"Tell her that," he said when he finally stopped coughing. As soon as he said it, Drew wished he'd kept his mouth shut. He didn't want the family knowing he and Kim were having any problems.

Amber regarded him curiously. "I will."

She got up to pour herself some fresh coffee, and after topping off Drew's cup, she asked, "Do you believe people can change?"

"I don't believe we can change other people, but I think someone can change himself if he wants to badly enough. Do you want to talk about it?" Drew asked, dropping all pretense that they were talking about a hypothetical situation, a hypothetical person.

"Not really." She shrugged. "Maybe. I don't know." She gave him a sideways glance. "It's not easy admitting to yourself that you're selfish, self-centered and spoiled."

"Admission is the first step to recovery," he quipped, making an attempt to bring the smile back to her face.

"Been there, done that."

"What?"

"I'm seeing a shrink. When I finally sobered up after the little scene at that restaurant, I knew I'd really crossed the line, and it was time to clean up my act. I was hanging out with the wrong people and drinking too much."

"Drugs?"

"No," she said with an emphatic shake of her head. "No drugs. Gwen scared the bejesus out of me about drugs when I was a kid, but men—especially

men who were all wrong for me—now, that was another thing. I like men.''

Her smile came back, albeit somewhat defeated.
''Believe it or not, I don't make a habit of getting
involved with married men.''

Drew suspected she was referring to Marc Hanley,
the man she'd been with when she was arrested.
''Marc?'' he asked.

''Yeah. Marc is a lying, cheating, no-account son
of a gun. He told me he and Kathleen were finished,
that her baby wasn't his. There hadn't been anyone
for more than a year, and I was lonely.''

Tears filled her eyes and she looked up at the
slowly whirling fan. ''Lord, but I get so lonely....''
She swiped at the tears with her fingertips, lowered
her defiant gaze to Drew's and lifted her shoulders
in a shrug. ''Silly me, I believed him.''

''Don't be so tough on yourself,'' Drew said. ''We
all make mistakes.''

''Yeah, but some of us make more than our
share.''

''True. And sometimes we get older and wiser. I
think that's what's happened here.''

Amber laughed shortly. ''I'm not sure about the
wiser, but I'm definitely getting older. I look around,
and everyone my age has kids. Look at Molly. We're
near the same age, and she has two. And Shiloh...''

''Shiloh was older than you when she finally got
married and settled down.''

''Hey! I didn't say anything about getting married
and settling down.''

''You're talking about wanting kids.''

''Am I?''

''Sounds that way to me. And the new older and

wiser Amber, the one who wants to change—badly—wouldn't have those kids without a husband, would she?''

"Hoist by my own petard," she said dramatically. "The question is moot, my dear Drew, because there are no decent men left out there. I've dated them from coast to coast, and I should know."

"Maybe you're looking in the wrong places—or for the wrong kind of guy."

"Point taken. For what it's worth, I'm thinking of moving somewhere closer so I can see the family more often—once I tie up a few loose ends."

The news didn't surprise Drew as much as it might have. "'Loose ends' as in the clothing designer?"

"Who?" Amber asked with a frown.

"The clothing designer who wanted you to fund his boutiques," Drew said.

Amber's face turned nearly as white as the damask cloth covering the table. "Oh, yeah." She shrugged. "It doesn't look like I'll be able to get the money out of Dad, so I'll have to find a way to get rid of the jerk."

Drew didn't miss the worry hiding in her eyes. "He won't be a problem, will he?"

"No!" she said quickly. Too quickly, Drew thought. "Nothing I can't handle."

The familiar bravado was back, but Drew wasn't sure he believed her.

"Hi!"

Both Drew and Amber turned at the sound of Hannah's voice. She was dressed in shorts and a T-shirt, and she was alone. Her dark hair was an unruly tangle around her face. She held a brush and two hair clasps in her hand.

"Hi, sweetness," Drew said, holding out his arms for her. She ran to him, and he put her on his lap, where she promptly put the "hair fixes" as she called them beside Drew's plate and reached for the remains of his biscuit. He watched in pure delight as she crammed the butter-laden morsel into her mouth with her palm. Like her grammar, her manners needed a little work.

"Where's Cindy?" he asked.

"Sick," Hannah mumbled around a mouthful of food.

"No talking with food in your mouth," Drew reminded her. When she'd chewed up the biscuit and washed it down with a mouthful of his café au lait, he asked, "Where's Mommy?"

"Inna shower." She pushed back the curly hair that fell into her eyes with the flat of her hand, smearing butter across her forehead and into her freshly washed hair.

"Do you want me to fix your hair?" Amber asked, taking her napkin from her lap and stretching across to wipe the greasy glob away.

"Daddy do it."

"Oh, Hannah, Daddy doesn't do hair very well. Why don't you let Auntie Amber do it?"

"She wants *you* to!" she said to Drew, folding her arms across her chest and poking out her bottom lip. She looked so much like her mother, it brought a smile to Drew's lips.

"Okay," he soothed. "Hop down."

He set her on her feet and reached for the hairbrush. "What do I do?" he asked Amber.

"Part it down the middle, I guess. It won't be easy with a brush."

"Why should anything about this be easy?" Drew muttered, repeating the words he'd spoken to Kim the night before.

"What?" Amber asked.

"Nothing." He set his jaw and began to work at fixing Hannah's hair. Amber was right. Making a straight part wasn't easy with a brush, but he finally got it fairly even, and then started gathering Hannah's curly hair up into doggy ears. Finally, with Amber's help, several muffled curses and several "ouches" from Hannah, he got the hair clasps secured.

When he turned her to face him, Amber burst into laughter. Drew couldn't help but join her. One dog ear was a full inch higher than the other, and the center part was a good half inch off center. Not knowing what they were laughing at, but willing to join in the fun, Hannah flung herself at him and added her happy giggles to theirs.

"Not bad for a first time," Amber said.

"It'll have to do."

"What'll have to do?"

The question came from Kim, who stood in the open doorway, wearing a look of polite inquiry and baggy white slacks in a loose cotton weave. Drew noticed she'd aimed the question at her sister. She wouldn't even look at him.

"Hi, sis," Amber said. "We were talking about Hannah's hair. I wanted to do it, but no one but Drew could fix it for her. Look at Mommy, Hannah Banana," she coaxed. Then to Kim, she said, "Not bad, huh?"

"Not bad," Kim replied. "For a first time."

"Am I beautiful, Mommy?" Hannah asked, flut-

tering her eyelashes at Kim in what she called
"pretty eyes."

"Gorgeous," Kim said. She flicked a cursory
glance at Drew. "I'm sorry she interrupted your
breakfast. Cindy isn't feeling well, and I told Hannah
to watch cartoons while I showered."

"No problem," Drew said. "Like I told you last
night, I enjoy being with her. I want to do things
with her." He'd thought to remind her of what he'd
said the night before, but when the color drained from
her face, he wished he'd kept quiet. Darn it, he didn't
want her to think he was an ogre of some kind. He
was only trying to prove a point. Two points.

One. He loved Hannah and intended to be a father
to her for the rest of his life. Two, ditto for his feelings about Kim.

It looked as if she was about to make some sort
of reply when Gerald stepped onto the porch. "Good
morning, everyone!"

"Hi, Daddy," Kim said as he gave her a perfunctory kiss on the cheek. "Did you rest well?"

"Like the dead. I guess all those sleepless nights
finally caught up with me. I hope I haven't kept you
all from going ahead with breakfast."

"You didn't."

"Good. Drew, someone from Shreveport is on the
phone for you. Something about Bud Reeves."

Bud Reeves. The last of Maria Antonia's former
foremen he'd been trying to track down. "Great,"
Drew said, tossing his napkin to the table and rising.
"Excuse me."

Surprisingly, Kim scooted her chair back and rose,
too. "I need to talk to you."

"Can't it wait?" he asked, his gaze raking Gerald

and Amber's blatantly curious faces. "I really should take this call."

"I won't take but a minute."

"Sure." He made a sweeping gesture toward the doorway, and she preceded him inside. Out of range of Gerald's and Amber's hearing, he said, "What is it?"

"I just wanted to tell you that last night was—"

Drew had no doubts about what Kim intended to tell him. He didn't want to hear her say it was a mistake, that it never should have happened, because it wasn't a mistake and it should have happened long ago. He knew it, and she did, too. The only thing was, she wasn't willing to admit it. The only way he could think to stop her was to slip an arm around her waist, pull her close and kiss her.

She resisted, sliding her hands between them and pushing. Grim determination forced him to hold on more tightly as he slanted his mouth over hers and deepened the kiss. After a few seconds there was a change in them both. The resistance had drained from her, so there was no need to hold her so firmly. His own libido was screaming for a repeat of their session in Gerald's office.

When he drew back, the resolute expression on her face had changed to one of bemusement.

"I know what you were going to say," he said before she could formulate a comeback. "Last night wasn't bad, was it? For a first time."

Chapter Eight

Kim stared at Drew's retreating figure, her sense of bewilderment slowly changing to irritation—at him and herself. How could she ever hope to make him understand that she was serious about the divorce if she kept turning to putty every time he touched her? What was the matter with her, anyway?

You love him, that's what's the matter.

That was no news flash. And it didn't change the situation. But making love with him did. Making love with him not once, but twice. Kim raised her hands to her cheeks that flamed with hot color. If the old walls could talk, the two of them would be a hot topic of conversation for years to come.

Hot. Like the heat of him against her. Hot, like the feel of his skin beneath her fingertips. Hot, like the moist cavern of his mouth...

"Stop it!"

The sound of her own angry voice in the silence of the library sent the memories packing. Kim's face took on the mutinous look she'd passed on to Hannah—including the pouty lower lip—and she crossed her arms over tender breasts that still bore the faint red chafe marks left by Drew's whiskers.

When he'd left her in the office with the admonishment to figure out what he meant by his cryptic statement, she'd tried to do just that. But when she'd cleared away all traces of what they'd been doing, she had no more idea of what he meant than when he'd said it.

This morning was a different matter. After thinking about it for most of the night, she understood exactly what he meant. The reason she wanted the divorce was clear. She wanted Drew to have the freedom to look for his own happiness without a wife he didn't love holding him back. The reasons she'd made love with him were just as clear. She loved him and wanted him, and, as he'd suggested, she had, for once in her repressed twenty-seven years, gone after something she wanted without thinking of the consequences. She knew now that she'd wanted to have at least one memory to keep her company through the rest of her life.

On the other hand, Drew's motivation wasn't clear at all. He'd admitted to wanting her, too, and claimed to know what was behind her decision to make love with him. Then he'd tempered that remark with the comment that maybe it was only wishful thinking on his part.

What was wishful thinking? That she wanted him as much as he wanted her? That she was having second thoughts about ending their marriage? How was she expected to know, when she didn't have the slightest idea who he was or what he was thinking? They'd grown so far apart through the years.

Drew was a straightforward kind of man who liked to keep things uncomplicated. Maybe the reason he wanted to stay married to her was as simple as the fact that he didn't want the complications of a real marriage. He knew what to expect from her. If he could have the complete adoration of a child and engage in a little satisfactory sex along the way, so much the better. That must be the reason he was so opposed to the idea of divorce.

He did tell you to go ahead and get your divorce after you made love with him—if you still wanted one.

Yes, but he'd said that because he'd taunted her about not consummating their vows, and because he was angry—hadn't he? And what had he meant by "if she still wanted one"? She shook her head. She just didn't know anymore. The only thing she knew for certain was that she loved him and that she'd never find anyone else who made her feel what he did.

When she went back outside, Amber was alone at the table. Gerald had gone to make a phone call.

"Where's Hannah?" she asked.

"She said she needed to go to the bathroom," Amber said.

Kim reached for her coffee without bothering to sit down. "I guess I'd better round her up. I need to go into town."

"What's the hurry?" Amber asked, sounding surprisingly like Kim's mother, Gwen. "Have another cup of coffee and finish your toast, or you'll be running on empty.''

Kim didn't meet her sister's gaze. "I really need to get going. I've got a dozen errands to run today." She picked up her coffee cup and took a swallow.

"You can't ignore me forever," Amber said, leaning back in her chair with a grace and confidence that always made Kim feel young and gauche.

She felt her face grow warm with embarrassment. Like her husband, her sister was one who didn't pussyfoot around when something was on her mind. "I'm not."

"Sure you are. You haven't spoken more than ten consecutive words to me in the past six years."

"We were never close," Kim said, taking the defensive.

"No. Unfortunately."

Kim's gaze flew to her sister's. Genuine regret gleamed in Amber's eyes.

"I could never live up to your perfection, so I did everything in my power to belittle you, to make you feel like you were the outsider. But you weren't. I was."

Startled and confused by Amber's confession, Kim couldn't think of a thing to say but "You were always Daddy's favorite." Even she heard the resentment in her voice.

"And you were always Gwen's."

"She wasn't your mother."

"I know. And to give credit where credit is due, she seldom made a distinction between us. But I always knew, and when I found out about my own mother running around on Dad, I knew the badness in me was inherited."

"You aren't bad, Amber. Just willful and spoiled. That's Dad's fault. He'd never listen to Mom when she tried to make him see that by giving in to your every whim, he was doing you an injustice," Kim said, surprising herself by taking her sister's part.

Amber spread her arms wide. "And just look at me now."

There was nothing Kim could say to that.

"Look, we're both big girls. Let's lay all our cards on the table, okay?" Amber said. "You hate me."

Faced with owning up to her feelings, Kim knew it wasn't true. She'd often been jealous of Amber, often wished she could be as outgoing and natural-acting around people as her sister was…had wished she were as pretty, as vivacious. As they'd grown older and she began to see the toll Amber's life-style was taking on her, those feelings of envy had begun to change into a sort of sadness Kim refused to acknowledge and no small amount of embarrassment—especially when Amber made the front page of the tabloid. But she didn't hate her.

"I don't hate you."

"No?"

"No. I've been so angry with you I could have choked the life from you, but I've never hated you. Not really."

"I caused Dad's heart attack when I was arrested in L.A., didn't I?"

The directness of the question took Kim aback. "I always thought so," she said, taking a page from her sister's book and—for once—saying what she wanted with no thought for the consequences.

Amber nodded, and her eyes glittered with an unnatural brightness. "Yeah. That's what I thought. He was already tied in knots and worn out from Gwen's illness, and then I make headlines.'' She raised guilt-ridden eyes to Kim's. "Would it help if I said that that's when I hit rock bottom? That I've gotten help for my drinking?" She gave a short, bitter laugh. "My shrink says I've come a long way."

Suddenly Kim saw just how empty Amber's life had really been. For years, she'd been smack in the middle of one big party, and now it was over and she was reaping what she'd sown. There had been times Kim had railed against a nature that had kept her bound to her parents, especially after her mother died, but now those once-empty, boring years seemed like a haven.

"I was jealous of you," Amber said, clearly determined to settle their differences once and for all.

"I was jealous of you, too." It seemed necessary for Kim to repay Amber's honesty in kind. "You had it all. Looks, personality, charm."

"No," Amber said. "*You* had it all. Brains, an unselfish nature, a kind heart. Everyone thought you hung the moon. I see now that I behaved the way I did to get my share of attention from the parents."

"Negative attention is better than no attention, huh?" Kim asked.

"So they say." Neither of them spoke for several moments, and finally Amber said, "I might have had a child by now if things had been different. If I hadn't given it up for adoption."

Kim looked at her sister in shock. "I beg your pardon?"

"I was only twenty and in school at Baton Rouge when I came up pregnant. The jerk I was involved with told me it was him or the baby." Her lips twisted in a bitter smile. "I couldn't go through with the abortion, so I decided to go to Dallas to art school. I didn't come home until my baby was born.

Surprised, Kim thought of her own situation, and what she might have done if Drew hadn't agreed to marry her. Would she have considered an abortion or adoption rather than confess her sin to her father? "I had no idea."

"How could you? It's something I'm not proud of. Something I'm not sure I'll ever get over." Amber exhaled and plastered a false, bright smile on her face. "Enough of that! Why don't you let me baby-sit Hannah while you run your errands?"

"Oh, Amber, I don't know...."

"What's the matter, sis? Don't you trust me?"

"It isn't that," Kim said, though deep in her heart, she wasn't sure it was the truth. "She can be a real handful for someone who isn't used to kids."

"Tantrums if she doesn't get her way? Pouting? Never fear. I've had a lot of experience with that. I used to do it."

Something told Kim Amber's request meant a lot to her. Surely she could trust her with Hannah for the day. "Okay," she said. "She's all yours. I just hope you won't be sorry."

"I won't."

Amber looked as if she wanted to say something else. "What?" Kim asked.

"I'll be out of your hair the day after the party."

"Really? Why?"

"I've got to try and come up with that money." Amber slanted a calculating look at Kim. "I don't suppose you'd ask Dad for it for me, would you?"

"No," Kim said shortly. "I wouldn't." The softening she'd begun to feel toward Amber had vanished along with her sister's request.

"I wouldn't ask if I didn't really need it, sis," Amber said. "I'm getting desperate."

"What do you need it for?" Kim asked. "And don't say a string of boutiques. I know that's a lie."

"I can't say."

"Then I'm sorry," Kim said. "I won't do your dirty work for you. Daddy has enough to worry about, and in case you hadn't noticed, his money is a bit tight right now. You said it a little while ago. You're a big girl. You're going to have to learn to deal with your mistakes the way the rest of us do. Face them and fix them."

"Well, it was worth a shot." The words were spoken with a breezy nonchalance, and Kim hardened her heart to the despair she saw in her sister's eyes.

The phone call was from the private detective Drew had hired to try to find Bud Reeves, one of the foremen who'd worked for Maria Antonia the past three years. According to the P.I., the former Muldair employee was working on a farm in Doyline, a small town just outside of Shreveport.

As soon as he got all the information, Drew hung up and called the private pilot who often flew him back and forth from Kentucky. Luckily, Barney Blevins and his plane were free, and Drew made arrangements to leave before noon. By the time he returned to the breakfast table to tell everyone of his plans, Kim, Amber and Hannah were gone.

"Kim had some errands to run, and Amber offered to baby-sit Hannah since Cindy's still under the weather," Gerald explained when Drew asked where everyone had gone.

In spite of his excitement about soon being able to talk to Bud Reeves, Drew had to smile at the thought of Amber baby-sitting. A precocious two, and with more than her share of bossiness, Hannah was a handful.

"Do you think Bud Reeves will be able to tell you anything?" Gerald asked.

"I hope so. I'm as ready as you to get this cleared up and to put it behind us."

"When do you leave?"

"In an hour or so. Barney is flying me up to Shreveport."

"You'll be back this evening?"

"Yeah," Drew said. "If the good Lord's willing and the creek don't rise." The Southern saying sounded strange with an Irish lilt to it. "Will you tell Kim where I'm going?"

"Surely," Gerald said. "Have a safe trip."

"Thanks."

Drew found Bud Reeves in a double-wide mobile home near the training track at Doyline. Though he was clearly puzzled about why Drew had shown up on his doorstep Bud seemed glad to see him.

"Come on in and have a cup of coffee," he said after pumping Drew's hand a full thirty seconds. "The wife's gone to the store."

"Thanks. Coffee sounds good."

Drew followed Bud into the surprisingly spacious living room. Though the decor was a mishmash of different styles with a lot of country crafts that didn't appeal to Drew, the place was scrupulously clean.

"What brings you to this neck of the woods?" Bud asked as he went about filling the coffeemaker with water and measuring out the correct amount of grounds into a brown paper filter.

Drew couldn't see any sense in beating around the bush. "I guess you've heard about the Flight of Dreams scandal."

Bud laughed. "Who hasn't? I figured that gambling of Miz Perkins's husband's would get her into trouble sooner or later," Bud said. "I'm just glad I'm out of it."

This wasn't the first time someone had mentioned David Perkins's gambling problem. Though Gerald had told him about Maria's shaky finances, it was next to impossible to imagine her doing anything unethical. "That's why you left?"

Bud gave a derisive snort. "No. I left because I was asked to leave."

"She fired you?"

"Perkins did. Guess I was askin' too many questions."

"What kind of questions?"

"Like why she was lettin' those guys from Mexico handle the stallions when they didn't hardly know which end of the lead shank to hold on to. Like why she had them doing some of the breeding when I wasn't around. You know as well as I do that when you have a stud worth several million dollars, you don't want a contrary mare damaging the goods, so to speak."

"No," Drew said. "You certainly don't."

The last of the water sputtered into the coffeepot, and Bud got up to pour the dark, fragrant brew into two mugs.

Once his coffee was doctored to his taste, Drew posed another question. "Let's cut to the chase. You're saying Perkins let them handle the studs when you weren't around, which means you think something was going on."

Bud looked uncomfortable suddenly. "I really don't think I should say, Mr. McShane. I mean, Miz Perkins is your friend, and anything I might think is just speculation. I don't have a thing but gut feeling to go on."

"Sometimes that's a pretty good gauge," Drew said. "You're right, Bud. Mrs. Perkins is a friend, but you can speak freely. The Thoroughbred industry is important to me, the same way it is to all of us who make a living by it. If there's something going on that will undermine the integrity of that industry, then it needs to be stopped. I want to find out the truth about what's going on, and I want to clear Gerald Campion's name."

"I don't think Mr. Campion had any idea what Maria Perkins and her husband were doing."

"Which was?" Drew prodded gently.

Bud's face turned beet red. "Like I said, I don't have any proof, but I think she and Perkins were taking money to breed to Flight of Dreams, and then breeding to a couple of other studs with the same coloring. Since artificial insemination is a no-no, it would be a good way to collect more money—which I think they needed to pay his gambling debts."

As Bud talked, Drew's heart sank. Bud's reasoning was the same as his own, but Drew felt no satisfaction at knowing his hunch might be right. He simply couldn't believe Maria Antonia was capable of such a thing. But love had made a fool of many a person.

He should know. Thank God, it would be up to the police to sort it all out. Even though his name would be cleared, the news would hit Gerald hard if Maria was found guilty.

Drew finished his coffee and left, thanking Bud for the information. He drove the rental car back to the airport and had Barney Blevins fly him back home. During the flight, Drew decided to wait and tell Gerald about Bud's theory after Hannah's birthday tomorrow. He was looking forward to the party, and Kim and Amber had worked hard to make sure it was a success.

He wondered briefly what Kim thought about the kiss he'd given her that morning, and he decided that when he got back, he needed to have another talk with her. He was tired of playing games. He'd tell her how he felt, that he loved her, had always loved her, and if she said there was no chance, then he'd agree to a divorce.

Whoa, McShane. Don't forget the party. Right. Like the news about Maria, he could wait until after the party to bare his soul to Kim. There was no need putting a damper on the celebration when both conversations could wait.

Amber pulled into McDonald's and helped Hannah out of her car seat. So far, the day was a success, Amber thought as she watched her niece leap into the pit of colorful plastic balls. Hannah was potty trained—thank God!—and even though Kim had warned that she could be stubborn when she wanted her own way, so far Hannah had been an angel.

There was a curious ache in Amber's heart, and a bittersweet smile on her lips as she watched while

Hannah crawled through the tunnels of the playground and slid down the covered slide. If she'd made different choices, she could be watching her own child. Amber pushed that troubling thought away and waved at Hannah.

There'd been a moment, after their small altercation, that Amber had been afraid Kim would change her mind about letting her watch Hannah.

Why had she asked Kim to approach their father about the money?

It's called desperation, kiddo. Last resort. If you don't get the money soon, life as you know it will cease to exist.

She hadn't been surprised when her sister refused, something Amber realized was meant to be a character-building experience. But she had been surprised at the unexpected pain she felt when she saw the disappointment in Kim's eyes. The memory brought another pang of hurt. She'd realized a lot of things lately. She just hoped it wasn't too late in her life to put what she'd learned into action.

"Watch, Aunt Ammer!" Hannah cried, spreading her arms wide and falling face first into the sea of brightly colored balls.

"That's great, Hannah Banana!" Amber called.

"Cute kid. Your niece?"

The sound of the familiar masculine voice drove the smile from Amber's lips and the happiness from her heart. Slowly, as if she were afraid to actually see who stood next to her, she angled her head upward. She felt the color drain from her cheeks. As she expected, her worst nightmare—in the form of an attractive older man—stood smiling down at her. David Perkins.

"Hello, Amber."

"What are you doing here?" she asked.

"I came to see if we can't work something out about the money I asked you to get for me."

Even though her heart was pounding in her chest, Amber decided that her best bet was to brazen out the situation.

"I can't get the money, David." She met his gaze boldly. Her tone of voice seemed to be asking why he'd bothered to come. "Not right away. I thought I made that clear when you called yesterday."

Still wearing that falsely pleasant look, he tugged his sharply creased slacks up an inch and sat down at the small table across from her. "I understand your predicament," he told her, "but it doesn't change the fact that you were supposed to have the money a couple of weeks ago."

"I don't have any control over the situation my father is in, and I'm not going to ask him for that kind of money when his business practices are under scrutiny by the police."

"I don't have any control over my creditors, either," David said. "I need my money, and I need it now."

Amber forced a laugh she was far from feeling. "What's the matter? Did Maria refuse to ante up?"

When the color rushed to his face, Amber knew she'd scored a direct hit. She took little pleasure in the knowledge, though. David Perkins was generally unpleasant, and when he was angry he could be especially offensive. Still, she couldn't help the sardonic smile or her sarcastic "Gotcha!"

"On the contrary, Amber, I think I've got you,"

he told her smoothly. "If you don't come up with the money, I go to Gerald."

Amber's brief euphoria vanished along with her smile.

"Don't look so surprised. You knew all along that was the stake we were gambling for, and trying to run out on me was a mistake."

He reached out and gave her fisted hand a fatherly pat. "Surely you didn't think you could mislead me by hiding out with your family? Even if I hadn't seen that picture in the paper, it was only a matter of time until I found you."

Amber jerked free of his touch and felt what was left of her world begin to crumble around her. There was no way she could get the money from Gerald. She'd just have to hope he loved her enough. "I can't get the money, so do your worst."

"You're pretty cocky for a woman who owes so much money."

Forcing a bluster she didn't feel, Amber leaned forward. When she spoke, she enunciated each word clearly. "Let's call a spade a spade, David. Your little game is called blackmail. I don't *owe* you a dime."

He rubbed his smoothly shaven chin with his fingertips. "I guess that depends on how you look at it. And the way I look at it, Gerald Campion owes me."

"For what? You slept with his wife!" Amber had had enough. She grabbed her purse and stood, scanning the playground equipment for Hannah. She saw her peering down from a high tunnel.

"Hannah!" she called. "Come on down. Aunt Amber's ready to go."

Hannah smiled and waved from behind the safety

of a clear plastic bubble. Amber motioned for her to come down.

"Don't run off, Amber. We're going to come to some sort of agreement here."

She didn't even look at him. "I don't think so."

"What about your brother-in-law?"

"Drew?" she said, turning her shocked gaze to the man who seemed determined to ruin her life.

"Yes, Drew. He's got plenty of money. Maybe he'd lend it to you."

"I can't ask Drew McShane for a hundred thousand dollars, David. I'm not a particular favorite of his."

"He's a successful businessman. Put some sort of a business venture to him. Maybe he'll want to invest."

"Drew didn't get where he is by investing in stupid ventures. He'd want to see a whole ream of papers proving the investment was sound."

"Maybe you could offer him a little collateral." The suggestion was accompanied by a lewd look that raked Amber from head to toe.

Her stomach knotted. For all that she'd once been interested in Drew, what David hinted at disgusted her now. "You're sick. You know that, don't you? Drew loves my sister. I couldn't do that to her, even if either of us was so inclined—which we aren't."

"Why not?" David asked. "From what I hear, there isn't any love lost between you and Kim."

"Who told you that?" Amber asked sharply.

"I think it's pretty well known."

"Well, we're working on our relationship," Amber said. "And I don't plan to mess up what little progress we've made by trying to seduce her husband.''

"So you're developing a conscience. Interesting."

Before Amber could reply, Hannah came running up, a sandal clutched in each hand. "I can't put my shoes on," she said, holding them out to Amber and, at the same time, looking curiously up at David.

Amber sat Hannah up on the table and took the shoes.

"Who are you?" Hannah asked.

"I'm a friend of your Aunt Amber's."

"I wouldn't go so far as to say that," Amber corrected him.

The exchange went right over Hannah's head. "What's your name?" she asked.

"David. What's yours?"

"Hannah," she said, dimpling up at him. "Hannah McShane."

"Hannah," he said. "I like that."

"Give me your other foot, Hannah," Amber said, anxious to put as much distance as possible between her and the man busily charming her niece.

Hannah stuck out her bare foot.

"I'm going to have an ice-cream cone," David said. "Do you want one, Hannah?"

"Yeah!" she cried, her eyes bright with excitement.

"I'm sorry, Hannah," Amber said. "Not this time. We have to get back home."

"I want ice cream!" Hannah's face crumpled, and she began to cry.

"Now look what you've done," David scolded, giving Amber a triumphant look.

Ignoring him, Amber scooped Hannah into her

arms and started for the exit. She began to struggle and kick, yelling out that she wanted ice cream. A feeling of déjà vu swept through Amber. Having frequently pulled the same stunt herself as a child, she recognized Hannah's tantrum for what it was—manipulation, pure and simple.

"It's only an ice-cream cone." David's voice carried to her. "I'll get her the kiddie size."

Embarrassed, not having the slightest idea how to handle the situation, and more anxious to have Hannah stop causing a scene than she was to escape David's presence, Amber stopped, turned and pinned him with a hard look. "Fine. Get the darned ice-cream cone. But hurry."

David went into the building, and Amber turned her attention to Hannah. "Hush, Hannah," she whispered in a harsh tone. "You can have the ice cream."

Almost immediately, the tears turned to sniffles. Hannah wrapped her arms around Amber's neck and kissed her cheek. Amber felt her anger dissolve even as she recalled using the same ploy with her father. She hugged Hannah back. Amber knew she should stand firm when she told Hannah no, but a little spoiling couldn't hurt her, could it?

Maybe you'd better take a good look at yourself.

That was different, Amber thought as David came through the door carrying the ice cream. She'd been spoiled all her life. She consoled herself with the fact that she wouldn't be making a habit of giving Hannah what she wanted. After all, she wouldn't be around much longer.

"Here you go, angel," David said, handing the miniature cone to Hannah.

"Tank you," Hannah said, accepting the gift. Under any other circumstances, Amber would have been proud of her for remembering her manners.

For the next ten minutes, they sat at the table and David talked to Hannah. She told him about her birthday party and that she was having clowns and a pony and a tent. He teased her and joked with her and made her laugh while Amber sat watching them, wordlessly. David might have passed his prime, but there was no doubt that if he set his mind to it, he could charm the pants off anyone in skirts. It was easy to picture him as he would have been more than thirty years ago, easy to see why her mother had fallen for him.

Finally, Hannah finished her ice cream, and Amber wiped her niece's sticky hands and face with a pre-packaged towelette she took from her purse.

"See how happy she is," David said.

Amber didn't comment.

"You know, people are funny," he said in a thoughtful voice. "When they want something badly enough, they'll figure out a way to get it."

Amber glanced over at him. He was fingering a curly lock of Hannah's hair, but his gaze was fixed on Amber's. "And if they can't get it one way, they'll get it another. Just look at Hannah, here."

A shiver of apprehension she didn't understand swept through Amber.

David turned his attention back to Hannah. "Isn't that right, angel?" he cooed. Though she had no idea what he was talking about, Hannah smiled and nod-ded, pleased at the attention.

Feeling as spooked as if she'd just stepped into a minefield, and not sure why, Amber picked Hannah up and settled her on her hip.

"What's the rush?" David asked, his voice smooth and pleasant.

"Don't play games with me," Amber snapped, grabbing her purse.

"Believe me, Amber, this is no game." His smile was still firmly in place, but the look in his eyes was dead serious. "I want the money, and I intend to have it. One way or the other."

Chapter Nine

Kim was having a glass of tea on the back *galerie* when Amber and Hannah got home. She'd been on pins and needles all day. Judging from the smile on Hannah's face when Amber lifted her out of the car seat, all Kim's worries had been for nothing.

"Hi," she said as Amber climbed the steps, Hannah in her arms. A fine tension tightened Amber's lips, and there was a defeated look in her eyes that was totally out of place. "Rough day?" Kim asked.

"Hi," Amber said, handing the wriggling Hannah over to her mother. "Not too bad, actually." She smiled, but there was a definite lack of enthusiasm in the brief quirking of her lips.

"Was she good?"

"For the most part," Amber said. "Is there any more of that tea?"

"Sure." Kim poured her sister a glass of tea from

the frosty pitcher, feeling as if the conversation had been purposefully turned.

"We went to McDonald's," Hannah said. "I got a Happy Meal."

"Did you eat it all?" Kim asked.

Hannah nodded. "And I played in the balls."

"No wonder you look so whipped," Kim said to her sister. "She'd stay there forever if I'd let her. How did you manage to get her out of there without a scene?"

"It wasn't too bad."

"I had ice cream."

"You did?"

Hannah nodded again. "David bought it for me."

Kim cut a startled gaze to her sister's pale face. "You didn't tell me you were meeting one of your... friends when you asked to watch Hannah."

Another of those smiles flickered across Amber's mouth. "Don't get your panties in a wad, sister dear. It isn't like we indulged in wild decadent s-e-x in front of Hannah."

"I didn't think you had," Kim said quickly.

"Didn't you?" Amber sighed, as if she were tired not only of the conversation, but of everything. "He's just an acquaintance, and I didn't *plan* to meet him."

Seeing the sincerity in her sister's eyes, Kim knew she'd jumped to conclusions. "I'm sorry."

"As well you should be," Amber said primly. She took a swallow of her tea and set the glass back down. "I'm whipped," she said. "And I need a shower to pick me up. I guess I'm not in very good shape for keeping up with a two-year-old."

Kim felt a sudden urge to try to erase the look in

Amber's eyes. "If it's any consolation, she wears me out, too."

Amber smiled, and this one looked more like the real thing. "She's a sweetie." She stood, scooped up her glass of tea and, leaning over, dropped a kiss to the top of Hannah's curly head. Then she looked at Kim and said, "See you at dinner."

Amber was at the door when Kim called her name. She turned.

"Is something wrong? You seem worried."

"I'm fine," Amber said, but even as she said it, Kim knew it was a lie.

Drew wasn't home by dinnertime, and, as crazy as she knew it was, Kim worried that something had happened to Barney Blevins's small plane. Finally, as she was getting Hannah ready for bed, he called from his parents' to let her know he was back and that he'd be home soon.

"How was your day?" he asked. The nonchalance of the question was at odds with the emotions seething through her. She was all too aware of the way her heart began to sprint at the sound of his voice and that her fingertips were touching lips that seemed to remember the feel of his.

"Hectic," she told him. "I had a million last-minute things to do, but I think everything's set for tomorrow."

"Who took care of Hannah?"

"Amber."

If he was surprised, he didn't show it. "And how did Amber do?"

"She was exhausted, but I think she enjoyed it."

"It was good for her."

"Probably." Kim didn't tell him about their conversation and how, for the first time, she truly felt Amber might be trying to get her life straight. The softening she felt toward her sister—despite the fact that she'd asked Kim to hit their father up for money—was too new, too tentative to explore too deeply. Today was only a preliminary foray into a new relationship. It would take more heart-to-heart talks and seeing a real change in Amber's behavior before Kim was convinced her sister's change was sincere.

"I'll let you go," Drew told her. "Try to rest. We've got a big day ahead of us tomorrow."

"I know."

They said their goodbyes and hung up. Kim had a strong suspicion neither of them had said what they wanted. She took a shower, checked on Cindy and went to bed early. As usual, Kim had a hard time falling asleep, despite Drew's admonition about the upcoming party. This time, though, her thoughts were divided equally between her growing feelings for her husband and her conversation with Amber. She fell asleep uncertain where her relationship with either of them was headed.

But when she dreamed, it was of Drew kissing her and her returning that kiss....

It was near midnight when Drew let himself into the house. Once he'd made the decision about when to tell Gerald about Maria Antonia, he'd allowed thoughts of Kim to fill his mind. He was anxious to see the breeding scandal settled so he could actively pursue a relationship with his wife and convince her a divorce was the last thing they needed. The more he thought about it, the more certain he was that she had feelings for him. Why else would she respond the way she did whenever he kissed her?

He was about to pass the room where she slept when an overpowering urge to see her gripped him. He grasped the doorknob and turned it silently. The soft glow of the night-light near the dresser revealed Hannah on her back in one of the room's twin beds. She'd kicked her covers down around her feet. Kim slept in the other bed. Unlike Hannah, she lay on her side, one hand under the pillow, the other beneath her cheek.

As he watched, Hannah curled onto her side in a fetal position. Thinking she must be cold, Drew pulled the covers up over her. Then he bent down and brushed a kiss across the petal softness of her cheek. She mumbled something in her sleep and, fearful that he'd wake her, he stepped away. In the other bed, Kim shifted onto her back, as if Hannah's sleepy babbling had disturbed her. Just looking at his wife disturbed Drew.

Her long hair fanned out over the floral pillowcase, a skein of the softest gold, silky to the touch. But no more silky than her skin, he thought, noting how the strap of her gown had fallen over the smooth softness of her shoulder. He itched to pull it back in place— okay, maybe he just wanted to touch her—but shoved his hands into the pockets of his jeans to keep from succumbing to the impulse. As good as the sex was, and as certain as he was that she wouldn't refuse him if he instigated another night of lovemaking, he also knew they needed to have some serious discussion about the things they were both feeling.

Stifling a sigh of longing and regret, Drew bent

and touched Kim's lips with his. She gave a little groan and returned the pressure of his kiss. As small as it was, the sign of her capitulation, even in sleep, went to his head like fine Irish whiskey. He straightened and backed away before he woke her, his heart filled with new determination.

She was his, just as Hannah was his, and somehow, some way, he intended to keep them both.

The day of Hannah's party dawned gray and drizzly, but despite the weatherman's predictions, an obstinate sun dared to make brief, sporadic appearances. Kim kept hoping the sky would clear before the party began so the sunshine could dry the yard.

Hannah was beside herself with excitement. She'd been totally in awe when the tent had gone up the day before, and when Kim and Amber began to fill dozens of balloons with helium, she went wild.

A table was set up alongside one wall of the tent, and a bright yellow tablecloth became the backdrop for a clown-face cake with orange hair and a punch bowl that would be filled with red punch. There would be sandwiches for the parents. A pony ride, spiral slide and five clowns performing magic tricks would provide the entertainment. It promised to be quite a blowout. Kim thought it was too much for a child Hannah's age, but her dad and Drew seemed to want it, and she'd certainly heard no complaints from Hannah.

Molly and Garrett Rambler were the first to arrive. They both hugged Kim, and then, seeing the horrible Desmoulins twins climbing from their mother's Suburban, Garrett decided it was time for him and Rett to go and see what Drew was up to.

"I hate to leave you alone," Molly said, as the Desmoulins twins leaped from the sport utility vehicle. "But I think Laura Leigh and I will go up and check on Cindy."

"Coward," Kim taunted.

"I don't deny it," Molly said, pushing a lock of her red hair away from her face. "But Dad asked me to check on Cindy."

"Okay, you're forgiven," Kim said with a smile. "Just hurry back, okay?"

Molly winked. "Right."

Kim watched her friend leave, unaware of the wistful expression in her own eyes. Like Amber and her, Molly and Cindy had the same father, but different mothers. Unlike Amber and her, neither that, nor the difference in their ages, seemed to keep Cindy and Molly from a closeness that Kim sometimes envied.

"Stop that, you little brats!"

The shrill command came from Patti Desmoulins, who brushed past Kim and bore down on her four-year-old hellions with blood in her eyes. Kim turned as the terrible twins stuck their chubby fingers into their mouths. Evidently they'd just sampled the cake's icing.

No sooner had Patti taken each of them by the ear and escorted them outside the tent to give them a talking to, than Cade and Shiloh Robichaux and four-year-old Micah pulled up. Kim couldn't help noticing the beginning of a tummy beneath Shiloh's loose-fitting dress. Evidently, the Robichaux would soon be welcoming another addition to the family.

Kim was feeling another of those strange longings for something she couldn't quite put a name to when Shiloh enveloped her in a warm embrace.

"Where have you been keeping yourself?" she asked with her soft Tennessee drawl so different from that of her husband, who'd been born and raised in the area. "It's been a coon's age since I've seen you."

"I know," Kim said, feeling a pang of guilt for not keeping in closer touch with her friend. With all her friends. "I have no idea what I do with my time."

"I understand," Shiloh said. "Uh-oh! I see Micah trying to make a getaway. Let me go rescue Cade. I'll talk to you later."

"Sure," Kim said. Feeling more than a little melancholy, she watched as Shiloh crossed the yard to where the men—who had been joined by Molly and Laura Leigh—were gathered.

"Those kids have sure grown."

The sound of her mother-in-law's voice intruded on Kim's thoughts. "They certainly have. Time has a way of getting away, doesn't it?"

"That it does," Maureen said. "Why, just look at Hannah. If you and Drew plan on having another, you'd best get to it before there's too big of an age gap for them to enjoy each other."

This was the second time in as many weeks Kim's mother-in-law had hinted that it was time for her and Drew to have another child. Actually, Maureen's confession that Drew desperately wanted another child was one thing that had started Kim to thinking about the unfairness of their marriage.

Now her thoughts turned to the realization that, as of two nights ago, Drew's desire for a child might have become a reality. It was all she could do to keep from moving her hand to her abdomen. Was it possible that even now, Drew's baby was growing inside her?

"Maybe it's none of my business, but you do want another baby, don't you?" Maureen pressed. "You do want to have Drew's baby?"

Something in the older woman's voice sent warning bells ringing inside Kim's head. She turned to face Maureen. Her mother-in-law's face wore an anxious expression, and she wrung her plump hands.

"What do you mean?" Kim asked, but the guilt on Maureen's face was answer enough.

"Oh, dear! I've put my foot in it now, haven't I?"

"He told you," Kim said, posing the words as a fact instead of a question. "Drew told you that Hannah isn't his."

Maureen nodded miserably.

"When?"

Surprise leaped into Maureen's eyes. "When? Why as soon as the two of you married. Drew never could fool his dad," she said. "Cullen knew something wasn't right from the first. When he pressed, Drew told him the truth—though he didn't want to," she added, as if that might make a difference.

"You've known all this time and never said anything?" Kim asked incredulously.

"Well," Maureen said with a shrug of her plump shoulders, "what was there to say?"

"Neither of you minded that he married a woman pregnant by another man? One who…loved another man?"

"What does love have to do with anything?" Maureen said. "What young people today call love is a fickle thing at best. Real love comes with living through the hard times with someone. Cullen and I understood why you wanted to keep your pregnancy from your father, and we've all loved you—especially Drew—from the time you were born. We knew we'd love your child, too.''

"You haven't said anything to my father?"

"Not a word," Maureen said with a shake of her head. "Though I don't imagine he'd be as upset as you might think."

"Maybe not," Kim said, "but I'd rather he not know just now." *Now that I'm trying to end the marriage.*

"You do plan to tell him?"

"Of course I do," Kim said. But had she? Or had she convinced herself that Gerald's health was so bad he never needed to know the truth? Had she avoided the issue, hoping it would go away?

"The longer you put it off, the harder it'll be," Maureen chided gently. "Gerald Campion is a good man who loves you dearly. He never expected perfection from you, Kim. You're the one who demanded that of yourself."

Kim didn't comment. Again, she knew her mother-in-law was telling the truth.

"I know things between you and Drew aren't good just now."

The matter-of-fact observation sent Kim's startled gaze winging to her mother-in-law's.

"What's wrong is none of my business, but just remember that you can work things out if you want to badly enough."

Maureen didn't tell Kim it would break her heart— and Cullen's—if their son's marriage ended, but it was there in the pleading look in her eyes and the tension that molded her lips into a rigid line.

"I appreciate your concern, Maureen. Please believe me when I say that Drew's happiness is one of my greatest concerns."

"That's as it should be when you love someone."

Kim hoped the despair in her heart wasn't evident in her eyes. She wondered what Maureen would say about one-sided love. "And I want you and Cullen to know that, considering the circumstances, I'm very grateful for the way you've taken Hannah into your hearts and lives and treated her like your real grandchild."

Maureen took Kim's cold hands in hers. "Ah, but she is our real grandchild. Neither of us could love her more if it were Drew's blood running in her veins. That I promise you."

Kim blinked back the tears that prickled behind her eyelids. Afraid she'd start bawling if she said anything, she just squeezed her mother-in-law's fingers and murmured a soft "Thank you."

"You'd best be gettin' to your guests," Maureen said. "They're really starting to flock in."

A horn honked. Kim turned and saw two cars pulling into the driveway. She returned a wave. There was no time to indulge in wishful thinking or wallowing in regrets. It was Hannah's day. One Kim wanted to be perfect in every way.

Was she crazy? Amber asked herself an hour later. Had she really been entertaining the idea of giving up her carefree single life-style and looking for someone like Drew—or that good-looking Cade Robichaux or Garrett Rambler, for that matter—and settling down in a nice suburban house with the requisite two-point-five kids?

There were between fifteen and twenty children at Hannah's party, most of whom had been dropped off by parents with better things to do than stay and make sure their respective offspring didn't destroy Lafourche Farm.

Truth was, most of the attendees were being pretty well behaved, other than the Desmoulins twins—whom Amber was beginning to think were the spawn of Satan—and mouthy, rowdy Beau Simmons, who'd been dropped off by a patrol car bearing the insignia of the town's sheriff. Her lips curved into a bitter twist. Maybe they'd let him out of the slammer for the afternoon.

She looked around. It wasn't that they were really so bad, there were just so many of them! Even with Shiloh and Molly helping her, Amber felt as if she were being pulled in a hundred directions at once.

For the past hour, she'd made sure each child got a pony ride and caught them at the bottom of the slide. Someone from the sheriff's department was supposed to come and fingerprint the children so their prints would be on file. The idea had come from Cade Robichaux, whose sister, Chantal's baby had been stolen from the hospital soon after it was born, but so far, the parish fuzz was a no-show.

Currently, the clowns—apparently dredged up from two different party companies according to the logos on the two vehicles outside the tent—were juggling, pulling rubber chickens from battered hats, telling corny jokes and doing whatever it took to make young children laugh. Even the Desmoulins twins were entranced by the performance.

She saw a clown in a red-and-white polka-dot suit and with chartreuse hair carrying a unicycle slowly past the opening of the tent. He stopped suddenly, as if he were aware of her scrutiny. Their eyes met, and Amber imagined she saw guilt there. Then he shrugged and smiled, causing his white-and-red-painted mouth to curve in exaggerated parody of happiness. With a little wave, he tucked the unicycle under his arm and moved out of sight.

Amber frowned. Something didn't feel right, but before she could figure out what it was, she heard a child cry, "Stop it, Beau!"

Turning in the direction of the wailed command, Amber saw that Beau Simmons had left his seat and was trying to push a younger child aside so he could sit in the front row. Muttering dire threats against his absentee parents, Amber took him by the arm and plunked him back into the place he belonged. "Stay put," she whispered harshly into his ear, "or I'll—"

"You'll what?" the little thug-in-the-making asked with a belligerent tilt of his chin.

Knowing she had to make a believer of him or lose that particular battle altogether, Amber glanced around for inspiration. She was thinking of telling him she'd have the clown make him disappear when she saw the man in a brown uniform standing near the tent's entrance. The officer from the sheriff's department. She hoped he'd brought help, so they could do the finger printing and end the party.

The man, who looked vaguely familiar, was over six feet tall and as burly as a linebacker—though if his narrow hips and flat stomach were any indication, his bulk was all muscle, not flab. His light brown hair was cut short and brushed to the side. The square angle of his chin and jaw said without words that he was a man who didn't suffer fools kindly. His nose

looked as if it had been broken a time or two, and a
the thin white line of an old scar angled down his
lean cheek. If he hadn't been wearing the uniform,
she'd think he was on the other side of the law.

Seeing the handcuffs dangling from his belt, she
was struck with inspiration. "I'll tell you what," she
said to Beau Simmons. "I'm going to have that guy
over there come lock you up in those handcuffs and
drag you off to the parish jail!"

To her surprise, Beau Simmons began to laugh.
Then, wearing a smile that more closely resembled a
smirk, he waved at the man and called loudly, "Hey,
Uncle Cal!"

The giant in the brown uniform smiled at the boy,
summoning up deep grooves in tanned cheeks and a
network of sun-induced wrinkles around what looked
to Amber like golden brown eyes. The stern harsh-
ness faded from the officer's face, giving him the
look of an overgrown kid who'd just been granted
his heart's dearest wish. He waved and began to
saunter toward the boy.

Not knowing what the child would say about her
threat, Amber stifled the longing to flee from the tent.
She had a sneaking suspicion that Beau Simmons's
uncle wasn't the kind of man who took kindly to
anyone threatening his nephew. To make matters
worse, the giant coming toward her had moved his
attention from the boy to her.

Amber shifted uncomfortably beneath the pene-
trating probe of cool brown eyes that raked her from
the top of her head, over her summer-weight red cotton sweater and white slacks, to her bare feet, en-
cased in clunky-heeled slides.

Even though she was all too familiar with that brazen look, she felt a familiar heat warm the soles of her feet and ease upward over her body. The reason behind the sudden awareness boggled her mind. The man coming toward her was attractive enough in a rugged, manly sort of way, but even though he might be a diamond in the rough, she liked her men a bit more polished.

A yell went up from the crowd, and Amber glanced out to the ring in time to see a clown in baggy blue pants perch Hannah on his shoulders and proceed to ride the unicycle around the ring while the other clowns pretended to be knocked aside or tried to put obstacles in the way.

"Amber?"

Amber glanced back at the man who was looking at her with a cautious curiosity. Her gaze moved automatically to the name tag on his shirtfront. *Sheriff Caleb Simmons.*

She sucked in a sharp little breath. Caleb Simmons, better known as Cal. Cal Simmons was two years younger than she was, a boy from the wrong side of the tracks who'd driven to school in a beat-up Dodge pickup and worn jeans with holes in the knees before they became the trendy apparel kids favored today.

She remembered that even though he hadn't had the bulk of some of the players, he'd been the star quarterback of the junior varsity football team. She'd heard that he'd only gotten better as a junior and senior, good enough to be awarded a football scholarship to LSU. She wondered now if he'd made use of it.

But the thing she remembered most clearly was that he'd had a crush on her when she was a senior and he was a sophomore. He'd written her poems and left bouquets of wildflowers in her locker. Stuck-up and pretty high on herself, she hadn't known whether to feel sorry for him or be embarrassed at being the object of his affections. She remembered, too, that she hadn't been very nice to him. Now the memory of her cavalier treatment left her with a sick feeling in the pit of her stomach.

"Cal?" she asked in a voice hardly more than a whisper.

He nodded. No smile.

The corners of her lips arced upward nervously. "You've changed. I wouldn't have recognized you without your name tag."

"Yeah," he said. "I put on a little weight. Got a decent job and some respectability. *Voilà!* A brand-new Cal Simmons."

"She said she was gonna have you throw me in jail," Beau said, flicking Amber a challenging look.

Cal riffled the boy's hair, but the smile he turned on her was anything but affectionate. "Looks like you haven't changed at all," he observed. "What are you doing back here, anyway, Amber? Slumming?"

The not-so-subtle implication that she considered herself better than the mortals who made their homes in the area around Bayou Lafourche wasn't lost on Amber. Neither was the fact that Cal Simmons had obviously revised his favorable opinion of her. Hearing the mockery in his voice, seeing the disdain in his eyes, she felt a sharply exquisite pang of sorrow quiver through her. To hide it, she gave a jaunty lift of her eyebrows and said, "My family lives here, remember? I had to bring Hannah something from California for her birthday."

A part of her was aware that Drew was announcing that Sheriff Simmons himself had come and that it was time for the children to have their fingerprints recorded. As soon as they were finished, they could go get their refreshments and take their seats.

"That's my cue," Cal said. "Gotta go."

"Yeah. Sure." Another smile jittered across her lips. "It was good to see you, Cal," she said, years of ingrained manners surfacing from beneath the onslaught of guilt and something strangely like remorse that washed over her.

"Goodbye, Amber."

Without another word, he turned and left her standing there. Before Amber could do more than acknowledge that he hadn't pretended that it was nice seeing her again, she heard Kim call her name. Plastering a phony smile on her face, she headed toward her sister.

"Will you help with the refreshments?" Kim asked.

"Sure."

For the next thirty minutes she doled out slices of clown cake while Maureen and Shiloh poured punch and dipped ice cream. Unfortunately, it took a few minutes to fingerprint the kids, and, when the children were finished eating, there was nothing to keep them occupied while they waited for the others to catch up. The din inside the tent got louder and louder, and nothing Drew and his friends did seemed to solve the problem for long. The clowns were wandering around, engaging small groups of children with making balloon animals, but even that didn't impact the group as a whole. What they needed was structured supervision, Amber thought.

She spied the clown she'd seen outside the tent earlier and was struck again with an anxiousness she didn't understand. Shrugging it off, she wiped the icing from her fingers. She'd go ask him if he and his buddies could corral the kids back to the slide and keep them occupied until everyone finished eating and Hannah began to open her presents. Another request for cake held her up for a few seconds, and when she looked again, the clown was gone.

Twenty minutes later, Kim glanced at her watch. Cal Simmons's tardiness had caused the party to run later than planned. Parents who had left their children were beginning to arrive to pick them up. Unconcerned that the affair was running late, they gathered good-naturedly to watch as Hannah opened her birthday presents and laughed with the children as the clowns made silly comments or acted out ridiculous pantomimes with the toys and clothes.

Hannah, who was ensconced in the middle of the circus ring among a small mountain of colorfully wrapped gifts, announced that she needed to go to the bathroom.

"You're almost finished unwrapping your presents. Can't you wait till you're finished?" Kim asked, while parents smiled in understanding and some of the older children snickered.

Hannah shook her head.

"Okay then," Kim acquiesced with a sigh. "I'll take you."

Hannah's lower lip went out and she shook her head. "No! I do it."

Kim cast Drew a questioning look. He shrugged. Hannah's independent nature aside, Kim knew that the excitement and lack of an afternoon nap had taken its toll on her daughter's normally pleasant nature. There was no sense causing a scene.

"Fine," Kim said. "But hurry."

Hannah nodded and started for the opening of the tent. "Don't forget to wash your hands," Kim called after her. "And come right back. You still have lots of presents to open."

"Okay," Hannah called over her shoulder.

While the guests waited for the birthday girl to return, Kim wandered around apologizing for the delay. The children ran around chasing one another and yelling at the tops of their lungs. The Desmoulins twins each opened one of Hannah's gifts. Wanting to thrash the little monsters—or maybe their mother for having so little control over them—Kim smiled politely and said it was all right.

Beau Simmons pushed another little boy into a mud puddle, and his uncle Cal announced that since Beau didn't know how to behave, he had to go home. Kim had to give Cal credit for doing his best by Beau since his mother walked out on him and his sister.

Deciding that the best part of the party was over and that their children had inflicted enough misery on the company, several parents gathered up their kids, thanked Kim for a good time and followed Cal's lead.

After five minutes she began to worry. Where was Hannah? Kim considered the possibility that her daughter might have had an accident and was trying to repair the damages alone. Or maybe with her short attention span, she'd forgotten she was supposed to return to the party. With a sigh, Kim left the tent and started across the rain-wet lawn.

At the house, she checked the bathroom that connected the garage with the mudroom. No Hannah. Kim poked her head in the main downstairs bathroom and saw no sign of her daughter there. She was about to head for the stairs when she saw movement outside the window. Stepping fully into the room so she could get a better view through the wavy glass of the old wood window, she saw a clown in a red-and-white-striped outfit carrying a laughing Hannah toward a blue minivan. Kim was so stunned that all she could do was blink and try to comprehend what it meant.

A nanosecond later the full implication of what was happening before her very eyes banished the surprise and gave birth to a fear more intense than anything she'd ever experienced. Dear sweet heaven! That clown was taking Hannah away. He was *kidnapping* her! Without thinking beyond the driving need to get her little girl back, Kim reached for the window's old-fashioned lock. As she struggled with it, she never took her eyes from the scene unfolding before her.

When the clown reached the van—which wasn't more than thirty feet from the window—Kim gave a moan of frustration. He set Hannah on top of the hood and pulled off his red nose. The window lock gave as he ripped off the chartreuse-green clown wig and Kim's finger slipped, tearing off a nail down to the quick. She was too paralyzed by astonishment to acknowledge the pain.

The clown was David Perkins, Maria Antonia's husband. Kim had met him briefly at a party in Kentucky a little more than a year before. There was no mistaking that mane of silver hair or the straight, aquiline nose. It was definitely David. But why was he taking Hannah? Fresh panic fueled her struggle to open the window, which was one of the tall kind so common to old houses. Thankfully, her father hadn't resorted to countless coats of paint through the years, and the sash slid up on the second shove.

Bending over, Kim screamed Hannah's name. Both she and David looked toward the house. Hannah smiled and waved. David didn't smile, though. He snatched Hannah off the hood and put her into the front seat on the driver's side, scooting her over and climbing into the van himself.

"David, no!" Kim cried. "Stop!"

Stooping, she shoved hard at the aluminum screen—so hard it flew from the window and Kim tumbled through with a startled shriek. As she plunged toward the ground, she grazed a nandina bush and landed on the plush St. Augustine grass with nothing to break her fall but her outstretched hands. Her knees skidded across the wet grass and one wrist turned, twisting beneath her weight painfully.

Kim got her bearings in time to see David reverse the van and take off, the tires spitting pieces of white seashells like a battered fighter spitting a mouthful of shattered teeth. Ignoring the burning throb of her wrist and finger, she pushed herself to her knees. The van was headed down the long lane that led to the road. He was getting away! Taking Hannah to God only knew where. A hot rush of tears sprang into her eyes, but she was only marginally aware of that phenomenon.

Kim had no idea what David Perkins planned to do with Hannah, but she knew she had to try to stop

him. She limped around the back of the house to the
garage with as much speed as her banged-up knees
would carry her and yanked open the door of her
Explorer. Never more thankful that she usually forgot
to take the keys out of the ignition even though her
father had been cautioning her about it for years, Kim
climbed inside, started the engine and backed out of
the garage.

Away from the house, she pressed harder on the
accelerator. Darn it! The blue van was pulling farther
and farther ahead. She had to get round the next
curve so she could see which way he went on the
highway. Fury and a fierce protectiveness filled Kim.
Her mouth settled into a straight line. Her eyebrows
drew together in a frown of concentration. David Perkins wasn't going to take her baby without a fight.

Where the heck was Hannah? Drew wondered after checking his watch for the second time in as many
minutes. She'd had plenty of time to go to the bathroom. Several times. He looked around for Kim and
didn't see her anywhere. Maybe she'd gone in to see
about Hannah. His frustration growing, he spotted
Amber clearing away the remains of the cake and
punch.

"Do you mind going inside to see what the heck
Hannah's doing in there?" he asked. "The natives
are getting restless, and I don't mind telling you I'm
more than ready to send them all home."

"That makes two of us," Amber said with a relieved smile. "I'll be back in a jiffy."

A few minutes later, Drew was talking to Cade and
Garrett when he heard Amber call his name. He
turned toward the opening of the tent, his heart racing

suddenly. Something in the tone of her voice told him something was wrong. Very wrong. Her blue eyes were wide and anxious in the paleness of her face. He considered and rejected half a dozen scenarios as she flung herself at him.

"What is it?"

"It's Hannah!" Amber said, tears springing into her eyes. "Dad and I looked all over the house. We can't find her anywhere!"

Chapter Ten

"What do you mean, you can't find her?"

The words were calm, but the pure fear Drew saw in Amber's eyes ignited a reciprocal panic inside him. It was a fear he had to control, because some inherent sense told him that if he didn't, Amber would go to pieces before his eyes. The murmur that rippled through the parents still milling around had a shocked, ominous note and warned him that if he didn't take control, he'd have mass hysteria on his hands.

"She may have gone upstairs to see Cindy," he suggested.

Amber shook her head. "I already checked. Dad and I looked through the whole house. She isn't there. No one heard her come inside."

Drew fought back another wave of alarm. "Did you see Kim?"

"Kim?" Amber asked with a frown. "No. Why?"

Fighting his own escalating anxiety, Drew dragged a hand down his cheek. "She went off somewhere after Hannah went inside. I haven't seen her since."

"Hannah's probably wandering around out here," Garrett Rambler suggested. "Most likely Kim missed her and went to look for her. Do you remember that time your sister Megan's Sean came up missing?"

They'd looked everywhere for Sean and finally found him sleeping in the barn, on top of some hay bales. He'd followed one of the barn cats, who was moving her kittens, and had fallen asleep watching them play.

Drew nodded. "Everyone was wild with worry for the better part of an hour, but in the end it was nothing."

Like most kids her age, Hannah's attention span *wasn't* good, but it was hard to imagine anything making her forget the stack of birthday presents still left to open. Still, Garrett's assessment made sense. It also went a long way toward calming the panic that had risen sharply when Drew realized that no one knew Kim's whereabouts, either.

Feeling somewhat better, he turned to the knot of parents standing a few feet away. "Those of you who want to stay and help look for Hannah, we appreciate it. Those who can't, the party is over. We're glad you could come."

In the end, the Ramblers, Robichaux, and five other parents agreed to stay and search. Drew paired them up and sent them to various areas of the farm, cautioning them to search carefully. Cade Robichaux volunteered to question the people from the tent company, who were waiting to start taking down the canvas. Drew himself would question the clowns, who were casting curious glances his way as they loaded their gear into the van outside the tent. Shiloh took the remaining children inside to watch television while their parents looked for Hannah.

Amber had just gone to break the news of what was happening to Gerald, when one of the clowns separated himself from the group and headed for Drew, his hand outstretched.

"I couldn't help overhearing what's going on," the man said, after introducing himself. "We'll be glad to help if you need us."

"Thanks. I appreciate that. Did you by any chance see anything? Like my little girl going to or coming from the house, or anyone suspicious hanging around?"

"I didn't see anyone hanging around who shouldn't have been," the clown said with a slow shake of his head. "But there was one thing we all thought was a little strange."

"Strange?" Drew asked. "What do you mean?"

"It's probably nothing," the clown said, "but there was an extra clown."

Drew's heart plummeted. "An extra clown? What do you mean?"

"There were five of us who came out here from Clownin' Around. We were unloading our things when this other van pulls up and another clown gets out. We didn't have any idea who he was, but he said Mr. Campion wanted an extra man to help keep the kids occupied."

Beneath the heavy greasepaint, the clown's regret was evident. "I guess one of us should have said something to you, but—"

"Where is he now?" Drew interrupted.

"I don't know. The van's gone. Normally, I wouldn't have thought much of it—" He shrugged. "It's nothing to us how people spend their money. But with your little girl gone…"

His voice trailed away as Drew's mind absorbed what he'd just heard. Hannah was missing. Kim was missing. And now they were missing a clown—an *extra* clown. Maybe he'd watched too much television, but he didn't like the sinister implication of what he'd just been told. When Amber came back, he'd ask how many clowns she'd hired. It might just be an honest mix-up, and Hannah and Kim might be just around the corner, but he didn't think so.

"Daddy still hasn't seen Hannah or Kim." Amber's breathless voice brought the nasty turn of Drew's thoughts to a screeching halt.

Drew swore. "Is he okay?"

Amber nodded. "He's worried, but he took it better than I expected."

"Good."

"Does this mean there are three people missing?" the clown asked.

The question startled Drew. He'd forgotten the man was still standing there.

"What do you mean, three people?" Amber asked.

"Well, I guess technically that other clown isn't missing, he's just gone," the helpful clown said.

"What clown?" Amber's gaze shifted from the clown to Drew. Growing trepidation filled her eyes. Sensing an emotional storm on the horizon, the clown excused himself.

Careful to keep his voice neutral, Drew related what he'd been told. As he spoke, the color drained from Amber's face, and the uncertainty in her eyes was overtaken by a rush of horror. She swayed, and he reached out to catch her.

"It may just be a coincidence," Drew said, alarmed by her reaction.

Amber shook her head. Her fingernails dug into the flesh of his upper arms. "No," she told him in a voice filled with dawning understanding and an unshakable certainty. "He took them."

"He? He, who?"

Still clutching his arms, Amber leaned back so she could look at him. "The missing clown."

Drew couldn't hide his surprise. "The clown? Why would the clown take Hannah and Kim?" Even as he asked the question, he knew the answer. He was a wealthy man. His own horror grew, even as his mind tried to reject the idea. Was it possible that someone had actually kidnapped his wife and child?

"It's obvious," Amber said. "Money."

"Sure I have money, but there are a lot of people out there with more. Why me?"

Amber seemed to wilt before his eyes. "It's my fault," she said, meeting his eyes with grim determination shining in hers.

"Your fault?"

"He was blackmailing me."

"Blackmailing you?"

A weary, halfhearted smile claimed Amber's lips briefly. "You're starting to sound like a stuck record, Drew."

"And I'm starting to feel as old as one," he added. "What do you mean you were being blackmailed? Why would this clown guy want to blackmail you?"

Amber crossed her arms across her breasts, pressed

her lips together to still their trembling and threw her head back to gaze up at the clouds drifting aimlessly across the sky. When she had her emotions under control she offered Drew a wobbly smile. "Maybe I should start at the beginning."

"Maybe you should," he said, nodding.

"Did Kim tell you I called Daddy wanting money?"

Drew nodded again. "Yeah. When she first got to Kentucky. She said some man wanted you to finance a string of boutiques or something."

"That was a lie. I was being blackmailed."

"Why? What did you do?"

Amber gave a bitter laugh and shook her head. "So you just automatically assume I did something that needed covering up. I expected more from you, Drew."

There was no disguising the hurt in her eyes. "I'm sorry," Drew told her. "That wasn't very diplomatic or very nice."

"No, it wasn't. Will you just let me tell my story and hold your comments till the end?"

"I'll try."

"Good enough." She exhaled harshly. "Well, as you also probably know, Daddy refused to give me the money. I thought that if I came here I could bring him around."

"I'm not going to ask why you didn't go to the police."

"Thank you. Anyway, all hell had broken loose with Maria Antonia and the breeding scandal and everything, so I couldn't bring myself to ask him. I was afraid he might have another heart attack or something. But I thought that since I was here, I'd stay a couple of weeks or so. I could buy myself some time and at least hide out for a while.''

"Don't tell me," Drew said. "Let me guess. Mavis Davenport's article came out in the paper, this guy saw it and figured out where you were.''

"You got it!" Amber said with a mirthless smile. "He called here. I put him off. Then he shows up out of the blue.'' She fixed an apologetic gaze on Drew. "It's a long story, but the abridged version is that he followed me to McDonald's the day I took Hannah there.''

"So he knew who she was?''

"Definitely. He bought her ice cream and charmed her with his teasing. He's good at that.'' When I told him I couldn't get the money, he suggested that I get it from you in exchange for sex.''

"What!''

"Yeah. Sweet of him, huh? I told him that not even I was rotten enough to sleep with my sister's husband for money. Then he made a comment that implied there were lots of ways to skin a cat.'' She rubbed her upper arms as if she were suddenly chilled. Her eyes were as bleak and cold as his fields in the winter. "It gave me a funny feeling at the time, but I had no idea he'd do something like this.''

"There's no way you could have known, Amber,'' Drew told her, hoping to lighten the burden of self-loathing and ease the brittle tension binding her.

"Thanks,'' she said, "but that doesn't make me feel a whole lot better. When I got home, Hannah mentioned meeting David to Kim, who was understandably ticked off. I was feeling pretty shaken and extremely desperate, so I asked her if she'd talk to Daddy for me. She told me I was a big girl and I needed to figure out how to get myself out of the fixes I was in like everyone else does.''

Drew nodded, his mind whirling with the things she'd told him. ''And you think that this guy came here dressed like a clown and took Kim and Hannah so he could get the money he wanted.''

''That's exactly what I think.'' She shook her head. ''I saw him earlier, outside the tent, and I thought there was something wrong with the way he was acting. I even thought there was something familiar about him, but then I had a minicrisis to take care of and I forgot all about it.''

''How would he know about the party and the clowns?''

''Hannah told him.''

Drew swore.

''I'm sorry. I never meant for anything to happen to Hannah. I never dreamed he'd do anything like this,'' Amber said, the tears she'd been holding back finally making an escape.

Drew took her hands in his. ''I know you didn't,'' he said. ''What you say makes sense, but I have to know who this guy is and what he has on you so we can take the information to the police.''

Amber's face lost its last bit of color. Her blue eyes held a torment straight from hell. ''It's David Perkins.''

''David Perkins? Maria's husband?''

Amber nodded. ''He's my real father.''

The statement was so unexpected that for a second or two Drew could only stare at her. Then disbelief set in. ''What do you mean, he's your real father? Gerald Campion is your father.''

''Actually, he isn't. It seems David and my mother

were lovers in college. He was from around here and was at LSU on scholarship. When she got pregnant, he wouldn't marry her, so she slept with Gerald and pawned the baby—yours truly—off as his.''

A loud gasp sent both Drew and Amber whirling around. Gerald stood a few yards away, his face deathly white, an expression of stunned disbelief on his face, his palm pressed against his chest as he crumpled to the ground. Amber's anguished cry was drowned out by the painful thudding of Drew's own heart. Dear God, he thought, as he and Amber rushed forward. Gerald must have heard it all.

Kim's mind raced as she followed the van. David Perkins turned onto a highway that she knew was little more than a connection between one Podunk town and another. After a couple of miles, the van made a right turn onto a gravel road bearing a sign in the shape of a black cow, standing on an arrow labeled Tobias Angus Farm.

Kim was vaguely familiar with the area, though it had been years since she'd been down the parish roads. Since high school, actually. One of her friends had lived in the area. Where was David Perkins going? Where was he taking her baby?

"Calm down, Kim," she muttered aloud. "You've got to think this through. There has to be some logical reason why he'd take Hannah."

Money.

Of course. Money. And who needed money? Who was desperate for money? Amber. Kim's heart sank. Amber needed money, and that explained why Hannah was the target. David Perkins must have been the man who'd bought Hannah ice cream at Mc-

Donalds—Amber's *acquaintance*. They must have been in on it together.

The thought that her sister might have been responsible for Hannah's abduction had barely taken root when a new thought popped into Kim's mind.

How did Amber know David? Kim knew her sister liked men, but David was *much* older than Amber. And besides, he was Maria's husband, and lived hundreds of miles from California.

Another thought hit her. Dear God! Maria was in financial trouble and David gambled. But Maria was an old family friend who adored Hannah. It was unthinkable that she was capable of something so heinous as kidnapping or that she'd deliberately cheated people by using another stallion just for the money.

Kim's deliberations were brought up short when she rounded a curve—going far too fast—and came face-to-face with a *Y* in the road. She slammed on her brakes and the Explorer fishtailed in the loose gravel, coming to rest near the weed-covered shoulder.

Trembling with the knowledge that she could have had an accident, Kim climbed out of the car and went to the roadside to take stock of the situation. Because of the rain, there was no dust. New gravel had been added to the road recently or the potholes had been smoothed out by a motor grader, making tire tracks impossible to make out. There weren't even any mud holes with cloudy water to give her a clue that a vehicle had passed recently. To her untrained eye, it was impossible to discern if a car had gone down either road in the past few minutes.

She pushed the hand with the mangled nail and rapidly swelling wrist through her hair and felt the stickiness of blood on her forehead. The scrape didn't hurt nearly as much as her broken nail, she thought, sucking on her throbbing appendage as she tried to decide which way to go.

A crow flew by, its raucous cry startlingly loud in the stillness. She heard a sound behind her, but before she could turn, an arm snaked around her waist and a hand clamped painfully over her mouth. She tried to scream, but the only sound that came through her bruised mouth was a panicked, muffled gurgling. She kicked and felt a thrill of satisfaction when her assailant swore in pain.

"Stop fighting me, Kim." David Perkins panted the words into her ear. "Stop fighting me and keep your mouth shut, and I'll let you go."

Kim stilled instantly. Just as quickly, he took his hand from her mouth. She whirled to face him, fury contorting her face, hate squeezing her heart. She noticed that he'd shed his costume and wiped the greasepaint from his face. Probably while he was waiting for her.

After making a succinct commentary about his mother's lineage, Kim asked, "What do you think you're doing?"

"It's a simple matter of economics, Kim. Nothing personal. I need money. Fast. Amber couldn't come up with it, so after I met your charming daughter the other day, I came up with this little plan."

A glimmer of understanding flickered in Kim's mind. "You're the man Amber wanted the money for."

"Right."

"I don't suppose there was ever going to be a string of boutiques."

"Hardly."

"Then why does Amber owe you money?"

"I believe the word is blackmail," David told her, a slight smile on his attractive face."

"Blackmail? What can Amber have done that's so bad she could be blackmailed for it?" Even though her sister had pulled some stunts through the years, Kim couldn't imagine her taking part in anything *that* terrible.

"Actually, the only thing she did this time was have the misfortune to be sired by me instead of Gerald, a small matter I told her I'd take up with him if she didn't get me the money."

Kim was so stunned by David's statement that she couldn't think of a ready comeback.

"I know it's hard to believe, but I was involved with Melody Hartley in college."

Kim listened while he told her how her father had been lied to and later cheated on. She shook her head. It was too much to try to comprehend. The most important thing was getting Hannah back home safely. The second most important thing was the realization that Amber had played no part in David Perkins's plan.

"Let's go," he said, jerking his head toward a stand of trees.

Kim shook her head. "Not until you tell me what you're going to do."

"I'm going to make a call and ask for a ransom."

"Ransom?" She laughed. "Amber wasn't lying. My father is broke."

"Your husband isn't. I'm sure McShane won't mind shelling out, say...a hundred grand to see his precious little girl and his pretty wife back in one piece.''

Kim couldn't argue with that. Even though things might not be good between the two of them, she knew Drew would walk on hot coals for Hannah.

''How did you get her to go with you?''

''She remembered me,'' David said with a pleased smile. ''She even called me by name. I told her I'd take her to McDonald's to play.''

''Where is she?'' Kim demanded. ''I want to see her.''

''She's in the van, sleeping.''

Kim saw no sign of the van. ''Where's the van?''

''Down that logging road.''

There was nothing but trees on either side, but she saw the road he was talking about winding through the lush maze of trees and vines. For the first time Kim realized just how isolated the area was. She cursed herself for not telling someone what had happened and longed for the flip phone in her purse back at the house.

The sound of an approaching vehicle brought a sudden tension to David's features. He gestured toward the logging road. ''Go on to the van while I take care of whoever this is,'' he commanded in a harsh voice. ''And don't try anything stupid.''

''Go to hell.''

He surprised her by pulling a .38 from behind his back. ''Stop trying to be so tough and just do it!''

Shocked by the sight of the gun, Kim turned and ran down the road, cursing him as she went. She had to figure out how to get word to Drew—or better yet, Cal Simmons—and she had to find a way to get Hannah away from David before things got ugly.

Within a few dozen yards and a couple of turns, the blue van came into sight. Kim glanced in the window and saw that Hannah was slumped over and sleeping soundly in the front seat. A wave of love and thankfulness swept through her.

Thank God David had fastened her seat belt. Kim's first inclination was to grab Hannah and take off through the woods, but a remnant of sanity told her that action would be foolhardy at best. There wasn't enough time to get any kind of lead, and she couldn't carry Hannah very far without giving out. No, she'd just have to wait for a better opportunity.

Sighing with frustration, she opened the rear door, climbed inside and found herself looking squarely at a cellular phone mounted on the floor between the seats. A quick glance over her shoulder told her she had at least a few seconds to try to contact someone.

She reached for the phone without bothering to close the door. Who should she call? Drew or the law? The law, she decided. They were better equipped to deal with things like this, and they could tell her family what was going on. She thought of dialing 911, but she didn't want just anyone responding. She wanted Cal Simmons. She trusted him, and he'd understand how she felt because of his relationship with his niece and nephew. Kim rang the operator and asked to be connected to the Lafourche Parish Sheriff's Department.

"And hurry!" she said. "This is an emergency."

In a matter of seconds, a nasal voice said, "Sheriff's Department. Rowell speaking."

"I'd like to speak to Sheriff Simmons, please."

"Cal is gone for the day, but I can have him call you."

Kim felt like screaming. Like crying. She did neither. "No!" she said sharply. "Just tell him Kim McShane called. Have him call my husband. Hannah is okay—"

"Lady, can you slow down? And start at the beginning," the man on the other end of the line said. "I don't have the vaguest idea what you're talking about."

"I don't have time to explain!" Kim snapped in a low, harsh whisper. "We're someplace near the Tobias farm."

The sharp snap of a twig stopped her midsentence. Kim slammed the receiver back in place and leaped out of the car in a flash, careful to close the door behind her. When David strode into view mere seconds later, she was picking her way back toward the van through a tangle of berry brambles and vines, pants unzipped and pretending to tuck her shirt in.

"What are you doing?" he asked.

She flung him an insolent look. "What does it look like I'm doing?"

He scowled. "Get in. Let's get out of here."

Kim followed and opened the door to the van. In the front seat, Hannah stirred. "What are you going to do with us?" Kim asked.

"Take the two of you someplace where we won't be found and make a phone call."

Kim climbed into the back seat and closed the door behind her. She only hoped her own phone call would generate some sort of response.

Chapter Eleven

The first thing Drew and Amber did after Gerald's collapse was to get him inside and give him one of his tablets to put under his tongue. After a few minutes, the pasty tint of his face returned to its normal healthy tone.

Feeling the crisis had passed, Amber went to the kitchen to make her father a cup of tea, and Drew excused himself. Father and daughter had much to say to each other, and he didn't think he should be around to hear whatever recriminations or apologies might be offered. Besides, he wanted to call Cal Simmons.

Cal didn't run in the same social circles as the Campions, but his older brother, Dean—Beau's dad—had been a fishing buddy of Drew's throughout their high school years. Dean Simmons had died in a crop dusting accident three years earlier. His wife,

Georgina, had taken the quarter of a million dollars of his life insurance money and gone to look for a new husband in Europe, leaving her two children, Beau and Claudia, for Cal to raise.

Since Dean had died, Cal had taken his brother's place whenever Drew came back to Louisiana and wanted to spend some time fishing for black bass, but since Cal had been elected sheriff he didn't have as much free time as he once had. When Drew called the office and Deputy Rowell said Cal was out for the rest of the day, Drew felt no compunction about calling his friend at home. Cal picked up on the first ring.

"Hannah and Kim are gone," Drew said without a proper hello. "We think they've been kidnapped."

Cal gave a short hoot of laughter. "Is this some sort of a joke?"

"Look, Cal!" Drew said, his frustration and fear finding an outlet in anger. "It's no joke. My wife and daughter are gone. We've searched the farm. They aren't here. So why don't you just get in that shiny sheriff's car of yours and haul your butt over here?"

Drew's anger went a long way toward convincing Cal of the seriousness of the situation. "Okay," he said. "Just stay calm. I'll see if my neighbor can keep an eye on the kids, and I'll be right over."

"You do that."

"Can I ask one question?"

"I suppose."

"Do you have any idea who might have had a reason to take off with Hannah and Kim?"

"I don't, but Amber thinks it's the same guy who's been blackmailing her."

"Blackmailing h—"

Drew hung up before Cal could ask him anything else. He wanted the sheriff on the scene. There'd be plenty of time for explanations once he got there.

Drew started for the kitchen to get himself a fresh cup of coffee and was stopped by the pile of presents stacked just inside the doorway of the foyer. Someone had brought Hannah's gifts inside. He stared at the packages while his heart pounded painfully in his chest. Some were open; some weren't. The colorful wrappings mocked the misery that grew inside him like some dark and fatal disease.

There were stuffed animals and pretend makeup... *"Look Daddy! Am I bootiful?"*...a purse...*"I gots a whole dodder, Daddy"*...a gold heart necklace, an assortment of dolls and a fairy in a wispy costume with iridescent wings inspired by some sort of lily. Drew went to the pile of presents and picked up the box. Something about the shape of the lily fairy's nose reminded him of Kim...and Hannah. And the wings! Their glittery ability to change in the light definitely reminded him of his daughter. Silly one minute. Then put out and pouty. Loving the next. His Hannah might well be a fairy, so fanciful and fey was she. And Kim. Ah, his earthbound Kim needed to spread her wings. Needed to learn to fly.

He could help her, if she'd let him.

Dear God, he loved them both so much. He'd never known just how much until now. Though he'd longed for a life with Kim, just knowing she was here had been a source of joy and comfort. Now she was gone to God knows where. And Hannah. The child Justin had given Kim before his death. Drew knew he couldn't love Hannah any more than he would had he sired her himself.

Where were they? Where had David Perkins—or whoever—taken them? Drew blinked back the threat of unmanly tears and replaced the box on the pile of gifts. He was surprised to see that the edges were crushed where he'd gripped them.

With Drew gone, an uncomfortable silence filled the room while Gerald sipped his Earl Grey and Amber tried to think of something to say. The first emotion she'd experienced when she realized her father had overheard her conversation with Drew about David Perkins was guilt. But that feeling was soon driven aside by a rush of concern for the man who'd raised her. She'd never forgive herself if her carelessness caused her dad to have another heart attack.

"Tell me about David Perkins blackmailing you."

The sound of Gerald's voice echoed in the silence of the room. It was a reasonable request, but compliance with the simple command threatened the very cornerstone of her existence. "Now isn't the time to talk about this, Daddy. You don't need the stress."

"Maybe I don't need the stress," Gerald said, setting his cup and saucer down on the coffee table, "but we seldom get from life what we really need, do we?"

"No."

"I heard what you told Drew about David being your real father." He rubbed his cheek with his palm. "I won't say it wasn't a shock, but a lot of things make sense now." He sipped at his tea in silence for several minutes. There was nothing Amber could say.

"Tell me about you and Kim."

Amber forced herself to meet his gaze. "What about us?"

"I've known for years you weren't close, but until recently, I had no idea there was so much hard feeling between the two of you."

"It's just a personality clash," she said. "Kim and I have never seen eye to eye on anything. She's the straight arrow. I'm the loose cannon. She even blames me for causing your heart attack and sending Gwen to an early grave. Strangely enough, that's one thing I'm inclined to agree with her on."

"You're referring to the article about you in that tabloid."

"Yes."

"We've never talked about that."

Shame flooded Amber's face with heat, and her heart beat out a sluggish, agonized rhythm, but she only shrugged, as if the whole thing were unimportant. "There never seemed to be a good time."

"The paper said you were with a married man."

"Yeah. Like father, like daughter, huh?" she said in a mocking tone.

"You're referring to David, I suppose."

"Who else?"

"Amber," Gerald said, holding her gaze with the gentleness of his. "I may not have been there at your conception, but I *am* your father, and I've loved you as much as I've loved Kim."

The tenderness she saw in his eyes sent another surge of tears to hers. "Thank you for that."

Fighting the impulse to bawl like a baby, she crossed her arms over her breasts and lifted her chin. "Marc—the guy I was with in L.A. told me he hadn't lived with his wife for several months, and that he'd filed for a divorce."

"And you believed him?"

"I didn't have any reason not to."

Gerald nodded. "Did it ever occur to you or Kim that maybe I'd have had a heart attack that day, anyway? I was terribly worried about Gwen, and the doctor had told me her days were numbered."

Gerald was being his usual fair self, which only made Amber feel worse. Tears stung her eyes, but for once she refused to let them fall.

"Despite your feelings to the contrary, you aren't a bad person, Amber. Spoiled, undoubtedly, but that's my fault, not yours. It would do me no more good to beat myself up for indulging you for so many years than it would to try to make up to Kim for the lack of attention I gave her. I know I haven't been the best father in the world. Both of you have suffered as a result of my shortcomings." A deep sigh lifted his chest. "But there's nothing I can do now but say I'm sorry and hope you'll both forgive me."

"There's nothing to forgive," Amber said, her voice breaking.

"I don't think your sister shares that sentiment." He waved his hand in the air. "I'm pretty sure she feels I've treated you differently than I have her." There was genuine remorse in his eyes. "Kim was so quiet and so easy to deal with. I think she felt less loved because she always thought you were prettier, more outgoing—"

"And always demanded—and got—your attention."

Gerald nodded. Amber was mulling that over when

the phone rang. Her father answered it with a short "Hello."

The tension on his face relaxed immediately. "Maria. How nice of you to call. Oh, the party was fine, but we have a problem. Hannah and Kim are missing."

Feeling the walls closing in around her, Amber wrenched open the French doors that led to the porch and stepped through, needing the feel of the cool breeze against her hot cheeks, needing the moment of peace to gather herself.

This was all her fault! If she hadn't come back here, David wouldn't have followed her, and Hannah would be playing with her birthday presents or sleeping off the excitement of her party. A brand-new guilt burrowed a place in Amber's heart, but she knew feeling sorry for herself wouldn't help anyone. She blinked back the tears and took a deep breath. Her father and Drew would need her. She couldn't fall to pieces now. When she thought she had her emotions under control, Amber went back inside. Gerald was staring at the telephone receiver in his hand.

He looked up with a slight smile. "Maria said to call if there was anything she could do."

"That was nice of her." Amber picked up her coffee cup. The liquid had grown as cold as her heart.

"I didn't say anything about the possibility that David might be involved," he said.

"Good. No sense in her worrying until we know for sure."

"Let me see if I have this straight," Gerald said. "David was blackmailing you…telling you he'd come to me with the information about him being your biological father if you didn't come up with the money. And you didn't want me to find out. Why?''

"I was afraid Kim was right," Amber said. "That I was responsible for your heart attack, and I was afraid that if you found out about mom's deception, it might cause you to have another one, especially since you were under so much stress from the problems with Flight of Dreams. And," she added, her gaze sliding away from his, "I didn't want you to think less of me."

"How could that make me think less of you?"

"I'm the one who *always* messes up," Amber said, self-directed anger in her voice.

"Amber, none of this is your fault. It's your mother's. You're the innocent party here."

"Well that's a first," she said with a shaky laugh.

Gerald smiled. "So you think David took Hannah and Kim for ransom."

"It's the only explanation I can think of," Amber said. "He said he had creditors. Probably loan sharks. He told me that if I couldn't come up with the money there were other ways a person could get what he wanted."

Before Gerald could comment, Drew burst through the doorway. "Cal's on his way," he said. "But come take a look at what I found in the bathroom."

"What?" Amber asked, a new fear filling her.

"The window is up and the screen is off, and it looks like someone had a wrestling match in the nandina bush."

The first thing Cal Simmons did when he arrived was to acquaint himself with all the facts of the case. He asked Amber why David Perkins was blackmailing her, and considered Drew's theory that the extra clown and Perkins could be one and the same.

While Amber seemed hesitant about repeating her story to an outsider, Drew suspected it was easier to tell Cal than it had been to explain the situation to Gerald. Cal listened intently, asked an occasional question and made notations in a small spiral-bound pad.

"I think the clown—whoever he is—may have taken them from the bathroom," Drew offered.

"Why do you say that?"

"The window is open and the shrubs outside it are a mess, as if there was a struggle or something."

A few minutes later, Cal stood in the middle of the bathroom, his hands on his hips as he surveyed the open window. He squatted and looked at the area outside, then eased his legs over the sill and dropped to the ground.

Drew wondered what Cal was doing when he picked up the aluminum screen and turned it one way and then the other, carefully examining all the edges.

"The screen wasn't taken off from the outside. It was pushed out by someone inside the bathroom," he announced.

"How do you know?" Drew asked.

Cal carried the screen over to Drew. "First, the ground outside here is wet enough to show footprints, and I don't see any but mine here near the window, which is where someone would have to stand to take the screen off from the outside."

He turned the screen. "See the top? It doesn't hook over anything. The screen is held in place at the top by sliding it into those grooved doohickeys on the facing, and one of them is gone.'' He turned the screen. ''See how the mesh is stretched and bowed?''

Drew nodded.

''That, and the fact that it was lying on the ground a considerable distance from the window suggests that it was pushed and pushed hard. So hard, the person fell out and landed on the bush.''

''What are you saying?'' Drew asked.

''I don't think anyone took Hannah from the bathroom.'' Cal's beeper chose that moment to go off. He glanced at the number. ''I'll be right back. I've got to check in with the dispatcher.''

The trio in the bathroom watched through the window as he disappeared around the house.

''What do you think it means?'' Amber asked.

Drew and Gerald shook their heads. They stood around in the small room for a couple of minutes while a strange awkwardness grew. Finally, unable to take the silence any longer, Amber turned to shut the window. It was halfway down when she noticed something lying next to the lock at the top of the sash. She picked it up and regarded it with a growing misery.

''What is it?'' Drew asked.

''It looks like a broken fingernail,'' she said, pushing the words out around the emotion clotting her throat. ''And the nailpolish is the color Kim was wearing.''

Cal came back around the house, going to where the drive curved between two trees. Then he crossed back to the bathroom window, stopping every now and then to examine the ground. His face held a look of grimness it hadn't worn before he'd gone to make his call.

"I don't know what it meant, but I found a broken fingernail," Amber said. "I'm sure it's Kim's."

Cal hoisted himself back into the room and took the piece of fingernail from her. He gave the top of the sash a thorough going-over before he finished shutting the window.

"The nail broke off down to the quick," he said. He pointed to the lower pane of the top half of the window. "There's a smear of blood here." Cal turned to face them. "The call was from the dispatcher at the station," he said. "He said I got a call from Kim almost an hour ago."

Amber's gasp of surprise was almost drowned out by Drew's and her father's startled "What?"

"Rowell told her I was gone for the day. She left a message, and he almost didn't call me because he thought it was a crank call from one of my girlfriends or something."

A dull red stained Cal's face and neck above his T-shirt. "Then, a little later, he got a call from a guy named Gus Langley, who said he saw a guy in a green Explorer sitting at the fork in Wingfield Road. Gus took the license number and Rowell has already run it. It's Kim's."

Drew uttered a mild curse. "I can't believe I didn't notice if Kim's vehicle was in the garage or not," he said.

"You had a lot on your mind," Cal told him. "Anyway, Gus asked the stranger if he was having car problems, but he said it was nothing but a flat and that he'd just finished changing it. So Gus went on about his business. When he came back forty-five minutes later, the Explorer was still sitting there. The door was open and there wasn't a soul in sight. He thought something was fishy, so he called the Sheriff's Department. When my deputy heard about the abandoned car, traced the plates and connected it with Kim's call, he decided that maybe he ought to let me know what was going on."

"What did Kim tell him?"

"Something about being in a van and the Tobias farm and cows, and then she hung up before Rowell could get anything out of her."

"Tobias farm and cows," Drew said thoughtfully. "She must have been somewhere near the Tobias Angus Farm. It's over on Wingfield Road."

"Yeah," Cal said. "That's what I thought."

"Is she all right?" Gerald asked.

"She didn't say. But she said Hannah was okay."

"So Kim and Hannah are together," Gerald said.

"Yeah," Cal said. "But I don't know how. He stared at the window, the smear of blood showing plainly now that the lower sash was closed. Then he stared at the fingernail he held in his hand.

"Kim came in here to check on Hannah and saw this David Perkins or whoever it was take off with her," he said at last, conviction in his deep voice. "She pushed through the window, trying to stop them. Somehow, the kidnapper managed to get hold of her, too. She must have gotten access to a phone— a cell phone probably, since she mentioned being in a van—to let me know what happened. The perp probably came back, so she didn't get to say much." He turned his brown-eyed gaze from Gerald to Drew to Amber.

"Makes sense," Drew said.

Cal nodded. "I'm going to head out the direction of the Tobias place."

"I'm going with you," Drew told him.

"Drew—"

"Don't even think about telling me no, Cal."

Cal didn't look too happy about the ultimatum, but he gave a nod. "Okay. But only because I'm doing this in my capacity as a friend." At Drew's quizzical look, Cal added, "I'm not in uniform. If I were, I wouldn't be handling this the way I am."

"Thanks."

"If Drew's going, so am I," Amber announced. Since the whole episode was her fault, she felt as if she should be there.

For the first time since he'd arrived, Cal gave her more than a cursory glance. "No."

The look in his eyes and the vehemence of his refusal told Amber she'd be a fool to contradict him. Even though disobedience had often been her downfall, she'd learned long ago there were ways to get around direct commands. "Okay," she said with a shrug.

Cal looked suspicious of her easy capitulation, but instead of pursuing the subject, he turned to Drew. "Let's go."

As soon as they were out the front door, Amber bolted up the upstairs. She came down a couple of minutes later carrying her purse and a lightweight jacket.

The phone rang, and Gerald answered with a curt "Hello." After a couple of seconds, he covered the mouthpiece and mouthed the words *the kidnapper*. Instinctively, Amber moved closer, though there was nothing she could do.

"Yes. Yes. I understand perfectly," Gerald said.

"We'll be here." His eyes were bleak as he turned off the phone.

"What did he say?"

"He has Hannah and Kim. They're both fine. He wants a quarter of a million dollars in unmarked bills. He'll call and tell us when and where to take the money." Gerald's smile lacked humor. "And he said not to call the police."

"Did it sound like David Perkins?" she asked.

"I can't be sure," Gerald said. "I've only spoken with him a few times, and then only briefly."

Amber headed for the door.

"Where do you think you're going?"

"To see what I can do to help."

"Cal told you to stay put, Amber."

"I know. I can't explain it, but I feel like I really need to be there, Daddy. Besides," she added when she saw that her argument hadn't swayed him, "someone needs to tell Cal we heard from the kidnapper."

"He's going to be pretty upset with you."

"I know," Amber said with a weary smile. "But it won't be the first time."

Amber had been driving around for more than an hour when she spotted Cal's cruiser parked off the road a good four miles from the Tobias Angus Farm. If she'd been coming from the other direction, she'd never have seen it.

"Still doing what you want and everyone else be damned, huh, Amber?" he asked when she pulled to a stop behind the parish vehicle and climbed into the back seat.

The accusation stung, but Amber swallowed her

hurt and said, "I came with news." She told Cal and Drew the kidnapper had called and what he'd said.

Cal snorted in disbelief. "Pretty standard stuff. The guy's been watchin' too much TV." He leveled a stern gaze on her. "You brought the news, now get in your car and go back home."

"No," she said, her refusal as firm as his had been earlier. "I want to be here…to help."

"How?"

"I don't know," she said. The desperation in her voice was evident, even to her. "If it's David, and I believe it is, maybe I can talk to him, convince him to let them go."

"What makes you think he'll listen to you?"

"Maybe he won't. But it's worth a try."

"It could be dangerous. Animals get unpredictable when they're cornered."

"What's he going to do to me? I'm his flesh and blood."

The expression in Cal's eyes told her he wasn't convinced that she'd be anything more than a nuisance, but at least he didn't tell her again to leave. Taking his silence for surrender, she asked, "Do you know where he is?"

A satisfied smile toyed with the corners of Cal's finely shaped mouth. Amber's heart took a tiny, unexpected lurch.

"Yeah," Drew said. "There's a blue van sitting in back of the farmhouse over the next hill. Coincidentally, the house is none other than the old Perkins place."

"He used to live here?"

"Yep," Cal said with a pleased nod. "Mama Perkins's little chick has come home to roost—which makes him stupid, careless or extremely arrogant. If he was thinking halfway straight, he'd have done a better job of hiding the van.''

''Maybe that will make our job easier,'' Amber said.

''*My* job,'' Cal said. ''You're going to stay right here while I do what I have to do.''

''What's the plan?'' Drew asked.

''First, I'm going to check and make sure they're in there, then I'm going to call for backup, and then I'm going in to get that piece of scum.''

Kim was sitting with Hannah on an old sofa, trying to keep her entertained. She had gone through her repertoire of fairy tales and was searching her mind for more nursery rhymes. When they ran out, she wasn't sure what she'd do to keep Hannah occupied.

Even as she recited the age-old poems, Kim was wondering if her message had been passed on to Cal Simmons. Since David had brought them to the abandoned house, she had planned and discarded a dozen ways she might make a getaway. Besides being concerned about herself and Hannah, Kim was anxious about what the news of the kidnapping might do to her dad. And Drew. He'd be crazy with worry about Hannah.

He'll be worried about you, too. You know that.

Tears prickled beneath her eyelids. She did know it. She knew something else, too. She was a fool. If she'd learned anything from all this it was that she owed it to Drew and herself to be honest about her feelings. She loved him and wanted him in her life, and when all this was over—and she had to believe they would be back at LaFourche Farm soon, all safe and sound—she would tell him so. He wanted to stay married to her. If they both tried, maybe what he felt for her could change into something more.

"I'm hungry," Hannah whined, looking up at her with wide, soulful eyes.

"We'll get something soon," David said smoothly.

He'd been unfailingly nice to Hannah, though Kim suspected his patience was running out as his nervousness grew. Unfortunately, with that innate sense all kids seemed to have, Hannah was picking up on the tension in the air.

"Mommy..." Hannah wailed.

David shot Kim a sharp look that said without words for her to keep Hannah quiet.

"Sh, sweetie," she said. "Do you remember Bobby Shaftoe?"

Hannah shook her head, and Kim began to recite the rhyme. She was on the second verse when David's name was called on a bullhorn outside the house.

His shocked gaze flew to hers. He cursed her in a low, angry voice that made Hannah cringe at her side. "You called them, didn't you?"

Kim had never been good at poker. She knew her face gave her away.

"I should have known you were lying when you came out of those bushes acting all innocent and put out."

"You may as well give up," Kim said.

"Shut up!"

"You don't say 'shut up,' do you, Mommy?" Hannah asked. "That's not nice."

"It's okay, sweetie."

"Come out with your hands up, Perkins," Cal Simmons said, the sound amplified in the evening air. "Don't make me have to come in after you."

Throwing Kim a chilling look, David went to the window and pushed back the tattered curtain. Kim knew that if she wanted to get Hannah out before something terrible happened, she'd have to make her move soon. She stood and went to the window flanking the other side of the door, making a pretense of looking to see where the voice was coming from. David was too concerned about what might be going on outside the house to notice.

Hannah followed, winding her fist tightly into the cotton of Kim's beige slacks, her thumb firmly in her mouth. Kim's heart throbbed painfully. She'd never known Hannah to suck her thumb. It broke her heart to think of the damage this might cause her innocent child.

Kim looked out the window, letting her gaze pan the expanse of yard and the trees beyond. Dusk was settling in. It would be dark in another ten or fifteen minutes. She had to make a break—and soon.

"We know you just wanted the money, Perkins," Cal said. "So far it's just kidnapping. Come on out before you make things worse on yourself."

David moved to the other side of the window, putting his back to Kim.

Hannah pulled her thumb out long enough to whine that she wanted to go to McDonald's, that David had promised.

"Make her shut up!"

The command gave Kim good reason to pick up Hannah. "Sh!" she soothed, smoothing her hair and pressing a kiss to her baby-soft cheek. "We'll get something to eat soon."

Kim didn't know if she could make good on the promise or not, but the main thing was to mollify Hannah for the moment. Holding her close, Kim edged to the door and turned the knob as quietly as possible. Hoping to have the advantage of surprise, she wrenched the door open and was through it in a flash.

From somewhere in the yard, she heard someone scream her name and realized it was Drew. Her feet skimmed the ground. If she could just get to Drew, everything would be all right.

"Stop or I'll shoot." The deadly calm of David's voice stopped Kim in midstride. He wasn't panicky or freaked out. He was in control, and he meant what he was saying.

Kim pressed Hannah's face against her shoulder and turned toward him slowly. He stood in the doorway, the gun leveled at her. From a distance that seemed like miles, she heard Amber sobbing and yelling for him to let them go. She heard Cal—without the bullhorn now—calling for David to drop the gun. Heard Drew call her name. She was aware of an owl hooting, of the way her legs trembled, of the warmth of Hannah's breath against her neck and the tightness of the arms clinging to her. She was acutely aware of the desperation in David Perkins's eyes.

"Put her down."

Kim shook her head.

"For God's sake, let her go, David!" Amber screamed. She must have left her hiding place because Kim heard Cal shouting for her to come back.

David swung the gun away from Kim toward Amber. "Stay back!" To Kim, he said, "Put the kid down or I'll shoot your sister."

Amber's shocked gasp mingled with Kim's. "You won't do that," she said, but the look in his eyes told her otherwise. Hopelessness was a powerful motivation. She should know.

David sauntered closer, moving the gun's aim from Amber back to Kim. "You don't want to try me. Now, put her down."

He was right. Kim set Hannah down but held firmly to her daughter's shoulders. Hannah pressed her back against Kim's legs.

"Come here, Hannah," David said. His handsome face wore his most charming smile.

"No." Her lower lip came out in a familiar mutinous gesture. "You're not nice."

"I thought you were hungry and wanted to go to McDonald's," David said, dangling his choicest carrot in front of her pert little nose.

Hannah looked up at Kim, who kept her gaze locked with David's, searching for any change in expression, no matter how subtle.

"Come here, Hannah. Now."

Accustomed to obeying adult commands, the firmness worked where the wheedling hadn't. Hannah jerked free and started running toward David.

Drew and Amber screamed her name in unison with Kim. The next seconds seemed to take place in surreal slow motion. Kim had taken one step forward when Amber sprang in front of Kim with a feral cry of rage. Even as she fell, Kim saw David pivot slightly, saw Amber throw up her arms in a gesture of defense as old as time.

Kim hit the ground at the same time she heard the

loud boom of the gun and a woman's maniacal scream. She saw the look of surprise on Amber's face as she crumpled to the grass. It was only later that Kim would realize the cry of denial was her own.

Chapter Twelve

Kim knelt at the altar of the hospital chapel, more because her legs wouldn't hold her than because she was prostrating herself before God—though she'd done that, too. She'd begged God to forgive her for the way she'd treated her sister. Prayed Amber would forgive her, too. Kim's eyes burned from the tears she wanted to let fall but couldn't. Her throat ached painfully, though it wasn't as painful as the agony ripping at her heart.

Images of Amber were burned into Kim's memory: the hurt expression on her sister's face when Kim had accused her of taking Hannah along while she met a man at McDonald's. The desperate look in Amber's eyes as she'd pleaded for Kim to help her find the money she needed. Amber pushing her aside, flinging up her arms and taking a bullet that was meant for Kim. If she lived to be a thousand, she'd never forget the sickening lurch of her stomach when she'd seen her sister fall....

Drew had been right to tell her to get over her petty feelings. And she had. Finally. There was nothing like the threat of losing someone to put things into perspective.

"They said I'd probably find you here."

Kim raised her head, looked over her shoulder and saw her father standing in the doorway. She pushed to her feet with a smile that wobbled as much as her legs. "Hi."

Gerald entered the small room and, taking her arm, steered her toward a chair. He sat down next to her. "I just came from Amber's room."

"How is she?"

"About the same. She hasn't come around yet."

"Have you heard from Drew since he took Hannah home?"

"No." Gerald regarded Kim thoughtfully. "But we had a long talk while the doctors were checking Hannah over."

Something in her father's voice—or maybe it was the considering expression in his eyes—caused her to go very still.

"Why didn't you tell me Hannah was Justin's?"

The bluntness of the question left Kim speechless. Breathless. She felt as if someone had sucked all the air from the room.

When she didn't answer, Gerald asked, "Were you so afraid of me?"

"No!" Kim said quickly, wondering how he could even think such a thing. "It wasn't that. It's just that it was so soon after your heart attack and Mama's death."

"And the write-up in the tabloid about Amber."

Kim nodded. "I didn't want to cause you any more grief or worry. And I didn't want you to think less of me." The last was confessed in a shamed whisper.

"So you lied to me instead."

Again, the bluntness of his words stunned her. "At the time, it seemed like the best thing to do."

"That's the thing, honey," Gerald said with a sad sort of smile. "Most of the things we do generally seem like the best thing. At the time."

His point wasn't lost on Kim.

"So you and Drew went into a loveless relationship for my sake?"

"If you've talked to Drew, you know all this," Kim said.

"I know why he did what he did," Gerald told her. "Now I want to hear your side."

"Then the answer is yes. At least that's what I thought. I knew Drew didn't love me—not that way—and I didn't think I loved him. But I've been doing a lot of thinking the past few months, and I've come to suspect that maybe I was wrong about that. Maybe I've always loved him."

Gerald gave a sorrowful shake of his head. "I'm so sorry for you both."

"What I did was wrong. I see that now," she said. She took a deep breath and plunged. There was no use trying to hide the rest of it. "I realize that this marriage isn't fair to him, so you may as well know that I went to Kentucky to ask him for a divorce. We agreed to wait until everything is settled with the investigation."

"Because you didn't want to put me under any more strain?"

"Yes."

"I see," Gerald said. "What about Hannah? She's crazy about Drew."

"I don't plan for things to change between them. He's her father in every way that counts."

"I'm glad you see that." He rubbed a hand down his face. "I'm so sorry," he said again.

"For what?" Kim asked.

"For not seeing how much stress *I* put on *you* all these years. You were always here, always dependable, always willing to go the extra mile. You made it so easy for me to lean on you. I've known for a long time that it was wrong of me to take advantage of you that way."

Once more, Kim was left without a response.

"Drew McShane is a good man," Gerald said, meeting her troubled gaze with a steady earnestness.

Kim's laugh was short and strained. "Believe me, I know that. I do love him, and I've decided to try to talk to him…tell him I've changed my mind, that I want our marriage to be a real one. But Drew is pretty angry with me right now. I don't know if talking will do any good."

"There's always 'I'm sorry,'" Gerald said. "Don't forget that. For two little words, they're awfully powerful."

Kim's eyes filled with tears. "I know."

Gerald rose and gave her an awkward pat on the shoulder. "I've preached enough. I'm going home to get some rest. Are you coming?"

"Not just yet," Kim said. "I want to stay until Amber wakes up."

Gerald nodded. "See you later, then."

"Yeah." Kim watched him go, and with the soft

closing of the door, the protective dam of denial she'd built around her heart so long ago burst. The sob that ripped painfully through her throat came from somewhere deep inside her. Her soul, no doubt.

She buried her face in her hands and cried. She wept for all the years she'd refused to cry, because Amber had used tears to manipulate. For all the things she'd said and done that had hurt her sister...and ultimately herself. For things she wished she *had* said and done. For too many long, lost years with Amber and with Drew. For the loss of her mother and Justin. For the return of the daughter snatched from under her very nose. And for the husband she had tossed so carelessly away.

"Don't cry."

Kim stood at the window of Amber's room, watching the first pink rays of dawn stain the gray of the morning sky. The soft command had her swiping at tears that had been falling unexpectedly throughout the night. It was almost as if once she'd given in to the need to cry, she couldn't turn the tears off.

Now she turned from the window and regarded her sister, who lay pale and still against the blinding whiteness of the hospital pillowcase. Kim wasn't sure what she'd expected from Amber after the scene at the Perkins place, but it wasn't a look of concern for her own welfare. Certainly not a smile—however weak it might be.

Kim neared the bed, drawing in a deep breath to settle her nerves and give her courage. There were things that needed to be said to Amber. Things that should have been said long ago. "How do you feel?"

Amber passed the tip of her tongue over her dry lips. "Groggy."

"It's the pain medicine," Kim said.

"Did they get David?"

"Yeah. Cal locked him up in the parish jail."

Amber's blue eyes darkened with sudden memory. "Is Hannah okay?"

"A little shaken up," Kim said. "But she's fine. The doctor looked her over, gave her a little something to make her sleep. Drew's at home with her."

"You should be there, too."

"No," Kim said. "I needed to be with you."

Clearly, the admission surprised Amber. She looked uncomfortable suddenly.

"You saved our lives," Kim said. "I don't know how to thank you."

"Aw, shucks," Amber drawled in a slurred voice. "It was nuthin', ma'am."

Kim's laughter was dismayed and amazed. She shook her head. "How do you do it?"

"Do what?"

"Keep that smart mouth and that attitude after you take a bullet that came inches from killing you."

"That's why I keep it," Amber confessed. "If I show myself any pity, I'll fall to pieces." Kim saw the sudden glitter of tears in her sister's eyes. "It got my face, didn't it?"

Kim nodded, her face solemn. "You raised your arms in what Cal called a defense reaction. The bullet went through your upper arm. Barely missed the bone. Grazed your cheek. A couple of inches higher or inside and you'd be in the morgue."

"So long, Hollywood," Amber quipped.

"You had one of the best plastic surgeons. He says you shouldn't have much scarring."

Amber drew an unsteady breath. "To tell you the truth, sister dear, I don't really care about my face at the moment."

Kim felt the threat of those wretched tears again. "I wish I were," she said.

"Were what?"

"Your sister dear."

They looked at each other in the growing light of a new day, the distance of six feet and a lifetime of resentments between them.

"Me, too," Amber told her.

Despite the flip answer, the confession, combined with the serious look in Amber's eyes, lightened the load of guilt weighing down Kim's heart. It gave her the courage to say the things she knew she must. "You were always the prettiest, most popular."

"And you were the smartest and most respected."

"Daddy gave you everything you wanted. I always resented you for that."

"Things," Amber said with a nod. "And permission to do things he probably shouldn't have. He gave you his time. His attention. I resented you for that."

They were silent, letting their confessions sink in. Finally, Kim said, "For just a moment or two, I thought you were in on Hannah's kidnapping."

Surprise flickered in Amber's eyes, which were growing less muddled and more pain-filled by the moment. "Why?"

"Because I knew you needed that money, that you were desperate for it. I guess I wanted to think the worst of you. I've used you as my excuse for not

taking charge of my own life for way too many
years.''

"And I just ran away from my problems,'' Amber
said. "Or tried to. That's what I was doing when I
came home. Running away. Trying to hide from David because he wanted the money and I couldn't get
it. He's my biological father,'' she added.

It was Kim's turn to be surprised.

"It seems that David and my mom were an item
in college. He wouldn't marry her when she got pregnant, so she pawned me off as Gerald Campion's
baby while David went to California. Evidently, he
grew up in the house where he took you and Hannah,
but he was called D.J.''

"How did he meet Maria?''

"He's a gigolo and a gambler who was partial to
the ponies,'' Amber said. "He hung out with the racing crowd in California, Kentucky and New York,
romancing wealthy widows. When Larry died he hit
on Maria.''

"But how did he find out about you?'' Kim asked.

"Remember when my picture came out on the
front page of *Tattle Tales*?''

"How could I not?''

"Yeah,'' Amber said. Her mouth twisted in a parody of a smile—whether from bitterness or pain, Kim
couldn't be sure. "Well, he saw me, realized I was
the spitting image of my mother and that I must be
his loving daughter. He happened to be in a money
crunch, and he knew Daddy was loaded, so he came
out to L.A. and looked me up. This was before he
conned Maria into marrying him. I guess he thought
I'd be an easy touch, and I guess he was right. He's
been hitting me up periodically ever since, which was

why I kept hitting Daddy up. Most recently, he said that if I didn't cough up a hundred thousand dollars, he'd tell Dad that he was my biological father.''

Kim's eyes widened. "He was blackmailing you?"

Amber nodded. "I know my reasoning may be skewed, but I'd rather have had Dad think I was a no-account spendthrift always asking him for money than for him to find out I wasn't his." Her eyes clouded with tears. "Like you, I figured that deal in the tabloid brought on his heart attack, and I didn't want to think I'd be responsible for his having another one."

Kim couldn't help the sad smile that claimed her lips. In her own strange way, Amber had been trying to protect their father, too. Maybe she had changed. And maybe she'd been wrongly judged.

"I imagine David has spilled his guts to Cal about what he was up to," Amber said.

"I imagine so. Cal seems like a really sharp guy."

"Yeah," Amber said with a tired smile. "Who'd ever have believed good old Cal would go so far? I always had him figured for a poor, dumb jock."

"You don't make sheriff by being dumb."

"I know. So much for preconceived notions. But I was just a teenager when I made that judgment," Amber said. "And obviously Cal has come a long way. He's turned into a real stud muffin, too."

"Is that interest I hear in your voice?" Kim didn't ever remember a time in the past she'd felt comfortable enough with her sister to tease her.

"Are you kidding!" Amber managed a weak laugh. "Cal and I would be like Goldie Hawn and Kurt Russell in *Overboard*."

"Just asking."

A comfortable silence fell between them. In spite of Amber's talkativeness, Kim could tell her sister was in pain. "You're hurting, aren't you?"

"It's my heart as much as my face and my arm," Amber said. "I hate that Dad found out the truth, you know? Heck, I hate that I found out. I was just beginning to feel like I was getting my life together, and then all this happens. I was even considering getting my own place and moving back here."

"What's stopping you?"

"Dad may not want to have anything to do with me now that he knows I'm not really his," Amber said.

"Don't be ridiculous!" Kim chastised. "It takes more than donating sperm to make a father. Gerald Campion is as much your real father as he is mine."

As she spoke the words, she realized just how true they were. Gerald was as much Amber's father as Drew was Hannah's.

A single tear slithered down Amber's cheek. "Thanks." She sniffed and swiped it away with her uninjured hand.

Kim saw the strain around Amber's mouth. Uncertain if it was from their conversation or the pain she was bound to be feeling as the medication wore off, Kim said, "You need to get some sleep."

"I'm hurting too darn bad."

"I'll call the nurse."

Amber nodded. In a matter of minutes the nurse had administered the medication and left them alone again. "Try to rest," Kim said.

"I will, but I'm cold."

Kim went to the bed and pulled the thermal blanket up over her sister's shoulders.

"Thanks," Amber said. Her sorrowful gaze met Kim's. She held out her good hand, and Kim took it in hers. "I'm sorry, Kim. For everything. For not being the kind of sister and daughter I should have been."

"I'm in no position to throw stones."

"And for inadvertently dragging Hannah into my mess."

"That wasn't your fault. Cal says David has no prior convictions for kidnapping or anything but fleecing unsuspecting women. There's no way you could know what he planned to do."

"Maybe not, but it doesn't change the fact that he held a gun on you, or that either one of you could have been hurt or killed." The tears sprang into her eyes again. "I pray this doesn't scar Hannah."

"She's young and adaptable. If we notice any unusual behavior, we'll see to it."

"You're being awfully decent about this."

"You took a bullet for me and my daughter," Kim said, urging a smile to her lips and squeezing Amber's hand. "I'm not likely to forget it." The pressure was returned, but weakly. "I'd like to start over, Amber. If we can."

Amber's eyelids drooped. "I'd like that, too."

In seconds, the even tenor of her breathing told Kim she was sound asleep. There was so much more she'd wanted to tell Amber, so many things to apologize for. And she wanted to repay her sister's honesty with her own by telling her about Justin and Hannah and how she'd come to be married to Drew.

Maybe tomorrow, she thought. At least they'd made a good start.

Kim was on her way to her car when she ran into Cal at the elevator.

"You look like something the cat dragged in," she said.

Offering her a wry grin, he rubbed at the twenty-four-hour growth of whiskers shadowing his lean cheeks. "Thanks. You don't exactly look like Little Mary Sunshine."

Kim smiled wearily. "Touché."

"How's Amber?" he asked.

"They just gave her a pain shot and she went out like a light. She was awake quite a while, though."

Cal shook his head. "That's one gutsy woman. I'd never have suspected Amber Campion had the stuff heroes are made of."

"Me, either," Kim said, "but either Hannah or I might be six feet under if she hadn't taken that bullet."

Cal's eyes held a grim conviction. "Yeah, and she'd be six feet under if that guy was a better shot."

Kim didn't want to think about how close a call it had been, but like Cal, she couldn't seem to stop thinking about it. "Did you find out why he resorted to kidnapping?" she asked.

"Loan sharks. When Amber couldn't come up with the blackmail money, he figured Drew would be good for it, and decided to up the ante. Perkins was also behind the breeding mix-up. He said Mrs. Perkins had no knowledge of what he was doing."

"Which was what, exactly?" Kim asked.

Cal told Kim Drew's version of how Perkins had

scammed the people by taking the money for breeding to the good stud, then having the workers from Mexico breed to another one. "By hiring Mexicans who spoke little or no English and foremen who spoke no Mexican, he cut down on the chance of anyone finding out what he was up to. And if a foreman started questioning him about why they weren't at the breeding sessions or started getting suspicious, Perkins fired them. He was in a lose-lose situation. When he realized he'd gotten all he could from Amber and saw Hannah, he came up with the idea of kidnapping her. I think he threw the plan together on the spur of the moment. His problem was that he's not a real criminal type. He's a slimy gigolo who can charm the pants off a woman and talk her out of her money, but he doesn't have the mind-set it takes to plan and pull off something like a kidnapping. I knew he was sloppy when he didn't hide the van."

"Thank God for that."

"It made finding him easier," Cal admitted, "but we'd have located him sooner or later."

"We appreciate everything you've done, Cal."

He grinned, a heart-stopping, sexy smile, and turned on the Southern charm. "Just doin' my job, ma'am."

"Thanks."

"Sure thing. How's Hannah?"

"She seems fine. Drew took her home."

"I hope she doesn't have any lingering scars," Cal said. "I see way too many kids with hurts they have no business feeling."

Kim knew his niece and nephew were included in that statement. "Yeah."

He shifted from one foot to the other. "Speaking of scars, what about Amber's face?"

"The E.R. doctor called in a top-notch plastic surgeon. He seems to think there'll be minimal scarring."

"Good," he said with a nod. "She's a pretty woman, and I'm not sure how she'd take it if her looks were ruined."

Kim arched her eyebrows. "She's proved to be a surprising lady. She might handle it better than any of us think."

"I hope so." Cal smiled. "I'm going to go check on her."

"Good idea," Kim said. "Keep us informed about what's happening with David Perkins."

"You bet." They said their goodbyes and Kim headed for home.

Amber was sleeping when Cal entered the room. Her left arm, the one that had taken the slug from Perkins's .38, was bandaged and in a sling. The white patch across her left cheek was a stark reminder of how close she'd come to buying the farm. Without her bold red lipstick, her skin looked pale. Her short blond hair was mussed, but it only made her look sexier.

Whoa! Where on earth had that come from? he wondered. He already felt like a fool for coming to see her and had asked himself for the dozenth time exactly why he had. Hadn't he learned his lessons from Amber Campion long ago?

It wasn't as if he'd been suffering from unrequited love all this time. He'd found his grown-up love at twenty-three, and that relationship had ended four years later. Actually, her rejection back in high school had helped him see that he needed to make something of himself. And he had.

Amber stirred, bringing his thoughts back from the past. She tried to turn to her side. "No!" she groaned. "Stop!"

In two long strides, Cal was at her bedside. He reached out and pushed gently on her good shoulder. "Lie still," he said. "It's okay. Shh."

She opened her eyes at the sound of his voice. They were cloudy with sleep and glazed with the peculiar glassiness that accompanied pain medication.

"Cal?" His name came out as a croak.

"Yeah?"

She held out her hand and he took it in his. "You saved my life."

He grimaced. "Hardly."

If anything about the confrontation the evening before bothered him, that was it. He should have done more. Should have had a better handle on the situation, but Amber hadn't reacted in any predictable way. Neither had Perkins, for that matter.

Cal looked down at Amber and realized that she'd drifted back to sleep. He pulled his hand free of hers, but couldn't resist dragging the backs of his knuckles over her cheek and across the lush fullness of her mouth.

Moments later, he was gone from the room, just as Amber would soon be gone from Louisiana.

When Kim got back to the house, she found Gerald at the table on the back porch having breakfast.

"Where is everyone?" she asked after assuring him that Amber was okay.

Gerald shifted uncomfortably. "Hannah's still asleep. Drew left."

Kim felt as if the bottom had dropped out of her world. "Left?" she echoed. "Where did he go?"

"He said he had to go drive up to north Louisiana to talk to Reeves again about testifying against Perkins. Then he was catching a flight back to Kentucky." The look in Gerald's eyes was brutally frank. "I suggest you fly to Kentucky and have that talk with your husband, if you want to save your marriage."

"Fly!" she said, terrified at the very thought. "I can't fly!"

"Of course you can. Just because Justin was killed on a plane, doesn't mean that you or anyone else you know will ever suffer the same fate."

"Intellectually, I know that," she said, "but I just can't."

"You would if you'd seen the look in his eyes when he left here," Gerald said. "He loves you. Hannah, too."

She gave a small gasp of surprise. "How do you know he loves me?"

"I've always known. I can't believe you didn't see it. Go after him, Kim. You'll never find out if it's true or not if you don't ask him."

With her father's statement ringing in her ears, Kim went upstairs. Cindy had gone home with Molly and Garrett to recuperate from her cold, and the second floor of the house seemed as empty as Kim's heart. She slipped into the room to check on Hannah and found her still sleeping soundly, her hands tucked under her sleep-flushed cheek.

Compelled by a rush of love and thanksgiving so strong it threatened to buckle her knees, Kim knelt beside her daughter's bed and laid her head against the child's back. There was something reassuring about the thumping of her innocent heart, something innately precious in her soft, childish snoring.

After long moments spent thanking God for delivering her child and her sister from a terrible fate, Kim brushed the tears from her cheeks and headed for the bathroom. Maybe she could sort out her feelings about Drew and what she should do about his leaving while a hot shower beat the weariness from her body.

She was stripping off her clothes when she saw the note lying on the bed. A feeling of déjà vu swept through her as she recalled leaving the note on Drew's mirror a week before. Her fingers trembled as she reached to pick it up, and her heart beat out a doomsday rhythm.

Kim

I've gone back to Kentucky, via a quick stop in Doyline to make sure we can count on Reeves's testimony. Your dad is upset about Amber and David, but I believe he's dealing with it as well as can be expected. Under the circumstances, I felt it only right to tell him the truth about Hannah and Justin. Since David's confession has cleared Gerald, there's not much reason to drag out our marriage any longer, so you may as well go ahead and get your divorce. It's my sincere hope that what Amber did for you and Hannah will make you stop and take a good look at your relationship with her. From time to time, we all need second chances. I wish things could have turned out differently between us, but more than anything, I want you to be happy.

                                                    Drew

Kim crushed the note in her hand and pressed her fists to her mouth to hold back a wail of anguish. Why hadn't she realized how painful it would be to end something in such a cold, impersonal way? No wonder Drew had been so furious when he'd met her in the garage the night she'd driven in from Kentucky.

And, oh God, why had she let her jealousy and resentment—even her feelings of duty—keep her from seeking her own happiness? She'd let those feelings stunt her emotionally, just as her father's indulgence had crippled Amber's ability to grow into a responsible adult.

She recalled hearing her mother say that parents just did the best they could. Kim hadn't understood what Gwen had meant at the time, but now that she was a parent, the meaning was crystal clear. Even parents made mistakes. Everyone made mistakes. All you could do was hope they weren't too damaging. As Drew said, you had to get over it if you were hurt and hope you didn't hurt anyone else too badly.

The scene at the Perkins farm had taught her that life was too short and relationships far too precious to waste a single moment of it on petty misunderstandings or hurt feelings.

So what was she going to do about Drew?

"What do you want?" *"What would make you happy?"* The memory of Drew asking those questions surfaced from someplace deep in her mind.

"You," she said out loud. "I want you. You make me happy."

"I'm sorry...two powerful little words... He loves you, Kim... You'll never find out if it's true or not if you don't go ask him...."

Her decision made, Kim headed for the shower. Her stomach churned with apprehension. Her heart was filled with a fragile hope.

Late that night, Drew pulled beneath the portico in front of his house and turned off the engine. He dreaded going inside and tried not to think of how empty and silent it would be when he stepped through the door. It was a beautiful old house, made to be filled with the laughter of half a dozen kids and the voices of a boisterous, happy family. Unfortunately, it might be years before that happened. He wasn't naive enough to think he'd never meet anyone else he could love, but he knew it would be a long time before that happened. And there would never be anyone he loved quite the way he loved Kim.

He got out of the vehicle, slamming the door behind him. Suddenly the light on the porch went on and the front door flew open. A woman—Kim?— sailed down the steps, her hair flying out behind her. Drew was too stunned by the fact that she was there—had beat him home—to be more than marginally impressed as she rounded on him with full-fledged feminine fury.

"How dare you leave me a *note* telling me to go ahead and get a divorce," she said, punching him in the chest with her forefinger.

As she had earlier, Drew experienced an eerie feeling of déjà vu. His second reaction was to note that she was angry. Why? Hadn't he just given her what she wanted?

"I thought that's what you wanted."

"How do I know what I want when you make me so crazy?"

He realized that the words sounded more confused than angry. Or, he thought, seeing the misery and uncertainty in her eyes, it was *bemused.*

"*I* make *you* crazy?" he said, thinking of the way she'd made love with him with such wild recklessness and then treated him so coolly afterward. There were other things that drove him crazy, too, but he couldn't remember them with her standing so close and the familiar scent of her hair filling his nostrils...robbing him of thought and awakening the urge to plow his hands through the thick, straight mass and kiss her senseless.

"Yeah," she said indignantly, her lower lip jutting out like Hannah's. "You make me crazy."

The words were soft, filled with wonderment, not anger.

"How?" he demanded. Like her, there was little fire in the question.

"By telling me things about myself that make me furious even when I know you're right. By doing this."

She stood on tiptoe, slid her hands up his chest to clasp the back of his neck and surged against him, pressing herself to him from knee to chest and fusing her open mouth to his with a heat and hunger that caught him off guard and sent his libido into overdrive.

Her hands seemed everywhere. Unbuttoning his shirt, undoing his belt, threading through his hair to hold his head still while she devoured his mouth with hers. Taken by surprise, Drew could only let her have her way.

They never made it to the house, but Drew found out that, like desktops and battered couches, the back seat of a vehicle sufficed in a pinch.

Later, when he found the strength to speak, he lifted himself on one elbow and looked into her eyes. They were filled with supreme satisfaction. A contented smile hovered on her lips.

"Does this mean we aren't getting a divorce?" he asked, his own mouth curving into a smile.

The expression in her eyes grew serious, uncertain. Her voice quavered when she spoke. "Hannah misses you, Drew. She wants you with her. Deep down, I've always known it, but the past couple of days has made me see that she truly is as much your child as mine."

He only nodded. "What about you? What do you want?"

"You," she said without hesitation. "I love you, Drew. I've always loved you. If what just happened means you love me—even a little—I want to try to make our marriage work."

He used one finger to brush a lock of hair away from her eyes. "What just happened doesn't mean I love you a little. It's just a small part of how much I love you," he said.

Kim lifted her hand to his cheek. "I'm sorry."

"For what?"

"Everything stupid and wrong I've done."

He knew then that she'd made her peace with Amber and whatever demons that drove her. It took a strong person to admit fault. A stronger one to do something about those mistakes. A sudden thought hit him.

"How did you get here?"

"I flew."

"On an airplane?"

"No, silly," she said, her expression perfectly deadpan. "On my broom."

Drew was so shocked by the fact that she'd actually confronted her fear of airplanes to come to him that the sarcastic quip went right over his head.

"It was a joke, Drew," she said, waving her hand in front of his face. "You know?—a joke. Ha. Ha. I was making fun of myself."

He'd never known her to joke before. She'd always taken life so seriously. He looked deeply into her eyes, trying to fathom what had happened to change things, and saw her smile fade to uncertainty.

"Don't stop smiling," he said, still filled with a growing wonder. "It looks good on you."

"It does?"

"Yeah," he said. "Real good. You mean you actually got on an airplane and *flew* here to try and reconcile with me?"

"I'd walk over hot coals to be with you," she told him.

The seriousness he heard in her voice banished the last lingering doubt, leaving more room for his growing joy. He smiled. "A nice gesture, but the real question is would you have sex in a bed with me?"

"What?"

"It occurred to me that we've never had sex in a bed."

"Well," she said, pretending to contemplate the suggestion. "I might. Under certain conditions."

"What's that?"

"You carry me up."

And he did.

Epilogue

The Kentucky hills rolled out beyond the miles of white board fence, as far as the eye could see. Mares with swollen bellies nibbled at the tender shoots of grass, and new-born foals frolicked about on fragile sticklike legs. Birdsong filled the April air, while baby rabbits played hide and seek in clumps of sweet smelling narcissus.

A table boasting a pink cloth sat in the midst of the flowering white garden, between the gazebo and the fish pond with its softly gurgling fountain. A rainbow of pastel plates, cups and napkins were arranged on the table, which was dominated by a round cake with lavender frosting piped with pink, white and yellow roses that cascaded over the sides like the drift of white thrift that tumbled over the rocks bordering the flagstone path. A candle in the shape of a three sat atop the cake.

Hannah was on her knees in the chair behind the cake, her elbows propped on the table, her dimples flashing as she hammed it up for the adults wielding the cameras and camcorders that were recording the events surrounding her third birthday.

Never much good with a camera, Kim was content to sit with her feet propped up and let her father, Drew and his parents do the honors.

"Isn't she adorable?" Maureen McShane said to her husband. The eyes fixed on her granddaughter glowed with love.

"Precious," Cullen agreed.

"I want cake," Hannah said, tired of the posing.

"Not yet, sweetness," Drew told her. "Mom wants to wait for Aunt Amber."

Kim cast him a look that said without words that they might be waiting 'til eternity, and they both grinned, knowing there was no malice in the thought. Amber had changed considerably, but punctuality still wasn't her strong suit.

Hannah's giggle drew Kim's attention back to the table. Her daughter cast a mischievous look at Drew, scooped up a yellow rose and popped it into her mouth.

"Hannah!" Kim chastised.

Hannah only laughed and dragged her finger through another flower.

Struggling to control her own laughter, Kim asked, "Did you get a picture of that, Drew?"

"Yep," he said. "It should be a dandy."

"Do you want to let her open her presents while we wait?" Gerald asked.

"Sure," Kim said with a weary sigh. "Why not?"

Hannah leaped down from the chair and settled

next to the gifts Kim had stacked on a quilt earlier.
She watch as Hannah chose a present and tore at the
bow. This birthday was a far cry from last year's.
Kim said a silent prayer of thankfulness that her
daughter was safe and well.

She felt Drew's arms slide around her waist, or
what was left of her waist, since she was a full nine
months pregnant, and five days past her due date. As
always, when he touched her, she felt a thrill of desire, and total contentment. She tipped her head back
against his chest and smiled up at him. A year ago,
she would never have believed her life could be so
full, or that she could be so happy, but since she'd
made her peace with Amber and moved to Kentucky
to be with Drew, every facet of her life had taken on
new meaning. The love surrounding her was a gift
so priceless, she never forgot to be thankful for it.

"Have I told you today that I love you?" Drew
asked, his hands moving over her stomach with the
same tenderness she'd often seen him use on the
horses.

"Yes, but I don't mind if you're redundant."

"I love you. And you look gorgeous in that peachy
color."

"Why thank you, sir."

Her belly knotted beneath his hands, and she
sucked in a sharp breath. "Ouch!" he said. "How
do you feel?"

Her eyes met his. "Like I'm going to have the
baby. Soon."

The tenderness in Drew's eyes vanished. "You're
kidding."

She shook her head.

"That wasn't one of those false labor pains?"

"No."

"Then we'd better go to the hospital," he said, his voice rising.

"What is it?" Maureen said.

"Kim's in labor."

"Calm down, Drew," she said. Her smile encompassed her dad and her in-laws. "We have plenty of time. I'm not going anywhere until we have cake and ice cream."

"Then let's get on with it," Drew said, picking up Hannah and carrying her back to the table. He plunked her onto the chair. "Light the candle, Dad," he barked. "Mom you cut the cake. Make a wish, Hannah."

"Drew!" Kim wailed.

"It may be best for you to get on to the hospital," Maureen said. "You weren't in labor that long with Hannah, and she was your first. Your second often comes even faster."

"I'm fine."

"Sorry! I know you won't believe me, but my taxi got stuck in this traffic jam."

The apology came from Amber, who was scurrying down the path, almost dragging a huge, stuffed bag from a popular toy store. She looked harried, hurried, gorgeous, and not the least bit concerned that she was holding up the party.

"Happy Birthday, Hannah Banana." She dropped the bag on the quilt, gave Kim a hug, then moved on to Drew and the others.

"Kim's in labor," Maureen said. "She wanted to wait until you got here to cut the cake."

"Oh." Amber offered Kim an apologetic look. "Sorry, sis." She went to Hannah and gave her a smacking kiss on the cheek. "So what are we waiting for, kiddo? Let's do it!"

She broke into "Happy Birthday," and everyone joined in. It escaped no one that Kim was stricken with a hard contraction in the middle of the song.

With his eyes fixed on Kim's pale features, Drew spoke to Hannah, "Go on, sweetness. Blow out the candle."

"What's wrong with Mommy?"

"She's about to have your baby sister or brother," Drew said. "Now blow out your candle so we can cut the cake."

Hannah puckered her lips.

"Wait!" Kim cried. "Make a wish."

"I did already," Hannah said. "I wished for a—"

"Don't tell," Cullen cautioned, "or it won't come true."

"—baby sister," Hannah finished.

"Drew, my water just broke."

"What?"

"My water just broke."

Without a word, he swung her up into his arms and started for the house. "I haven't had any cake."

"Forget the darned cake. We're going to the hospital."

"Not now."

"Now. Gerald, you call the doctor," Drew bellowed over his shoulder. "The number is next to the phone. Dad, run upstairs and get the suitcase."

"I'll get some towels," Maureen said, scurrying past them.

Kim glared at Drew. "I'm not going."

"Wanna bet?" he said, his tone as implacable as the look in his eyes.

"I can walk," Kim said. "Put me down."

"Fat chance!"

"Are you making fun of me?"

"I wouldn't dare."

Amber and Hannah watched the others disappear down the path. Amber poised the cake server above the cake. "Which piece do you want?"

"I want flowers," Hannah said.

"Me, too." Amber cut into the cake. "So you wished for a baby sister, did you?"

"Uh-huh," Hannah said, reaching for a plastic fork. "Boys are yucky."

"Yeah, sometimes," Amber agreed. "And it would be nice to have a sister. It is nice to have a sister. I hope you get your wish."

"Me, too. Can I have some ice cream, Aunt Amber?"

"Sure. There's more than enough for the two of us. How about some nuts?"

Drew called three hours later to tell Hannah her birthday wish had come true. Her new sister weighed almost eight pounds—the biggest girl in the nursery—and was twenty-one inches long. They would call their new child Gwendolyn Maureen, after both her grandmothers.

Hannah announced that she was going to call her new sister Gweneen. And for a long time, she did.

*   *   *   *   *

Silhouette

SPECIAL EDITION ®

TM

That's My Baby!

**Don't miss these poignant stories coming to
THAT'S MY BABY!—only from
Silhouette Special Edition!**

December 1998 THEIR CHILD
                    by Penny Richards (SE# 1213)
Drew McShane married Kim Campion to give her baby
a name. Could their daughter unite them in love?

February 1999 BABY, OUR BABY!
                    by Patricia Thayer (SE# 1225)
Her baby girl would always remind Ali Pierce of her
night of love with Jake Hawkins. Now he was back—
and proposing marriage!

April 1999 A FATHER FOR HER BABY
                    by Celeste Hamilton (SE #1237)
When Jarrett McMullen located his long-lost runaway
bride, could he convince the amnesiac, expectant
mother-to-be he wanted her for always?

THAT'S MY BABY!
*Sometimes bringing up baby can bring surprises...
and showers of love.*

Available at your favorite retail outlet.

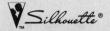

Silhouette ®

TM

Look us up on-line at: http://www.romance.net   SSETMB2

Silhouette® SPECIAL EDITION®

AND BABY MAKES THREE:
THE NEXT GENERATION:

The Adams men and women of Texas all find love—and parenthood—in the most unexpected ways!

Bestselling author Sherryl Woods continues to captivate with her popular series about the headstrong heroes and independent-minded ladies of charming Los Pinos, Texas:

November 1998: THE COWGIRL & THE UNEXPECTED WEDDING (SE #1208)
Could fit-to-be-tied cowboy Hank Robbins convince mule-headed mother-to-be Lizzie Adams to march down the aisle?

December 1998: NATURAL BORN LAWMAN (SE #1216)
Justin Adams was a strictly by-the-book lawman—until he fell in love with a desperate, devoted single mom on the run!

February 1999: THE UNCLAIMED BABY
(Silhouette Single Title)
The family saga continues with a passionate, longer-length romance about a fateful stormy night that changes Sharon Adams's life—forever!

March 1999: THE COWBOY AND HIS WAYWARD BRIDE (SE #1234)
Rancher Harlan Patrick Adams would do just about anything to claim stubborn Laurie Jensen—mother of his infant daughter—as his own!

Available at your favorite retail outlet.

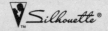

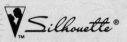

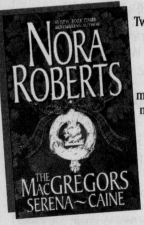

Silhouette®

SPECIAL EDITION™®

COMING NEXT MONTH

es 1217

edition suhrkamp
Neue Folge Band 217

Seit Mitte der siebziger Jahre erlebt mann mit wachsendem Befremden, wie frau die deutsche Sprache instandbesetzt. Früher fand sie keinen Raum in dieser Herr-berge, genannt »Muttersprache« (ausgerechnet). Inzwischen jedoch hat frau sich eingerichtet und mit der Sanierung begonnen. Die Regeln der Grammatik, morsches Gebälk, werden feminisiert und dadurch humanisiert. Am Mauerwerk, dem Wort»schatz«, wird zur Zeit viel geklopft und geprüft, was noch brauchbar ist, was hinaus muß und was wo neu eingesetzt werden soll.

Die feministische Linguistik entlarvt die Geschichte und Struktur der Sprachen als Männergeschichte und Männerstruktur. Sprachen als Bauwerke, von Männern errichtet, damit Männer darin wohnen und sich wohlfühlen können.

Die feministische Linguistik fundiert und dokumentiert die sprachkritische, sprachschöpferische und sprachpolitische Arbeit der Frauen.

Über die Männersprache Englisch – Manglish – sind bereits mehrere Monographien erschienen. Speziell zum Deutschen gibt es bislang nur die wissenschaftlichen und journalistischen Arbeiten der Konstanzer Linguistin Luise F. Pusch, die hier erstmals gesammelt vorgelegt werden.

Luise F. Pusch, geboren 1944. Habilitation für Sprachwissenschaft 1978. Seit 1979 Heisenberg-Stipendiatin. Aufsätze und Bücher zur Grammatik des Deutschen, Englischen, Italienischen und Lateinischen. Spezialgebiete: Kontrastive Linguistik, Übersetzungswissenschaft, feministische Linguistik. Herausgeberin des Bandes *Feminismus – Inspektion der Herrenkultur. Ein Handbuch* (edition suhrkamp 1192).

Luise F. Pusch

Das Deutsche als Männersprache

Aufsätze und Glossen
zur feministischen Linguistik

Suhrkamp

Für Irmela und Hans Schmidts

edition suhrkamp 1217
Neue Folge Band 217
Erste Auflage 1984
© Suhrkamp Verlag Frankfurt am Main 1984
Erstausgabe
Alle Rechte vorbehalten, insbesondere das der Übersetzung,
des öffentlichen Vortrags
sowie der Übertragung durch Rundfunk und Fernsehen,
auch einzelner Teile.
Satz: Philipp Hümmer, Waldbüttelbrunn
Druck: Nomos Verlagsgesellschaft, Baden-Baden
Umschlagentwurf: Willy Fleckhaus
Printed in Germany

2 3 4 5 6 – 89 88 87 86 85

2/20/86 *jl*

Inhalt

Einleitung
Von der Linguistik zur Feministischen Linguistik
Ein persönlicher Bericht

In meinem Paß steht: »Der Inhaber dieses Passes ist Deutscher.«
Ich bin aber kein Deutscher. Hätte ich je in einem Deutschaufsatz
geschrieben, ich sei »Deutscher«, so wäre mir das Maskulinum als
Grammatikfehler angestrichen worden.

Ich bin Deutsche. Es müßte also heißen: »Der Inhaber dieses Passes ist Deutsche.« Nein, das ist auch falsch. Zwar gilt es nicht als
Fehler, wenn ich, obwohl weiblich, über mich sage: »Ich bin der
Inhaber dieses Passes.« Genauso korrekt ist aber *Inhaberin*. Und
zusammen mit *Deutsche* ist **nur** *Inhaberin* richtig: »Die Inhaberin
dieses Passes ist Deutsche.«

Im Paß meines Bruders steht derselbe Satz wie in meinem. Er hat
sich nie daran gestört. Wieso sollte er auch? Der Satz ist ihm auf
den Leib geschneidert. Aber wenn da stünde »Die Inhaberin dieses
Passes ist Deutsche«, so wäre das nicht nur falsch, sondern eine
Katastrophe. Die Paßbehörden würden sich vor Männerbe-
schwerden kaum retten können, denn welcher Mann läßt sich
schon gern »Inhaberin« und »Deutsche« schimpfen?

Weibliche Bezeichnungen sind für Männer genauso untragbar wie
weibliche Kleidungsstücke. Und doppelter Papierkrieg ist für Be-
hörden zu aufwendig, also werden uns Frauen die männlichen Bezeichnungen zugemutet. Es ist die einfachste Lösung. Frauen sind
erstens geduldig, und zweitens sind männliche Bezeichnungen sowieso viel schöner und kürzer und praktischer und irgendwie edler
und überhaupt allgemeiner.

Ich bin Linguistin. Oder bin ich Linguist? Mal bin ich dies, mal
jenes; ich habe mich längst daran gewöhnt. Eins aber steht fest:
Meine Mutter war Sekretärin und nicht Sekretär. Sie hat den Sekre-
tärinnenberuf ausgeübt und führt jetzt ein Rentnerdasein. Oder ist
es ein Rentnerinnendasein? Schließlich führen Rentnerinnen ein
ganz anderes Dasein als Rentner. – Meine Mutter ist vielleicht eine
Ausnahme; sie ist Studentin der Philosophie – oder auch Student.
Mal dies, mal jenes.

Ich stelle fest: Meine Muttersprache ist für Männer bequem, klar und eindeutig. Das Reden über Männer ist völlig problemlos in dieser Männersprache. Schwierig, kompliziert und verwirrend ist nur das Reden über Frauen. Mutter Sprache ist auf meine Existenz etwa so gut vorbereitet wie Vater Staat auf die Existenz von Behinderten. Als »Problemgruppe« dürfen wir uns mit offenkundigen Behelfslösungen herumschlagen, die als »Grammatik« nicht weiter diskutiert werden. Denn schließlich: Wer wäre auch für Grammatik verantwortlich zu machen?

Als Frau und Linguistin interessieren mich nun folgende Fragen:

1. Wie kommt es, daß die deutsche Sprache so ist? War sie schon immer so? Welche Personen/ Personenkreise/ gesellschaftlichen Strömungen/ geschichtlichen Ereignisse/ didaktischen Maßnahmen/ sprachregelnden Verordnungen usw. sind möglicherweise für ihren heutigen Zustand verantwortlich?

2. Sind andere Sprachen auch so?

3. Wieso sind weibliche Bezeichnungen für Männer untragbar, männliche Bezeichnungen für Frauen jedoch nicht?

4. Welche anderen Bereiche der Sprache – außer den Personenbezeichnungen – sind noch männlich geprägt?

5. Welche psychischen, kognitiven, gesellschaftlichen und politischen Konsequenzen hat es für uns Frauen, daß unsere Muttersprache eine Fremdsprache ist?

6. Welche psychischen, kognitiven, gesellschaftlichen und politischen Konsequenzen hat es für Männer, daß ihre Muttersprache eine Vatersprache ist?

7. Warum beschweren sich nicht mehr Frauen über die Frauenfeindlichkeit der deutschen Sprache? Warum gab es früher keine Diskussion über diesen Skandal?

8. Was können wir tun? Wie können wir aus Männersprachen humane Sprachen machen?

Die herkömmliche Sprachwissenschaft kann solche und ähnliche Fragen nicht beantworten, weil sie sie nicht stellt. Das ist auch kein Wunder, denn sie wird, wie jede Wissenschaft, überwiegend von Männern verwaltet. Und warum sollten Männer ohne Not einen Tatbestand als Problem erkennen und behandeln, der ihnen nur Vorteile bringt?

Die männlich geprägte Linguistik hat es sogar vermocht, **ihre** Auffassung von Sprache auch in den Köpfen von Linguistinnen so fest zu verankern, daß nicht sie als Begründerinnen der Feministischen Linguistik* anzusehen sind, sondern frauenbewegte »Laiinnen«, Nichtlinguistinnen, deren allgemeines Unbehagen in der Herrenkultur die Herrensprache von Anfang an selbstverständlich mit einbezog.

Gleich 1973 las ich den inzwischen klassischen Aufsatz »Language and women's place« von Robin *Lakoff*. Ich fand ihn sehr interessant, aber er regte mich nicht zu eigenständiger Forschung auf dem damit eröffneten neuen Gebiet an. Außerdem hatte ich damals auch weisungsgemäß über andere Themen zu forschen, z. B. über Nominalisierungen konjunktionaler Nebensätze. 1976 kam ich zur Frauenbewegung, las Simone *de Beauvoir*, Betty *Friedan*, Kate *Millett* und Alice *Schwarzer*, abonnierte *Emma* und *Courage* – und immerzu fiel es mir wie Schuppen von den Augen. Nächtelang war ich wütend über vergewaltigende und prügelnde Ehemänner, über die systematische Benachteiligung der Frau im Beruf, über den alltäglichen Sexismus in Lehrbüchern und in den Medien. Aber Sexismus in der Sprache – nein, das war für mich kein Thema, obwohl ich von den »Laiinnen«, gerade als Sprach-Fachfrau, ständig darauf angesprochen wurde. Das neue Prono-

---

* Die Feministische Linguistik, Anfang der siebziger Jahre von US-Amerikanerinnen begründet, inzwischen international verbreitet und seit 1978 auch in der Bundesrepublik beheimatet, hat zur Zeit zwei Themenschwerpunkte: Sprachsysteme und Sprechhandlungen, oder kürzer: Sprachen und Sprechen. Ich beschäftige mich in den hier zusammengestellten Aufsätzen und Glossen mit Sprachen, vor allem mit dem Deutschen.

Hinsichtlich des Sprechens untersuchen wir, welche typischen Redestrategien Frauen und Männer haben. Das Ergebnis der bisherigen Untersuchungen ist, daß Frauen in Gesprächen **aller** Art, ob es sich nun um Familiengespräche am Frühstückstisch oder um große Fernsehdiskussionen handelt, von Männern unterdrückt werden. Männer unterbrechen Frauen viel häufiger als umgekehrt, und sie reden viel länger als Frauen. Gelingt es Frauen doch einmal, zu Wort zu kommen, so verweigern Männer ihnen diejenigen Bekundungen aufmerksamen Zuhörens, ohne die ein Gespräch zum Monolog wird und stirbt.

Die erste umfassende Darstellung dieses Gebiets der Feministischen Linguistik in deutscher Sprache veröffentlichte meine Freundin und Kollegin Senta *Trömel-Plötz* 1982 unter dem Titel *Frauensprache – Sprache der Veränderung*. Sehr empfehlen möchte ich auch Fritjof *Werners* Dissertation (1983) *Gesprächsverhalten von Frauen und Männern* – eine differenzierte Analyse der komplizierten Mechanismen in Gesprächen, deren wir uns zumeist kaum oder nur ganz vage bewußt werden. – In Kürze erscheint, herausgegeben von Senta *Trömel-Plötz*, die Aufsatzsammlung *Gewalt durch Sprache: Die Vergewaltigung von Frauen in Gesprächen*.

men *frau*, das ich in feministischen Texten nun allenthalben las, fand ich lustig, schön frech und aufsässig, aber nicht eigentlich wichtig – weil ich die Supermaskulinität von *man* auch nicht so wichtig fand. Denn die Linguistik, wie ich sie gelernt hatte, interessiert sich zwar dafür, was Ausdrücke bedeuten, aber nicht dafür, was es für Menschen subjektiv und objektiv bedeutet, daß Ausdrücke gerade das bedeuten, was sie bedeuten. Die herkömmliche Linguistik kritisiert Sprache nicht, sondern sie beschreibt sie. Und mit dem Beschreiben allein hat sie tatsächlich reichlich zu tun, denn Sprachen sind äußerst komplizierte Systeme, über die wir erst sehr wenig wissen.

Die Linguistik erlegt sich diese Selbstbeschränkung vermutlich auch deswegen auf, weil sie etwas vom Glanz der Naturwissenschaften erben möchte. Die Naturwissenschaften beschränken sich bekanntlich auf beschreibendes Erklären ihrer Gegenstände, da Kritik sinnlos ist. Sprache ist aber kein Natur-, sondern ein historisch-gesellschaftliches Phänomen und als solches auch kritisier- und veränderbar. Nach Auffassung von Feministinnen nicht nur kritisier**bar**, sondern extrem kritik**bedürftig** – und reformbedürftig.

Es bedurfte wohl radikalfeministischer Verve, Unbekümmertheit, Subjektivität und entschlossener Parteilichkeit, um zu dieser Auffassung über Sprache zu kommen. Sonst hätte sie sich kritikfähigen Frauen sicher schon eher aufgedrängt. Es ist aber nicht nur die herkömmliche Linguistik, die solche Gedanken nicht gerade fördert, sondern auch unser aller Alltagsbeziehung zu Sprache. Sprache wird uns im Kindesalter einverleibt etwa nach dem Motto: »Was auf den Tisch kommt, wird gegessen.« Zwar lernen wir, daß wir »schmutzige« Ausdrücke nicht verwenden und *mir* und *mich* nicht verwechseln sollen, aber daß wir **von uns aus** etwas Sprachliches rundheraus ablehnen könnten, wird uns weder beigebracht noch vorgemacht. Eine »natürliche« Ausnahme bilden die Eigennamen. Manche mögen bestimmte Namen einfach nicht leiden. Ich z. B. finde *Yvonne* »affig« und würde ungern so heißen (alle Yvonnen mögen mir verzeihen!). Aber es wäre mir von allein niemals eingefallen, gegen ein Pronomen *(man)*, eine Endung *(-in)* oder gegen ein Genus (Maskulinum) zu rebellieren. Dergleichen sprachliche Einheiten sind für die meisten so abstrakt und außerbewußt, daß sie dafür überhaupt keine Gefühle, weder positive noch negative, entwickeln können.

Jedenfalls galt das bis vor kurzem für die meisten Frauen. Männer dagegen waren schon immer emotionaler. Es gibt für sie **einen** allergischen Punkt in der Sprache: das Femininum. Wird ein Mann als Verkäuferin, Hausfrau, Fachfrau, Beamtin, Ärztin, Dame, Deutsche, Inhaberin o. ä. bezeichnet, so bringt ihn das völlig aus der Fassung. Es ist ihm etwa so gräßlich, wie wenn er mit Vornamen *Rosa* hieße oder neckisch in den Po gekniffen würde.

Die Folge der männlichen Allergie gegen das Femininum ist dessen nahezu vollständige Verdrängung aus der Sprache, mit anderen Worten: die sprachliche Vernichtung der Frau, denn ihre genuine sprachliche Existenzform ist das Femininum. Es fängt scheinbar harmlos an: Wenn Ute Schülerin ist und Uwe Schüler, dann sind Ute und Uwe Schüler, nicht Schülerinnen – denn Uwe verträgt das Femininum nicht. Es geht und geht nicht an, ihn mit der Bezeichnung »Schülerin« zu kränken, selbst wenn -zig Schülerinnen seinetwegen zu Schülern werden müssen. Da bereits **ein** Knabe mittels seiner Allergie beliebig viele Mädchen sprachlich ausschalten kann, kann frau sich leicht ausrechnen, was die männliche Hälfte der Bevölkerung gegen die weibliche ausrichten kann. Ein Wunder, daß wir überhaupt noch hin und wieder einem Femininum begegnen. (Für Besserwisser: Ich beziehe mich selbstverständlich auf feminine Personenbezeichnungen und nicht auf Feminina wie *die Neutronenbombe*.)

Unerbittliche Empfindlinge sind die schlimmsten Tyrannen, besonders gegen Rücksichtsvolle. Feministinnen haben das klar erkannt, die Rücksichtnahme aufgekündigt und eine Großaktion »Rettet das Femininum« gestartet. Wie läßt es sich am besten retten, wiederbeleben und weithin verbreiten? Natürlich durch eine gezielte Allergie gegen das Maskulinum.

Die Rettungsaktion hat seit Mitte der siebziger Jahre schon erstaunliche Erfolge gezeitigt. Immer mehr Frauen schlossen sich ihr an und lehnten es kategorisch ab, sich selbst und andere Frauen mit einem Maskulinum zu bezeichnen oder bezeichnen zu lassen. Die geistig und emotional weniger motivierte und agile Umwelt reagierte auf ihre unerhörten Thesen und eigenwilligen Neuerungen mit Überraschung, Belustigung, Spott, Befremden, Abwehr oder Ignorierung – je nach Temperament.

Ich reagierte mit einer Mischung aus Sympathie und Befremden – letzteres hauptsächlich berufsbedingt.

Meine – wie ich jetzt finde, reichlich späte – Bekehrung von der

Sympathisantin zur Aktiven gelang schließlich einem Kollegen namens Kalverkämper. Eigentlich hatte er den irregeleiteten Frauen den rechten Weg weisen wollen. Aber nicht jedermann ist zum Wegweiser berufen, zumal in Zeiten, da jedefrau sich ihren Weg lieber selbst sucht. Mich jedenfalls führten seine Belehrungen stracks in die entgegengesetzte Richtung. Ich schrieb eine Antwort auf seine Mahnschrift, und im Zuge dieser ersten intensiven gedanklichen Auseinandersetzung mit den feministisch-linguistischen Standpunkten erkannte ich, **wie** brisant und intellektuell faszinierend das neue Gebiet ist.

Das ist jetzt, im September 1983, vier Jahre her. In diesen vier Jahren habe ich mit meiner feministisch-linguistischen Forschung meinen Fachkollegen zwar anscheinend nicht viel Freude und meiner Disziplin keine Ehre gemacht, aber ich habe mich mit meiner Arbeit wohler gefühlt und besser identifizieren können als je zuvor. Außerdem freut es mich natürlich, daß meine Artikel neuerdings von mehr als fünf Personen gelesen werden.

»Je wichtiger ein Gegenstand ist, um so lustiger muß man ihn behandeln«, sagt Heine. Er muß es ja wissen als Außenseiter von Geburt.

Aufsätze

Von Menschen und Frauen

Wer ja sagt zur Familie,
muß auch ja sagen zur Frau.
Helmut Kohl, 1983

1 Meditation über ein Kanzlerwort

»Wer A sagt, muß auch B sagen«, so lautet ein deutsches Sprich-
wort. Mir wurde es zum erstenmal entgegengehalten, als ich lieber
spielen wollte als auf meine kleine Schwester aufpassen. Hatte ich
mir nicht ein Schwesterchen gewünscht? Nun, dann hatte ich ge-
fälligst auch die Unbequemlichkeiten in Kauf zu nehmen.

Unser Kanzler hat den deutschen Sprachschatz um eine bedeut-
same Variation dieses Sprichwortes bereichert. Aus dem dürren
»Wer A sagt...« machte er ein strahlendes »Wer ja sagt...« – aber
das harte Wort *muß* blieb!

Niemand wird freilich gezwungen, A zu sagen bzw. ja zur Familie. Erst wenn – freiwillig! – ja zur Familie gesagt wurde, muß auch
in den sauren Apfel B gebissen, das Ja zur Frau gesagt werden.

Mir als Frau will es allerdings nicht in den Kopf, daß das Ja zur
Frau vom Ja zur Familie abhängig ist wie das B-Sagen vom A-Sa-
gen. Sagen wir – als Menschen – nicht geradezu zwangsläufig ja
zum Menschen, egal ob wir zur Familie ja oder nein sagen? Wieso
braucht es überhaupt neben dem unbedingten Ja zum Menschen
noch ein bedingtes Ja zur Frau?

Ich muß den Kanzler mißverstanden haben. Vielleicht meint er
mit *Frau* nicht die Frau im allgemeinen, sondern die Ehefrau.

Also nochmal: »Wer ja sagt zu seiner Familie, muß auch ja sagen
zu seiner Frau.« – Ich hänge an meinen Eltern und Geschwistern.
Doch, ich sage ja zu meiner Familie. Aber nicht zu meiner Ehefrau,
denn ich habe keine.

Das also kann der Kanzler auch nicht gemeint haben.

Es bleibt nur ein Schluß: Der Kanzler hat nicht zum Volk gesprochen, sondern zu sich selbst. Er hat sich ermahnt, ja auch zu seiner
Frau zu sagen, weil er ja zum Rest seiner Familie sagt.

Das ist schön von ihm, aber hätte er sich nicht etwas präziser ausdrücken können? Etwa so: »Wenn ich ja zu meiner Familie sage,
muß ich auch ja zu meiner Frau sagen.« Auch diese Version ist noch

eigentümlich, weil das Ja zu seiner Familie nach gängiger Logik seine Frau einschließt – aber trotzdem: damit wäre mir schon viel Grübeln erspart geblieben.

Aber möglicherweise klang ihm das zu privat, nicht staatsmännisch genug. Was er sich selbst zurief, wollte er als Landesvater zugleich allen Landeskindern zurufen. Nur hat er dabei vergessen, daß nicht alle Landeskinder, die ja zur Familie sagen, auch ja zu ihrer Frau sagen können, weil nämlich viele keine haben. Frauen haben keine Frau, Kinder haben keine, unverheiratete Männer haben keine.

Das sind schätzungsweise 70 bis 80 Prozent der Bevölkerung, die er da vergessen hat. Wie konnte das geschehen?

2 Der Mensch in seinem Widerspruch

Helmut Kohl hat überhaupt nicht 70 bis 80 Prozent vergessen, sondern nur etwa 15 Prozent: die männlichen Kinder und die unverheirateten Männer. Die restlichen ca. 53 Prozent sind Mädchen und Frauen, und die hat er nicht vergessen, sondern nicht mitgerechnet.

Mit »Wer ja sagt zur Familie« sind nicht Tiere oder Gegenstände gemeint, sondern Menschen. Nur Menschen können ja sagen. Und alle Menschen, die ja sagen zur Familie, sind gemeint.

Was nun die Frauen betrifft, so steht bis heute nicht eindeutig fest, ob sie Menschen sind. Bekanntlich stehen in der Bibel zwei verschiedene Schöpfungsberichte, und ausgerechnet in diesem zentralen Punkt, ob die Frau nun ein Mensch sei oder nicht, widersprechen sie sich und lassen uns mit dem Widerspruch allein in alle Ewigkeit.

In Genesis 1.27 heißt es: »Und Gott schuf den Menschen ihm zum Bilde, zum Bilde Gottes schuf er ihn; und schuf sie einen Mann und ein Weib.« Schuf Gott nun einen oder zwei Menschen? Die Stelle ist sprachlich etwas seltsam.

In Genesis 2 ist nur von **einem** Menschen die Rede, von **dem** Menschen:

Vers 7: Und Gott der Herr machte den Menschen aus einem Erdenkloß, und er blies ihm ein den lebendigen Odem in seine Nase. Und also ward der Mensch eine lebendige Seele.

Vers 8: Und Gott der Herr pflanzte einen Garten in Eden gegen Morgen und setzte den Menschen hinein, den er gemacht hatte.

Vers 16: Und Gott der Herr gebot dem Menschen und sprach...

Vers 18: Und Gott der Herr sprach: Es ist nicht gut, daß der Mensch allein sei; ich will ihm eine Gehilfin machen, die um ihn sei.

Vers 22: Und Gott der Herr baute ein Weib aus der Rippe, die er von dem Menschen nahm, und brachte sie zu ihm.

Vers 23: Da sprach der Mensch: Das ist doch Bein von meinem Bein und Fleisch von meinem Fleisch; man wird sie Männin heißen, darum daß sie vom Manne genommen ist.

Das Wort *Mensch* (hebr. *adam*) hat also in der Bibel zwei Bedeutungen. Aus Genesis 1.27 folgt, daß Männer und Frauen Menschen sind. Beide zusammen sind Ebenbild Gottes.

Aus Genesis 2 folgt dagegen, daß der Mensch ein Mann ist und daß es neben dem Menschen als seine Gehilfin noch »das Weib« bzw. »die Männin« gibt. Ihr blies Gott keinen lebendigen Odem in die Nase. Ob sie also wie der Mensch eine lebendige Seele ist, muß bezweifelt werden. Aber »menschlich« darf sie wohl genannt werden, denn sie ist ja Fleisch vom Fleische des Menschen, und wir unterscheiden ja auch sonst streng zwischen menschlichen und tierischen Produkten.

Vom Menschen in Genesis 2 wird übrigens nicht gesagt, daß er das Ebenbild Gottes ist.

Der Widerspruch zwischen Genesis 1 und 2 ist unauflöslich, und die Folge davon ist: Unklarheit, Unsicherheit über den Status der Frau, und zwar in Permanenz, von den Anfängen bis heute.

Ein ungeheuer diffiziles Problem, auch sprachlich: Als Tier oder Pflanze kann die Frau nicht eingestuft werden, denn die Bibel sagt ja klipp und klar, sie sei ein Mensch. Als Mensch kann sie aber auch nicht eingestuft werden, denn die Bibel sagt ebenso klipp und klar und wiederholt es nachdrücklich: Der Mensch ist der Mann.

Die sprachliche Lösung, die für dieses Problem gefunden wurde, kann nicht anders als genial bezeichnet werden.

Eine global und seit Urzeiten gültige Sprachregelung sorgt dafür, daß die Bezeichnungen für die Bestimmt-Menschen (Männer) wahlweise die Vielleicht-Menschen (Frauen) einschließen können.

Wir empfinden das zwar durch die lange Gewohnheit als selbstverständlich oder banal, keineswegs als »genial« – es ist aber trotzdem einzigartig und auch die einzige Möglichkeit, mit dem uns auferlegten Widerspruch zu leben, ihn lebendig zu erhalten, statt ihn eigenmächtig zu leugnen oder wegzudefinieren, wie wir es sonst so gern mit Widersprüchen tun. Wir hätten ja, in dem verständlichen Streben nach Widerspruchsfreiheit, einfach einseitig beschließen können, daß der Begriff ›Mensch‹ auf Frauen zutrifft oder aber nicht zutrifft, ähnlich wie wir die Männer immer ein- und die Tiere immer ausschließen und dort kein Kuddelmuddel dulden. Sätze über Menschen, die Männer aus- oder Tiere einschließen, lehnen wir als abweichend oder unsinnig strikt ab:

? Alle Menschen werden Schwestern.
? Mit der Geschlechtsreife wird der Mensch gebärfähig.
? Die Deutschen sind tüchtige Hausfrauen.
? Manche Menschen gebären lebende Junge, andere legen Eier.
? Die Menschen bewegen sich auf zwei oder vier Beinen oder mit
   Hilfe von Floßen oder Flügeln fort.

Anders bei den Frauen. Sie können entweder ein- oder ausgeschlossen werden. Beides ist recht:

Alle Menschen werden Brüder.
Die Portugiesen behandeln Frauen schlecht.
Die Deutschen sind tüchtige Soldaten.
Ein Mensch ohne Frau ist überhaupt kein Mensch.
Die Menschen unterscheiden sich von den Tieren durch ihre
Sprachfähigkeit.
Beim Menschen spricht man nicht von »Männchen und Weibchen«, sondern von »Mann und Frau«.

Im »Lied der Deutschen« von Hoffmann von Fallersleben, das wir »Deutschlandlied« nennen, heißt es in der zweiten Strophe:

Deutsche Frauen, deutsche Treue,
Deutscher Wein und deutscher Sang
Sollen in der Welt behalten
Ihren alten schönen Klang,
Uns zu edler Tat begeistern
Unser ganzes Leben lang:
Deutsche Frauen, deutsche Treue,
Deutscher Wein und deutscher Sang.

Ähnlich wie die Gehilfin des Menschen »menschlich« genannt werden darf, dürfen die Frauen der Deutschen »deutsch« genannt werden. Die Deutschen lassen sich von deutschen Frauen zu edler Tat begeistern. Auch deshalb sagen sie ja zur Frau, nicht nur weil sie ja zur Familie sagen, Herr Bundeskanzler!

Und weil das alles möglich, üblich und rechtens ist in unserer Sprache, sagen wir Frauen nein zu dieser Sprache.

1983

Der Mensch ist ein Gewohnheitstier,
doch weiter kommt man ohne ihr*

Eine Antwort auf Kalverkämpers Kritik an Trömel-Plötz'
Artikel über »Linguistik und Frauensprache«

Vorbemerkung 1984: Dieser (mein erster feministisch-linguistischer) Artikel hat, wie schon am Untertitel abzulesen, eine Vorgeschichte, die interessierte Leser-innen in der Fachzeitschrift *Linguistische Berichte* nachlesen können (*Trömel-Plötz* 1978 und *Kalverkämper* 1979; s. Bibliographie). Ich habe ihn jedoch bewußt so abgefaßt, daß er weitgehend auch ohne Kenntnis dieser Vorgeschichte, »aus sich heraus«, verständlich sein sollte.

Trömel-Plötz hatte 1978 in ihrem Beitrag die wichtigsten Positionen der Feministischen Linguistik vorgestellt. *Kalverkämper* fühlte sich dadurch aufgefordert, ihr und damit allen gleichgesinnten Linguist-inn-en zu erklären, was Linguistik wirklich ist und daß die Probleme, die wir diskutieren wollten, wenn nicht überhaupt Scheinprobleme, so doch mindestens keine linguistischen Probleme seien.

Wir hätten seinen Beitrag nachsichtig ignorieren können, hielten es aber strategisch für besser, nun unsererseits eine Kritik seiner

---

* Es ist immer etwas peinlich, witzig gemeinte Formulierungen bemüht zu erklären, aber es ist mir in dieser Sache wichtiger, verstanden zu werden, als Peinlichkeiten zu vermeiden. Also: Der Titel ist ein Versuch, die folgenden einschlägigen Gedanken und Assoziationen in einem griffigen Spruch zusammenzufassen:

   a) Assoziation an *Bescheidenheit ist eine Zier, doch weiter kommt man ohne ihr.* Aufruf an uns Frauen: Stellen wir weiter unsere »unbescheidenen« Forderungen an »das Sprachsystem«. Bescheidenheit gilt als spezifisch weibliche Tugend, doch wie der Spruch zu verstehen gibt, kommen wir damit nicht weit. Der Spruch verletzt, hier um des Reimes willen, kühn die Regeln der deutschen Grammatik. **Wir** haben noch wichtigere Gründe, uns einengende Regeln nach Bedarf zu ignorieren und neue aufzustellen.

   b) *Der Mensch* ist ein Fall eines generisch verwendeten maskulinen Nomens – einer der Hauptgegenstände in der Argumentation von *Trömel-Plötz* und der Kritik von *Kalverkämper.*

   c) *Der Mensch ist ein Gewohnheitstier* – auch in »seinem« Umgang mit »der Sprache«. Anspielung auf den Gemeinplatz, daß Sprache auf Konvention beruht. (Vgl. hierzu *Lewis* 1969.)

   d) Der Mensch (mask., generisch verwendet, Unterbegriff) mag ein Gewohnheitstier (neutr., Oberbegriff) sein – aber deswegen ist eine Kundin noch lange kein Kunde.

Darstellung zu publizieren, da das Gesamtgebiet »Feministische Linguistik« damals in der Bundesrepublik noch jung und relativ unbekannt war und vielen gezielten, in der Regel jedoch nur mündlich kursierenden Mißeinschätzungen seitens männlicher Kollegen ausgesetzt war.

1 Einleitung: Wie Kund' und Katze[1]

Man[2] stelle sich folgendes vor: Herr Kalverkämper kommt in ein Geschäft. Auf seiner Schulter sitzt eine Katze (weiblich). Der Verkäufer sagt zu ihm: »Sie sind heute schon die dritte Kundin mit einem Kater.«

Was ist passiert? Ein Ereignis, das man (mindestens) auf zweierlei Weise analysieren kann – linguistisch und sozialpsychologisch.

A. Linguistische Analyse

Der Verkäufer macht zwei Fehler, die linguistisch gesehen demselben Typ angehören:

1. Fehler: Er referiert auf ein Individuum männlichen Geschlechts (Herrn Kalverkämper) mit einem femininen Gattungsnomen *(Kundin)*, obwohl für dieses Individuum ein geschlechtsspezifisches maskulines Gattungsnomen *(Kunde)* und ein geschlechtsneutrales, ebenfalls maskulines Archilexem *(Kunde)* zur Verfügung stehen:

e) *... ein Gewohnheitstier, doch weiter kommt man ohne ihr* – nämlich ohne die Gewohnheit. Hier werden (natürlich wieder zu höherem Zwecke!) zwei Grammatikregeln verletzt: Erstens die schon oben unter (a) erwähnte, zweitens die Regel, die es verbietet, sich mit einem anaphorischen Element auf ein Antezedens zu beziehen, das Teil einer »anaphorischen Insel« (»anaphoric island«) im Sinne von *Postal* 1969 ist. *Gewohnheit* ist hier Teil der anaphorischen Insel *Gewohnheitstier*.

f) *... weiter kommt man ohne ihr:*
1. (je nach Geschlecht zynische oder betrübte) Lesart: »Weiter kommt mann ohne frau«
2. (hoffnungsvolle, kooperative) Lesart: »Weiter kommt man ohne Gewohnheit«. Soll heißen: Frauen und Männer können zufriedener werden, wenn sie frauenignorierende Sprachkonventionen aufdecken und sinnvoll abändern.

Für Teilnahme, Kritik, Anregungen und Unterstützung im Zusammenhang mit dieser Arbeit ein herzliches Dankeschön an: Traudel Barobier, Hilde und Rolf Fieguth, Lily von Hartmann, Maria-Theresia Jung, Ursula Klein, Mike Roth, Christine und Christoph Schwarze, Arnim von Stechow, Senta Trömel-Plötz, Maurice Vliegen und Ursula Zumbühl.

```
                der Kunde
        der Kunde        die Kundin
```

(Die Grafik übernehme ich von *Kalverkämper* (59).)

2. Fehler: Er referiert auf ein Individuum weiblichen Geschlechts (die Katze) mit einem maskulinen Gattungsnomen *(Kater)*, obwohl für dieses Individuum ein geschlechtsspezifisches feminines Gattungsnomen *(Katze)* und ein geschlechtsneutrales, ebenfalls feminines Archilexem *(Katze)* zur Verfügung stehen:

```
                die Katze
        die Katze        der Kater
```

Linguistisch gesehen hat Herr Kalverkämper also keinen Grund, sich gegenüber der Katze benachteiligt zu fühlen. Mit anderen Worten: Wenn der Katze kein Unrecht geschah oder nur geringfügiges, so geschah auch Herrn Kalverkämper kein oder nur geringfügiges Unrecht.

B. Sozialpsychologische Analyse

Der Verkäufer begeht einen schweren Fehler (d. h. er verletzt eine Grundregel sozialen Verhaltens) und einen geringfügigen, den man als Skurrilität einstufen kann.

1. Fehler: Er identifiziert einen Mann als Frau. Herr Kalverkämper, der korrekt gekleidet ist, kann daraus nur schließen, daß der Verkäufer entweder verrückt ist oder ihn auf den Arm nehmen will.

2. Fehler: Der Verkäufer identifiziert eine Katze als Kater. Die Katze merkt es nicht. Herrn Kalverkämper wird die Fehlidentifikation relativ gleichgültig sein. Er wird sich vielleicht wundern und den Verkäufer fragen: »Wie kommen Sie darauf, daß es ein Kater sein soll?«

Fazit: Ob eine Fehlidentifikation einen sozialen Verstoß darstellt oder nicht, hängt nicht notwendig von den sprachlichen Mitteln ab, mit denen sie durchgeführt wird. Es hängt davon ab, welches Bewußtsein das fehlidentifizierte Individuum von seiner Identität hat. Da die Katze kein Bewußtsein ihrer Identität hat[3], ist sie auf diesem Gebiet sozusagen nicht »beleidigungsfähig«, Herr Kalverkämper hingegen sehr wohl.

Die »Normalform« dieser Anekdote hätte so ausgesehen, daß eine Kundin den Laden mit einem Kater betritt und der Verkäufer sagt: »Sie sind heute schon der dritte Kunde mit einer Katze.« Der Kater hätte nichts gemerkt. Nicht einmal Kater Murr hätte etwas zu murren gehabt; er mußte sich lange schon daran gewöhnen, unter dem Archilexem *Katze* subsumiert zu werden. Und die Kundin? Sie hat vermutlich die Ohren schon so voll Männersprache, daß sie fast ertaubt ist und die Sache ganz normal findet. Handelt es sich aber unwahrscheinlicherweise um eine Frau mit einem noch oder wieder hörfähigen Ohr für sprachliche Diskriminierungen, so stehen ihr zwei Wege offen: Sie kann schweigen und etwa so überlegen: »Nun ja, ich bin zwar eine Frau, also ein Kundin, aber die beiden anderen werden wohl Männer gewesen sein, und der Verkäufer wußte sich anscheinend nicht besser zu helfen. Schwamm drüber – nicht der Verkäufer ist frauenfeindlich, sondern die Sprache.« Sie kann aber auch den Verkäufer zur Rede stellen und sagen: »Wieso Kunde? Sehe ich vielleicht aus wie ein Mann, oder was wollten Sie damit sagen? Als Verkäuferin sind Sie eine Niete, Verehrteste!« Der Verkäufer wird es nun schwer haben, falls er nicht zufällig linguistisch gebildet ist und den persönlichen Vorwurf geschickt auf »die Sprache« abwälzen kann (diese Strategie ist bei Linguisten – Kalverkämper eingeschlossen – sehr beliebt, die mit dem Thema »Frauensprache« konfrontiert werden). Wie dem auch sei – in keinem Fall aber hätte die Frau einen Anlaß, den Verkäufer für verrückt zu halten, also den Weg zu beschreiten, der Herrn Kalverkämper für seine Identitätssicherung breit offenstand. Dafür sorgen die Besonderheiten unseres deutschen Sprachsystems, mit denen *Trömel-Plötz* sich auseinandersetzt.

2 Wahrgenommenwerden, Beachtetwerden, Identifiziertwerden und Gemeintsein

Herr Kalverkämper und die Katze wurden in dem obigen Sketch von dem Verkäufer zwar fehlidentifiziert, aber immerhin wahrgenommen. In Vis-à-vis-Situationen ist Wahrgenommenwerden die Voraussetzung dafür, daß man (richtig oder falsch) identifiziert wird.

23

Es ist für alle Menschen existentiell wichtig, von anderen Menschen wahrgenommen, beachtet und in ihrer Identität bestätigt zu werden. Das wissen wir alle aus Erfahrung: Wir sind irritiert bis verletzt, wenn wir von Leuten, die uns persönlich kennen, mit falschem Namen angesprochen werden (Fehlidentifikation); wir vertragen es nicht, wenn man im Krankenhaus von uns als »dem Magengeschwür auf Zimmer 217« spricht; wir erleben oft den berechtigten Zorn und/oder die Verzweiflung von Kindern, die von Erwachsenen nicht wahrgenommen werden und nun mit allen Mitteln versuchen, auf sich aufmerksam zu machen, oft sogar nach der Devise: »Besser unangenehm als gar nicht auffallen.« Politisch machtlose und deshalb nicht wahrgenommene Gruppen greifen nach derselben Devise in letzter Zeit immer häufiger zum Terror.

Diese Alltagserfahrungen und -eindrücke werden von sehr unterschiedlichen Wissenschaftszweigen aufgearbeitet, bestätigt und theoretisch erklärt, am eindrucksvollsten vielleicht von der modernen Schizophrenieforschung (*Laing* u. a.), der Kommunikationstheorie (*Watzlawick* u. a.), der psychoanalytischen Narzißmustheorie (*Kohut, Miller* u. a.), der Hospitalismusforschung (*Spitz* u. a.), der psychoanalytischen Aggressionsforschung (*Fromm* u. a.) und von der sozialpsychologischen Identitätstheorie und -forschung in der Nachfolge von *G. H. Mead*. Die Sozialpsychologie unterscheidet mit und seit *Mead* 1934 zwischen dem spontanen Teil des Selbst (»I«) und dem sozialisierten Teil des Selbst (»Me«). Den sozialisierten Teil des Selbst nennt man auch Identität. Identität ist das Ergebnis eines Zusammenwirkens von Identifizierungen durch andere und Selbstidentifikation (Aneignung der Identifizierungen). Herr Kalverkämper ist zeit seines Lebens als »Mensch« und als »männliches Wesen« identifiziert worden, seit einiger Zeit auch als »Wissenschaftler« und »Linguist«. Infolgedessen wird er sich auch selbst so identifizieren, machen diese Identitäten zusammen mit noch anderen nun seine Gesamtidentität aus. Wird die Identität »männliches Wesen« von einem Verkäufer zufällig einmal nicht bestätigt, so wird das Herrn Kalverkämper nicht weiter erschüttern, es wird nicht zu einer Identitätskrise führen.

Identifiziertwerden ist also die Voraussetzung zur Gewinnung einer Identität, die wiederum die Voraussetzung für psychisches, soziales, wenn nicht sogar biologisches Überleben ist (vgl. *Durkheims* Studie über Anomie und Selbstmord (1897)). Bestätigung der Identität durch andere (Richtig-Identifiziertwerden) ist notwendig zur Bewahrung und Aufrechterhaltung dieser Identität. Frauen befanden und befinden sich aber häufig in der schizophrenogenen Lage, daß ihnen sogar die Identität »menschliches Wesen« nicht bestätigt wurde oder wird (von anderen Teilen ihrer jeweiligen Gesamtidentität zu schweigen) – einfach deswegen, weil sie als Mitglieder der Spezies Mensch und anderer Gruppen, denen sie faktisch angehören, nicht wahrgenommen werden. Ich bringe zunächst zwei Beispiele.

Erstes Beispiel: Mit dem *du (sollst deinen Vater und deine Mutter ehren, nicht töten, nicht stehlen, nicht ehebrechen,* etc.) der Zehn Gebote soll sich die ganze Menschheit angesprochen fühlen, so lehrt uns die Kirche. Doch beim zehnten Gebot dann, *Du sollst nicht begehren deines Nächsten Weib* etc., muß frau schließen, daß sie mit dem *du* nicht gemeint ist (es sein denn, sie ist lesbisch), daß sie somit wahrscheinlich auch in den anderen Geboten nicht gemeint war und daß sie folglich als Mensch überhaupt nicht wahrgenommen wurde, wohl aber als Besitz des Menschen = Mannes – auf einer Stufe mit seinem Haus, Acker und Vieh.

Zweites Beispiel: Ich gehe ins Büromateriallager der Universität Konstanz. Auf dem Weg dorthin werde ich von vielen wahrgenommen, mit freundlichem Gruß beachtet, mit freundlicher Anrede identifiziert. Dann aber erblicke ich in der Materialausgabe folgende Vordrucke:

Universität Konstanz   775 Konstanz, den

Sehr geehrter
Dear

Ich bedauere, daß von dem von Ihnen gewünschten Artikel
I regret that reprints of the article you requested

keine Sonderdrucke mehr zur Verfügung stehen.
are no longer available.

Mit den besten Grüßen
Sincerely yours

Universität Konstanz   775 Konstanz, den

Sehr geehrter Herr
Dear Sir
Monsieur

Für die freundliche Übersendung eines Sonderdruckes Ihrer
Arbeit:
I would greatly appreciate receiving a reprint of your article:
Je vous serais très obligé, si vous vouliez bien m'envoyer un
tirage à part de votre article intitulé:

wäre ich Ihnen sehr zu Dank verpflichtet. Mit den besten Grüßen
Yours sincerely
Avec nos remerciements et l'expression de nos sentiments les
meilleurs

Wer auch immer diese beiden Texte ersonnen und ihre tausendfache Vervielfältigung angeordnet haben mag, er/sie hat die Existenz forschender und publizierender Frauen in Konstanz und anderswo nicht wahrgenommen und damit diese Frauen selbst ignoriert.[4] Ein wesentlicher Teil meiner Identität (»forschendes Mitglied der Uni Konstanz«) wird hier von der Institution, der ich angehöre, nicht bestätigt (eindeutiges Indiz dafür ist das mask. *obligé* in dem zweiten Vordruck). Ich befinde mich damit in einer ähnlich paradoxen Lage wie Herr Kalverkämper in meiner Einleitungsanekdote. Die Anekdote war aber frei erfunden und total absurd. Mein Erlebnis ist weder erfunden noch absurd; es ist vielmehr typisch und steht hier für viele derselben Art, von denen ich seitenlang berichten könnte. Und die Vordrucke betreffen und treffen mit ihrem durch die Mehrsprachigkeit als international definierten Adressatenkreis nicht nur ein Einzelindividuum, sondern alle Frauen in meiner Berufssituation. Wir alle werden durch derartige Akte des Ignorierens permanent in unserer Identität beschädigt, denn wir können nicht den an sich zwingenden Schluß ziehen, daß die Institutionen verrückt sind – ihr Verhalten ist ja so schrecklich »normal« und alltäglich.

Was hat das alles nun mit Sprache zu tun? Sehr viel. Das deutsche

Sprachsystem z. B. mit seinen im Bereich der Berufs- und sonstigen Personenbezeichnungen ausschließlich maskulinen »Archilexemen«[5] enthält, wie *Trömel-Plötz* ausführt, aufgrund seiner semantischen Struktur für Männer mehr Chancen des Gemeintseins und damit des Identifiziertwerdens als für Frauen. »Rein semantisch«, das bestätigt auch *Kalverkämper,* enthalten Sätze wie

Der/Ein Berliner ist schlagfertig.
(Die) Berliner sind schlagfertig.

wegen ihrer zwei Lesarten (»alle, die in Berlin wohnen«, »alle Männer, die in Berlin wohnen«) für Männer zwei Chancen des Gemeintseins und für Frauen eine. Gewichtet man nun noch das Ausschließlich-Gemeintsein als doppelte und das Mitgemeintsein als einfache Chance, so haben Männer dreimal so viel Chancen wie Frauen.

Man kann also unser deutsches Sprachsystem in diesem Bereich mit einer Lotterie vergleichen, in dem Männer mit jedem Los gewinnen (mit beiden Lesarten gemeint sind), Frauen aber nur mit jedem zweiten. Noch treffender ist vermutlich der gewichtende Vergleich mit einer Lotterie, bei der Männer mit der einen Hälfte der Lose doppelt gewinnen (nämlich auf Kosten der Frauen) und mit der anderen Hälfte einfach, Frauen hingegen bei der einen Hälfte der Lose leer ausgehen und bei der anderen nur eine einfache Gewinnchance haben.

Soweit die »rein linguistische« Seite dieses ungerechten Spiels. Es wird nun oft argumentiert, daß der Situations- oder sprachliche Kontext diese historisch gewachsene und objektiv gegebene, aber erst seit kurzem öffentlich diskutierte und wissenschaftlich beachtete Chancenungleichheit der Frau klar ausgleiche, kurz: daß wir Frauen doch selbstverständlich immer mitgemeint seien. Dazu ist gleich mehreres zu sagen:

1. Wie *Stanley* (1977) am Beispiel des englischen generisch gebrauchten *he* nachgewiesen hat, ist es im Gegenteil oft so, daß der Kontext, ähnlich wie der Kontext der Zehn Gebote, den Frauen klare Information liefert, daß sie keineswegs gemeint sind, also eine Niete in der Lotterie gezogen haben, eine Verletzung ihrer Identität hinnehmen müssen. Für das Deutsche habe ich das nicht näher untersucht, aber die folgenden, während einer einstündigen Lektüre gefundenen Belege stimmen mich nicht optimistischer als *Stanley:*

(1) Dennoch können wir, wenn wir beispielsweise *einen Menschen* in die obere Mittelklasse einordnen (ohne etwas anderes von *ihm* zu wissen und vielleicht, ohne *ihn* jemals gesehen zu haben), mit ziemlicher Sicherheit etwas über die Aufteilung *seines* Haushaltsgeldes aussagen, die Anzahl *seiner* Kinder erraten, die Lage *seiner* Wohnung und die Art und Weise, wie *er seine* Ferien verbringt. Das ist aber noch nicht alles. Wir können auch in vielen Punkten auf *seine* politische Einstellung schließen, wir vermuten *seine* Religionszugehörigkeit und die Art der Bücher, die *er* liest. Wir können sogar voraussagen, ob **er mit seiner Frau** bei Lampenlicht oder im Dunkeln Verkehr haben wird... (*Berger* und *Berger* 1976: 92).

(2) *Der Leser* stelle sich einmal die eigene Person als *Erneuerer* der Grammatik oder des Wortschatzes vor. Vielleicht kann *er* in *seiner* nächsten Umgebung, *seiner* Mikrowelt, manchmal bescheidenen Erfolg erzielen. Tatsächlich war *ihm* der wohl schon in *seiner* Kindheit beschieden. Die Familie hat vielleicht etwas von *seinem* kindlichen Kauderwelsch in die interne Familiensprache übernommen. Als *Erwachsener* kann man ähnliche Miniatursiege erringen, wenn man sich **mit seiner Frau** ... auf eine bestimmte Formulierung einigt (*Berger* und *Berger* 1976: 52).

(3) Und die Art des »Verstandes« oder des »Denkens«, die *dem Einzelnen* zur Gewohnheit gemacht wird, ist dementsprechend auch im Verhältnis zu *Menschen seiner* eigenen Gesellschaft so ähnlich und so verschieden wie die gesellschaftliche Lage, wie die Stellung im *Menschen*geflecht, in der *er* auf- und in die *er* hineinwächst, ähnlich und verschieden von anderen, wie *seine* und *seiner* Eltern und *seiner* wichtigsten *Modelleure* Funktion. Die Langsicht *des Buchdruckers* oder *des Maschinenschlossers* ist eine andere als die *des Buchhalters,* die *des Ingenieurs* eine andere als die *des Verkaufsdirektors,* die *des Finanzministers* verschieden von der *des Chefs der Heeresleitung*... (*Elias* 1969: 380).

(4) Interessanterweise scheint sich eine stillschweigende Übereinkunft in der populären Auffassung von Lebensgeschichten entwickelt zu haben, in denen ein fragwürdiges *Individuum* seinen Anspruch auf Normalität beweist, indem es seinen **Besitz von Frau und Kindern** anführt, und sonderbarerweise

auch, indem es glaubhaft macht, daß es Weihnachten und Thanksgiving mit ihnen verbringt (*Goffman* 1967 (1963): 16).

(5) Institutionen ... nehmen sich nicht nur das Recht, *einen Frevler* zu züchtigen, sondern auch, *ihn* moralisch zu maßregeln. Selbstverständlich gibt es von Institution zu Institution Gradunterschiede der moralischen Erhabenheit. Diese Unterschiede kommen gewöhnlich im Strafmaß, das *dem Frevler* auferlegt wird, zum Ausdruck. Der Staat als Institution kann *ihn* unter Umständen vernichten. Die Mitbewohner *seiner* Wohnsiedlung dagegen schneiden vielleicht nur **seine Frau** bei geselligen Veranstaltungen (*Berger* und *Berger* 1976: 52). (Hervorhebungen von mir.)

Solche Texte lesen sich für uns Frauen wie Krimis, spannend bis zur »Auflösung« des Falls. Doch, wir sind trotz der ständigen Maskulina und der fehlenden Feminina mitgemeint, so dürfen/müssen wir die ganze Zeit wähnen, denn auch wir haben ja Haushaltsgeld, Wohnung, Ferien, politische Einstellung, Religionszugehörigkeit, Umgebung, Mikrowelt, Kindheit, Verstand, Denken, Stellung im Menschengeflecht, Lebensgeschichten etc. etc. Aber all diese Identifikationsmöglichkeiten waren nur raffinierte Fallen, um die Schlußpointe »Frauen sind out« um so dramatischer auf uns wirken zu lassen.

Dieser Befund ist für Frauen in mehrfacher Hinsicht empörend, entmutigend oder belustigend – je nach Temperament, Ichstärke und Stimmungslage.

a) Wenn selbst eindeutig geschlechtsneutrale Ausdrücke wie *du* (Zehn Gebote), *Mensch* (Text 1 und 3) und *Individuum* (Text 4) ohne weiteres auf Männer allein referieren können, kann frau mit ziemlicher Sicherheit schließen, daß Ausdrücke wie *der Leser, der Erneuerer, der Erwachsene* (Text 2), *der Einzelne* (Text 3) und *der Frevler* (Text 5), die schon von ihrer Semantik her die Lesart »Männer allein« zulassen, erst recht auf Männer allein referieren werden (und in den Texten tun sie das ja auch). Die Semantik der letztgenannten Ausdrücke läßt die Lesart »Männer allein« deshalb zu, weil es die femininen Pendants *die Leserin/Erneuerin/Erwachsene/Einzelne/Frevlerin* gibt.

b) Belustigend und vielleicht sogar schmeichelhaft könnte frau es finden, daß auch nicht an sie gedacht wird, wenn von »fragwürdigen Individuen« (Text 4) und von »Frevlern« (Text 5) die Rede ist.

29

Da aber auch frau hin und wieder frevelt und sich fragwürdig verhält und dann auch die Folgen zu tragen hat, da ihr **dies** Ausgeschlossensein in der Praxis also keineswegs nützt, wird sie auch derartige Fälle als Symptome des generellen »geistigen Gynocids«[6] deuten müssen.

c) Bei den Produzenten der obigen Texte handelt es sich durchweg um Autoren mit eindeutig emanzipatorischen Absichten und Überzeugungen, die ganz entschieden Stellung gegen Diskriminierung von Schwarzen, Behinderten und anderen sozial benachteiligten Gruppen beziehen. Aber den besagten Gynocid begehen sie alle.

2. Weiter ist zu dem Argument, Frauen seien doch selbstverständlich immer mitgemeint, zu sagen: Ein Akt des Meinens ist, sofern er auf Personen zielt, ganz offenbar dann mißlungen, wenn diese Personen sich trotz aller guten Absichten der/des Meinenden nicht gemeint fühlen und dafür handfeste Gründe (Ambiguität, Kontext, Erfahrungswerte) angeben können. Sollen solche Meinens-Akte in Zukunft besser gelingen, müssen andere (also nicht ambige) Formulierungen gewählt werden etwa in der Art, wie *Trömel-Plötz* sie für das Deutsche vorschlägt und wie sie für das Englische schon seit 1972 in den von *Trömel-Plötz* angeführten *Guidelines* großer amerikanischer Verlage und Berufsorganisationen in aller Deutlichkeit und Detailliertheit vorgeschlagen oder vorgeschrieben werden. Wenn diese Vorschläge und Vorschriften befolgt werden, ist wenigstens linguistisch garantiert, daß das Meinen gelingen kann, daß Frauen sich wirklich angesprochen fühlen. Es gibt dann natürlich immer noch genug außersprachliche Faktoren (vor allem soziale und politische), die dem Gelingen entgegenstehen können – in dem Punkt sind *Kalverkämper*, *Trömel-Plötz* und ich uns wohl einig.

3 Zu *Kalverkämpers* Kritik im einzelnen

3.1 *Au weia!*

Gar herbe Kritik mußte sich meine Freundin und Kollegin da aber anhören! So harte Worte, daß ich mich als Sympathisantin und mitfühlender Mensch direkt selbst getroffen fühlte. »Unlinguistisch« (60) soll sie vorgegangen sein; sie redet »plakativ« (60), begeht

»Mißgriffe in der Argumentation« (60) und »Methodenfehler« (62); sie »läßt Grundprinzipien der ... Semantik und der Linguistik überhaupt außer acht« (62), leistet sich eine »unzulässige Verwechslung von Sexus und Genus« (62, 68), ihre Argumentation ist »willkürlich« (62, 68), und schließlich ist sie auch noch »agitatorisch« (67) und wissenschaftlich unredlich (62,68). Schlimm, schlimm!

Und nun wollen wir uns mal ansehen, was an diesen vernichtenden Vorwürfen dran ist.

3.2 Unlinguistisch?

»Unlinguistisch« nennt *Kalverkämper* die Kritik von *Trömel-Plötz* an unserem überkommenen Sprachsystem, weil sie die Arbitrarität des sprachlichen Zeichens mißachte. »Unlinguistisch« ist folglich auch, da sie von denselben Prinzipien und ähnlichen Beobachtungen ausgeht und dieselben Ziele verfolgt, die gesamte von Linguistinnen und Linguisten geleistete neuere Forschung zum Thema Sexismus und Sprache, die inzwischen eine kleine Bibliothek füllt.

Ich wünschte, ich wüßte so genau wie anscheinend *Kalverkämper*, was linguistisch ist und was nicht. Sprache hat so viele Eigenschaften und Funktionen, daß mir der pluralistische Ansatz zu ihrer Erforschung der einzig angemessene scheint. Die Sozio-, Psycho- und Ethnologie interessiert sich mit Recht für Sprache, und daher gibt es die Sozio-, Psycho- und Ethnolinguistik – Disziplinen, von deren Forschungsergebnissen die »reine Linguistik« nur profitieren kann. Vielleicht bekommen wir demnächst noch Astro-, Bio-, Etho-[7], Geo- und Theolinguistik hinzu – ich wäre gespannt, was sie mir Neues zu sagen hätten. Eine feministische Linguistik aber haben wir offenbar schon seit einiger Zeit (grob: seit 1970). Sie scheint kräftig zu gedeihen und sich nicht darum zu scheren, daß *Kalverkämper* sie »unlinguistisch« schilt. Ob er es weiß oder nicht: Sie nimmt bei großen amerikanischen Linguistikkongressen einen immer breiteren Raum ein (vgl. *Trömel-Plötz* 1979).

Was nun das ehrwürdige Dogma von der Arbitrarität des sprachlichen Zeichens betrifft, so wurde ich schon als Kind eines Besseren belehrt, als mann mir erklärte, Herren seien herrlich und Damen dämlich. Damals hätte ich das Dogma gern parat gehabt, um mich zu wehren.

De Saussure, der Vater des Dogmas, ist übrigens viel weniger dogmatisch als *Kalverkämper.* Er sagt folgendes:

> Das Band, welches das Bezeichnete mit der Bezeichnung verknüpft, ist beliebig; [. . .] So ist die Vorstellung »Schwester«[8] durch keinerlei innere Beziehung mit der Lautfolge *Schwester* verbunden, die ihr als Bezeichnung dient; sie könnte ebensowohl dargestellt sein durch irgendeine andere Lautfolge. [. . .] das Bezeichnete »Ochs« hat auf dieser Seite der Grenze als Bezeichnung *o-k-s,* auf jener Seite *b-ö-f* (bœuf). (79)

An diesen Feststellungen habe auch ich bis vor kurzem nicht gezweifelt (sie berühren im übrigen das, was *Trömel-Plötz* und die gesamte feministische Linguistik will, überhaupt nicht, wie ich weiter unten zeigen werde). Aber im Juni 1979 habe ich zwei interessante Vorträge von *J. R. Ross* gehört: »Grenzen der Arbitrarität des sprachlichen Zeichens« und »Le signe n'est pas arbitraire«. Auf den Befunden von *Cooper* und *Ross* 1975 aufbauend, hat *Ross* (auch ein »Unlinguist«?) da, mit streng linguistischen Mitteln, ganz andere Ergebnisse als *de Saussure* zutage gefördert. Nach seinen Untersuchungen scheint etwa die Vorstellung »ich« nicht ohne Grund gerade durch die Lautfolge *ich* bezeichnet zu werden. Der Trick bei *Ross'* Überlegungen ist, daß er *ich* nicht mit *I, je, io, jeg, ego* etc. vergleicht, sondern mit *du, I* mit *you* und so fort. *Ross* geht sogar so weit, einen »Sounder« im menschlichen Sprachzentrum zu postulieren, der unsere Kernvorstellungen in die »richtigen, passenden« Laute umsetzt.

Wie also neueste (wohlgemerkt: linguistische!) Forschungen ergeben haben, ist unser Dogma von der Arbitrarität des Zeichens anscheinend revisionsbedürftig. Einer Arbeit, die es »mißachtet«, kann also die Mißachtung nicht mehr gut als unlinguistisch angekreidet werden – eher erweist sich der Tadel als Bumerang.

Außerdem hat weder *Trömel-Plötz* noch sonst eine feministische Sprachkritikerin gegen das Dogma in der obigen Minimalformulierung unlinguistisch aufbegehrt. Keine Frau hat etwa gequengelt, sie wolle lieber, sagen wir, mit *Glau* bezeichnet und angesprochen werden, weil ihr die Lautfolge *Frau* nun mal nicht zusage.

Was die Feminist/inn/en am Sprachsystem beschäftigt, sind im wesentlichen

a) Referenzprobleme, die m. W. vorher weder von *de Saussure* noch von der Referenzsemantik überhaupt gesehen wurden. **Diese**

Probleme vor allem diskutiert *Trömel-Plötz* im Abschnitt II (»Frauen und das Sprachsystem«) ihres Artikels.

b) »Assoziationsreihen« *(de Saussure)*, paradigmatische Beziehungen zwischen Zeichen also – Beziehungen, hinsichtlich derer *de Saussure* selbst das Zeichen nicht mehr als »arbiträr, beliebig, unmotiviert«, sondern als »relativ motiviert« einstuft:

> Nur ein Teil der Zeichen ist völlig beliebig; . . . **das Zeichen kann relativ motiviert sein.**
> So ist *elf* unmotiviert, aber *dreizehn* ist es nicht im selben Grade, weil es an die Glieder denken läßt, aus denen es zusammengesetzt ist, und an andere, die mit ihm assoziiert sind, z. B. *drei, zehn, vier-zehn, drei-und-zwanzig* usw. (156)

Schäfer und *Dichter* sind laut *de Saussure* »relativ motivierte« Zeichen, weil sie »die einfachen Wörter *Schaf, dichten* ins Gedächtnis rufen«, *Käfer* und *Trichter* dagegen sind »unmotiviert« (156f). Was rufen nun die Maskulina *man* und *jedermann* den Frauen ins Gedächtnis? Richtig – das Wort *Mann*, und es gibt inzwischen zahllose Texte und Kontexte, in denen diese Assoziation störend bis widersinnig wirken muß. In solchen Kontexten verwendet frau deshalb lieber und sinniger *frau* und *jedefrau*.

Mir ist nur ein einziger Fall bekannt, wo Frauen ein (vermutlich, s. o. *Ross*) echt unmotiviertes Zeichen kritisiert haben – aufgrund einer linguistisch »falschen« Assoziationsreihe (Paradigmabildung). Es ist der Fall des Wortes *history*, das einige in *herstory* umbenannt wissen wollten, was denn auch von *R. Lakoff* 1973 als Verirrung kritisiert wurde (ich find's eher lustig).

»Falsche« Assoziationsreihen liegen den meisten Wortspielen zugrunde (vgl. *Gynocid)*, vom Kalauer bis zur hochpoetischen, Worte und Begriffe »verdichtenden« Metapher. Apropos Kalauer: Genauso kreativ wie der traditionelle männliche Chauvinismus (ich erinnere an die »herrlichen Herren« und »dämlichen Damen«) ist der neue Antifeminismus. Die letzten Schöpfungen, die mir zu Ohren gekommen sind, lauten *Gebärvater* und *manche und frauche*. Da die Sprache nicht von Linguist/inn/en, sondern von »Laien« »gemacht« wird, müssen wir nun abwarten, welche dieser Kreationen sich durchsetzen. Wenn ich die Lage richtig beurteile, haben *herstory, frau* und *Gynocid* bessere Chancen als *Gebärvater* und *manche und frauche*.

Laut *Kalverkämper* »krankt die von Frau *Trömel-Plötz* vorgelegte Fragestellung in ihrem Vorgehen und Ergebnis daran..., daß Grundprinzipien der struktural-funktionalen Semantik und damit der Linguistik überhaupt außer acht geblieben sind« (62). Zu diesen Grundprinzipien gehören für ihn neben dem soeben abgehandelten Dogma von der Arbitrarität des Zeichens auch die Begriffe ›Neutralisation‹, ›Opposition‹ und ›Archilexem‹.

Auch dieser Tadel erweist sich als Bumerang, weil er zeigt, daß *Kalverkämper* die Fragestellung von *Trömel-Plötz* überhaupt nicht verstanden hat – sie ist allerdings für Linguisten auch ziemlich ungewohnt, ja geradezu revolutionär und von theorieaffizierender Bedeutung, wie ich bereits mehrfach angedeutet habe.

Es geht *Trömel-Plötz* eindeutig um ein referenzsemantisches Problem, um die Frage nämlich, ob Aussagen mit Personenbezeichnungen **aller** *Art*, von denen es in den Grammatiken und in der Linguistik bisher hieß, sie referierten entweder auf Personen beliebigen Geschlechts oder auf eine Person beliebigen Geschlechts, **tatsächlich** in der postulierten Weise funktionieren. Zum Untersuchungsgegenstand gehören folglich viele Ausdrücke, auf die die Begriffe ›Opposition‹ und ›Neutralisation‹ überhaupt nicht anwendbar sind, wie z. B. *man, wer, jemand, Mensch, Passagier*. Da der Untersuchungsgegenstand ganz anders definiert ist, als *Kalverkämper* es wahrgenommen hat, sind denn auch nicht die von ihm favorisierten lexikologischen Begriffe das angemessene Analyse-Instrumentarium, sondern die von *Trömel-Plötz* verwendeten referenzsemantischen Begriffe ›generisch‹, ›Referent‹, ›distributiv‹, ›universal‹ und ›kollektiv‹.

Überhaupt kennt sich *Kalverkämper* in der Referenzsemantik, insbesondere mit dem Begriff ›generisch‹ nicht aus, wie seine »Argumentation« und schließlich die Rede von dem »generisch gebrauchten Nomen im Plural« (63) mit den dort angeführten Beispielen klar belegen. Um so mehr verwundert es, wenn uns aus solcher Unkenntnis folgende Belehrung sprießt: »Was Frau *Trömel-Plötz* ›generisch‹ und ›geschlechtsindefinit‹ nennt, kann in der strukturalen... Semantik systematischer beschrieben werden« (58).

Nur in einem Teilbereich des Untersuchungsgegenstandes, bei den paarigen Personenbezeichnungen vom Typ *der/die Spre-*

cher/in, der/die Angestellte hätten die laut *Kalverkämper* vernachlässigten Begriffe mit verwendet werden können, allerdings ohne daß sich dadurch am Analyseergebnis irgendetwas geändert hätte: Die jeweilige maskuline Bezeichnung hat generisch zwei Lesarten (»Männer allein« sowie »Männer und Frauen«) und die feminine nur eine (»Frauen allein«).

Im Rahmen einer feministischen Wortschatzanalyse (die aber bei *Trömel-Plötz* nur ein Thema am Rande war, p. 56, 1–4) ist natürlich der Begriff ›Archilexem‹« außerordentlich interessant – aber nur, wenn man ganz anders fragt als *Kalverkämper,* bzw. wenn man überhaupt fragt, denn *Kalverkämper,* der »sich dem wertfreien und vorurteilslosen struktural-systematischen Zugang zum Phänomen ›Sprache‹ verpflichtet fühlt« (55), stellt ja nur fest: »Solche Prozesse sind in den natürlichen Sprachen nichts Besonderes« (59). Da aber in den Sprachen nun einmal unsere grundlegenden Wertvorstellungen kodifiziert sind, lohnt es sich immer, diese Vorstellungen auch mit linguistischen Mitteln aufzudecken, etwa wie *Lakoff* und *Johnson* 1979 und 1980 es mit verblüffenden Resultaten vorexerziert haben. Eine nach versteckten Wertungen forschende Analyse hätte hier also zu fragen: Zu welchen Oppositionspaaren gibt es Archilexeme, zu welchen nicht? Welches von zwei Oppositionsgliedern trägt den Archi-Sieg davon? Es ist kaum anzunehmen, daß die Wahl arbiträr ist, und schon ein kurzes Hinsehen liefert interessante Aufschlüsse. Bei den Personenbezeichnungen ist alles klar: Wenn es ein Archilexem gibt, dann ist es das Maskulinum. Bei den Nutztieren wird anscheinend das nützlichere Geschlecht zum Archi: *HUHN/Hahn, GANS/Gänserich, ENTE/Enterich, Erpel, KUH/Stier, Ochse, ZIEGE/Ziegenbock.* Bei den Raubtieren der männliche Gegner des Mannes (das starke Geschlecht?): *LÖWE/Löwin, WOLF/Wölfin, BÄR/Bärin, TIGER/Tigerin, LEOPARD/Leopardin.* Bei den relativen Adjektiven wird dasjenige zum Archi, das das Mehr der jeweiligen Dimension bezeichnet: *Wie GROSS/? klein, LANG/? kurz, BREIT/ schmal, DICK/? dünn, ALT/? jung, SPÄT/? früh ist es?* Das Archilexem *Tag* hat gegenüber *Nacht* die positiveren Konnotationen. Zum Archi wird also anscheinend das jeweils Wichtigere, Größere, Positivere. Wie schön für uns Frauen.

Kalverkämpers Behauptung, Sexus habe nichts mit Genus zu tun (62), ist natürlich ein so hanebüchener Unsinn, daß er selbst sie nicht durchgehend aufrechterhalten mag und sich da lieber widerspricht, indem er einräumt: »Das soll allerdings nicht kategorisch besagen, daß die Sprachgemeinschaften in Einzelfällen nicht doch eine Beziehung zwischen Genus und Sexus, zwischen Sexus und Genus erstellen« (60).

Das, was *Kalverkämper* »Einzelfälle« nennt, sind vor allem die Personenbezeichnungen – der Untersuchungsgegenstand von *Trömel-Plötz* also und derjenige Sprachausschnitt, dem zur Zeit das Hauptinteresse der feministischen Linguistik und Sprachpolitik gilt (vgl. die oben erwähnten *Guidelines*). *Trömel-Plötz* »verwechselt« nicht Sexus und Genus, sondern sie analysiert gezielt die Beziehungen zwischen der grammatischen Kategorie Genus und dem Sexus der Referent/inn/en – unter besonderer Berücksichtigung der Fälle, wo beide Kategorien miteinander in Konflikt geraten:

?? Hallo Frauen, wer von euch kann mir sein Fahrrad leihen?

?? Herr Kalverkämper ist eine wissenschaftliche Leuchte, über deren Ausführungen sich ihre Kolleginnen und Kollegen ziemlich gewundert haben.

Wie das zweite Beispiel zeigt, gibt es auch hin und wieder Konflikte zwischen männlichem Geschlecht und femininem Genus, aber sie sind in unserer speziellen deutschen Sprachlotterie (vgl. oben Kap. 2) vergleichsweise selten.

In anders zentrierten Studien über Referenzprobleme werden »gestörte« Beziehungen zwischen der grammatischen Kategorie Numerus und der Anzahl der Referent/inn/en analysiert:

* Meine Familie ist ein/e Frühaufsteher/in.
* Meine Familie sind Frühaufsteher/innen.
  My family are early risers.
* Jeder blieb sitzen. Er wartete nämlich auf eine Zugabe.

Konflikte zwischen Numerus und Anzahl werden üblicherweise durch Paraphrasen gelöst: *In meiner Familie sind alle Frühaufsteher/innen* (o. ä.). Diesen Lösungsweg schlägt auch *Trömel-Plötz*, wie die gesamte feministische Linguistik, für Konflikte zwischen grammatischem und natürlichem Geschlecht vor. *Kalverkämper* hält dem entgegen, das bedeute eine »erhebliche kommunikative Erschwernis« (64) und führe zu »unökonomischen Schwerfälligkeiten«. Dazu ist zweierlei zu sagen:

1. Der Gesichtspunkt der Ökonomie ist bei einer Diskussion über menschliche Grundrechte (zu denen das Als-Mensch-Respektiert- und Identifiziertwerden gehört) offenbar unangemessen. Renten und die Erhaltung sogenannten »lebensunwerten Lebens« mögen für »die Volkswirtschaft« auch unökonomisch sein – aber das ist wohl kein Grund, gegen sie zu plädieren.

2. Es scheint da eine »richtige« und eine »falsche« sprachliche Ökonomie zu geben. Richtige Ökonomie ist z. B. die in den oben abgebildeten Konstanzer Vordrucken manifestierte – allgemeiner: die Beibehaltung frauenignorierender Formulierungen. »Falsche Ökonomie« wäre es hingegen, die mit dem Wort *Fräulein* verbundene Verschwendung von Papier, Druckerschwärze und Sprechenergie aufzugeben. Falsche Ökonomie wäre es wohl auch, einfach *Trömel-Plötz* zu schreiben statt immerfort *Frau Trömel-Plötz* – wieviel Tippenergie wurde da vergeudet (vermutlich aber bloß von einer Frau)!

Diese Befunde lassen zwei Interpretationen zu, die einander nicht ausschließen: eine »ideologiekritische« und eine »allgemein menschliche«.

a) Ideologiekritische Interpretation:

Es geht überhaupt nicht um sprachliche »Ökonomie« oder »Schwerfälligkeit«, sondern um die Aufrechterhaltung der überkommenen sozialen Klassifizierungen, die in den Anrede- und Bezeichnungsasymmetrien ihren sprachlichen Niederschlag finden. Diese Asymmetrien (Frauen werden anders behandelt als Männer) gibt es nämlich in, linguistisch gesehen, sowohl »ökonomischer« als auch »unökonomischer« Ausprägung.

Ökonomisch: *Liebe Kollegen*
(statt *Liebe Kolleginnen und Kollegen*)
die Studenten
(statt *die Studentinnen und Studenten*)
Unökonomisch: *Herrn/Frau/Fräulein* (statt *Herrn/Frau*)
Frau Trömel-Plötz (statt *Trömel-Plötz*)

b) »Allgemein menschliche« Interpretation:

Nicht die vorgeschlagenen Umformulierungen sind »schwerfällig« (sie sind ja bisweilen kürzer als die gängigen Formulierungen), sondern **wir** sind es. Es ist sehr beschwerlich, umzudenken und umzulernen und so alte und eingefleischte Gewohnheiten abzulegen. Das gilt für Frauen wie für Männer, für Sympathisant/inn/en und Aktive wie für Gegner/innen der Frauenbewegung. Ich selbst erlebe es, besonders seit dem Schreiben dieses Artikels, als täglichen Konflikt zwischen theoretischem Selbstanspruch und Trägheit, Unaufmerksamkeit, Gewohnheit. Ich sage weiter Sätze wie *Es ist schwer,* **seine** *Gewohnheiten zu ändern* – und meine damit nicht etwa nur die von *Kalverkämper*. Schriftlich aber genüge ich meinen eigenen Ansprüchen schon besser als mündlich, weil ich da bewußter formuliere und mehr Zeit habe. Und die feministische Sprachkritik richtet sich ja auch vor allem gegen den »veröffentlichten« Gebrauch sexistischer Sprache in den Massenmedien, Lehrbüchern, Gesetzestexten, amtlichen Vordrucken und Verlautbarungen. Privat begangene Sprachsünden mögen noch eine Weile als läßlich durchgehen, aber offizielle und öffentliche wiegen schwer, weil sie jeweils die Hälfte der Betroffenen (oft eine riesige Anzahl Frauen) »unterbuttern«. Wir wollen angesprochen und explizit benannt werden, um sichergehen zu können, daß auch an **uns** gedacht wurde. Wir wollen, kurz gesagt, beim Gemeintsein dieselben Chancen haben wie Männer.

Soll nun aber statt *die Bürger, die Urlauber* etc. immerfort, bei jedem Vorkommen, *die Bürgerinnen und Bürger, die Urlauber und Urlauberinnen* gesagt werden? Das würde vermutlich auf die Dauer wirklich ziemlich beschwerlich sein und schwerfällig wirken. Es gibt bessere, auch »ökonomischere« Strategien, die aber für unseren Sprachraum im einzelnen erst noch ausgearbeitet werden müssen.

Dabei können die englischen *Guidelines* uns wertvolle Anregungen liefern. Nützlich ist auch aufmerksame Zeitungslektüre: Sensible und problembewußte Schreiber/innen finden da manchmal einfache und elegante Lösungen, auf die unsereins vielleicht nicht so schnell gekommen wäre. In einem am 9. Juli 1979 (p. 20 f.) im *Spiegel* abgedruckten Text von *Wehner* fand ich z. B. eine ausgewogene Mischung von »Geschlechtersplitting« und »ökonomischer« Archilexemverwendung. Durch das vorangegangene Splitting werden die Archilexeme (für mein Empfinden) hinreichend disambiguiert:

> Denn der Kandidat wird wissen, daß es vielen *Bürgerinnen und Bürgern* kalt den Rücken herunterläuft, wenn sie an seinen Durchmarsch zur Macht denken. (20)
> Es ist die Pflicht der in Betrieben und Gewerkschaften aktiven *Frauen und Männer,* diesen Dirigierversuchen von oben die Grundlage zu entziehen. (21)
> Nur die *Wählerinnen und Wähler* haben es noch in der Hand, ob die jetzt abgeschlossene Entwicklung der letzten zehn Jahre ein Dauerzustand wird. Schneidende Wahlniederlagen sind das einzige noch verbliebene Mittel zur Reform der CDU/CSU.
> Daß die *Wähler* diese Chance nützen können, hängt von uns Sozialdemokraten sehr stark ab. (21)
> (Hervorhebungen von mir)

Eine speziell das Deutsche untersuchende feministische Linguistik kann aus solchen Dokumenten viel lernen und allgemeine Umformulierungsrichtlinien aus ihnen ableiten, die z. B. auch den Faktor Textkohärenz mit einbeziehen, der **ständiges** Geschlechtersplitting überflüssig macht. *Kalverkämpers* Sorge bezüglich der »unökonomischen Schwerfälligkeiten«, die sich aus der Befolgung feministischer Formulierungsvorschläge ergeben würden, beruht also auf Kurzsichtigkeit und undifferenziertem Verallgemeinern, das wiederum auf fehlendes mitmenschliches Interesse schließen läßt. Eben deshalb wollte ich ihm mit dem Rollenspiel der Einleitungsanekdote und mit den übrigen persönlichen Anspielungen im Text eine Gelegenheit zum Empathie-Training geben. Der Nichtlinguist *Wehner* ist ihm an Einfühlungsvermögen weit überlegen. Er probiert's halt mal aus und zeigt durch die Praxis, daß *Kalverkämpers* Sorge völlig unbegründet ist: Sein Text ist nicht die Spur schwerfällig und erfüllt doch die Grundforderungen feministischer Sprachkritik.

4 Schlußwort

Ich habe nur drei zentrale Punkte der Kritik von *Kalverkämper* aufgegriffen, weil es sich dabei um Einwände gegen die feministische Linguistik handelt, die ich so oder ähnlich schon öfter gehört habe. Die übrigen Vorwürfe *Kalverkämpers*[9] lassen sich in derselben Weise erledigen, aber ich verzichte gern darauf, das hier vorzuführen[10], zumal ich ihm auch zu Dank verpflichtet bin. Seine unsägliche Kritik war für mich der Anstoß, mich endlich von der Sympathisantin zur Aktiven zu mausern. Fortan werde ich mich intensiv an der Frauensprach-Debatte beteiligen, auf die er so gern »einen beruhigenden Einfluß« ausüben wollte (56). Ich habe während der Arbeit an der hier vorgelegten Gegenkritik gemerkt, daß diese Debatte zum Interessantesten und theoretisch wie praktisch Folgenreichsten gehört, was die Linguistik derzeit an Themen zu bieten hat.

Beruhigung? – Nein: Unruhe(stiften) ist die erste Bürgerinnenpflicht.

1979

Anmerkungen

1 Die Einleitung widme ich Christoph Schwarze, der in Gesprächen über Frauensprache öfter das Beispiel *Katze* bringt. Das feminine Genus des Archilexems *Katze* war mir allerdings nur ein geringer Trost dafür, daß ich in Uni-Gremien mit der Anrede »Liebe Kollegen« erfaßt werde, und so mußte ich weiter über Katzen, Kunden und Kollegen nachdenken.

2 Mit *man* beziehe ich mich auf Personen beiderlei Geschlechts, mit *frau* auf Personen weiblichen Geschlechts und mit *mann* auf Personen männlichen Geschlechts.

3 Es tut mir leid, wenn ich mit dieser Ansicht Andersdenkende (Tierfreundinnen und -freunde?) vor den Kopf stoße.

4 Vgl. *Trömel-Plötz* 1979.

5 Die Archilexeme zerfallen, grob geordnet, in zwei Gruppen:
a) solche mit femininem Pendant auf *-in: KUNDE/Kundin, UNTERNEHMER/Unternehmerin*, etc.
b) solche, die aus Adjektiven und Partizipien abgeleitet sind und bei denen die Unterscheidung zwischen Maskulinum und Femininum im

Plural morphologisch neutralisiert ist: *DER/die Gefangene, Betreffende, Kranke, Jugendliche*, etc.

Die mask. Archilexeme sind neben den Pronomina nur ein Teilaspekt des Gesamtproblems »Wie wird im Deutschen auf Frauen referiert?« Ein anderer Teilaspekt sind die mask. Personenbezeichnungen ohne feminines Pendant: *Mensch, Gast, Passagier, Lehrling, Zwilling, Flüchtling, Säugling*, etc., von denen es heißt, sie referierten auf Personen beiderlei Geschlechts.

Für diese Gruppen und Untergruppen sowie weitere Gruppen müssen im Rahmen einer feministischen Liguistik unterschiedliche Paraphrasierungsvorschläge entwickelt werden, desgleichen für je verschiedene Mitglieder einzelner Gruppen, je nach ihrer Semantik, Verwendung und Verwendungshäufigkeit.

6 Vgl. Mary Daly 1978 *Gyn/ecology: The Metaethics of Radical Feminism*. Boston.

7 Vgl. *Pusch* 1978.

8 Frau nimmt überrascht und erfreut zur Kenntnis, daß hier einer der Väter der modernen Linguistik eine seiner zentralen Ideen anhand des schönen Wortes *Schwester* (im Original: *sœur*) erläutert.

9 Bei seiner letzten Attacke (*Kalverkämper* gönnerhaft belehrend: »Mit diesem propädeutischen Wissen ausgerüstet, ergibt sich ein adäquater Zugang...« (65)), die ebenso wie die vorigen danebengeht, zitiert er als Kronzeugen *Harweg*. Ich gestehe freimütig, daß ich jenes Buch von *Harweg* nicht gelesen habe. Meine erste und letzte *Harweg*-Lektüre war ein Aufsatz von 1973, in dem mit Hilfe der Linguistik erstaunliche Erkenntnisse erarbeitet werden. Gegenstand der Betrachtung sind die Betonungsverhältnisse in den Sätzen (p. 42 f.):

(4) Hier in der Gegend ist gestern eine álte Fráu von einem júngen Mánn überfallen worden.

(5) Er ist gestern zu Háuse geblieben, weil er kránk war.

(6) Er hat in den letzten Ferien eine Seminárarbeit geschrieben, die über dréihundert Séiten lang war.

Diese Sätze kommentiert *Harweg* wie folgt (43 f.):

Einen solchen Kontrast suggerierende Sätze aber sind die Sätze (4)–(6), Sätze, von denen die beiden ersteren, da ihre Verbindungen aus Kern und Zweitsatellit eigentlich keine außergewöhnlichen Sachverhalte bezeichnen, einen solchen Kontrast allerdings zu Unrecht suggerieren. Diese beiden Sätze sind denn auch strenggenommen ungrammatisch und müßten durch andere Beispiele – etwa die Sätze *Hier in der Gegend ist gestern ein júnger Mánn von einer álten Fráu überfallen worden* bzw. *(Du,) der Karl (der) hat seine Fráu erschlagen, weil sie nicht rechtzeitig das Éssen auf dem Tisch hatte* – ersetzt werden. Satz (6) demgegenüber enthält tatsächlich eine außerge-

41

wöhnliche Kern-Zweitsatellit-Kombination und suggeriert seinen Kontrast somit zu Recht. Ihn wollen wir deshalb etwas genauer analysieren.

Wir aber wollen jetzt mal was anderes genauer analysieren. Frau erfährt hier also:

a) Es ist nichts Außergewöhnliches, wenn eine alte Frau von einem jungen Mann überfallen wird.

b) Wenn eine alte Frau von einem jungen Mann überfallen wird, so ist das ebenso »gewöhnlich«, wie wenn »er« zu Hause bleibt, weil »er« krank ist.

c) Wenn »er« eine Seminararbeit von 300 Seiten schreibt, so ist das ungewöhnlicher, als wenn ein junger Mann eine alte Frau überfällt.

d) Ungewöhnlich ist nur, wenn eine alte Frau einen jungen Mann überfällt. Und wenn Karl seine Frau erschlägt, so ist das erst dann ungewöhnlich, wenn er es aus dem genannten Grund tut: weil sie das Essen nicht rechtzeitig auf dem Tisch hatte.

Das Grauenhafte an diesen Ausführungen ist, daß *Harweg*, statistisch gesehen, vollkommen recht hat. Aber Überfälle junger Männer auf alte Frauen und Morde von Ehemännern an ihren Ehefrauen sind nicht in erster Linie statistisch, sondern ethisch und juristisch relevante Vorfälle und als solche keineswegs »gewöhnlich«, genausowenig wie sie es für die Opfer sind. Die linguistische Phantasie, die gerade solche Beispiele produziert (es gibt genügend andere »gewöhnliche« und »ungewöhnliche« Sachverhalte), ist ethisch defekt und frauenfeindlich. Der »wertfreie Kommentar« dieser Beispiele ist reiner Zynismus.

10 Ein besonders lustiges und aufschlußreiches Kapitel, das über die Kalverkämpersprache, wird nun in meiner Schublade vermodern. Das Thema war ja auch Frauensprache, und die Kalverkämpersprache ist eine Extremform der Männersprache. Als solche ist sie allerdings für die feministische Linguistik eine so reiche Beleg-Fundgrube, daß sie in zukünftigen Analysen den ihr gebührenden Platz eingeräumt bekommen muß und wird. Auffälligstes Kennzeichen der Kalverkämpersprache ist ihre eigentümliche Wissenschaftsmetaphorik. Die Wissenschaft wird anscheinend als eine Art Gottheit aufgefaßt, etwas unabhängig von Menschen und menschlichen Interessen Existierendes. Menschen sind nur dazu da, dieser Gottheit zu dienen. Ketzer/innen werden unter Berufung auf die Gottheit erbarmungslos verfolgt und ihr zum Opfer dargebracht.

Der Piloterich
Ein Beitrag der außerirdischen Linguistik

Neulich war ein Wesen von einem fremden Stern hier. Auf jenem Stern gibt es keinen Geschlechtsunterschied, deshalb sollte das Wesen untersuchen, wie wir sprachlich mit diesem Unterschied zurechtkommen. Es hatte den Auftrag, mit dem Deutschen zu beginnen und eine objektive strukturale Beschreibung anzufertigen mit dem Titel (sinngemäß übersetzt): »Wie wird im Deutschen auf Frauen und Männer referiert?« Die Beschreibung sollte so einfach, allgemein und genau wie möglich sein. Das fremde Wesen nahm sich zunächst die Bezeichnungen vom Typ *Arzt/Ärztin* vor und erstellte folgenden Bericht:

A: *Bestandsaufnahme*

Die Gesetzmäßigkeiten im Bereich des Referierens mit Personenbezeichnungen vom Typ *Arzt/Ärztin* lassen sich mit einem einzigen Satz erfassen:

1. Eine Gruppe von Personen ist eine »männliche Gruppe«, d. h. es wird auf sie mit dem Maskulinum referiert, wenn sie **mindestens einen** Mann enthält.

Aus diesem einen Satz lassen sich alle weiteren Besonderheiten ableiten:

2. Eine Gruppe von Personen ist eine »nichtmännliche Gruppe«, d. h. es wird auf sie mit einer vom Maskulinum abgeleiteten Form (sog. »Femininum«) referiert, wenn sie **keinen** Mann enthält.

3. Auf ein Mitglied einer männlichen Gruppe wird mit dem Maskulinum referiert.

4. Auf ein potentielles Mitglied einer männlichen Gruppe wird mit dem Maskulinum referiert (Beispiel: *Der Gewinner steht noch nicht fest.)*

5. Auf ein Mitglied einer nichtmännlichen Gruppe wird mit dem sog. »Femininum« referiert.

6. Ein Mann ist immer Mitglied einer männlichen Gruppe, da er durch seine Mitgliedschaft jede nichtmännliche Gruppe zu einer

männlichen macht. (Von einem Arzt wird nie gesagt: »Er ist Ärztin.«)

7. Eine Frau kann sowohl Mitglied einer männlichen als auch einer nichtmännlichen Gruppe sein. (Von einer Frau kann man sagen: »Sie ist Arzt/Ärztin« – je nach Gruppenzuschreibung.)

8. Frauen »zählen« nur als Mitglieder nichtmännlicher Gruppen: Eine Gruppe von zehn Sängerinnen enthält zehn Frauen. Eine Gruppe von zehn Sängern enthält neun bis null Frauen.

B: *Kommentar*

Die deutsche Sprache liefert ein befremdend verzerrtes Bild der Realität, in der sich folgende Arten von Gruppen finden:

Weibliche Gruppen

Gemischtgeschlechtliche Gruppen $\longleftarrow$
          überwiegend Frauen
          fifty-fifty
          überwiegend Männer

Männliche Gruppen

Für die deutsche Sprache ist aber das Klassifikationskriterium nicht, ob eine Gruppe Frauen enthält, und schon gar nicht, wie viele. Klassifikationsgrundlage ist, ob eine Gruppe einen Mann enthält oder nicht. Der sprachliche Raster, der der Realität übergeworfen wird, sieht so aus:

Weibliche Gruppen	–M
Gemischtgeschlechtliche Gruppen $\longleftarrow$ überwiegend Frauen / fifty-fifty / überwiegend Männer Männliche Gruppen	+M

Es ist also nur folgerichtig, daß die Sprachwissenschaft auf jenem Planeten überwiegend mit den Merkmalen /+ M/ und /– M/ operiert. Der für die objektiv beobachtbare Realität sinnvolle, nichtableitende Begriff ›weiblich‹ (+ F(eminimum)) hat sprachlich in diesem Bereich, dem die meisten deutschen Personenbezeichnungen zuzuordnen sind, kein begründbares Korrelat. Die Endung *-in* »bedeutet« nichts anderes als ›nichtmännlich‹ im oben definierten Sinn.

Geradezu absurd ist allerdings die von der Sprachwissenschaft auf jenem Planeten vertretene Behauptung, Maskulina wie *Geiger, Student* könnten ähnlich wie *Gans, Maus* geschlechtneutral, »unmarkiert« verwendet werden. Dabei wird verkannt, daß Maskulina **nur** auf männliche Gruppen und deren Mitglieder, im oben definierten Sinne, referieren können. Wirklich geschlechtsneutral ist ein Ausdruck logischerweise erst dann, wenn er auf rein weibliche (nach dortigem sprachlichen Raster: »nichtmännliche«) **und** rein männliche **und** gemischtgeschlechtliche Gruppen (und deren Mitglieder) referieren kann.

Die Frauen des deutschen Sprachraums versuchen in letzter Zeit, die im Kern diskriminierende *in*-Form durch vermehrten Gebrauch aufzuwerten. Es ist möglich, daß diese »weiche« Politik erfolgreich und sinnvoll ist. Denkbar sind allerdings auch radikalere Strategien.

Zum Beispiel könnten die Frauen die weibliche Gruppe als referenzsemantische Grundeinheit setzen und auf Männer mit abgeleiteten Formen referieren, wie es im Tierreich den Gänse- und Mäuserichen geschieht: *die Pilot, der Piloterich, die Piloten.*

1979

Das Deutsche als Männersprache
Diagnose und Therapievorschläge

> ... dann ein Weib hat allzeit zwen nachteil,
> da ein man zwen vortail hat.
>
> *Martin Luther*

1 Einleitung

Vor einiger Zeit schickte mir der Leiter des Instituts für deutsche Sprache, Dr. Gerhard *Stickel*, eine Stellungnahme zur sprachlichen Form von Diplomgraden, um die ihn das Ministerium für Wissenschaft und Kunst Baden-Württemberg gebeten hatte. Das Ministerium hatte sich erkundigt, ob es angeraten sei, Diplomgrade offiziell auch in der »weiblichen Form« (*Diplom-Bibliothekarin* etc.) zu verleihen.[1] *Stickel* unterwies die Ministerialen geduldig und umsichtig dahingehend, daß ihr Problem keines ist, daß diese Anwendung der Wortbildung auf Diplomgrade geradezu selbstverständlich ist und völlig mit der Gebrauchsnorm des Deutschen in Einklang steht. Nach Ablieferung des Gutachtens waren ihm aber Zweifel an seiner Empfehlung gekommen. Daher bat er mich in seinem Begleitbrief, den ich hier mit seinem Einverständnis in Auszügen wiedergebe, um einige Auskünfte aus weiblicher Sicht:

> ... Was die männlichen und weiblichen Personen-, Rollen- und Funktionsbezeichnungen angeht, bin ich in der Zwischenzeit unsicher geworden. Von mehreren skandinavischen Gewährsmännern und -frauen habe ich gehört, daß in Schweden und Dänemark zumindest die ›morphologische‹ Tendenz gegenläufig ist, obgleich es im Dänischen und Schwedischen ähnliche Movierungsmöglichkeiten wie im Deutschen gibt. Dort sind es gerade die Frauen, die Wert darauf legen, *Lehrer* und *Ingenieure* zu heißen, und nicht *Lehrerinnen* und *Ingenieurinnen,* gerade weil sie auch sprachlich nicht diskriminiert werden wollen. Es käme schließlich auf entsprechende berufliche Fähigkeiten und Kenntnisse an, und nicht auf das Geschlecht.
>
> Aus England erfuhr ich gerade, daß dort Stellenanzeigen, in denen auf das Geschlecht der Bewerber explizit Bezug genommen wird, verboten sind, im Unterschied zur Bundesrepublik, in der die meisten Zeitungen drei Rubriken haben: Stellenange-

bote/-gesuche männlich *(Textilingenieur)*, weiblich *(Textilinge-nieurin)* und gemischt *(Textilingenieur/-in)*.

Ich bekomme deshalb den Verdacht nicht los, daß möglicher-weise durch die Forcierung des Gebrauchs »geschlechtmarkier-ter« Personenbezeichnungen zwar einerseits dem Wunsch der Frauen nach deutlichem Gemeintsein entsprochen wird, ande-rerseits aber in all den Fällen Sexusmarkierungen gebraucht werden, in denen es gerade auf das Geschlecht nicht ankommen darf.

Ich habe keine Repräsentativerhebung angestellt, aber mit mehreren Frauen (auch hier im IdS) gesprochen. Einige äußer-ten sich ähnlich wie die erwähnten Skandinavierinnen. Die Ver-wendung von Berufsbezeichnungen in der ›weiblichen‹ Form sei ihnen lästig, sei eine typisch männliche Koketterie und sei vor allem dann zu beobachten, wenn Frauen in ihrem professionel-len Status nicht ganz ernst genommen würden, wenn aus ir-gendwelchen Gründen gezielt an ihre Weiblichkeit appelliert werde.

Als Mann bin ich für derartige Einstellungen nicht hinreichend sensibilisiert. (Kommentar L. F. P.: Ein wahrhaft bemerkens-werter Satz! Eine Einsicht, wie ich sie bisher noch nie von einem Mann gehört, sie mir aber immer zu hören gewünscht habe.) Daß Artikel 3 des Grundgesetzes immer noch nicht hinreichend verwirklicht ist, weiß ich. Aber könnte es nicht sein, daß dem verfaßten Benachteiligungsverbot sprachlich besser entspro-chen würde, wenn ›weiblich‹ markierte Bezeichnungsformen für alle Berufe und Funktionen, die geschlechtsunspezifisch sind (und das sind ja fast alle) grundsätzlich vermieden würden? Die Bezeichnungen würden dann – was sie jetzt zweifellos noch nicht sind – geschlechtsneutral, weil es dann kein Geschlechts-paradigma mehr gäbe. Es käme dann auch nicht zu einer Virili-sierung/Maskulinisierung der Frauen. Dies wäre freilich ein erheblicher Eingriff in die Morphologie und die tendenzielle Gebrauchsnorm des Deutschen.

Ich würde mich freuen, wenn Sie mir ein paar Sätze zu dieser Frage schreiben könnten.

Auf diese Anfrage habe ich *Stickel* zunächst vorläufig geantwortet und diese Antwort inzwischen zu dem folgenden offenen Brief ausgebaut:

Zu Ihrer Frage: Soll die movierte Form forciert werden, ihr häufiger und systematischer Gebrauch gefordert, praktiziert und unterstützt werden – oder soll sie im Gegenteil ganz abgeschafft werden mit dem Ziel, dadurch die nicht-movierte (»unmarkierte«) Form mit echter Geschlechtsneutralität auszustatten?

Ich finde, beide »Parteien« haben recht, wenn sie meinen, die jeweils andere Lösung sei schlecht. Beide Parteien haben aber unrecht, wenn sie die jeweils eigene Lösung gut finden. Sinnvoll wäre höchstens die Frage, welche der Lösungen das kleinere Übel ist. Es ist wie mit allen Alternativen, vor die sich Frauen in patriarchalischen Systemen gestellt sehen – und die deutsche Sprache ist wie die meisten anderen Sprachen ein patriarchalisch organisiertes System. Die Crux ist immer die, daß bei solchen Alternativen die »männliche Seite des Problems« unangetastet bleibt oder bleiben soll. Nehmen Sie die Parallele »Entscheidung zwischen Familie und Beruf«. Solange Männer sich nicht vor dieselbe Alternative gestellt sehen (für sie verbindet sich beides problemlos), bringt **jede** getroffene Wahl für die Frau schwere Nachteile.

Fazit: Nur wenn die Situation der Männer gleichzeitig mit geändert wird, ist eine gerechte Lösung für Frauen möglich. Auf die (deutsche) Sprache übertragen bedeutet das: Nur wenn die Bezeichnungen für Männer gleichzeitig mit geändert werden, ergeben sich gleiche sprachliche Chancen für Frauen und Männer.

Das Problem – gleiche Chancen des Gemeintseins – ist zwar theoretisch-linguistisch nicht ganz einfach zu lösen, aber theoretisch lösbar ist es gewiß. Schwierig ist erst die Praxis, aber darauf gehe ich später ein.

2 Diagnose: Welche Mittel der Geschlechtsspezifikation besitzt das Deutsche, und wie werden sie gegen Frauen eingesetzt?

Vor dem Lösungsvorschlag hier zunächst eine onomasiologische Analyse des Problems.

Die Spezies Mensch kann man unter dem hier interessierenden Gesichtspunkt betrachten als Klasse prinzipiell gleich organisierter Entitäten, die in zwei Hälften zerfällt: eine weibliche und eine männliche. Um das Wortfeld der Bezeichnungen für Menschen von einer neutralen Warte aus beurteilen zu können, empfiehlt es sich, eine ähnlich strukturierte Klasse von Entitäten zum Vergleich heranzuziehen, z. B. die Klasse der paarweise vorhandenen, symmetrisch angeordneten Körperteile. Bei den Menschen gibt es also zwei Arten der Geschlechtszugehörigkeit, weiblich und männlich, bei den paarweise vorhandenen Körperteilen zwei Arten der Situierung, links und rechts. Sehen wir uns das Wortfeld »Körperteilbezeichnungen« an, so stellen wir fest, daß es nur solche Lexeme gibt, die von der Situierung abstrahieren. Soll die Situierung spezifiziert werden, so kann das nur mittels Hinzufügung der Attribute *link-* und *recht-* geschehen:

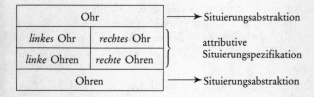

Ganz genauso funktioniert (zumindest theoretisch) der größte Teil der Personenbezeichnungen des Englischen, wie ein Vergleich der folgenden Konfiguration mit der obigen klarmacht:

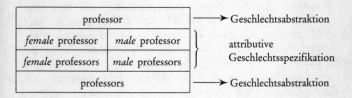

Wir sehen, daß das System der Körperteilbezeichnungen keine der beiden Hälften bevorzugt bzw. diskriminiert und daß das Englische mindestens theoretisch die Voraussetzung für ein nicht diskriminierendes Bezeichnen von Personen besitzt. Nur ist es leider auch im Englischen unüblich, beide Hälften der Menschheit so unparteiisch zu behandeln wie beide Hälften der meisten Körperteilpaare (bei Händen und vielleicht auch Beinen und Füßen gibt es eine kulturbedingte gewisse »Rechtslastigkeit«). Weibliche Menschen werden im Englischen etwa so behandelt wie linke Hände in allen Sprachen. So wie *Hand/hand/main/mano* etc. in den meisten Kontexten ›rechte Hand‹ bedeutet (vgl. *Sie gab mir die Hand / They shook hands* etc.), so referieren engl. *professor/doctor/ clerk/farmer/employee,* …bekanntlich in den meisten Kontexten auf männliche Menschen.[2]

Doch zurück zum Deutschen: Das Deutsche greift zur Spezifikation der Geschlechtszugehörigkeit gleich auf drei grammatische Subsysteme zurück:

1. Lexikon: a) die Attribute *weiblich* und *männlich*
   b) lexeminhärente Geschlechtsspezifikation in Paaren wie *Schwester, Bruder – Mutter, Vater.*

2. Grammatische Kategorien: die Genera Femininum und Maskulinum.

3. Wortbildung: Suffixe zur Spezifikation des weiblichen Geschlechts.

(Während im Englischen die lexikalischen Mittel der Geschlechtsspezifikation überwiegen, überwiegen im Deutschen die im engeren Sinne grammatischen (Genussystem und Suffix-Ableitung).)

Zunächst einmal ist festzustellen, daß es – anders als bei den Körperteilbezeichnungen, die **alle** situierungsabstrahierend sind – nur ganz wenige Personenbezeichnungen gibt, die geschlechtsabstrahierend sind, wenn man berücksichtigt, daß das Genus Bestandteil der Bezeichnungen ist und daß es in diesem Wortfeld in der Regel geschlechtsspezifizierende Funktion hat. Geschlechtsabstrahierend sind z.B. *Kind, Säugling, Mensch, Person* sowie die Komposita auf *-kraft: Lehr-, Hilfs-, Fach-, Spitzenkraft.* Sie sind es deswegen, weil sie weder zur Klasse der geschlechtsspezifizierenden Lexeme (s. u.), noch zur Klasse der Personenbezeichnungen mit Differentialgenus[3] gehören (Typ *die/der Abgeordnete*), noch die *-in*-Movierung erlauben (aus unterschiedlichen Gründen, die ich hier nicht aufzählen will).

Der obigen *Ohr*-Grafik entspräche für *Kind* und *Mensch* folgendes:

Kind/Mensch		→ Geschlechtsabstraktion
weibl. Kind/Mensch	*männl.* Kind/Mensch	} attributive Geschlechtsspezifikation
weibl. Kinder/Menschen	*männl.* Kinder/Menschen	
Kinder/Menschen		→ Geschlechtsabstraktion

Nun sagen wir aber bekanntlich selten Sätze wie:

D. *weibliche Mensch/Kind verabschiedete sich von dem männlichen Menschen/Kind.*

Wir sagen statt dessen:

Die Frau/Das Mädchen verabschiedete sich von dem Mann/Jungen.

Anders als bei den Körperteilbezeichnungen ist die Spezifikation des Subklassifikationsmerkmals bei vielen Personenbezeichnungen inhärent:

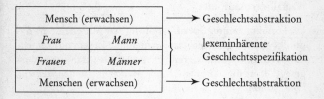

Mensch (erwachsen)		→ Geschlechtsabstraktion
Frau	*Mann*	} lexeminhärente Geschlechtsspezifikation
Frauen	*Männer*	
Menschen (erwachsen)		→ Geschlechtsabstraktion

Bei geschlechtsspezifizierenden Lexemen führt eine zusätzliche attributive Geschlechtsspezifikation zu pleonastischen oder kontradiktorischen Ausdrücken, vgl. *männlicher/weiblicher Vater.*[4] Redundant, aber nicht zu Pleonasmen führend, ist das jeweilige Genus solcher Lexeme: Die Bezeichnungen für weibliche Menschen haben (mit wenigen Ausnahmen: *Mädchen, Weib, Fräulein*) feminines Genus, die Bezeichnungen für männliche Menschen (mit wenigen und bemerkenswerten Ausnahmen: *Tunte, Tucke, Schwuchtel*) maskulines Genus, vgl.:

die Schwester, der Bruder
die Tochter, der Sohn
die Mutter, der Vater
die Tante, der Onkel

Diese »redundante Geschlechtsspezifikation« mittels des Genus unterscheidet z. B. das Deutsche und die romanischen Sprachen vom Englischen und den skandinavischen Sprachen.

Die bisher vorgeführten Grafiken weisen trotz ihrer unterschiedlichen Belegung eine wichtige Gemeinsamkeit auf: ihre Struktur ist symmetrisch. Das heißt: Wenn (in den beiden mittleren Feldern) die Situierung oder die Geschlechtszugehörigkeit spezifiziert wird, so **beiderseits** und mit denselben grammatischen Mitteln:

a) attributiv: *linkes/rechtes Ohr / weibliches/männliches Kind*

b) lexeminhärent: *daughter, son*

c) lexeminhärent plus Genus: *die Tochter, der Sohn.*

Die Abstraktion von Situierung oder Geschlechtszugehörigkeit ist gekennzeichnet

a) bei attributiver Spezifikation in den Mittelfeldern: durch Wegfall der Attribute

b) bei lexeminhärenter Spezifikation in den Mittelfeldern: dadurch, daß das geschlechtsabstrahierende Lexem mit keinem der geschlechtsspezifizierenden formal identisch ist; anders gesagt: es ist nicht ambig – *Kind: Mädchen, Junge. Mensch: Frau, Mann.*

Wir kommen nun zu der Gruppe der deutschen Personenbezeichnungen, die aus Adjektiven und Partizipien abgeleitet sind: *d. Jugendliche/Abgeordnete.* Die Geschlechtsspezifikation geschieht hier allein mittels des Genus; sie ist nicht lexeminhärent. Die Lexeme dieser Gruppe besitzen das sogenannte Differentialgenus: *die* oder *der Jugendliche* können wir sagen, je nach Geschlecht der jugendlichen Person. Zum Vergleich: Bei *Mensch/Person* können wir zum selben Zweck nicht zwischen *die* und *der Mensch/Person* wechseln. Wir müssen entweder ein anderes Lexem wählen *(Frau/Mann)* oder attributiv spezifizieren: *weibliche/männliche Person.*

Schema für die Personenbezeichnungen mit Differentialgenus:

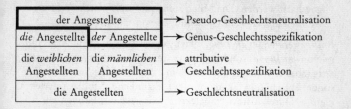

Ich unterscheide in meiner Kommentierung der Grafiken zwischen ›Geschlechtsabstraktion‹ und ›Geschlechtsneutralisation‹. Unter ›Abstraktion‹ verstehe ich eine Relation zwischen Bezeichnung und Bezeichnetem (Wörtern und »Dingen«). Die Dinge haben Eigenschaften (d. h. sie sind weiblich oder männlich, links oder rechts situiert), von denen wir wissen, daß sie sie haben und die uns wichtig sind. Wir besitzen aber Wörter zur Bezeichnung dieser Dinge, die von diesen Eigenschaften abstrahieren.

Unter ›Neutralisation‹ verstehe ich eine Relation zwischen Bezeichnungen. Ich betrachte den Plural (etwa: *die Abgeordneten*) als sekundär gegenüber dem Singular *(die/der Abgeordnete)*. Im Singular besteht ein grammatischer Spezifikationszwang, aber diese Spezifikation wird in der Pluralform ›neutralisiert‹.

Wir begegnen hier zum erstenmal einer asymmetrisch belegten Konfiguration (vgl. das stark umrandete Feld). Die Asymmetrie betrifft allerdings vorerst nur den Singular-Teil; später behandle ich Konfigurationen, die im Singular **und** im Plural asymmetrisch belegt sind. Die Asymmetrie des obigen Systems besteht darin, daß die Bezeichnungen für das männliche Individuum und für ein Individuum gleich welchen Geschlechts identisch »ausfallen«. Vom rein formal-linguistischen Standpunkt aus ist nicht einzusehen, wieso das System gerade diese Gestalt annehmen mußte. Theoretisch hätte auch das Femininum für die Neutralisierungsaufgabe ausersehen werden können, mit demselben Resultat einer asymmetrischen Konfiguration. Was jedoch formal am meisten befremdet, ist, daß nicht das Neutrum gewählt wurde, wo wir es doch nun einmal haben. Hierzu ein kleiner Ausflug in die Vergangenheit. In den Lebenserinnerungen des armen Mannes im Tockenburg, Ulrich *Bräker,* steht folgendes zu lesen:

Im Winter 63 gebar mir meine Frau *eine Tochter,* und 65 *noch eine.* [. . .] auf der Stelle mußten / . . . / etliche [Geißen] herbeigeschafft werden. Die Milch stund mir und *meinen drei Jungen* trefflich an . . .[5] (Hervorhebungen von mir.)

Bräker verwendet *die Jungen* hier ganz offensichtlich nicht als Plural von *der Junge,* sondern (so vermute ich) von *das Junge.* Eigenartig (aber es wundert uns trotzdem kaum), daß *die Jungen* als Personenbezeichnung heute nur auf männliche Kinder referieren kann. – Durch historisch belegte Praxis gestützt, können wir folgern: Wird die Geschlechtsspezifikation allein durch das Genus gewährleistet, so sollte auch die Neutralisation mittels Genus, und zwar Genus Neutrum, erfolgen. Ich komme im Abschnitt 3 darauf zurück.

Nach diesen notwendigen systematischen Vorarbeiten nun zum Anlaß Ihrer Frage und Kernpunkt der Diskussion, den sogenannten movierten Formen. Im Schema sehen sie wie folgt aus:

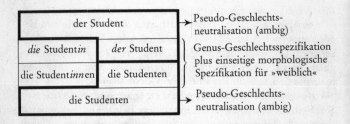

Es ist auf den ersten Blick erkennbar, daß dieses System in punkto Symmetrie eine eklatante Fehlkonstruktion ist. Formal betrachtet ist es absurd und unökonomisch. Man stelle sich zum Vergleich etwa vor, wir würden die linken Körperteile mit *der Fuß, der Schenkel, der Auge, der Bein* benennen und die rechten mit *die Füßin, die Schenkelin*[6], *die Äugin* und *die Beinin!*

Wie so manche sprachliche Absurdität läßt sich auch diese historisch erklären. Das formal gesehen unökonomische und absurde System ist ökonomisch und sinnvoll genau dann, wenn die männliche Hälfte der Menschheit als Norm gilt und im Zentrum des Interesses steht und die weibliche Hälfte von der männlichen abhängig ist und auch so wahrgenommen wird.

Für Derivationen gilt allgemein, daß das Denotat der derivierten Form in irgendeiner Weise dem Denotat der Grundform **zugeordnet** ist, von diesem Denotat her seinen eigentlichen Sinn bezieht. Weil Eva aus Adams, des Mannes, Rippe geformt wurde, **deshalb** soll sie »Männin« heißen, belehrt uns die Bibel mit bemerkenswerter linguistischer Klarsichtigkeit. Oder nehmen wir die Grundform *England* und die abgeleitete Form *Engländer*. Ein Engländer ist jemand, der aus England stammt; er ist durch die Bezeichnung *Engländer* deutlich dem Land England **zugeordnet**. Gäbe es das Wort *England* nicht, so auch nicht das Wort *Engländer*. Und weiter, entsprechend: Gäbe es nicht das Wort *Engländer,* so auch nicht das Wort *Engländerin*. Allgemein: Gäbe es nicht die maskulinen Grundformen, so auch nicht die abgeleiteten Formen auf -in.

Wie aber ist eine Engländerin ihrer »Grundform«, dem Engländer, wie eine Ärztin dem Arzt usw., »zugeordnet«? Wieso bringt die deutsche Sprache hier eine Abhängigkeitsrelation zum Ausdruck, die uns etwa bei Körperteilbezeichnungen völlig widersinnig vorkäme?

Die Geschichte der Entstehung, Funktion, Funktionsaufspaltung (s. u.) und Ausbreitung des Motionssuffixes -in aus feministischer oder wenigstens weiblicher Sicht ist noch nicht geschrieben. Für die Zwecke dieses offenen Briefes habe ich mich zunächst nur oberflächlich orientieren können. Natürlich sind alle älteren sprachhistorischen Arbeiten und auch die meisten neueren von Männern verfaßt, und wie wir Frauen inzwischen wissen, sind deren Forschungsergebnisse, Rekonstruktionen und Interpretationen, vor allem soweit sie uns, hier: Bezeichnungen für uns, betreffen, mit Vorsicht zu genießen.[7] Rein androzentrische (d. h. verfälschende) Sehweise prägt z. B. die folgende Feststellung von *Henzen* (1965: 152): »Wie schon angedeutet ..., bildet das Idg. persönliche Feminina aus Maskulinen mittels reinen *a*-Stammes (lat. *lupa, domina, puella*).« (Was hier vorliegt, ist natürlich **kein** Ableitungsverhältnis *dominus → domina,* sondern Differentialgenus: Beide, *domin-a* und *domin-us,* sind vom Stamm *domin-* abgeleitet.) – Solcherart »belehrt«, mögen wir verständlicherweise auch den meisten anderen »objektiven« Forschungsergebnissen männlicher Sprachhistoriker zu unserem Thema nicht mehr recht trauen. Über das Gotische, für das -ini (Vorläufer des -in) nur ein einziges Mal belegt ist[8], werden wir von *Wilmanns* (1899: 217) wie folgt unterrichtet:

Persönliche Feminina lassen sich wie die persönlichen Masculina oft teils auf Verba, teils auf Substantiva mit unpersönlicher Bedeutung beziehen, z. B. *pflega* Pflegerin zu *pflëgan, hîwa* Gattin zu **heiws* Haus. Aber sie sind doch nicht von gleicher Ursprünglichkeit wie die Masculina, setzen vielmehr im allgemeinen Masculina voraus und sind von ihnen abgeleitet. Das Femininum-Suffix erscheint als ein Mittel, dem Masculinum gegenüber das natürliche Geschlecht zu bezeichnen. Natürlich folgt daraus nicht, daß jedes Femininum der Art auf ein Masculinum zurückgeführt werden müsse.

Frau fragt sich hier erstaunt: Wenn das Femininum-Suffix das natürliche Geschlecht bezeichnet, welches Geschlecht bezeichnet dann das Masculinum? (Vgl. auch den Schluß meines Briefs.)

Das Gotische scheint ein relativ unparteiisches Bezeichnungssystem (Überwiegen des Differentialgenus) besessen zu haben. Allerdings werden wir darüber wieder sehr androzentrisch informiert:

Zu jedem schwachen Masculinum mit persönlicher Bedeutung, mögen sie von Substantiven oder Verben abgeleitet sein, kann ein entsprechendes Femininum gebildet werden; z. B. g. *arbjô* Erbin zu *arbja, garaznô* Nachbarin zu *garazna; swaihro* Schwiegermutter zu *swaihra*. (*Wilmanns* 1899: 217)

Logischerweise kann dann auch »zu jedem schwachen Femininum ein entsprechendes Masculinum gebildet werden« – aber so lesen wir es nicht, natürlich.

Garazno ›Nachbarin‹ neben *garazna* ›Nachbar‹ und *hêrra* ›Herrin‹ neben *hêrro* ›Herr‹ sind für *Henzen* (1947: 152) »deutlich movierte« Formen. Woran ihm das deutlich wurde, bleibt unerfindlich.

Nach dem Einzelbeleg *Saurini* ›Syrerin‹ zu *Saur* ›Syrer‹ im Gotischen findet man die *-in(na)*-Form im Althochdeutschen sehr häufig, und sie hat sich bis heute immer mehr ausgebreitet (vgl. *Henzen* 1965: 153 f.). Warum das so ist – darüber machen sich unsere männlichen Sprachhistoriker keine Gedanken; jedenfalls habe ich außer bei dem erstaunlichen Radikalfeministen *Baudouin de Courtenay*[9] nirgends auch nur den Anflug eines wissenschaftlichen Kopfschüttelns über diese merkwürdig einseitige morphologische Geschlechtsspezifikation gefunden. Es scheint, daß sie männlicherseits als »selbstverständlich und natürlich« empfunden wird – obwohl ja das Gotische offenbar sehr gut ohne sie auskam. Im Laufe der Zeit begann die Bedeutung des -in sich aufzuspalten – ich würde eher sagen: -in begann sein wahres Gesicht zu zeigen, dasjenige, das sein Vorhandensein sprachlogisch erst rechtfertigt und das uns heute diese Form als extrem diskriminierend erkennen läßt. Hören wir dazu *Wellmann* (1975: 107 und 117). Er unterscheidet nach semantischen Gesichtspunkten ein -in[1] von einem -in[2]. Das Motionsmorphem -in[1] »überführt Maskulina in Feminina und ergänzt den Basisinhalt um das Merkmal ›weibliches Geschlecht‹« (frei nach *Wellmann*). Eine ganz andere Funktion erfüllt das Suffix -in (bei *Wellmann*: -in[2]) jedoch in Bildungen wie *die Marschallin* (Rosenkavalier), *Luise Millerin, Agnes Bernauerin, die Höfrätin Berndt* (Feuchtwanger), *die Pastorin Höhlenrauch* (Th. Mann). Hier bedeutet es nichts weiter als ›Frau (oder Tochter) des X‹; es symbolisiert die Zuordnung zu bzw. Abhängigkeit von einem Mann. Eine semantisch vergleichbare Funktion haben nur noch die Suffixe zur Bildung von Patronymika: *Wälsung* ›Sohn des Wälse‹, *Friedrichsen* ›Sohn Friedrichs‹. Diese Suffixe sind erwartungsgemäß aufgrund der Emanzipation der Söhne nicht mehr produktiv und überleben nur noch in Eigennamen. Analog müßte die Emanzipation der Frau also eigentlich zum Absterben des -in führen.

Da das Suffix -in nur in der letztgenannten Bedeutung sprachsystematisch überhaupt einen Sinn ergibt, möchte ich hier kühn behaupten, daß diese angeblich später entstandene Funktion von Anfang an seine eigentliche war. All die so früh (Ahd.) belegten *Gräfinnen, Königinnen, Kaiserinnen, Wirtinnen* – was waren sie anderes als Frauen von Grafen, Königen, Kaisern, Wirten?! Von **dieser** ursprünglichen Bedeutung aus mag sich dann die andere entwickelt haben. Eine Fürstin, eigentlich nur »Frau des Fürsten«, mag bei Fortsein oder nach Ableben des Gatten auch einmal Fürstenfunktion gehabt haben; die »Frau Glaserin« Lichtenbergs[10] mag im Handwerksbetrieb ihres Mannes mitgearbeitet haben und fast so etwas wie ein »weiblicher Glaser« gewesen sein.

Ich glaube, es lohnt sich, diese Hypothese an den Quellen, ohne männliche Vermittlung, zu überprüfen. War jene einzelne *Saurini*, Syrerin, nicht vielleicht ganz einfach die Frau eines Syrers? – Die ebenfalls gut belegten *Bärinnen* und *Löwinnen* etc. lassen sich mit dieser Hypothese natürlich nicht direkt erklären, wohl aber indirekt: das androzentrische Weltbild ordnet ja auch sonst das meiste nach eigenem Maßstab.

> Kuhreiher sind treue Vögel. Ähnlich wie Schwäne, treiben sie es lebenslänglich mit einer Partnerin. (*PZ* »Politische Zeitung« der Bundeszentrale für Politische Bildung, Nr. 33/1983, S. 15)

Noch ein Nachtrag: Zwar haben unsere männlichen Kollegen das -*in* ohne weiter nachzufragen zu Protokoll genommen, aber es gibt doch Dinge, die auch ihnen Kopfzerbrechen bereiten. Ich denke, das folgende Zitat bildet einen würdigen Abschluß dieses historischen Exkurses:

> Aber auch viel Neueres macht uns Kopfzerbrechen [. . .]. Wie steht es nur um die anscheinend so eindeutigen movierten Feminina? Von jeher besteht da Schwanken zwischen *Frau Pfarrer* und *Pfarrerin* (früher mit derselben Bedeutung); und heute kann man auf Buchtiteln lesen *Studienrat* und *Studienrätin* [. . .]. Für *Wustmann*, der sich über diese Damen mit männlichen Titeln sehr aufregt, gehört ein *Frl. Doktor* zu den Sprachdummheiten. Hier und in allen Fällen wie *Spezialärztin, Direktorin, Referendarin, Verwalterin, Vertreterin* stünde einem folgerichtigen Verfahren nichts im Wege, sofern nur das zartere Geschlecht es selbst wünschte. Dadurch könnte man übrigens endlich eine *Frau Doktorin Meyer* von einer *Frau Dr. Meyer* unterscheiden und neuerdings eine wirkliche *Pfarrerin* von einer *Frau Pfarrer*. Aber wie kennzeichnen wir einen weiblichen *Kaufmann* oder *Obmann*? *Kauffrau* klingt etwas ungewöhnlich (trotz *Gemüse-, Eier-, Milchfrau* [. . .]) und könnte einen unliebsamen semantischen Nebenton haben. Vielleicht *Kaufmännin, Obmännin?* Sagen wir doch anstandslos *Landsmännin*, unbekümmert um den Widerspruch in -*männin*. (*Henzen* 1965: 116f.)

Soweit also das Henzensche Standardwerk im Jahre 1965. Immerhin – die Zeiten haben sich inzwischen doch schon dahin geändert, daß niemand mehr es wagen würde, diesen Stoff in so plumper und peinlich »neckischer« Weise zu erörtern. Und die Rede von »sofern nur das zartere Geschlecht es selbst wünschte« erscheint als Verdrehung oder naive Verkennung der wirklichen Gegebenheiten angesichts der Tatsache, daß Ministerien die »männlichen Titel« gesetzlich verordnen und erst Sprachgutachten einholen »müssen«, bevor dem erklärten Wunsch der Frauen (eventuell) entsprochen werden »kann«.

Festzuhalten bleibt also, daß die movierte Form zur Bezeichnung weiblicher Menschen eine sprachliche Diskriminierung sozusagen ersten Ranges darstellt. Das hochproduktive Suffix *-in* konserviert im Sprachsystem die jahrtausendealte Abhängigkeit der Frau vom Mann, die es endlich zu überwinden gilt. Auch sprachlich.

Wenn nun aber nur die movierte Form abgeschafft und sonst nichts geändert wird, so erhalten wir folgendes System:

der Ingenieur		← Geschlechtsabstraktion
der *weibl.* Ingenieur	der *männl.* Ingenieur	attr. Geschlechts-spezifikation
die *weibl.* Ingenieure	die *männl.* Ingenieure	
die Ingenieure		→ Geschlechtsabstraktion

Rein formal ist gegen diesen Vorschlag also nichts einzuwenden, und ich nehme an, daß Sie diesen formalen Aspekt im Sinn hatten, wenn Sie schreiben: »Die Bezeichnungen würden dann – was sie jetzt zweifellos noch nicht sind – geschlechtsneutral, weil es dann kein Geschlechtsparadigma mehr gäbe.« In der Tat, die oben abgebildete Konfiguration ist in den entscheidenden formalen Eigenschaften identisch mit unserem Muster an Symmetrie, den Körperteilbezeichnungen. Man vergleiche noch einmal:

der Arm		→ Situierungsabstraktion
der *linke* Arm	der *rechte* Arm	attributive Situierungs-spezifikation
die *linken* Arme	die *rechten* Arme	
die Arme		→ Situierungsabstraktion

Trotzdem gibt es schwerwiegende Gründe, weshalb dieser Vorschlag abzulehnen ist:

1. Maskulines Genus hat im Deutschen, wie wir alle wissen und wie in den Grafiken ausführlich abzulesen, bei Personenbezeich-

nungen geschlechtsspezifizierende Funktion, sei diese nun redundant *(der Mann)* oder nicht *(der Angestellte)*. In diesem Punkt unterscheiden sich die Körperteilbezeichnungen mit ihren bedeutungsirrelevanten verschiedenen Genera *(die Hand, der Arm, das Bein)* **grundsätzlich** von den Personenbezeichnungen. Deshalb sind die beiden letzten Grafiken auch nur dann identisch zu nennen, wenn man sie aus ihren Funktionszusammenhängen herauslöst. Auch ein E hat in E-Dur eine völlig andere Funktion als in F-Dur.

Der Vorschlag **kann** also nur dazu führen, daß die alte, von Frauen angegriffene Praxis erhalten bleibt und noch verstärkt wird: Das Maskulinum legt die Referenz »männlich« nahe – je mehr grammatisch erforderliche Maskulina *(er, sein, ihm, der, dessen, dem, ...)* in seinem Gefolge auftreten, um so mehr. Frauen werden sprachlich noch weiter unsichtbar gemacht.

2. Das Referieren auf Frauen wird noch mehr »Genus-Vergewaltigung« nötig machen als bisher. Sollen die Pronomina sich nach dem grammatischen Geschlecht (Maskulinum) oder nach dem natürlichen Geschlecht (weiblich) richten? Sollen wir sagen *Unser (weiblicher) Ingenieur und ihr Mann* oder *... und sein Mann?*

3. Es wird sich in unserer Welt der Männer schwerlich die Praxis durchsetzen (lassen), immer dann korrekt die attributive Spezifikation anzuwenden, also immer *der männliche Student, die männlichen Rechtsanwälte* zu sagen, wenn Männer gemeint sind. Vielmehr ist klar abzusehen, daß die Praxis sich weiter und nun noch verstärkt des folgenden asymmetrischen Systems bedienen wird:

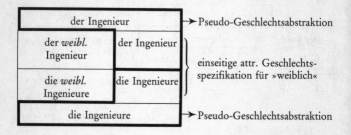

Soweit die Problemanalyse, und nun zu meinem Lösungsvorschlag.

3 Therapievorschläge

Was wir tun müssen, um ein funktionsfähiges und gerechtes symmetrisches System herzustellen, ist ganz simpel:

> Abschaffung des *-in*-Suffixes – aber nicht etwa der femininen Personenbezeichnungen!

Statt die *Studentin/Lehrerin/Ingenieurin* einfach immer *die Student/Lehrer/Ingenieur*, etc.!

Wenn wir Frauen listig vorschlagen: »Wir schaffen einfach das *-in* ab, ansonsten bleibt alles, wie es ist« – so stimmt das zwar formal, aber den Männern wird es trotzdem ungemütlich werden, denn damit wird, obwohl wir »nur die Bezeichnungen für uns leicht abändern«, zugleich in männliches Terrain gewaltig hineinregiert. Abschaffung des *-in* ist nämlich in der Auswirkung dasselbe wie »Feminisierung« vieler bisher rein maskuliner Bezeichnungen: Wörter, die immer total maskulin waren, können plötzlich auch feminin sein und feminine Pronomina nach sich ziehen.

Wie stark die Vorstellung »männlich« mit der sogenannten »unmarkierten« Form verknüpft ist, zeigt sich erst, wenn frau diese Form auch für das Femininum »beansprucht«. Anders läßt es sich kaum erklären, wieso »Abschaffung der movierten Form« bisher immer (offenbar auch von engagiertesten Feministinnen, von denen ja keine auf diese einfache »Usurpationsidee« gekommen ist) gleichgesetzt wurde mit »Abschaffung der femininen Bezeichnungen«. Dabei sind das – linguistisch gesehen – zwei völlig verschiedene Dinge.

Durch den simplen Trick der Abschaffung des *-in* (und der übrigen femininen Suffixe *-ess (Stewardess), -isse (Diakonisse), -issin (Äbtissin), -(eu)se (Masseuse)* erhalten wir zunächst folgendes System:

der Student		→ Pseudo-Geschlechtsneutralisation
die Student	*der* Student	Genus-Geschlechtsspezifikation
die *weibl.* Studenten	die *männl.* Studenten	attributive Geschlechtsspezifikation
die Studenten		→ Geschlechtsneutralisation

Textbeispiel:

Sie ist eine gute Student. Ihre Leistungen sind beachtlich und ihre Professor ist sehr zufrieden mit ihr. Früher war sie übrigens Sekretär bei einer Architekt.

Das System entspricht jetzt dem Paradigma *die/der Angestellte* – Plural immerhin schon garantiert geschlechtsneutral. Für die Masse der *-er*-Ableitungen ergibt sich das morphologische Problem, daß der Plural und das Femininum Singular noch homonym sind:

Meine Lehrer ist/sind nett.

Ausweg: dem Plural dieser Formen wird ein *-s* angehängt: *die/der Lehrer, die Lehrers.* Das hat zusätzlich den erheblichen Vorteil einer Assoziationsbremse: Die jahrhundertealte Tradition, die uns bei *die Dichter/Künstler/Arbeiter/Handwerker* etc. bisher ausschließlich an Männer denken läßt, wird formal abgeblockt. Es reicht, wenn Ausdrücke wie *die Bibliothekare/Professoren/Rechtsanwälte* etc. etc. weiterhin, aufgrund der langen sprachlichen Tradition, in erster Linie an Männer denken lassen.

Bleibt das Problem des sogenannten »unmarkierten« Maskulinum Singular (vgl. das obere Feld der letzten Grafik) zu lösen – wie Sie wissen, ein Problem, mit dem sich vor allem die angelsächsische feministische Linguistik herumschlägt. Im Deutschen haben wir es auch, nur beschäftigten uns vorerst noch schlimmere Probleme – z. B. die femininen Suffixe. Da das Englische kein grammatisches Geschlecht hat, konzentrieren sich feministisch-linguistische Forderungen und Vorschläge auf das »generisch« gebrauchte *he* (sowie auf die Komposita mit *-man (postman, chairman, congressman)*). Was nützt den Engländerinnen und Amerikanerinnen ihr schönes symmetrisches System, wenn es Usus ist zu sagen: *Any doctor/lawyer... he... his...?!* Die amerikanischen Guidelines schlagen vor, so oft es geht auf den Plural auszuweichen (geht nach Abschaffung der femininen Suffixe auch im Deutschen) und ansonsten die Pronomina gerecht zu wechseln, wo auf »the doctor/student« im allgemeinen referiert wird. Das geht im Deutschen nicht, weil wir das grammatische Geschlecht beibehalten – und das sollten wir, weil sonst die gesamte Wortstellung aus den Fugen gerät.

Aber wir haben ja im Deutschen, wie schon einmal gesagt, noch das Neutrum! Ich schlage also folgendes Paradigma vor: *Die/*

der/das Professor. Das Professor etc. soll in all den Fällen gesagt werden, wo Präjudizierung eines der beiden Geschlechter diskriminierend wäre.

das Professor		Geschlechtsabstraktion
die Professor	*der* Professor	Genus-Geschlechtsspezifikation
die *weibl.* Professoren	die *männl.* Professoren	attributive Geschlechtsspezifikation
die Professoren		Geschlechtsneutralisation

Anbei Paragraph 3 Abs. 2 der Zulassungs- und Immatrikulationsordnung der Universität Konstanz – auf Neudeutsch:

Dem Zulassungsausschuß gehören an:
1. das Rektor als Vorsitzendes oder das Prorektor für die Lehre als dessen Stellvertreter
2. zwei Professoren
3. ein Angehöriges des wissenschaftlichen Dienstes
4. ein Student
5. das Leiter der Studentischen Abteilung

Ein Beschluß des Senats der Universität Konstanz vom 20. 2. 80:

Den Vorsitz der Gemeinsamen Kommission für das Lehrerbegleitstudium soll das Dekan der Philosophischen Fakultät führen. Es kann sich durch das Prodekan der Philosophischen Fakultät vertreten lassen.

Anmerkung zu möglichen »tierischen« oder »dinglichen« Assoziationen beim Vernehmen des Neudeutschen: Beim Vernehmen des Jetztdeutschen haben wir Frauen immer so »männliche« Assoziationen und mögen's nicht sehr. Aber mann findet das ja nicht schlimm. – Weiter: Eine immerhin denkbare Rektor, Dekan oder Prodekan (zur Verdeutlichung: ein weibliches Rektor etc.) müß ja mit denselben »tierischen« Assoziationen leben.

Die hier vorgeschlagene Umstrukturierung tut dem deutschen Sprachsystem nicht mehr Gewalt an als dieses System uns Frauen antut. Läßt sich eine solche Umstrukturierung durchsetzen? Wenn mensch es will, bestimmt – ähnlich wie sich Sprachreformen

(Norwegen: Nynorsk) und Rechtschreibreformen (Dänemark) durchgesetzt haben. Es würde wahrscheinlich eine gewisse Übergangszeit der Unsicherheit, der ständigen Fehler und Versprecher und der Belustigungen geben – aber so was legt sich, wenn die neuen Formen vertraut geworden sind. Wenn die öffentliche Sprache (Schule, Medien, Gesetzgebung etc.) konsequent nach diesem Muster gehandhabt würde, würde die private Sprache bald nachziehen.

Eine der wichtigsten Konsequenzen der hier entworfenen Neuregelung sehe ich darin, daß wir Frauen uns auf diese Weise »die Bausteine der Wortbildung (zurück) erobern« würden. Die Wortbildung operiert in dem hier interessierenden Bereich ausschließlich mit maskulinen (auch »unmarkiert« genannten) Basiselementen, vgl. *ärzt-lich, schriftsteller-n, künstler-isch, jurist-isch, Meisterschaft,* etc. *Ärztin-lich, künstlerinnisch* geht nicht, gibt's nicht. Wenn aber diese Stämme fortan auch als Feminina gebraucht würden, wären sie und damit auch die Ableitungen wirklich »geschlechtsneutral«, würde die Assoziation »weiblich« nicht mehr sprachsystematisch erschwert und die Assoziation »männlich« nicht mehr so sehr begünstigt.

Nehmen wir aber einmal den wahrscheinlicheren Fall an, daß eine derartige Umstrukturierung gar nicht erst erwogen wird, sogleich als lächerlich, undurchführbar etc. abgelehnt wird. Welche der zur Wahl stehenden Strategien – Abschaffung oder Forcierung des Femininums plus *-in* – ist dann das kleinere Übel?

Ich plädiere mit aller Entschiedenheit für die Forcierung, obwohl die femininen Suffixe, wie ich gezeigt habe, hochgradig diskriminierend sind. Aber die Geschichte kennt viele Fälle, in denen Termini, Kennzeichnungen u. ä., die ursprünglich diskriminierende Funktion hatten, »neutralisiert« oder gar zum Gütezeichen wurden. Etwa die Waren-Kennzeichnung »Made in Germany« oder Bezeichnungen wie *Proletarier, Blacks, Lesben, Schwule, Krüppel.* Wenn solche Kennzeichnungen von der sprachlich ausgegrenzten Gruppe mit Stolz übernommen und forciert statt vermieden wurden, füllten sie sich mit neuem »Wert« und »Sinn«, zunächst für die Gruppe selbst, dann auch für die anderen, die für sich beansprucht hatten, die Norm zu sein.

Zum Schluß noch ein paar Bemerkungen zu dem Trend, den Sie für das Skandinavische und Englische und auch bei deutschen Frauen beobachtet haben und den ich »Trend zur Geschlechtsabstraktion« nennen möchte. Das übergeordnete Ziel ist ja immer: Gleiche Chancen des Gemeintseins und Identifiziertwerdens für Frauen und Männer. Die Wege, auf denen dies Ziel zu erreichen ist, sind von Sprache zu Sprache verschieden, weil die Sprachsysteme verschieden sind. Gleichheit heißt also: Entweder kein Geschlecht spezifizieren oder beide, je nach Systemhintergrund. Besitzt eine Sprache kein grammatisches Geschlecht, wie das Englische, so ist attributive oder sonstige Spezifikation in der Regel diskriminierend, wenn sie (und das ist die Praxis) einseitig bleibt: *female/woman doctor/lawyer* ist so diskriminierend wie *postman* und *chairman,* wenn das jeweilige Pendant unüblich ist *(male/man doctor, congresswoman).*

Daß die Skandinavierinnen die movierte Form ablehnen, ist die aussichtsreichste Strategie, da ihr Genussystem ja nicht zwischen Femininum und Maskulinum unterscheidet (genus commune für weibliche und männliche Personenbezeichnungen, neben dem genus neutrum)[11]. Morphologische Spezifikation für Frauen allein ist daher »Ausgrenzung aus der Norm«.

Für das Deutsche gilt hinwiederum die Strategie: Beide Geschlechter benennen – nicht nur das männliche! Wenn die Unterscheidung zwischen Femininum und Maskulinum das gesamte Personenbezeichnungssystem durchzieht, dann muß verhindert werden, daß eines der Genera das andere im Plural und im »generischen Singular« »vertreten« kann.

Und nun noch eine ganz schwierige Frage: Welche der nachstehenden Substantive bezeichnen Menschen?

Büchsenöffner, Schornsteinfeger, Korkenzieher, Staubsauger, Automat, Diplomat, Bovist, Dentist, Praktikant, Hydrant, Motor, Autor, Direktor, Transistor.

Antwort: Alle und nur die, die eine *-in*-Movierung erlauben.
Vielleicht wäre es doch ungünstig, das *-in* abzuschaffen. Wir brauchen es offenbar, um Männer von Maschinen, Pilzen und dergleichen unterscheiden zu können.
Das ist nicht etwa eine voreingenommene feministische Interpretation harmloser Sprachtatbestände – nein, der gewiß nicht als Feminist verschriene Kollege *Brinkmann* ([2]1971: 24) sieht es genauso:

Anders als Werkzeug- und Vorgangsbegriffe *(Bohrer, Fehler)* haben diese [. . .] Bezeichnungen die Möglichkeit zu einer weiblichen Variante *(Berlinerin, Schweizerin)*, und insofern sie diese Variante haben, eignet ihnen männliches Geschlecht.

1980

Anmerkungen

1 Senta *Trömel-Plötz* und mir wurde 1978 von der Universität Konstanz der Titel *Privatdozent* verliehen. Ob wir uns auch *Privatdozentin* nennen dürfen, wissen wir nicht.

2 Vgl. hierzu auch *Hellinger* 1980 a.

3 Den Terminus ›Differentialgenus‹ übernehme ich von *Wienold* 1967.

4 Daß die Adjektive *weiblich* und *männlich* nicht nur auf das Geschlecht, sondern darüber hinaus auch auf ein Rollenklischee referieren können (vgl. *ein sehr männlicher Mann*), lasse ich hier außer acht.

5 Zitiert nach *Lahnstein* (1977: 68).

6 *Schenkelin* ist bei Carl *Spitteler, Olympischer Frühling*, Jena 1919, Bd. 2, S. 296, belegt: *Doch als nun Aphrodites Kühnheit sich vermaß, / Daß sie auf Heras leeren Thronsitz lachend saß, / Rief Zeus: »Auf! Lüpf du deine losen Schenkelinnen, / Du lockre Gais, von Heras Ehrenstuhl von hinnen!* – Ich übernehme den Beleg von *Ljungerud* (1973: 146), der dazu verständnisinnig bemerkt: »Es mag dahingestellt sein, ob Aphrodites Schenkel nur des Reimes wegen ›Schenkelinnen‹ genannt werden, oder ob Zeus sie durch diese Form als besonders weibliche, zur Unzucht willfährige und anreizende Gliedmaßen charakterisieren will.« Ein imponierendes Beispiel schlüpfrig-männlicher Eintracht in »Dichtung« und »Wissenschaft«! Aus berufenem Munde erfahren wir hier endlich, was »diese Form« **wirklich** bedeutet. Anscheinend fügt sie nicht einfach, wie *Wellmann* (1975: 107) nüchtern mutmaßt, einem »Basisinhalt« das Merkmal »weibliches Geschlecht« hinzu. Es muß offenbar heißen »besonders weiblich, zur Unzucht willfährig und anreizend«. – Für derlei Phantasien dann Zeus verantwortlich zu machen, ist direkt rührend. Verantwortlich ist in erster Linie *Ljungerud* selbst – eventuell auch *Spitteler*.

7 Vgl. in *Trömel-Plötz* 1980 die zum Kapitel »Sexismus in der Linguistik« zitierte Literatur.

8 Vgl. *Wilmanns* (1899: 311) und *Henzen* (1965: 153).

9 *Baudouin de Courtenay* im Jahre 1923 (abgedruckt 1929): Diese in der sprache zum vorschein kommende weltanschauung, nach welcher das männliche als etwas ursprüngliches und das weibliche als etwas abgeleitetes aufgefaßt wird, verstösst gegen die logik und gegen das gerechtigkeitsgefühl. Und trotzdem ist sie so tief in die psychik von Europäern

und Semiten eingewurzelt, dass sie sogar in die künstlichen hilfssprachen übergegangen ist. So finden wir z. b. in Esperanto *bovo* nicht nur als ›rindvieh‹ im allgemeinen, sondern auch als ›stier‹ (? ›ochs‹) und *bovino* als ›kuh‹, *patro* als ›vater‹ und *patrino* als ›mutter‹ (1929: 231f.).

Die Arbeit *Baudouin de Courtenays* ist **sehr** lesenswert, nicht nur wegen seiner entschieden feministisch-linguistischen Position (und das 1923!), sondern auch wegen seines Einfallsreichtums, seiner scharfen Ironie und seines unorthodoxen, radikal persönlich gefärbten Stils. Fast möchte ich dieser Sprache das Ehrenprädikat »Frauensprache« zuerkennen (in dem Sinne, wie etwa die Kalverkämpersprache eine Extremform der Männersprache darstellt, vgl. die Anm. auf S. 42). – Den Hinweis auf diese Oase in der Wüste verdanke ich Petra *Gall*.
Nachtrag im Dezember 1983: Von Helmut *Walther* (Gesellschaft für deutsche Sprache) bekam ich eine Kopie des Kapitels 7 »Vorwalten des männlichen Geistes in der Sprache« aus *Götze* 1918. *Götze* schreibt (S. 47f.):
Ein Mädchen kann ein Luftikus genannt werden oder ein Springinsfeld, Guckindiewelt, Tunichtgut: niemand gibt sich die Mühe, eigene Worte für das weibliche Geschlecht zu bilden oder ihnen auch nur die Endung -in anzuhängen. **Schon diese Bildung mit -in ist im Grund ein Unrecht gegen die Frau,** so hat es schon Jacob Grimm empfunden, als er aussprach, das Maskulin stelle sich als das lebendigste, kräftigste und ursprünglichste unter allen Geschlechtern dar. Regelmäßig bildet, wo gewechselt wird, das männliche Geschlecht den Ausgangspunkt: *Herr, Fürst, Hund* sind ursprünglich, *Herrin, Fürstin, Hündin* abgeleitet, und nur ganz selten tritt das umgekehrte Verhältnis ein, wie bei *Witwer, Katzert, Gansert, Enterich* zu *Witwe, Katze, Gans* und *Ente.* Eine unmittelbare Folge davon ist, daß wohl von den männlichen Substantiven weitere Ableitungen gebildet werden können, *Herrlichkeit, fürstlich, hündisch,* nicht aber von den weiblichen. Immerhin geschieht aber doch hier für die Frauen etwas, während in anderen Fällen der Wechsel, auch wo er möglich wäre, unterbleibt, so daß Wörter wie *Schüler* und *Patienten* auch die *Schülerinnen* und *Patientinnen* mit vertreten, daß sich in die *Hörerliste* auch *Hörerinnen* eintragen müssen. Und auf der ganzen Linie behält Luther recht, wenn er in seiner Predigt vom Jakobustag 1522 sagt: *dann ein weib hat allzeit zwen nachteil, da ein man zwen vortail hat.*
(Hervorhebung von mir.)
Helmut *Walther* erhielt den Hinweis von Luise *Berthold* (1891–1983), ihrerzeit Professorin der Altgermanistik der Universität Marburg, die sich 1923 als eine der ersten deutschen Frauen habilitierte und die sich wiederholt zum Thema »sprachliche Diskriminierung der Frau« geäußert hat in Zeiten, da ringsum in der Germanistik noch alles schlief, vgl.

Berthold 1958, 1964 (1981) und 1983. Über Luise *Berthold* vgl. *Mulch* 1981 sowie *Dingeldein* und *Friebertshäuser* 1983.
10 *Lichtenberg* in einem Brief vom 5. 3. 1772: »Mein Wirt ist ein Glaser namens Metmershausen, die Frau Glaserin, die ich künftig immer Frau von Metmershausen nennen werde, scheint mir eine gute Frau zu sein [. . .].« Zitiert nach *Lahnstein* (1977: 70).

11 Das gilt nicht für das Nynorsk.

>»Eine männliche Seefrau!
Der blödeste Ausdruck seit Wibschenged
Über Gerd Brantenbergs *Die Töchter Egalıas*

Gerd *Brantenberg* ist eine im deutschen Sprachraum (noch) unbe-
kannte Autorin. Ja, eine Autor-**in** – ich unternehme mit dem Ein-
leitungssatz nicht den Versuch, die deutsche Sprache feministisch
umzufunktionieren und den Ausdruck *Autorin* auf einen Mann
anzuwenden als Reaktion darauf, daß *Autor* ja auch für Frauen gebraucht wird. Solches Vorgehen wäre zwar durchaus im Sinne der
Autorin, es ist in diesem Fall aber nicht nötig, weil Gerd *Brantenberg* eine Frau ist. *Gerd* ist ein weiblicher Vorname im Norwegischen.

Auf dem Umschlag der deutschen (nicht der norwegischen) Fassung steht: *G. Brantenberg.* Der Roman wendet sich in erster Linie
an Menschen mit einem entwickelten feministischen Bewußtsein
(natürlich auch an solche, die es werden wollen). Bei dieser Zielgruppe konnte der Verlag von der Erfahrungstatsache ausgehen,
daß männliche Autorschaft das Interesse und den Kaufwunsch
nicht gerade anregt (»Von Männern haben wir nun nachgerade genug gelesen!«). Also wird Gerd bei uns diplomatisch als G Punkt
eingeführt. Die Assoziation »männlich«, die ihr Vorname bei un-
vorbereiteten Deutschsprachigen unweigerlich hervorruft, wäre
auch in der Tat völlig irreführend, denn dieses Buch konnte nur aus
einer weiblichen Betroffenheit heraus entstehen.

Das norwegische Original erschien 1977, die deutsche Übersetzung im Mai 1980. Einen Monat später, im Juni, wollte ich das
Buch mit meinen Studentinnen und Studenten diskutieren – da war
es bereits vergriffen! Ich erkläre mir den enormen Verkaufserfolg
damit, daß *Egalia* ein Lesebedürfnis befriedigt, das im allgemeinen
von feministischer Literatur eher frustriert wird: Selten hatten wir
bisher was zu lachen; hier aber wird feministische Theorie und Erfahrung in Form einer ungeheuer witzigen, bissigen und scharfsin-
nigen Satire auf das Patriarchat vermittelt. Ein kluges und geist-
reiches Buch, voll überraschender und entlarvender Einfälle und
Beobachtungen, voll konstruktiver Phantasie. Uneingeschränkt
zu empfehlen, ja ein Meilenstein des Feminismus, finde ich, wie

Beauvoirs *Le deuxième sexe*, Milletts *Sexual politics*, Schwarzers *Der kleine Unterschied...*, Janssen-Jurreits *Sexismus* und Dalys *Gyn/ecology*.

In den *Linguistischen Berichten* wurden bisher noch keine Romane rezensiert, schon gar nicht feministische. Obwohl Literatur doch gewiß etwas mit Sprache zu tun hat, haben die Linguist/inn/en dies Feld lange den Literaturwissenschaftler/inne/n überlassen (nach einem kurzen Erblühen der Textlinguistik Anfang der siebziger Jahre).

Das jetzt wieder erwachende linguistische Interesse an literarischen Texten ist ein Ergebnis der Gesamtarbeit der Frauenbewegung. Frauen haben erkannt, daß unsere Sprachen, wie verschieden auch immer strukturiert, allesamt Männersprachen sind. Sie gehen nun daran, diese zunächst gefühlsmäßige Erkenntnis breit zu belegen, u. a. anhand linguistischer Analysen von Texten aller Art.[1]

Die Töchter Egalias nun stellt den m. W. ersten Versuch dar, einen Text in einer »Frauensprache« zu verfassen, also in einer Sprache, die es nicht gibt, die neu erfunden werden mußte. Es ist jedoch nicht diejenige »Frauensprache«, die wir suchen oder gerne haben wollen, eine Sprache also, in der Frauen sich »einfach nur« als eigenständige Subjekte, kurz: als Menschen, artikulieren (können). Nein, die Sprache der Töchter Egalias ist eine Sprache von Machthaberinnen, wie unsere diversen Männersprachen (Norwegisch, Deutsch, Englisch, Französisch, Italienisch, Spanisch, Russisch, Tschechisch, Chinesisch, Japanisch, etc., etc.) Sprachen von Machthabern sind. Das bedeutet: die Regeln der Männersprache Norwegisch (für die Übersetzung: Deutsch) werden listig und sinnig auf den Kopf gestellt, uns spiegelverkehrt vorgeführt, mit dem einzigen Ziel, die Sprache des Patriarchats durch die lexikalischen und grammatischen Überraschungsschocks als solche erkennbar zu machen, schlagend zu entlarven. »Spiegelverkehrt« und »auf den Kopf gestellt« heißt hier: In Egalia ist die Frau die Norm und der Mann die Abweichung, der Abhängige – politisch, sozial und, folgerichtig, auch sprachlich. Zur Illustration aus der Fülle der Beispiele eines, das mich besonders nachhaltig »schockiert« hat. Beim ersten Lesen begriff ich's gar nicht, so fremdartig und »verkehrt« wirkt und klingt es: Eine Frau ruft an, und am anderen Ende der Leitung meldet sich jemand mit: »Herr Cheftaucherin Ödeschär«. Der brave Hausmann Ödeschär darf sich in Egalia mit dem Titel

»Cheftaucherin« seiner Gattin schmücken. Solcher erheirateter Titelschmuck war und ist außerhalb von Egalia bekanntlich ein rein weibliches »Privileg«. So bewegt z. B. mein Doktortitel auch heute noch manche zu der herzigen Frage: »Ach, Ihr Mann ist wohl Arzt?«

Egalia ist ein Buch, das man unter vielerlei Aspekten untersuchen kann – eine reiche Quelle z. B. für Seminar-, Magister-, Doktorarbeiten etc. Obwohl ich mich hier auf die rein linguistischen Aspekte beschränken muß, kann ich sie unmöglich in der Gründlichkeit behandeln, die sie verdienen. Vor allem kann ich die rein linguistisch besonders interessanten Gesichtspunkte, die sich aus einem Vergleich der deutschen Übersetzung mit dem norwegischen Original ergeben, nur andeuten. Es ist aber eine ausführliche kontrastive Analyse der sprachlichen Besonderheiten von *Egalias døtre / Die Töchter Egalias* geplant, die Katrin *Lunde*, Universität Tromsö, und ich gemeinsam schreiben wollen.

Wie gesagt ergibt sich die besondere Sprache des Buches folgerichtig aus dem besonderen Inhalt. Egalia ist eine matriarchalisch organisierte Gesellschaft, in der die Machtverhältnisse umgekehrt sind wie bei uns. Die hierzulande männliche Rolle haben dort die Frauen und umgekehrt. In Egalia gebären zwar immer noch die Frauen die Kinder, aber die Männer *bekommen* sie – zur Pflege und Aufzucht. Das Buch beginnt mit dem provokanten Satz: »Schließlich sind es noch immer die Männer, die die Kinder bekommen!« – dessen egalitanischen Sinngehalt (s. o.) frau[2] erst allmählich beim Weiterlesen erfaßt. Männern wird von Frauen mitgeteilt: »Du bekommst ein Kind!« Die Institution Ehe gibt es nicht; statt dessen existiert die Institution Vaterschaftsschutz (norw. *farskaps-beskyttelse*, schlecht übersetzt mit *Vaterschaftspatronat*[3]), die Frauen dem Mann ihrer Wahl anbieten können. Will eine Frau den Vater ihres Kindes nicht als Bettgefährten, Haushälter und Erzieher der Kinder, so »bekommt« er entweder das Kind trotzdem und findet sich damit in der sozial elenden Rolle eines ungeschützten Vaters, oder ein anderer Mann bekommt es zusammen mit dem Vaterschaftsschutz, dem Lebensziel und Traum aller Männer. – In Egalia kommt es relativ häufig vor, daß Frauen Männer vergewaltigen. Sind diese noch jung, so müssen sie sich u. U. von ihrer Mutter sagen lassen, sie seien selbst schuld; sie hätten halt nicht so einen aufreizenden PH tragen und nachts einfach im Wald herumgehen sollen.

Es ist die **Selbstverständlichkeit,** mit der diese Unerhörtheiten, ja Ungeheuerlichkeiten vorgetragen werden, die uns beim Lesen anfangs am gründlichsten verwirrt und schließlich am nachhaltigsten beeindruckt und belehrt. Der von *Brantenberg* angestrebte und erzielte Lerneffekt der gesamten, langen Lektüreerfahrung ist der, daß uns **unsere** Bedingungen, die des Frauseins im Patriarchat, allmählich oder auch schlagartig genauso fremd, absurd, unerhört und ungeheuerlich vorkommen.

Und so auch unsere Sprache – hier: das Norwegisch oder Deutsch (je nachdem), das wir sprechen, besser: zu sprechen gezwungen sind. Gerd *Brantenberg* zeigt uns, wie sehr das Norwegische eine Männersprache ist, indem sie den »herrschenden«, mann-zentrierten Sprachgebrauch systematisch zu einem »frauschenden« frauzentrierten umfunktioniert. Sie extrapoliert aus dem Norwegischen ein »Norwegalitanisch«, wie ich es einmal nennen möchte. Die deutsche Übersetzerin Elke *Radicke* stand vor der schwierigen Aufgabe, dieses Norwegalitanisch in ein Deutsch-Egalitanisch zu übersetzen. Sie mußte sich also bei der Übersetzung praktisch ständig auf drei Sprachen gleichzeitig beziehen: erstens auf die Männersprache Norwegisch, zweitens auf *Brantenbergs* Norwegalitanisch, drittens auf die Männersprache Deutsch. Ich möchte diese komplizierten Bezüge anhand einer Grafik verdeutlichen:

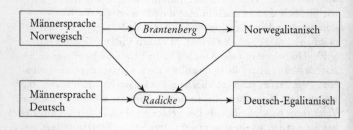

Wie *Brantenberg* und *Radicke* ihre jeweils unterschiedlich determinierten Um- bzw. Übersetzungsprobleme gelöst haben, soll wie gesagt Gegenstand einer kontrastiven Studie sein (*Lunde* und *Pusch*, in Vorb.). Im Rahmen dieser Rezension möchte ich nur auf das Deutsch-Egalitanische eingehen. Zunächst ein Auszug aus dem Lexikon:

Männersprache Deutsch	Deutsch-Egalitanisch
s. ermannen	s. erweiben
Vater werden	e. Kind bekommen; in glücklichen Umständen sein
zeugungsfähiger Mann	freier Samenspender; Verhütungspillennehmer
Mensch	die Wibsche
menschlich	wibschlich
Unmensch	Unwibsche
herrschen	frauschen
Herrschaft	Frauschaft
patriotisch	matriotisch
Hoden	Schambeutel
brüderlich	schwesterlich
Lehrerzimmer	Lehrerinnenzimmer
Bauerngeschlecht	Bäuerinnengeschlecht
Ritterstand	Ritterinnenstand
Herr der Lage (geschlechtsneutral)	Dame der Lage (geschlechtsneutral)
Allmächtiger!	Allmächtige!
O Gott!/Mein Gott!	O Göttin/Meine Göttin!
Mann! (Interjektion)	Weib!
den Weg wie seine Westentasche kennen	den Weg wie ihre Kitteltasche kennen
Teufel, Luzifer	Luzia
Weiß der Teufel!	Weiß Luzia!
Blödmann (geschlechtsneutral)	Blödfrau (geschlechtsneutral)
Nebenmann (geschlechtsneutral)	Nebenfrau (geschlechtsneutral)
Schwängerung einer Frau ohne deren Einverständnis/Wissen	P-Betrug (P wie Pille, Präservativ oder Pimmel)
primus inter pares (geschlechtsneutral)	prima inter pares (geschlechtsneutral)

Dieser lexikalische Auszug macht deutlich, inwiefern die Frau in Egalia und folglich im Egalitanischen als Norm gilt und der Mann als Ausnahme. Grammatisch schlägt sich dies vor allem darin nieder, daß im Deutsch-Egalitanischen durchweg das Femininum statt des Maskulinums generisch verwendet wird:

> (Ermahnung an einen Mann:) *Keine* kann das Ei essen und zugleich das Küken haben wollen. (p. 7)

> In der Natur frauscht ... das Gesetz des Dschungels. Das ist Krieg aller gegen alle, wobei *die Stärkere* immer gewinnt und *die Schwächere* immer hungert oder stirbt. (p. 16)

ich hab *keine*, mit *der* ich reden kann ... (p. 34)

Im Prinzip konnte *jede* Mitglied werden (p. 39)

Seine Beine wurden ganz schlapp – wie bei *einer Dreijährigen,
die* sich zu laufen weigert und vom Papa getragen werden will.
(p. 60)

Keine durfte es sehen, *keine* durfte es wissen (p. 62)

(Trost an einen Mann:) Sowas kann auch *der Besten* passieren,
Kleiner.

Immer führen sie *eine* hinters Licht. (p. 96)

Petronius träumte oft davon, daß er in einer Fischerhütte wohn-
te, wo nie *eine* kam und ihn störte. (p. 102) (Hervorhebungen
von mir)

Da in Egalia selbstverständlich die Frauen alle bei uns männlich besetzten Berufssparten fest in der Hand haben, gibt es bestimmte
Wörter nicht, die uns geläufig sind, z. B. *Seemann, Zimmermann,
Steuermann, Kaufmann.* Ein Junge, der gern Seefrau werden
möchte, wird von seiner Schwester ausgelacht:

»Haha! Ein Mann soll Seefrau werden? Denkste!« Neunmal-
klug fügte sie noch hinzu, daß der Widersinn doch schon in den
Wörtern liege. »Eine männliche Seefrau! Der blödeste Aus-
druck seit Wibschengedenken. Ho, ho! Vielleicht solltest du
Schiffs*junge* werden? Oder Zimmer*mann*? Oder Steuer*mann*?!
Ich lach mich tot!« (p. 8)

Bekanntlich enden viele skandinavische Nachnamen auf *-(s)sen*
bzw. *-(s)son.* In Egalia enden sie auf *-tochter;* der erste Bestandteil
ist immer ein Mädchenname: *Listochter, Monatochter.* Und so lesen wir: »Kristoffer Bram, geb. Listochter, ging mit Liebe und
Wärme in seinem Hausmannsdasein auf.«
  In dieser Tour geht es munter fort – unmöglich, alle Spitzen gegen
das Patriarchat hier aufzuführen. Frau sollte sich schleunigst ans
Lesen machen und selbst sehen und lachen. Es empfiehlt sich Vor-
lesen in trautem Freundinnenkreis. Zwei Männer, gute Freunde,
gestanden mir übrigens, sie hätten das Buch bald weggelegt, die
Sprache sei ihnen zu penetrant, und überhaupt alles.
  Quod erat demonstrandum. Gerd *Brantenberg* und Elke *Radik-*

ke, die Übersetzerin, konnten kaum sinnfälliger bestätigt werden. Penetrant, in der Tat – ist für uns Frauen diese Männersprache, und überhaupt alles.

1981

Anmerkungen

1 Vgl. etwa *Hiatt* (1976) und *Schulz* (1978).
2 *Radicke* »übersetzt« das norwegalitanische *dam*, eine Entsprechung zu norw. *man* ›man‹, mit *dam*. Besser wäre natürlich *frau* gewesen. Insgesamt gibt es aber bei *Radicke* weit mehr gute, eigenständige und kreative Problemlösungen als Schnitzer und Inkonsistenzen. Mehr dazu in *Lunde* und *Pusch*, in Vorb.
3 Die Übersetzung *Vaterschaftspatronat* ist geradezu sinnwidrig; sinngemäß wäre allenfalls *Vaterschaftsmatronat* gewesen. Das ist deswegen bedauerlich, weil es sich beim Vaterschaftsschutz in Egalia um eine zentrale Institution handelt und das Wort daher dauernd vorkommt.

Katrin *Lunde* möchte ich sehr herzlich danken für ihre fachfraulichen Auskünfte über das Norwegische und das Norwegalitanische. Ulrika *Jäger* verdanke ich den begeisterten Hinweis auf das Buch.

Frauen entpatrifizieren die Sprache
Feminisierungstendenzen im heutigen Deutsch[1]

> Deutschland braucht Kerle, auf die man sich
> verlassen kann. *Helmut Schmidt, 1982*

> Eine neue Sprache muß eine neue Gangart haben,
> und diese Gangart hat sie nur, wenn ein neuer
> Geist sie bewohnt. *Ingeborg Bachmann*

1 Einleitung: Das Gesetz »Weiblich gleich zweitrangig«

Seit Ende der sechziger Jahre gibt es die neue Frauenbewegung.
Ausgehend von den USA (im Anschluß an die Bürgerrechtsbewe-
gung) hat sie sich im Laufe der siebziger Jahre zu einer starken in-
ternationalen Bewegung entwickelt. Wie jede politische Bewegung
befaßt auch sie sich eingehend mit Sprache; vor allem übt sie
Sprachkritik in sowohl konstatierend-analytischer als auch in
»umstürzlerischer«, d. h. sprachschöpferischer Weise: Die Herrschaft des männlichen Prinzips in der Sprache wird entweder kri-
tisch festgestellt[2] oder durch das Erfinden und Verwenden neuer
Regeln und Redeweisen gebrochen.[3] Im deutschen Sprachraum
dürfte das neue Indefinitpronomen *frau* anstelle des oder neben
dem früher alleinregierenden *man* die provokanteste und bekann-
teste Sprachneuerung sein.

Feministische Linguistinnen haben festgestellt, daß die in unserer patriarchalischen Kultur allgemein geltende Regel »weiblich
gleich zweitrangig« für das Gebiet Sprache in extremer Weise
gültig ist.[4] Ich möchte dieses Gesetz zunächst mit zwei Beispielen
illustrieren.

Vor einiger Zeit unterhielt ich mich, wieder mal, mit einem Kollegen über das heiße Thema »Frauensprache – Männersprache«. Ich
erzählte ihm von der in etlichen Frauengruppen inzwischen üb-
lichen Praxis, statt des bisherigen »geschlechtsneutralen« Maskulinums ein geschlechtsneutrales Femininum zu benutzen. Nach
herrschendem Sprachgebrauch seien wir beide ›Linguisten‹, ›Wissenschaftler‹. Nach den neuen Regeln seien wir dagegen beide Linguistinnen, er eine männliche und ich eine weibliche. Der Kollege
meinte dazu ganz spontan und emotional, nein, das gefiele ihm nun

aber überhaupt nicht. Als ich ihn nach den Gründen für seine Reaktion fragte, konnte er keine nennen. Es ging ihm »einfach nur« ganz gewaltig gegen den Strich, gegen die Natur sozusagen.

Kein Wunder, meine ich: Er hatte eine Abwertung erfahren, war sprachlich als »weiblich« klassifiziert worden – für Männer, in unserer Kultur, anscheinend noch immer »das Allerletzte«.

Ich werde in diesem Aufsatz das geschlechtsneutrale oder »umfassende« Femininum so verwenden, wie sonst das Maskulinum verwendet wird. Wenn ich von ›Linguistinnen‹ oder ›Leserinnen‹ rede, sind Männer also immer mitgemeint. Wenn ausschließlich Frauen oder ausschließlich Männer gemeint sind, heißt es ›weibliche‹ bzw. ›männliche Linguistinnen/Leserinnen …‹.

Dieses Vorgehen hat einerseits didaktische Gründe, andererseits möchte ich Form und Inhalt meiner Aussagen zur Deckung bringen.[5]

Zweites Beispiel für die Regel »weiblich gleich zweitrangig«: Es gibt eine Formel für Lobsprüche mit folgender Struktur:

Er/Sie ist ein zweiter x.

Die x-Stelle kann gefüllt werden mit Namen berühmter Männer, z. B.:

Er/Sie ist ein zweiter Einstein/Picasso/Heifetz/Gandhi/ …

Für Kinder lautet das Lob:

Er/Sie ist ein/unser kleiner Einstein/Picasso/ …

Soll eine Frau oder ein Mädchen gelobt werden, so kann an der x-Stelle auch der Name einer berühmten Frau stehen:

Sie ist eine zweite/unsere kleine Marie Curie/Mutter Teresa/ …

Für Frauen finden wir das Lob außerdem in folgender Form:

Erica Jong ist ein weiblicher Henry Miller.

Die Umkehrung jedoch »funktioniert nicht«. Der junge Brahms wäre vermutlich beleidigt gewesen, hätte Freund Schumann seine pianistischen Fertigkeiten wie folgt gepriesen:

Johannes Brahms ist eine männliche Clara Schumann.

Hätte Dinu Lipatti zu einer »männlichen Clara Haskil« hochgelobt werden können oder irgendeine unserer männlichen Nachkriegslyrikerinnen zu einer »männlichen Ingeborg Bachmann«? Ich kann es mir schwer vorstellen, denn auch ich habe zunächst die Gesetze der herrschenden symbolischen Ordnung erlernt und verinnerlicht.

Ein Satz wie »Paul Celan war eine männliche Ingeborg Bachmann/Nelly Sachs« **kann** innerhalb unseres semantischen Systems einfach keine gelungene Laudatio sein, weil »Feminisierung« eines Mannes gleichbedeutend ist mit Deklassierung. Frauen hingegen können nicht auf einen zweiten Rang verwiesen werden, weil sie sich dort bereits befinden. Sie können durch »Maskulinisierung« allenfalls »emporgehoben« werden.

Soweit die Hintergründe, ganz knapp skizziert. Jede und jeder wird einsehen, daß es nur eine einzige Strategie geben kann, diese zugrundeliegende semantische Mechanik aufzubrechen: Aufwertung des Femininums durch selbstbewußten, konsequenten und forcierten Gebrauch. Genau das tue ich hier, und genau das haben viele Frauen hierzulande und anderswo in den letzten Jahren getan. Sie sprechen und schreiben inzwischen schon erheblich anders als es noch vor 20, 15 oder 10 Jahren üblich war, und dieses Anders-Sprechen hat unübersehbare Konsequenzen auch für die sogenannte »Gemeinsprache«. Vor unseren Augen vollzieht sich ein bemerkenswerter und linguistisch hochinteressanter Sprachwandel, dessen Grundzüge ich in diesem Aufsatz beschreiben und mit Beispielen belegen werde.

Zuvor jedoch möchte ich untersuchen, inwieweit und in welcher Form dieser von Frauen initiierte Sprachwandel von meinen männlichen Kolleginnen registriert wird.

2 Maskulinguistik in der Bundesrepublik: Frauensprache? Fehlanzeige!

Nach meiner Auffassung ist die von Frauen in den vergangenen zehn Jahren geleistete sprachkritische, sprachpolitische und sprachschöpferische Arbeit der zentrale und wohl auch rein linguistisch auffälligste Beitrag zum laufenden Sprachwandel. Linguistisch relevant und von den übrigen Beiträgen grundsätzlich verschieden ist er aus folgendem Grund: Der »normale« Sprachwandel betrifft vor allem den Wortschatz – alte Wörter und Redewendungen verschwinden aus der Gemeinsprache, neue kommen hinzu – der bekannte und normale Vorgang, wie schon immer gehabt. Der von Frauen in Gang gesetzte Sprachwandel hingegen bringt nicht nur laufend neue Wörter und Begriffe hervor[6], sondern er **verändert unser System grammatischer Regeln,** vor allem im Bereich der Kongruenz. Es geht diesmal ans oder ums »Eingemachte«, um die (patriarchalische) Substanz, nicht nur um lexikalisches Beiwerk. Eigenartigerweise aber werden diese sozusagen grundlegenden (einen neuen Grund legenden) Veränderungen von den mit der deutschen Sprache offiziell befaßten Institutionen kaum zur Kenntnis genommen. Als Beispiel möchte ich die Gesellschaft für deutsche Sprache anführen mit ihrem Publikationsorgan *Der Sprachdienst*. Im zweimonatlich erscheinenden Sprachdienst werden regelmäßig die »Neuerwerbungen« der deutschen Sprache registriert und kommentiert. 1978 erschien in zwei Abteilungen ein Aufsatz von Uwe *Förster*, hauptamtlichem Mitarbeiter der Gesellschaft für deutsche Sprache, mit dem Titel »Wortzuwachs und Stilempfinden im Deutsch der siebziger Jahre«.[7] In dieser an sich verdienstvollen, interessanten und gründlichen Arbeit findet sich **kein einziges Wort** über den Beitrag der Frauenbewegung zum »Wortzuwachs und Stilempfinden(!) der siebziger Jahre«. Und das, obwohl der Autor über die wahrscheinlich reichste Quelle an Informationen über den laufenden Sprachwandel verfügt, die es in der Bundesrepublik gibt, wie er selbst bekundet:

> Wo findet man Neologismen? Will man sich nicht auf Zufallsfunde verlassen, so muß auf ein Korpus zurückgegriffen werden. Mein Korpus ist die Zeitschrift *Der Sprachdienst* (DS). Die Sprachpflegezeitschrift wendet sich an sprachlich interessierte Leser aller Berufskreise in mehr als vierzig Ländern der Erde. Von ihnen erhält *Der Sprachdienst* ein ebenso reges wie differenziertes Leserecho. Seit seinem ersten Erscheinen im Oktober 1957 widmet er seine besondere Aufmerksamkeit dem, »was noch nicht im Wörterbuch steht«, zur Zeit vor allem unter der Rubrik »Auffälligkeiten«.
> Jede Wörterbuchredaktion findet im *Sprachdienst* Material. Das zeigt ein Blick in das gerade abgeschlossene WbGeg. (das sechsbändige *Wörterbuch der deutschen Gegenwartssprache* von Klappenbach & Steinitz, Ostberlin 1961–1977 – L.F.P.) ebenso wie der Vergleich verschiedener Auflagen der *Duden-Rechtschreibung* oder des *Deutschen Wörterbuchs* von Gerhard Wahrig (Gütersloh). (1978a: 66)

Allerdings legt sich *Förster* in seiner Darstellung folgende Beschränkung auf:

Unter welchem Gesichtspunkt sollen nun die Neologismen betrachtet werden? Unter dem Gesichtspunkt ihrer wortbildnerischen Produktivität. Zur Debatte steht also nicht Kurioses, sondern Symptomatisches. (1978a: 66)

Möglicherweise ist die »wortbildnerische Produktivität« der Frauen in den siebziger Jahren von ihm nicht erfaßt worden, weil sie für ihn in die Rubrik »Kuriosa« fällt. Dies tut sie anscheinend auch für Broder *Carstensen*, der von 1978 bis 1982 zu Beginn jeden *Sprachdienst*-Jahrgangs die wichtigsten Neuzugänge des vergangenen Jahres vorstellte und kommentierte.[8] *Carstensen* aber hat Spaß am Kuriosen; er will seinen Leserinnen (vor allem den männlichen) so köstliche Unterhaltung nicht vorenthalten. Nicht daß er etwa die Sprache der Frauenbewegung an den Quellen studierte, etwa mal *Emma* oder *Courage* selbst in die Hand nähme! An sein Ohr dringt diese Sprache nur vermittelt über die seltenen und in der Regel verzerrten Resonanzen im *Spiegel* und anderen Organen der Männerpresse. In seinem 1978er Beitrag, der die Serie einleitet, schreibt er, es liege

in der Natur der Sache, daß dieser Überblick nicht vollständig sein kann und daß die Auswahl der Wörter des Jahres weitgehend subjektiven Kriterien unterliegt. (1978: 1)

Natürlich kann frau *Carstensen* nicht zwingen, auch feministische Publikationen zu berücksichtigen. Wissenschaftlich nicht annehmbar ist es jedoch, wenn diese Selbstbeschränkung eindeutig Fehlinformationen der Leserinnenschaft zur Folge hat. So berichtet *Carstensen* gleich zweimal über die (US-amerikanische) feministische Diskussion zum Thema Wirbelsturm-Namen ((1978: 7) und (1979: 21)). Die Amerikanerinnen hatten gemeint, diese Wirbelstürme könnten ruhig auch mal männliche Namen bekommen. *Carstensen*, Professor der Amerikanistik, der allerdings die amerikanische Frauenbewegung genauso ignoriert wie die bundesdeutsche, meint aber, den *Spiegel* wiedergebend, der Vorschlag stamme von Alice *Schwarzer*. Sie hat vermutlich Wichtigeres zu tun, als sich mit den hierzulande eher seltenen Hurricanes zu befassen.

Weiter erfahren wir von *Carstensen*:

Der *Spiegel* vom 13. 11. 1978 löste ein in der deutschen Sprache seit langem offenes Problem: wie man weibliche Soldaten, Offiziere etc. nennt. Formen mit -*in* für Berufe und Tätigkeiten, die bisher nur oder überwiegend von den Männern ausgeübt wurden, dringen immer stärker vor, und die *Ministerin* hat inzwischen Eingang in die deutsche Sprache gefunden, aber die *Soldatin,* die der *Spiegel* in seiner Titelgeschichte 13mal erwähnte ..., fehlt bisher. (1979: 21)

Diese Fehlinformation geht ebenfalls auf die Feminismus-Abstinenz des Verfassers zurück. Nicht nur was im *Spiegel* steht hat »Eingang in die deutsche Sprache gefunden«. Das angeblich »seit langem offene Problem« löste nicht der *Spiegel,* sozusagen im Handstreich mittels einer Titelstory im Jahre 1978, sondern die (neue) deutsche Frauenbewegung in ihrer Gesamtheit schon weit früher. Sie ging dem »Problem« beherzt an die Wurzel und löste es gleich für **sämtliche** Maskulina. Mit anderen (linguistischen) Worten: Die Frauenbewegung machte – in einem Akt fröhlicher Anarchie – aus der bisher bestenfalls semi-produktiven Wortregel ›Movierung mit -*in*‹ eine produktive, d. h. uneingeschränkt an beliebigen Maskulina operationsfähige Regel. Wo der Mond zur Mondin, der Wind zur Windin und ein ruhender Pol zu einer ruhenden Polin wird, ist ein Routinefall wie die *Soldatin* wohl kaum als »offenes Problem« einzuordnen.

»Interessant ist auch die *Armeefrau*«, meldet *Carstensen* noch eine weitere *Spiegel*-Lesefrucht als Neologismus (1979: 21). Gut abgeschirmt, kann er nicht wissen, daß (zahllose!) neue Komposita auf -*frau*, mit und ohne Pendant auf -*mann*, ein wesentlicher Beitrag der Frauenbewegung zum »Wortzuwachs der siebziger Jahre« sind, daß der *Spiegel* da lediglich nachplappert.

Carstensen ist bekannt als jemand, der seine Arbeit mit äußerster Gewissenhaftigkeit und Sorgfalt betreibt. Daß er das Thema »Frauenbewegung und Sprachwandel« so nachlässig, ja schludrig behandelt, wie er wohl kein anderes behandeln würde, wird eher einen persönlichen und im übrigen unter seinen männlichen Kolleginnen weit verbreiteten Grund haben: Geringschätzung. Geringschätzigkeit ist denn auch der Grundton seiner diesbezüglichen Ausführungen, erkennbar schon an den Überschriften: »Weibliches und Kindliches« (1979: 21), »Emanzinnen« (1980: 20), »Dämliche Fräuleins« (1981: 25).

Die »dämlichen Fräuleins« stellen mit Genugtuung fest, daß die »Beobachtungen zum sprachlichen Geschehen 1982«, vorgelegt im

Sprachdienst 83/1–2 von Gerhard *Müller* und Helmut *Walther*, wesentlich frauenbewußter und -freundlicher geraten sind als die *Carstensen*schen Auslassungen.

3 Zur Geschichte und Motivation feministischer Sprachkritik und -politik in der Bundesrepublik

Nach dem Zusammenbruch der Naziherrschaft kam die große Entnazifizierung durch die Alliierten. Nicht nur die Deutschen wurden, mit mehr oder weniger Erfolg, entnazifiziert, sondern (z. B.) auch die Schulbücher. Daß unsere Schulbücher heute patriarchalisch geprägt sind, ist seit langem bekannt und wissenschaftlich breit belegt – eine der zahllosen wissenschaftlichen Leistungen der Frauenbewegung.[9] Eine Entpatrifizierung ist jedoch nicht in Sicht und von den Herren in den Kultusministerien auch schwerlich zu erwarten, so wenig wie zu erwarten war, daß sich das Naziregime etwa selbst entnazifiziert hätte.

Aber unsere Muttersprache! Sie wird uns nicht von Kultusministerien verordnet und vorgeschrieben. Sie manipuliert uns nicht nur – wir können sie auch ganz bewußt verändern. Wir erleben sie als etwas Fremdes, Erworbenes (wäre ich in Spanien aufgewachsen, spräche ich Spanisch als Muttersprache!) und zugleich Eigenes, Eingewachsenes. Normalerweise wird dieses Fremde schließlich als das Ur-Eigene anerkannt und verteidigt, wie eine ursprünglich aufgezwungene Gewohnheit, von der ich nicht mehr lassen kann oder will. Grundsätzlich hindert mich aber nichts, dies angewachsene Eigene als mir letztlich Übergestülptes, Fremdes zu erkennen. Dies getan, hindert mich nichts daran, Brauchbares von dem Fremden beizubehalten und Unbrauchbares, Schädliches durch wirklich Eigenes, meinen eigenen Bedürfnissen und Interessen Entsprechendes, zu ersetzen.

Genau dies tut die Frauenbewegung in ihren auf die Sprache bezogenen Aktivitäten. Der wichtigste, den Gesamtprozeß einleitende Schritt war wohl der der Bewußtwerdung: der »fremde Blick« auf das vorgeblich oder mutmaßlich »ganz Eigene«. Wer hat denn schon in den fünfziger oder sechziger bis weit in die siebziger Jahre darüber nachgedacht und daran Anstoß genommen, daß engl. *man*, frz. *homme*, it. *uomo*, span. *hombre* sowohl ›Mann‹ als auch ›Mensch‹ bedeutet?! Daß dt. *man*, entstanden aus *Mann*, auf

›Menschen im allgemeinen‹ referiert?! Niemand hat da »parasitäre Referenz«[10] gewittert, obwohl es in Wirtschaft und Werbung als großer Sieg gefeiert wird, wenn ein Markenname den gewaltigen Sprung zum Gattungsnamen geschafft hat (z. B. *Tempotaschentuch* für ›Papiertaschentuch im allgemeinen‹). Der entsprechende Sieg des Mannes über die Konkurrentin Frau lag schon so weit zurück, daß es keiner mehr bewußt war.

Es gehört zum soziologischen Grundwissen (leider nicht zum Allgemeinwissen), daß Herrschaft um so reibungsloser funktioniert, je weniger sie den Beherrschten bewußt ist. Schon Anfang der siebziger Jahre fingen einige frauenbewußte Frauen an, gegen die Dominanz des Männlichen auch in der Sprache die unterschiedlichsten Maßnahmen zu ergreifen – von der Schocktherapie des *frau* statt *man* bis zur sanften Geburt zahlloser Neubildungen auf *-in*. Die Reaktionen der übrigen Sprachgemeinschaft waren sehr unterschiedlich. Die meisten fanden solche Maßnahmen wohl schlicht »verrückt, aber harmlos« – die übliche Reaktion auf Neues und Fremdes, das uns »letztlich nichts angeht«, vor allem aber: unsere Ordnung nicht berührt oder gar bedroht. Sollten »die« doch ruhig *frau* statt *man* sagen und sich damit lächerlich machen. Aber dann, später, so ein blödsinniges Wort wie *Diplom-Kauffrau* auch noch offiziell als Titel zu verlangen, das ging ja schon ein bißchen weit. Das war nicht mehr nur »lächerlich« oder »verrückt« – diese Verkniffenheit wurde schon regelrecht lästig. Wörter zwangseinführen, andere zwangsabschaffen *(Fräulein)*, ehrwürdiges Namensrecht ändern – nur lästig, ärgerlich, unbequem. Und das ganze Gekeife und Getobe letztlich doch um nichts, Aggressionen an die falsche Adresse. Gut, die Frau mag ja wirklich benachteiligt sein, aber was soll das mit Sprache zu tun haben?! Ändert die Realität, dann ändert sich doch die Sprache automatisch. Es auf dem umgekehrten Wege versuchen zu wollen – einfach Schwachsinn!

Natürlich wollen wir »die Realität« ändern. Erstens **ist** Sprache, Sprechen, sprachliches Handeln heute wohl der zentrale Bereich dessen, was so »Realität« genannt wird[11], zweitens hat nie eine feministische Sprachkritikerin behauptet, sie wolle **nur** die Sprache ändern und den Rest dem gewöhnlichen patriarchalischen Lauf der Dinge überlassen.

Ich selbst habe die Sprache des Patriarchats sehr lange als »meine eigene« anerkannt und verteidigt. Noch 1976 benutzte ich Wörter wie *Brüderlichkeit* (statt *Mitmenschlichkeit*), ohne mir Böses dabei zu denken, und wurde von frauenbewegten Nicht-Linguistinnen des öfteren korrigiert. Lästig und zudringlich fand ich das damals – ich wußte ja schließlich, wie ich es gemeint hatte: bestimmt nicht diskriminierend. Ich wußte als Fachfrau auch besser, wie Sprache funktioniert – wo kämen wir denn hin, wenn wir, wie diese Laiinnen, alles so wörtlich nehmen würden. Derartige kleinkarierte Krittelei von Nicht-Fachfrauen rangierte bei mir auf derselben Stufe wie »sprachbewußte« Mätzchen à la *siebzehn Jahre jung* – die Betreffenden hatten eben keine Ahnung von der subtilen Funktionsweise relativer Adjektive bzw. von sprachlichen Mechanismen überhaupt.

Inzwischen bin ich gründlich eines Besseren belehrt worden. Das verdanke ich nicht nur diesen Frauen, sondern auch den Überreaktionen einiger Männer. Als Frau und Sympathisantin der Frauenbewegung hatte ich mir schließlich gesagt: Nehmen wir einmal an, daß an der Kritik doch was dran ist. Untersuche ich mal eine Weile nicht das italienische *gerundio* oder deutsche Sprachpartikel, sondern das System der Personenbezeichnungen im Deutschen in verschiedenen Mitteilungszusammenhängen. Je mehr ich also einfach »genauer hinsah«, um so mehr wurde mir klar, daß alles eigentlich noch viel schlimmer war, als es die anderen Frauen bis dahin wahrgenommen hatten. Immerhin vermittelt langes linguistisches Training doch einigen Scharfblick, wenn frau sich einen Objektbereich erst mal zur Analyse vorgeknöpft hat. – Zufällig ergab es sich dann, daß ich im In- und Ausland Vorträge halten sollte. Ich berichtete also von meinen neu gewonnenen Erkenntnissen. Bis dahin war ich gewohnt, daß meine linguistischen Beobachtungen und Ergebnisse mit freundlichem Interesse auf- und angenommen wurden. Nun waren die Reaktionen spürbar anders. Wahrscheinlich war es die implizite Aufforderung zur Änderung des eigenen Sprachverhaltens, die »nicht ankam« (um es gelinde auszudrücken). Registrieren, Beschreiben, ja – das ist genuin linguistisches Arbeiten, wie gehabt. Aber Kritisieren und Werten? Und noch dazu mit einem feministischen Interesse?

Man oder frau kann lange wegsehen oder die Augen verschließen, wie auch ich es lange getan habe. Aber wenn frau einmal die Augen geöffnet und genau hingesehen hat, kann sie erstens die dabei gewonnenen Einsichten nicht wieder vergessen und wird zweitens immer mehr Unrat entdecken. Es ist nach meiner Auffassung und der zahlloser Frauen und einiger Männer eine unumstößliche

Tatsache, daß unsere Sprache nicht nur von Anglizismen und ähnlichen anerkannten Ismen, sondern vor allem von Patriarchalismen[12] nur so strotzt, im Lexikon wie auch im engeren grammatischen Bereich. Erstaunlich ist nur, daß wir das so lange nicht gesehen haben. Erstaunlich ist auch, daß wir Frauen diese unsere vom Maskulinum beherrschte Sprache so lange als »unsere eigene« anerkannt haben und nicht schon viel eher zu einer gründlichen Entpatrifizierung und Feminisierung geschritten sind.

4 Die Hauptbereiche des Feminisierungsprozesses – Ein Überblick

4.1 Vorbemerkung zur Materialsammlung

Die im folgenden vorgestellten Daten entnehme ich meiner Sammlung von ca. 10000 Belegen, mit der ich im November 1980 begonnen habe und die kontinuierlich anwächst. Die Belege entstammen überwiegend der geschriebenen Sprache; ich berücksichtige aber auch alle einschlägigen Auffälligkeiten gesprochener Sprache, die mir begegnen. Die Sammlung dient mir als Grundlage für meine Untersuchungen zum Thema »Frauenbewegung und Sprachwandel«. Anders als bei Uwe *Förster* ist **mein** Korpus »die Sprache, die mich umgibt«, also alles, was mir an gedruckter Sprache unter die Augen und an gesprochener Sprache in die Ohren kommt. Diesbezüglich sind mein Vorgehen und meine Auswahl vermutlich ähnlich subjektiv wie die von *Carstensen*, nur ist mein Erkenntnisinteresse ein anderes, und meine Lektüre hat – meiner Aufgabenstellung entsprechend – **zwei** Schwerpunkte statt einen: Sprachliche Erzeugnisse des Patriarchats **und** der Frauenbewegung. Ich beobachte nicht nur *Spiegel, Stern, Zeit,* Funkzeitschriften, diverse Tageszeitungen, Hörfunk und Fernsehen sowie nichtfeministische Bücher verschiedener Epochen und Gattungen, sondern auch *Emma, Courage,* diverse weniger bekannte feministische Periodika und feministische Bücher. Die im folgenden vorgestellte Auswahl entstammt beiden Quellentypen, überwiegend jedoch meiner feministischen Lektüre.

4.2 Feminisierung der Pronomina –
Das Pronomen *frau* und die Folgen

4.2.1 *frau*

Das Pronomen *frau* begegnete mir zum erstenmal im *Frauenjahrbuch 1976*, wo es ständig vorkommt (viel häufiger als heutzutage in feministischer Literatur) – aber es ist schon früher entstanden:

> Mit dem wörtchen ›man‹ fängt es an. ›man‹ hat, ›man‹ tut, ›man‹ fühlt . . . : ›man‹ wird für die beschreibung allgemeiner zustände, gefühle, situationen verwendet – für die menschheit schlechthin. entlarvend sind sätze, die mit »als frau hat ›man‹ ja . . .« beginnen. ›man‹ hat als frau keine identität. frau kann sie nur als frau suchen. (*Stefan* 1975: 4)

Das Motiv für die »Erfindung« und den Gebrauch dieses Pronomens – es ist übrigens das Motiv für den **gesamten** Feminisierungsprozeß – leuchtet unmittelbar ein: Immer mehr Frauen lehn(t)en es ab, sich selbst oder andere Frauen mit einem Maskulinum zu bezeichnen. Als besonders entfremdend bzw. grotesk empfand frau solche Super-Maskulina wie *man* und *jedermann* in frauenspezifischen Kontexten (Schwangerschaft, Stillen usw.):

> Wenn *man sein* Kind stillt . . .

> Wie kann *man seine* Schwangerschaft frühzeitig selbst feststellen?

Statt dessen heißt es nun, stimmiger, in feminisiertem Deutsch:

> Bitte schreib doch *einmal,* daß frau auch eine Emanze sein kann, wenn frau nicht abtreibt. (*Emma* 83.5.62)

> Was kann frau tun, um nicht Phonotypistin werden zu müssen? (*Emma* 79.4.36)

> Wenn frau sich sonst ein Marzipanei oder eine Zigarettenschachtel kaufen würde, dann kaufe ich Emma. (*Emma* 83.5.62)

> Das feministische Parteiprogramm der Däninnen /kann/ frau doch nicht unbekümmert so abdrucken . . . (*Courage* 77.12.2)

> Edeltraud besuchte die Lämmermütter und stellte fest, daß frau als Schäferin beides sein muß: »hart wie ein Mann« und »›sensibel‹ wie eine Frau«. (*Emma* 79.5.4)

Wenn frau unterwegs ist, kann sie schlecht in den unhygieni-schen Waschräumen ihren Schwamm auswaschen. (*Courage* 77.12.57)

Was passiert heute frau eigentlich, wenn sie weder Kind noch... Verhütungsmittel will... (*Emma* 83.5.62)

(Die Siglen sind wie folgt zu lesen: »*Emma* 83.5.62« bedeutet »*Emma* Jahrgang 1983, Heft 5 (Mai), Seite 62«.)

Das Indefinitpronomen *frau* funktioniert übrigens ganz anders als *man*. Einerseits hat die semantische und entstehungsgeschicht-liche Nähe zum **Substantiv** *Frau* ihre grammatischen Konsequen-zen, andererseits haben sich stabile Regeln für den Gebrauch noch nicht herausgebildet – es wird viel herumgespielt und -experimen-tiert. Jedenfalls ist das Pronomen *frau* schon rein grammatisch so interessant, daß es eine sehr genaue Analyse verdient. Hier nur der Hinweis, daß *frau* im Nominativ sowohl durch *frau* als auch durch *sie* wieder aufgenommen werden kann (vgl. oben das zweitletzte Beispiel), wohingegen *man* nicht durch *er* pronominalisierbar ist:

Wenn man unterwegs ist, kann man/*er schlecht...

Die Dativform von *frau* heißt *einer* oder *frau*, die Akkusativform *eine* oder *frau*. *Man* hingegen variiert nicht zwischen *einem/einen* und *man* in diesen Kasus.

... sie/die SPD/sei nun mal das »kleinere Übel«. Und deshalb bliebe auch frau nichts anderes übrig, als sie zu wählen. (*Emma* 80.5.23)

Frau könnte ein Quiz darüber veranstalten, von... wem dieses Zitat stammt. Doch da bleibt einer der Humor leicht im Halse stecken. (*Emma* 83.5.45)

In London müßte man einkaufen! Da geht's einem gut. Da geht's sogar einer gut. (*Emma* 80.3.46)

Frau beachte auch die Stellung von *frau*:

Was passiert heute frau eigentlich?
Und deshalb bliebe auch frau nichts anderes übrig...

Die Stellung orientiert sich am Substantiv *Frau,* nicht am Prono-men *man*:

*Was passiert heute einem eigentlich?
*Und deshalb bliebe auch einem nichts anderes übrig...
Was passiert heute einer Frau eigentlich?
Und deshalb bliebe auch einer Frau nichts anderes übrig...

Das Pronomen *frau* oszilliert zwischen dem grammatischen Status eines Pronomens und dem eines Substantivs/einer Nominalphrase. Inzwischen gehen, in Analogie zu *Frau*, immer mehr Substantive diesen Weg, allen voran das Substantiv *Mann*. Es wird jetzt häufig klein geschrieben und/oder, wie *frau* und *man*, ohne Artikel benutzt, meist in ironisch oder kämpferisch verdeutlichender Absicht:

Was mann in Wiesbaden /Bundeskriminalamt/ über uns weiß. (*Courage* 79.10.8)

Buhfrau Alice, der mann... so gern die Scheiße vorrotzt... (*Emma* 80.7.63)

Mann nennt es Ausräumung. (*Courage* 77.6/7.24)

Wo käme Mann auch hin, wenn er nichtmal mehr ungestraft ein bißchen belästigen darf? (*Emma* 80.12.45)

Jeden zweiten Dienstag... wird jetzt... den erstaunten Seherinnen und Sehern präsentiert, wie Frauenherrschaft aussieht. Und weil Medien-Mann sie sich lieber nicht auf der Erde vorstellen will, wurde der Planet Medora erfunden. (*Courage* 77.4.21)

Auch *Mensch* wurde solcherart zum Pronomen:

Diese Leute kann mensch nur vor vollendete Tatsachen setzen. (*Emma* 80.12.62)

Subjektiv und ungerecht, wie mensch ist. (*Courage* 81.11.39)

Was macht mensch damit? (*Courage* 81.11.41)

Der Prozeß ist sehr ansteckend und greift auf immer mehr Substantive über:

Wie kann Bürger/in dem Rüstungswettlauf Steine in den Weg legen? (*Emma* 82.2.18)

88

4.2.2 jedefrau

Während *man* in feministischen Publikationen durchaus noch sehr häufig verwendet wird (weit häufiger als *frau* sogar), ist *jedermann* als Bezeichnung für »Menschen im allgemeinen« oder gar für Frauen selten oder nie anzutreffen.[13] Der Werbeslogan der *Courage* lautet: »Jedefrau braucht Courage.«

> Von Anfang an gründete sich die Macht der größeren Städte mehr auf den Handelsreichtum als auf das kleine Handwerk, das jedermann/jedefrau frei von feudalen Abgabelasten betreiben konnte. (*Courage* 76.2.17)

> Denn nicht jedefrau kann Abitur haben. (*Courage* 81.1.58)

> Courage-Abonnement – ein Geschenk für Jedefrau. (*Courage* 77.12 (Rücktitel))

Mehr und mehr scheint auch Männern die Angemessenheit von *jedermann* (und *man*) für »Mensch« fragwürdig zu werden:

> Man (und hier ist wirklich jedermann und jede Frau gemeint) sollte sich immer überlegen... (R. W. Leonhardt in *Die Zeit* Nr. 7 vom 12. 2. 82, S. 63)

4.2.3 jemand, die (... mir helfen kann)

In der *Emma* Nr. 12/1980 schreibt Gabi *Butz* unter dem Titel »Ich bin Malerlehrling« über ihre Schwierigkeiten in diesem Männerberuf. Sie schließt mit den Worten: »Wenn jemand vorhat, so etwas zu lernen, soll er es zumindest versuchen.« Wieso *er*? »Er« wird ja in diesem Beruf kaum auf die Probleme stoßen, mit denen »sie« zu tun hat!

Um solcher Sprachunlogik entgegenzuwirken, wird inzwischen *jemand* immer häufiger auch als Femininum verwendet:

> Vielleicht rufe ich mal jemand an, von der ich weiß, daß sie allein ist. (*Unsere kleine Zeitung* 80.12.13)

> Warum sollte es plötzlich jemanden geben, der zu trauen wäre? (*Courage* 78.6.2)

> Ich fühlte mich nicht angesprochen... von jemandem, die ich nicht kenne. (*Courage* 81.11.42)

Manchen Frauen klingt das *jemand* auch noch zu sehr nach *Mann*, und sie feminisieren es zu *jefrau* oder *jemande* (mündliche Belege). Oder sie benutzen, wenn es der Sinnzusammenhang zuläßt, statt *jemand* : *eine(r)*.

4.2.4 *Wer glaubt, sie sei mit »wer« gemeint, die irrt sich!*

Traditionellerweise wird das »geschlechtsneutrale« maskuline Indefinitpronomen *wer* gern wie folgt verwendet:

Wer zweimal *mit derselben* pennt, gehört schon zum Establishment. (Spruch aus APO-Zeiten)

Wer mit Katzen lebt, ist ihnen niemals *Herrchen*, wie man das dem Hund ist. (*Die Zeit* 83.22.56)

Ferienende in Nordrhein-Westfalen. Wer noch nicht zu Hause ist, wird sich an diesem Wochenende aus allen Himmelsrichtungen über die Autobahn gen Heimatort quälen. ... Vielleicht auf den letzten Drücker losgefahren, das Auto bis oben hin bepackt *mit Muttern*, Kindern, Koffern, Reiseandenken. (Günter Hoffmeister in *Neue Westfälische*, 18. 8. 83)

Wer das Echte liebt ..., wer überall *eine Schöne* für seine Töne findet – der raucht Gauloises. (*Gauloises*-Reklame, *Spiegel* 81. 4. 152)

Wer noch vor einigen Jahren zum Arbeitsamt ging, der tat dies oft, weil er mit seiner bisherigen Arbeitsstelle nicht mehr zufrieden war und sich erkundigen wollte, ob für *einen Mann* mit seinen Qualifikationen nicht etwas anderes vorhanden sei. (*Neue Westfälische*, 27. 2. 82)

Wer in Deutschland nur einen Hund, einen Kater oder einen Kanarienvogel hat, ist übel dran. ... Wer in Deutschland einen Hund und *eine Frau* hat, ist schon besser dran. Ärgert ihn der Hund, muß er nur rasch *die Frau* verprügeln – und alles ist wieder in Ordnung. (Daniel Doppler in *Die Zeit*, zitiert nach *Baumann* und *Fink* 1979: 26)

Alles klar, welches Geschlecht mit *wer* gemeint ist? Schließlich ist es ja auch nicht umsonst ein Maskulinum.

Daß das nicht immer so bleiben muß, zeigen viele mündliche Belege.

Wer ihre Hausaufgaben nicht macht, die muß eben zusehen, wie sie die Arbeit schafft. (mündlich)

Wer etwas gutfindet, was sie liest, weil sie sich damit identifizieren kann, sagt letzten Endes, daß sie sich gutfindet. (*Courage* 81.11.40)

Auch das Fragepronomen *wer* wird von Frauen feminisiert:

Wer von euch hat denn ihr Kind selbst gestillt? (mündlich)

Wer ist das, die da vorne mit der Eva redet? (mündlich)

Manche Frauen sind so klangsensibel, daß sie aus dem *wer* ein *wie* machen. Aus der Sequenz *wer – er – der* wird so ein *wie – sie – die*:

Wie glaubt, sie sei mit *wer* gemeint, die irrt sich aber! (mündlich)

Wie sagt, die Männerwelt sei schlecht, die hat wohl nur so ziemlich recht. (mündlich, frei nach Wilhelm *Busch*)

Aber es sind nicht nur die Frauen, die die Sprache des Patriarchats korrekturbedürftig finden. Eva Maria *Epple* von der *Courage* schickte mir folgenden Bericht:

Friedel war vor einem Jahr 5. Zu meinem Geburtstag hatte ich ein Kästchen mit Pralinen bekommen. Er fragte mich, von wem, und ich »antwortete«, um den Zeitpunkt der Gefräßigkeit noch etwas hinauszuschieben, »von wem wohl?« Er tippte nacheinander auf seinen Vater, auf meinen Vater, auf einen entfernten Bekannten, der vor längerer Zeit mal Babysitter bei ihm gewesen war, dann fiel ihm niemand mehr ein, so daß ich es ihm verraten mußte. Es war Erika. – Friedel fiel aus allen Wolken.« ›Von wer wohl?‹ hättest du mich dann fragen müssen.« (Brief vom 15. 4. 83)

4.2.5 jede, eine, keine

Am 25. Februar 1982 brachte Radio Bremen eine Fernsehsendung über Erika *Pluhar*, die mit ihrer Tochter Anna zusammenlebt. Die Interviewerin fragte die beiden Frauen: »Und wie lebt ihr heut so zusammen, ihr beiden?« Antwort von Anna: »Jeder für sich.« Frage der Interviewerin: »Jeder für sich, aber trotzdem miteinander?«

Zwei Frauen – jeder für sich?? Eindeutig Sprachunsinn, aber immer noch weit verbreitet. Und erklärlich, haben doch alle deutschsprechenden Frauen von Kindheit an gelernt, Maskulina ständig auf sich selbst und andere Frauen und Mädchen anzuwenden – bis hin zu solchen Fällen, wo es eigentlich gar nicht »nötig« wäre, da Feminina ja vorhanden sind: *jede/jeder; keine/keiner; eine/einer; die/der andere.* Auf dem Rückumschlag der deutschen Ausgabe von Nancy Fridays *My Mother My Self (Wie meine Mutter)*[14] ist zu lesen, daß »Mutter und Tochter das Faktum der Sexualität jeweils *beim anderen* offenbar nur schwer akzeptieren können«. Und in dem Faltblättchen, das jeder Packung o.b.-Tampons beiliegt, stand bis vor kurzem: »Die Menstruation ist bei jedem ein bißchen anders.« Die Firma ist inzwischen meiner Bitte um Korrektur gefolgt; seitdem heißt es: »Die Menstruation ist bei jeder Frau ein bißchen anders.«

Hier wird/wurde offensichtlich ein patriarchalisches Übersoll erfüllt. Der *Duden* erwartet das Maskulinum schließlich nur für gemischtgeschlechtliche Gruppen und weiß zugleich von früheren, gerechteren Zeiten zu berichten, die für Gemischtgeschlechtliches das Neutrum verwendeten:

> Die neutralen Singularformen vieler Pronomen können sich auf Substantive gleich welchen Genus und welcher Zahl beziehen [...].
>> *Fundevogel und Lenchen* hatten einander so lieb, daß, wenn *eins das andere* nicht sah, *es* traurig war (Grimm).
> Bei Nennung zweier Personen mit verschiedenem Geschlecht kann auch die maskuline Form des Pronomens stehen. Sie ist heute üblich: *Der Vater und die Mutter* waren einverstanden, *jeder* wollte mitfahren. (*Duden*-Grammatik [3]1973: 617)

Über rein weibliche und rein männliche Gruppen wird nichts gesagt. Sicher handeln wir Frauen ganz im Sinne der *Duden*-Grammatik, wenn wir dem einleitend vorgeführten Sprach-Unsinn Einhalt gebieten:

> Wie kommt eine zum Zeichnen? (*Emma* 80.12.4)

> Wenn eine eine Reise tut... (*Emma* 79.5.4)

> Was ist, wenn sich keine zu mir setzt? (Kontext: Müttergenesungswerk) (*Emma* 80.12.39)

Jede möchte ihre Gewohnheiten festhalten. (Gemeint sind Kate Millett und Sita, in einer Rezension über Milletts *Sita* (*Schreiben* 3, Mai 1978))

Ich finde Euch keineswegs zu abgehoben . . . Schließlich kann es nicht jeder recht gemacht werden . . . (Leserin an *Emma*-Redaktion) (*Emma* 80.12.63)

Jede von uns zahlt Steuern an den Bund (*Courage* 81.10.4)

Wie *jemand* oft durch *eine(r)* ersetzbar ist, so kann das Maskulinum *niemand* durch *keine(r)* ersetzt werden (s. o.). Vor fünf Jahren (1978), als die Diskussion über feministische Linguistik an den Universitäten gerade in Gang kam, berichtete mir allerdings ein sprachsensibler holländischer Gaststudent, er benutze für gemischtgeschlechtliche Gruppen lieber *niemand* als *keiner* (»Es ist niemand da«), weil *keiner* doch »so sehr männlich« klinge, mehr als *niemand.* An *keine* als Alternative (geschlechtsneutrales Femininum) dachte damals eben noch keine (oder keins).

4.3 Aus »Kollegen« werden »Kolleginnen und Kollegen« – Das Splitting

Bevor wir Frauen das umfassende, geschlechtsneutrale Femininum einführten und damit Männer sozusagen »verschwesterten«, haben wir es lange im Guten versucht und für das Splitting à la *Schülerinnen und Schüler* plädiert. Obwohl man uns immer wieder versichert hatte, wir seien doch selbstverständlich mitgemeint, wenn er von den *Autoren, Schriftstellern, Römern, Touristen* usw. redete, war mann es immer wieder selbst, der uns ernüchterte:

Denkt *der Normalbürger* an Szene, dann an jene, die ihm *seine Frau* macht, kommt er des Abends spät nach Haus, oder des Morgens früh, was noch schlimmer ist. (Anzeige »Tun Sie sich doch mal in der Berliner Szene um« des Verkehrsamtes Berlin. *Stern* 83.9.53)

Der Bilderbuchkandidat ist für viele Großfirmen schon heute *der 19jährige Gymnasialabgänger* mit Abiturnote 1,8 (zu klug ist verdächtig), *vom Wehrdienst freigestellt* und aus einem Beamtenhaushalt. (Das mt-journal, 29. 1. 83)

Kann *ein Mensch* wirklich acht Stunden am Tag liebevolle Zuwendung geben? Darf sich *ein Familientherapeut* scheiden lassen? Wie fühlt sich *ein Helfer,* der am Abend *von seiner Ehefrau* dieselben Klagen hört wie von seinen deprimierten Patientinnen tagsüber? (*Rowohlt*-Anzeige zu *Schmidbauer: Helfen als Beruf,* 1983)

Wir alle können nur leben, indem wir ständig Gedanken und Gefühle verleugnen. . . . Sicherlich weiß *der Autofahrer,* daß *er* in den nächsten Sekunden in einem Gewirr aus verbogenem Blech und splitterndem Glas unter gräßlichen Schmerzen sterben kann. Aber *er* verleugnet dieses Wissen. Gelingt es *ihm* nicht, . . . dann sagen wir . . . : *Dieser Mann* leidet an einer Phobie . . . (Wolfgang *Schmidbauer* in *Natur* 82.3.60)

»Nur« *Schriftsteller!* »Nur« *Menschen,* die den Politikern . . . so mißliebig sind, weil sie ihnen das eine voraushaben: die Kraft der Imagination . . . Jawohl, die Phantasie ist es, die den in militärischen Kategorien eingesponnenen Un-Denkern verhaßt ist. . . . Phantasie heißt: sich selbst, seine Eltern, *seine Frau,* die Kinder und Freunde in der Sekunde zu sehen, wo die Waffen . . . zerplatzen. (Walter *Jens* im *Stern* 1981.42.187)

Der Römer à la Hollywood . . . läuft, lüstern blickend, den intriganten *Weibern* hinterher. (*Spiegel* 80.51.192)

Ein Weiser sollte *seine Frau* verständig lieben. (*Seneca,* zitiert nach *Beuys* 1980: 82)

(Willy Brandt) hatte überlegt, wen er . . . *als neuen Regierenden* anbieten könne. Seine Idealfigur: Eine Persönlichkeit, die . . . Außerdem müsse *der neue Mann* . . . (*Spiegel* 81.4.19)

Frauen haben sie *(die Mongolen)* eine oder mehrere. (Chronisten der engl. Benediktinerklöster Burton und St. Albans. Zitiert nach *Borst* 1980: 19)

(Hervorhebungen von mir.)

Angesichts solcher Sprüche, deren Anzahl sich hier beliebig vergrößern ließe, ist es verständlich, daß wir unsere Konsequenzen ziehen und auf Splitting bestehen.

Abgesehen davon, daß wir es ablehnen, in alle Ewigkeit »verbrüdert« zu werden, fühlen wir uns mehr und mehr nur dann wirklich gemeint und angesprochen, wenn wir explizit genannt werden, d. h. wenn ein Femininum gebraucht wird.

Sogar »der Gesetzgeber« hat inzwischen auf die Sprachkritik der Frauenbewegung reagiert und folgendes Gesetz erlassen:

> Der Arbeitgeber *(sic)* soll einen Arbeitsplatz weder öffentlich noch innerhalb eines Betriebes nur für Männer oder nur für Frauen ausschreiben. (§ 611 b BGB)

Die Auswirkungen dieses Gesetzes auf die sprachliche Gestaltung der Stellenausschreibungen sind geradezu dramatisch zu nennen. Splitting, wohin frau blickt. Betrachten wir die Seite 36 der *Zeit* Nr. 8 vom 19. 2. 1982. Es finden sich folgende Fälle von Splitting:

des/der Amtsarztes/Amtsärztin
des/der Leiters/Leiterin des Gesundheitsamtes
stellv. Amtsarztes/stellv. Amtsärztin
Referenten/in für Hochschulpolitik
eine/n jüngere/n Redakteur/in
Diplom-Psychologe/in
Leiters/Leiterin der Stadtbücherei
wissenschaftl. Mitarbeiter/innen
wissenschaftl. Mitarbeiter/in
Professor/in
ein(e) Professor(in)
ein(e) Dozent(in)
zwei Dozent(inn)en
ein(e) Professor(in)
ein(e) Dozent(in)
ein(e) Dozent(in)
Erzieher/in
engagierte(n) Dipl.-Psych.(in) und Sozialarbeiter(in)

Den splittenden Ausschreibungen stehen die folgenden nichtsplittenden gegenüber:

Maskulina:
Arbeitsmediziner als Leiter des betriebsärztlichen Dienstes
Sozialpädagogen
Leitender Arzt (Orthopädie)
Leitender Arzt (Anästhesiologie)

Stelle des Leiters (Sozialpädagoge, Sozialarbeiter, Religions-
pädagoge, Diakon)
Erzieher

Feminina:
einer Sozialpädagogin oder einer Erzieherin
Erzieherin im Gruppendienst

Umschreibung:
Professur (C 4)

Ergebnis: Von insgesamt 27 fettgedruckten Angaben genau zwei
Drittel gesplittet, ein Drittel nicht gesplittet.

Auf S. 37 derselben *Zeit*-Nr. werden u. a. gesucht: Metallkund-
ler/innen, Werkstoffwissenschaftler/innen und Physikochemi-
ker/innen.

Wie frau sieht, läßt sich mit Hilfe eines Gesetzes mühelos ein
drastischer Sprachwandel erzielen. In der zweiten Auflage der
Dudengrammatik (1966) nämlich steht noch zu lesen:

Bei Berufsbezeichnungen und Titeln dringt die weibliche Form
sehr schwer durch:
Frau Schulze ist *Schlosser.* Fräulein *(sic)* Schmitt ist *Doktor* der
Philosophie.
Nur einige sind bisher üblich geworden...:
Sie ist eine tüchtige *Lehrerin, Ärztin, Schaffnerin.* (S. 624)

Siebzehn Jahre ist das erst her – und mutet an wie aus dem vorigen
Jahrhundert. – Weiter heißt es auf S. 628: »*Grete B., Rechtsanwalt*
(auch schon: *Rechtsanwältin*)«. Dieses *auch schon* klingt inzwischen fast genauso lächerlich, wie wohl vielen noch vor kurzem die
Geschäftsfrau, die *Kauffrau* – und der *Hausmann.*

Gegen die Praxis des Splittens werden immer wieder zwei Einwände vorgebracht, und zwar sowohl von Männern als auch von
Frauen:

(1) Es ist zu umständlich, plump, unelegant.
Früher entgegnete ich auf diesen Einwand, daß da, wo es um ele-
mentare Menschenrechte geht, »ökonomische« und Eleganz-
Erwägungen keine Rolle spielen sollten. Heute jedoch lenke ich
ein und gestehe, daß ich selber des ewigen höflichen Splittens
müde und zum ständigen Gebrauch des geschlechtsneutralen
Femininums übergegangen sei. Sehr ökonomisch im Vergleich
zum Splitten! Und sehr elegant auch, waren doch Eleganz und

Schönheit schon immer eher eine Domäne des weiblichen Geschlechts.

(2) Es gibt doch Sinnzusammenhänge, wo eine geschlechtsneutrale Form einfach eine Notwendigkeit ist, wo weder gesplittet noch feminisiert werden kann! Zum Beispiel:
Frauen sind *Bürger* zweiter Klasse.
Sind Frauen tatsächlich die schlechteren *Mathematiker*?
Sekretärinnenkongreß: Unser *Feind* sollte nicht die Kollegin sein!

Antwort: Auch solche verzwickten Fälle sind kein Problem mehr, wenn das geschlechtsneutrale Femininum sich durchgesetzt hat:
Männer sind Bürgerinnen erster Klasse.
Sind Männer tatsächlich die besseren Mathematikerinnen?
Unsere Feindin sollte nicht die weibliche Kollegin sein!

4.4 Feminisierung der Kongruenzregeln: Eine Frau ist eine Frau ist eine Frau

4.4.1 *Eine Kauffrau ist kein Kaufmann: Neue Komposita mit* -frau

Früher standen dem schier unübersehbaren Heer der Komposita mit *-mann* nur einige wenige (und bezeichnende!) Komposita mit *-frau* gegenüber: *Hausfrau, Putzfrau, Klofrau, Zugehfrau, Zeitungsfrau, Marktfrau, Gemüsefrau* – nicht zu vergessen die *Karrierefrau!* Diese für die Repräsentanz der Frau in »Realität«, Bewußtsein und Sprache symptomatische Sachlage hat sich gründlich geändert. Neben dem Motionssuffix *-in* ist *-frau* heutzutage vermutlich das produktivste Morphem überhaupt. Es gibt ja auch, weiß Göttin, viel aufzuholen.

Der Grund für diese Produktivität ist die neue Frauenöffentlichkeit, die in den siebziger Jahren entstanden ist. Frauen reden intensiv miteinander, über sich selbst und über andere Frauen. **Sie machen sich selbst zum Thema.** Sie interessieren sich für Frauen in allen Bereichen, seien es nun Unifrauen, Guerillafrauen, Medienfrauen, Architekturfrauen, Technikfrauen, SPD-Frauen und überhaupt Parteifrauen, Filmfrauen, Kirchenfrauen, Gorleben-Frauen, Gewerkschaftsfrauen, Musikfrauen, Friedensfrauen, Kunstfrauen, Punkfrauen, Grafikfrauen, Archivfrauen, abgebrochene PH-Frauen, Vorstandsfrauen, Apo-Frauen, anti-intellektuelle Bauchfrauen oder Ausnahmefrauen wie Simone de Beauvoir. Lauter Frauen, die es vorher nicht gab, jedenfalls nicht in deutschen Wörterbüchern. Und **weil** wir uns für sie interessieren und über sie sprechen wollen, bilden wir, frei und nach (ständig wachsendem!) Bedarf, die notwendigen Bezeichnungen. Uns interessieren nicht so sehr die Vorstände allgemein, sondern die (paar) Frauen in diesen Vorständen, die Vorstands*frauen* also. Nicht so sehr die Parteien allgemein, sondern die Partei*frauen*. Nicht so sehr die Kirche allgemein, sondern die Kirchen*frauen*. Und so weiter, überall.

Ein weiterer Grund für das sprunghafte Ansteigen der Komposita mit *-frau:* Gerade in den letzten Jahren sind innerhalb der Frauenbewegung zahllose nur von Frauen für Frauen betriebene Projekte entstanden: Frauenzentren, Frauenzeitungen, Frauenbuchläden, Frauenferienhäuser, Häuser für geschlagene Frauen, Frauen-Notrufe, Frauen-Mitfahrzentralen, Frauen-Reisebüros, Frauenkneipen, Frauencafés usw. Für die in diesen Projekten tätigen Frauen mußten neue Bezeichnungen geschaffen werden, und so gibt es jetzt die *Emma*-Frauen, die *Courage*-Frauen, die FFGZ-Frauen, die Zentrumsfrauen, die Notruffrauen. In den Frauenkneipen arbeiten Tresenfrauen und Küchenfrauen (ein altes Wort mit erneuerter Bedeutung), und unter den Gastfrauen gibt es Problemfrauen, die für die Kollektivfrauen bzw. Kneipenfrauen eben problematisch sind (die letzten sechs *-frau*-Belege aus *Emma* 81.2.12). Bei öffentlichen Aktionen können die Planungsfrauen und die Aktionsfrauen auf die Handzettelfrauen nicht verzichten. Und bei *Emma* oder *Courage* gibt es die Redaktionsfrauen, die Vertriebsfrauen, die Abo-Frauen und die Layoutfrauen und so weiter ad libitum, ohne Ende. Redaktionsfrauen sind auch etwas spezifisch anderes als Redakteurinnen, deren Arbeitsgebiet und -ablauf den männlichen Normen des Redakteur-Berufs *(sic)* entspricht. Redaktionsfrauen machen so ziemlich alles, was in der Redaktion an Arbeit anfällt, vom Kaffeekochen über die »eigentliche« Redaktionsarbeit bis zum Saubermachen.

Einmal vorhanden, greift die *frau*-Bewegung munter um sich. Umständliche Ausdrücke wie *berufstätige Frau* werden zu *Berufsfrau* vereinfacht:

> Eine Textileinkäuferin, sichere, selbständige Berufsfrau, wird nach ihrem Männerideal befragt. (*Courage* 77.4.21)

Unschöne (weil unweibliche) Neutra können mit Hilfe von -*frau* veredelt werden: *Mitglieder* werden zu *Mitgliederfrauen* (*Emma* 79.5.55) – anscheinend von solchen Frauen bevorzugt, die sich mit dem Wort *Mitgliederinnen* noch immer nicht so recht anfreundinnen können (ich gehöre auch zu diesen).[15] Auch für solche, die *Gästin* (noch) nicht mögen, ist *Gastfrau* eine willkommene Alternative (s. o.). Merke aber: Nur bei Neubildungen auf -*in/nen* ist Variation mit -*frau* problemlos (Typ *Gästin: Gastfrau* – *Mitgliederinnen: Mitgliederfrauen*). Sonst Gefahr der Verwechslung mit abzuschaffendem Wortgut bzw. -schlecht: *Ärztin* – gut! *Arztfrau* gehört eingemottet, solange der *Ärztinmann* noch nicht in Sicht!

Schon längst hat die *frau*-Bewegung auch die Männerpresse erreicht. Die von *Carstensen* verzeichnete *Armeefrau* ist bei weitem nicht die einzige Anwendung des Prinzips -*frau*. Einer meiner neueren Funde ist die *Rätselfrau* (die übrigens einer Feministin wohl nicht so schnell eingefallen wäre):

> Der Ufa-Star Sibylle Schmitz, im Goebbels-Deutschland als ... rothaarige Rätselfrau gehandelt, fängt in den fünfziger Jahren an zu trinken ... (*Spiegel* 82.8.199)

Ähnlich wie das Pronomen *frau* das Pronomen *mann* nach sich zog, so entstehen jetzt als Pendants zu den -*frau*-Komposita **neue** -*mann*-Komposita:

> Medienfrauen ehren Medienmänner. (*Emma* 81.1.20)

> Nun ist zwar sicherlich nicht jeder »Spiegel«-Mann ein Sokrates ... (*Emma* 78.11.26)

Womit wir bei dem Heer der alten *mann*-Komposita angekommen sind. Ein beträchtlicher Teil der neuen *frau*-Komposita, wenn auch bei weitem nicht der größte, ist analog zu diesen *mann*-Komposita gebildet, nach der Devise: Wir wollen nicht mehr mit einem Maskulinum bezeichnet werden, schon gar nicht mit *Mann*! Hilflosen männlichen Sprachforscherinnen wie *Henzen,* der noch im Jahre 1965 fragen konnte –

> Aber wie kennzeichnen wir einen weiblichen *Kaufmann* oder *Obmann*? ... Vielleicht *Kaufmännin, Obmännin?* (*Henzen* 1965: 117)

– haben die Frauen inzwischen tatkräftig den rechten Weg gewiesen: Den »weiblichen Kaufmann« kennzeichnen wir – ganz

einfach! – mit *Kauffrau*. Unbegreiflich heute, daß das noch vor
18 Jahren so undenkbar schien, daß allen Ernstes *Kaufmännin*
in Erwägung gezogen wurde. Weitere weibliche *mann*-Pendants,
die noch vor kurzem fremdartig wirkten und heute zum sprachlichen Allgemeingut zählen: *Geschäftsfrau, Fachfrau, Vertrauens-
frau, Kamerafrau*. Hingegen ist die *Staatsfrau* mir noch nicht offiziell begegnet, trotz Margaret Thatcher, Indira Gandhi, Golda
Meir und anderen.[16] Ich selbst benutze das Wort allerdings gern
und relativ häufig. Die *Bergfrau* fehlt meines Wissens auch noch –
vielleicht weil uns das Herumwühlen in Mutter Erde nicht so zu-
sagt? *Obfrau* und *Amtfrau* wollen anscheinend auch noch nicht so
recht raus, wohingegen die *Ombudsfrau*, im Zusammenhang mit
der öffentlichen Diskussion um ein Antidiskriminierungsgesetz,
uns schon ziemlich geläufig ist (*Emma* 82.2.9).

»Mein Bruder ist Jungfrau, ich bin Wassermann«, sagte neulich
eine. Darauf die andere, milde: »Ich bin auch Wasserfrau!« – Richtig, soll der jungfräuliche Bruder sein Sprachproblem alleine lösen,
aber: Eine Wasserfrau ist kein Wassermann!

Und all die Biedermänner, Saubermänner, Ehrenmänner, Dun-
kelmänner, Buhmänner, Hinter-, Vorder- und Nebenmänner,
Weihnachtsmänner, Schneemänner, Hampelmänner, Blaumän-
ner, Henkelmänner, Flachmänner, Walkmänner, Ballermänner,
Strichmännchen, Mainzelmännchen und Marsmännchen kommen
sicher durch die rastlos kreative *frau*-Bewegung auch noch zu einer
besseren Hälfte:

> nicht die ersten, die sich Alice Schwarzer . . . zur Buhfrau ausge-
> sucht haben . . . (*Courage* 79.9.58)

> Hampelfrau zum Ausschneiden (*Emma* 78.11.63)

4.4.2 *Eine Studentin ist kein Student, auch kein weiblicher*

In meiner Heimatstadt gab es, als ich noch zur Schule ging, ein
»Gymnasium« und ein »Mädchengymnasium«.

Bei Tanzveranstaltungen gibt es manchmal auch »Damenwahl«.

Neben »Rasierapparaten« werden auch »Damen-Rasierapparate«
angeboten.

1908 erlaubten die Männer den Frauen das Studium. Seitdem gibt
es neben den »Studenten« auch »weibliche Studenten«, neben den
»Ärzten, Rechtsanwälten, Wissenschaftlern, Akademikern, Pro-

fessoren« auch »weibliche Ärzte, Rechtsanwälte, Wissenschaftler, Akademiker«, ganz ganz selten auch mal einen »weiblichen Professor«.

1918 bekamen die Frauen in Deutschland das Wahlrecht. Seitdem gibt es neben den »Wählern« auch »weibliche Wähler«, neben den »Parlamentariern, Politikern, Staatssekretären und Ministern« auch »weibliche Parlamentarier, Politiker, Staatssekretäre«, ganz ganz selten auch mal einen »weiblichen Minister«. Einen weiblichen Bundeskanzler oder Bundespräsidenten? Nicht doch!

In den siebziger Jahren erlaubten die Männer der evangelischen Kirche Deutschlands den Frauen, das Pfarramt auszuüben. Seitdem gibt es neben den »Pastoren/Pfarrern« auch »weibliche Pastoren/Pfarrer« – aber »weibliche Bischöfe« noch nicht.

Wir sehen: Das Neue, Ungewöhnliche, nicht der Norm Entsprechende wird jeweils sprachlich gekennzeichnet. Die Norm – Gymnasium: nur für Jungen; Studenten, Pastoren usw.: Männer – bedurfte und bedarf keiner solchen Hervorhebung, im Fall des fehlenden Pendants zur »Damenwahl« anscheinend noch nicht mal eines Namens.

Nicht **immer** ist das Männliche die Norm. Parfüm für Herren z. B. ist eher die Ausnahme, daher gibt es neben den »Parfüms« noch die »Herrenparfüms«. Ob uns Frauen die ausgleichende Gerechtigkeit auf dem Kosmetiksektor aber auf die Dauer dafür entschädigen kann, daß wir sonst überall als Ausnahme, weil weiblich, eine sprachliche Sonderbehandlung erfahren?

»Weibliche Arbeiter, Köche und Lehrer« sind gegenüber den »Arbeiterinnen, Köchinnen und Lehrerinnen« eher eine Seltenheit, denn: Für Männer in der Fabrik arbeiten und kochen dürfen Frauen schon etwas länger, und der Beruf der Lehrerin war bis zum Anfang dieses Jahrhunderts der einzige »höhere« Beruf, den Frauen ausüben durften.

Seit einiger Zeit werden auch Männer im Haushalt und in den pflegenden Berufen tätig. Seither gibt es – nicht etwa »männliche Hausfrauen, Krankenschwestern und Hebammen«, sondern »Hausmänner«, »Krankenpfleger« und »Geburtshelfer«. Dem unerbittlichen Gesetz »weiblich gleich zweitrangig« sind die Männer mit bewundernswerter Schlauheit ausgewichen.

Männliche Linguistinnen werden nicht müde, den Frauen einzureden, die bisher aufgeführten Maskulina und zahllose andere maskuline Personen- und Berufsbezeichnungen seien auch »geschlechtsneutral«, »unmarkiert« verwendbar. Das stimmt. In Ausdrücken wie *weibliche und männliche Kandidaten, Bewerber* etc. wird, unbestreitbar, das Maskulinum »geschlechtsneutral« verwendet. Was allerdings bei dieser »abgehobenen«, klassisch-synchron orientierten Analyse als »unlinguistisch« unter den Tisch fällt, ist der oben skizzierte, langwierige und schmerzhafte historische Prozeß der Befreiung aus **realer** männlicher Unterdrückung, Bevormundung und Ausschließung aus allen Berufen und öffentlichen Ämtern. Es war erst dieser Befreiungsprozeß, der zu der heute beobachtbaren »Unmarkiertheit« geführt hat. Und »unmarkiert verwendbar« heißt ja nicht etwa, daß »Unmarkiert-Verwenden« gängige Praxis ist. Auch heute noch werden maskuline Personenbezeichnungen überwiegend genauso verwendet wie eh und je: als Bezeichnungen für Männer. Die für manche Vorkommen nachweisbare »Geschlechtsneutralität« derselben Maskulina dient höchstens patriarchalischen Verschleierungs- und Rechtfertigungsinteressen: Früher **wußten** wir wenigstens, daß wir nicht gemeint waren und nicht gemeint sein konnten. Sprachliche Form und Realität stimmten überein – diese Maskulina hatten ja nie etwas anderes bezeichnet als Männer. Heute wissen wir »eigentlich« auch, daß nicht von uns die Rede ist, aber nie ganz sicher (wegen der paar raffinierten Ausnahmen) – und vor allem können wir nichts mehr beweisen.

Warum heißt Zimbabwe heute »Zimbabwe« und nicht mehr »Rhodesien« nach seinem früheren Kolonialherrn Cecil Rhodes? Warum heißt Indonesien »Indonesien« und nicht mehr »Niederländisch-Indien« nach seinen ehemaligen Kolonialherren?

In den Nachrichten hören wir meist nicht »Zimbabwe«, sondern »Zimbabwe-Rhodesien«, damit auch diejenigen Bescheid wissen, die die politischen Entwicklungen nicht so schnell mitkriegen. – Auf viele Frauen nun wirken Ausdrücke wie *weibliche Hochschullehrer, Parlamentarier* ähnlich zwittrig und zwiespältig wie *Zimbabwe-Rhodesien.* Der Teil *weiblich* (bzw. *Zimbabwe*) steht für die neue, unter schweren Opfern erkämpfte Realität – der maskuline Teil (bzw. *Rhodesien*) erinnert an die alte, offiziell überwundene Ordnung, die doch noch überall mächtig ist.

Da Feministinnen die alte Ordnung abschaffen und nicht dazu beitragen wollen, sie in der Sprache zu konservieren, haben sie einen neuen Umgang mit dem Attribut *weiblich* etabliert. Der konservativ-patriarchalische, auch »korrekt« genannte Gebrauch von »*weiblich* plus Maskulinum« wie in

> Daß es auch anders geht, machen uns andere Länder vor, wie Schweden (22,6 Prozent weiblicher Parlamentarier) oder Norwegen (23,9 Prozent). (*Emma* 80.5.26)

wird mehr und mehr zurückgedrängt zugunsten des progressiv-feministischen »*weiblich* plus Femininum«:

> Dieser Beruf ist ziemlich neu für Mädchen aus meiner Gegend, obwohl es einige weibliche Kolleginnen geben soll. (*Emma* 80.12.41)

> Er konnte ... mit seinen Kollegen vergnügt zum geistigen Salto mortale ansetzen – über dem Netz, versteht sich – das die weiblichen Assistentinnen stets gespannt halten. (*Emma* 80.12.53)

> Die Tatsache, daß Island eine weibliche Präsidentin bekommen hat ... (*Emma* 80.9.58)

> »Sie sind meine erste weibliche Gesprächspartnerin bei einem Interview.« (Dirigentin Blankenburg in einem Rundfunk-Interview)

> Tatsächlich hat man in Hessen nicht gerade eifrig nach einer weiblichen Leiterin gesucht. (*Emma* 79.4.45)

Offenbar empfinden viele Frauen (ich schließe mich ein) die Redundanz dieser Konstruktion als kaum störend im Vergleich zu dem Verstoß, eine Frau mit einem Maskulinum zu bezeichnen.

4.4.3 *Leserinnenbriefe sind keine Leserbriefe*

Sibylle *Helferich*, Vorsitzende der soeben gegründeten Frauenpartei, stellte sich bei der Berliner Frauensommeruni 1979 im Rahmen einer Großveranstaltung dem Publikum mit folgenden Worten vor:

»Ich bin Tierarzt.«
Tobendes Gelächter des ganzen Auditoriums. Sibylle verstand erst nicht, was los war, und korrigierte sich dann: »Ich bin Tierärztin.«
Die Frauenpartei hatte einen schweren Stand an jenem Abend. Und Sibylles sprachlich mißglückter Einstieg hat das Unternehmen in den Ohren der meisten Anwesenden nicht gerade als ver-

trauenswürdig ausgewiesen. Die feministischen Sprachwächterinnen sind streng, das konnte ich da hautnah erleben, und Sibylle tat mir richtig leid. Sie hatte allerdings die **allerwichtigste** feministische Kongruenzregel verletzt:

Eine Sprecherin bezeichnet niemals
sich selbst mit einem Maskulinum!

Die patriarchalische Grammatik schreibt uns dagegen eher das Gegenteil vor – sie war es auch, an der Sibylle sich unkritisch orientiert hatte, und eben das wurde mit Spott quittiert.

Manche erinnert sich vielleicht noch an die Kongruenzregeln, die wir im Lateinunterricht lernten: »Das Attribut kongruiert mit seinem Bezugswort in Kasus, Numerus und Genus.« Beispiel: *puellarum urbanarum* ›der geistreichen Mädchen‹. *Puellarum* ist Genitiv, Plural, Femininum und *urbanarum* ebenfalls Genitiv, Plural, Femininum.

In den romanischen Sprachen spielen die Kongruenzregeln noch heute eine wichtige Rolle. Wo im Deutschen beide Geschlechter über sich aussagen können »Ich bin glücklich«, gilt im Französischen die Vorschrift, daß das Adjektiv im Genus mit dem Geschlecht der Sprechenden kongruieren muß. Die Französin sagt also: »Je suis heureuse«, der Franzose »Je suis heureux«. Vergleichbares haben wir im Deutschen nur bei den Adjektiven in attributiver Stellung *(eine glückliche Frau, ein glücklicher Mann)*. In prädikativer Stellung gibt es Kongruenzzwang nur bei einer kleinen Gruppe der Personenbezeichnungen – bei denjenigen, die aus Adjektiven und Partizipien abgeleitet sind (Typ *die/der Kranke, die/der Angestellte*). Die Deutsche sagt: »Ich bin Angestellte.« Der Deutsche sagt: »Ich bin Angestellter.« Wenn eine Deutsche sagt: »Ich bin Angestellter«, so ist das **grammatisch** falsch. Nicht falsch soll es dagegen sein, wenn sie sagt: »Ich bin Tierarzt.« (Ich erinnere an die *Duden*grammatik: »Grete B., Rechtsanwalt. Auch schon: Rechtsanwältin.«)

Feministinnen aber sind da, wie Sibylle *Helferich* schmerzlich erfahren mußte, **ganz** anderer Ansicht. Und sie gehen noch weiter. Immer zahlreicher werden die Beispiele, in denen Frauen, wenn sie über sich selbst und andere Frauen sprechen, die **Radikalversion** der feministischen Kongruenzregel anwenden. Sie lautet:

Verwandle alle maskulinen Personenbezeichnungen in feminine, sofern sie sich in irgendeiner Form auf Frauen beziehen.

Dies gilt auch dann, wenn die maskuline Personenbezeichnung **nur Teil** eines Wortes ist.

Nach dieser Regel wird z. B. *freundlich* zu *freundinlich*, *Freundschaft* zu *Freundinnenschaft* und *sich anfreunden* zu *sich anfreundinnen*. – Einige Belege:

Auf Eurer Überweisung darf die Kundinnennummer nicht fehlen. (*Courage* 81.7.2)

Frauen, die sich auf diese Arbeitsverträge einlassen, haben grob umrissen folgendes Arbeitnehmerinnenschicksal. (*Courage* 81.10.12)

Die Männer am Institut fordern von uns den Nachweis, wo ihre Theorien zu kurz greifen (. . .). Wir lehnen diese ergänzende Helferinnenrolle ab (. . .). (*Courage* 81.10.44)

Ich habe eine einjährige Sekretärinnenausbildung gemacht. (*Courage* 81.11.23)

Danach ging die Rednerin in Siegerinnenpose zu ihrem Platz zurück. (*Courage* 81.12.16)

Ich wollte freier sein, habe mich wieder junggesellinnenhaft benommen. (*Courage* Sonderheft Sexualität 1981, S. 60)

Was (. . .) soll denn nur so heldinnenhaft an der Prostitution sein? (*Courage* 81.4.59)

Ich fange im Herbst mit einer Heilpraktikerin-Ausbildung in München an. (*Courage* 79.7.59)

Was ist aus Eurem in früheren Heften formulierten Anspruch geworden, möglichst wenig Spezialistinnentum (. . .) und möglichst wenig Trennung von Hand- und Kopfarbeit bei Euren Mitarbeiterinnen zu erreichen? (*Courage* 80.8.59)

Die Stellung der Frau, insbesondere in Ostanatolien, ist ebenfalls in der Türkei ein Sklavinnendasein. (*Emma* 77.10.63)

sehr bald wird der literaturmarkt (. . .) vom schreibfluß einer einzigen frau, dieser *George Sand*, überschwemmt (. . .). der vielleicht erste fall von *imperialismus* einer autorinnenpersönlichkeit in der branche zeichnet sich ab. (*Courage* 80.8.22) die Genossin aus dem KSV, der Schrecken des ganzen Fachbereichs, in adretter Studienrätinkleidung, meiner alten Geschichtslehrerin, Fräulein Dr. F., zum Verwechseln ähnlich. (*Courage* 80.9.41)

Sie hat mich durchs Haus geführt, mich mit Besitzerinnenstolz vom Gymnastikraum durch das Schwimmbad in den Bastelraum gelotst (. . .). (*Emma* 80.12.37)

hier werden in oberlehrerinnenhafter Weise Punkte verteilt. (*Emma* 80.12.63)

Die Radikalversion der feministischen Kongruenzregel revolutioniert spielend das gesamte ehrwürdige System der deutschen Wortbildung. Auf der Ebene der Sprachpolitik leistet sie ähnliches wie spektakuläre feministische Aktionen: Sie sichert uns einen hohen Aufmerksamkeitswert, indem sie für unüberseh- und -hörbare weibliche Präsenz sorgt.

5 Eine neue Harmonie

Kongruenz heißt Übereinstimmung, Gleichförmigkeit, Harmonie. In der Sprache des Patriarchats bedeutete das: Die Welt kongruiert mit dem Mann. Der Mann hatte sich die Welt gedanklich so erklärt und geordnet und faktisch so eingerichtet, daß sie *ihm* **gleichförmig** war, mit *ihm* übereinstimmte, kongruierte. Sie war Geschlecht von seinem Geschlecht geworden. Von dem Mann auf der Straße über den Staatsmann bis zu Gott dem Herrn. Von den Muselmännern bis zu den Buschmännern. Von den Heinzelmännchen über die Mainzelmännchen bis zu den Marsmännchen. Vom Hampelmann über den Schneemann bis zum Weihnachtsmann. Vom Henkelmann über den Ballermann bis zu Little Boy und Fat Man, den Bomben auf Hiroshima und Nagasaki.

Es störte natürlich die Harmonie empfindlich, daß es neben dem männlichen noch »das andere Geschlecht« gab. Deshalb wurde es – hauptsächlich mittels der Grammatik – kurzerhand gleichförmig, kongruent **gemacht:** Neunundneunzig Lehrerinnen und ein Lehrer, das sind in »unserer« Sprache genau einhundert »Lehrer«. Im Französischen sind diese einhundert Personen nicht »elles«, sondern »ils«.

Der Mensch schlechthin – das kann nur ein Mann sein:

> Kein gesunder Mensch kann drei oder sechs Wochen ohne Frau auskommen (. . .). (Fußballtrainer *Rehhagel* über mehrwöchige Trainingslager. *Spiegel* 83.7.165)

> Jede Sprache entwickelt sich (. . .) nicht anders als jeder Mensch sich vom Kind zum Jüngling, vom Jüngling zum Mann und zum Greis entwickelt. (*Staiger* [8]1968: 208)

Die Frau mag selbst zusehen, wo sie bleibt. Entweder findet sie sich damit ab, dem männlichen Geschlecht zugezählt zu werden, oder damit, daß sie als Mensch nicht existiert.

Die Frau von heute lehnt beides ab. Die zugestandene Koexistenz als Mann gefällt ihr ebensowenig wie die Nichtexistenz als Mensch.

Endlich beginnt sie selbst zu sprechen, die Welt zu ordnen und zu benennen nach **ihrem** Maßstab. Sie bezeichnet sich selbst und andere Frauen nicht mehr mit einem Maskulinum. Die Feministische Kongruenzregel etabliert **eine neue Harmonie.** Mit der sanften Gewalt des Wassers unterspült sie die Fundamente der Sprache des Patriarchats und damit des Patriarchats selbst.

Eine Welt, die mit **beiden** Geschlechtern kongruiert (harmoniert), wird eine humane Welt sein.

1983

Anmerkungen

1 Revidierte Fassung eines Vortrags, den ich im März 1982 bei der 4. Jahrestagung der deutschen Gesellschaft für Sprachwissenschaft (DGfS) in Köln gehalten habe. Den in diesem Aufsatz entwickelten analytischen Raster für sprachliche Innovationsleistungen der Neuen Frauenbewegung in der Bundesrepublik habe ich erstmals vorgestellt im Dezember 1980 in einem Vortrag an der Universität Hannover zum Thema »Frauenbewegung und Sprachwandel«, später an den Universitäten Regensburg, Freiburg, Zürich, Bochum, Aachen und Düsseldorf.

2 Zum Deutschen vergleiche *Trömel-Plötz* 1978 und 1982, *Guentherodt, Hellinger, Pusch* und *Trömel-Plötz* 1981, *Hellinger* 1980a, *Guentherodt* 1980. Zum Englischen vergleiche *Key* 1975, *Thorne* und *Henley* 1975, *Miller* und *Swift* 1977 und 1980, *Nilsen, Bosmajian, Gershuny* und

Stanley 1977, *Lakoff* 1975, *Spender* 1980, *Kramarae* 1981, *McConnell-Ginet, Borker* und *Furmann* 1980.
Zum Französischen vergleiche *Yaguello* 1978.

3 Vgl. hierzu *Günthner* 1982, *Goop* 1982 und *Bartsch* 1982.

4 Vgl. *Schulz* 1975 und *Hellinger* 1980 a.

5 Susanne *Müller* vom Englischen Seminar der Universität Zürich gibt allerdings zu bedenken, ob die feminine Form als Bezeichnung für Männer nicht zu schade sei. Ein interessanter und schwerwiegender Einwand!

6 Vgl. hierzu auch *Hoffmann* 1979.

7 *Förster* 1978 a und 1978 b.

8 *Carstensen* 1978 bis 1982.

9 Vgl. u. a. *Brehmer* 1981 und 1983, *Zumbühl* 1981, *Benz* 1982, *Sollwedel* 1970, *Nohr* et al. 1983, *Hellinger* 1980 b, *Sarges* 1983.

10 Vgl. *Moulton, Robinson* und *Elias* 1978.

11 Vgl. hierzu *Berger* und *Luckmann* 1966, *Luckmann* 1979 und vor allem *Trömel-Plötz* 1982 und die dort zitierte Literatur.
Berger und *Luckmann* 1966 war übrigens für mich das seltsamste und zwiespältigste Leseerlebnis seit Jahren. Einerseits stimmt ihre theoretische Position über die Bedeutung der Sprache für die Erfahrung und Sicht der Welt hundertprozentig mit der Position der Feministischen Linguistik überein – ihre Argumente lassen sich auf viele Probleme, die Frauen mit der Sprache des Patriarchats haben, übertragen. Andererseits ist das Buch sowohl von der Sprache als auch von den Beispielen her durch und durch sexistisch und androzentrisch – weit mehr, als es in den sechziger Jahren »normal« war.

12 Diesen nützlichen Terminus verdanke ich Jutta *Wasels*.

13 Vgl. *Goop* (1982: 74). Sie hat bei Durchsicht des gesamten Jahrgangs 1981 der *Courage* nur einen einzigen Beleg für *jedermann* gefunden.

14 *Friday* 1979.

15 Vgl. meine Glosse »Mitgliederinnen« in diesem Band.

16 Nachtrag im Dezember 1983: Vor ein paar Wochen benutzte Franz-Josef Strauß *Staatsfrau* mit verblüffender Selbstverständlichkeit, als habe es das Wort schon immer gegeben. Für mich war es der erste »offizielle« Beleg (gehört bei einer TV-Übertragung seines Redaktionsbesuchs bei der *Zeit*).

Weibliches Schicksal aus männlicher Sicht
Über Syntax und Empathie

1 Einleitung

Die Anregung für das Thema dieses Aufsatzes bekam ich vor etwa einem Jahr in Zürich.

Ich hatte einen Vortrag über »Sprache, Geschlecht und Macht« gehalten. Es ging darin um die Kritik der Frauen an Sprache, Sprachverwendung und Sprachwissenschaft.

Gegen Schluß der Diskussion meldete sich eine Literaturwissenschaftlerin. Sie sagte, das sei ja alles gut und schön mit unserer Kritik an Ausdrücken wie *Fräulein Müller*, an *Maggie* statt *Premierministerin Thatcher* oder an *Mrs. John Brown* statt *Ms. Mary Brown*. Wir hätten ja recht. Aber wir gingen doch am wirklich Wesentlichen und Schlimmen ständig vorbei. Und sie begreife nicht, **warum** wir das täten. Wirklich verheerend sei doch, um nur **ein** Beispiel von vielen zu nennen, die »ganz normale« Berichterstattung über Vergewaltigungen, überhaupt über Gewalt gegen Frauen. Diese unglaublichen Verharmlosungen! Diese Gefühllosigkeit gegenüber den Opfern. Diese Einfühlung, statt dessen, in die Seele des Täters. Ihr jedenfalls käme es beim Lesen so vor, als würde der Frau durch solche Art von Texten, sogenannt objektive Berichterstattung, jeweils noch ein zweites Mal Gewalt angetan. (Nachtrag 1984: Ein konkretes Beispiel eines Journalustmordes behandle ich in der Glosse »Explosion einer geschundenen Seele«, in diesem Band.) Sie schloß mit der Frage, was ich denn, als gelernte Linguistin, zu **diesem** Tatbestand zu sagen hätte. Und wenn wir nichts dazu sagen könnten, wann die Linguistik sich endlich um das Thema kümmern würde.

Ich hatte tatsächlich nichts zu sagen. Dies ist von meiner Seite der erste Versuch, mich an das »Riesenthema« heranzuwagen. Soweit ich die gegenwärtige linguistische Diskussion in der Bundesrepublik überblicke, ist es überhaupt der erste Versuch.

Es geht, linguistisch gesprochen, um folgende Fragen:

1. Ist der pychologische Begriff der Empathie (Einfühlung) linguistisch überhaupt faßbar? Mit anderen Worten: Läßt er sich an

konkret beobachtbaren Eigenschaften genuiner Gegenstände der Linguistik wie Sätzen, Äußerungen und vor allem Texten (gesprochenen und geschriebenen) festmachen?

2. Wenn ja, wo genau ist Empathie lokalisierbar, diagnostizierbar? In der Wortwahl (Lexik)? In der Syntax, sei es die Mikrosyntax oder Syntax innerhalb von Sätzen oder die Makrosyntax, die Textstruktur?

Es läßt sich nachweisen, daß alle drei angesprochenen Gegenstände der Linguistik – Lexik, Mikrosyntax und Textstruktur – Träger von Empathie sein können. Ich möchte mich hier auf die Syntax konzentrieren, aus folgenden Gründen:

Für mich gehört die Syntax als Kernstück der Grammatik zu den Gebieten, für die ich mich, als Linguistin, »echt« zuständig fühle. Als Linguistinnen und Linguisten wissen wir, daß Disziplinen wie Literaturwissenschaft, Philosophie, Psychologie, Pädagogik, Soziologie, Geschichte, Medizin alle möglichen Gebiete beackern, die wir auch für uns reklamieren. Aber mit Syntax oder Grammatik haben diese Disziplinen meist nicht viel im Sinn. *Grammatik* ist sozusagen ein Reizwort – alle haben den Stoff in der Schule angeödet durchgestanden und sind eigentlich froh, wenn sie nichts mehr damit zu tun haben.

Entsprechend rudimentär ist meist das Allgemeinwissen über Grammatik und speziell Syntax. Besser gesagt: diese Gegenstände gehören nicht zu denen, über die man als gebildeter Mensch wenigstens in Ansätzen Bescheid wissen muß. Hochintellektuelle Leute, die mehrere Sprachen sprechen und Vorträge über Atomphysik, die Gesangstechnik des Belcanto und den französischen Poststrukturalismus halten können, wissen z. B. in der Regel nicht anzugeben, was der syntaktische Unterschied zwischen deutschen Haupt- und Nebensätzen ist und wie sich die Syntax des Deutschen in dieser Hinsicht von der Syntax des Englischen oder Französischen unterscheidet.

Daher meine ich, daß es für die Linguistik nicht nur eine lohnende und interessante Aufgabe ist, Empathiephänomene gerade in der Syntax zu untersuchen. Es ist auch eine Aufgabe, für die sie zuständig und kompetent ist, weit mehr als irgendeine der genannten benachbarten Disziplinen. Es bietet sich mit diesem Thema die Gelegenheit, einmal nicht Anregungen von anderen Disziplinen zu übernehmen und uns sozusagen anzuverwandeln, wie wir das in der linguistischen Pragmatik, der logisch-mathematischen Semantik, der Konversationsanalyse, der Psycho-, Sozio- und Textlinguistik getan haben und tun. Vielmehr können wir unser spezifisch linguistisches Training und Analyse-Instrumentarium für sowohl eigene Fragestellungen als auch für die anderer Disziplinen, vor allem der Literaturwissenschaft und Psychologie, fruchtbar machen.

2 Zur Illustration des Begriffs ›Empathiephänomene in Texten‹: Weibliches Schicksal aus männlicher Sicht

Bevor ich mich der ›technischen‹, im engeren Sinne linguistischen Seite meines Themas zuwende, möchte ich anhand von fünf Textbeispielen veranschaulichen, worauf die Kritik und die Frage jener Literaturwissenschaftlerin sich bezogen. Es geht in diesen Texten, wenn auch (vielleicht) nicht direkt um Vergewaltigung, so doch um einen ähnlich tragischen und typischen Aspekt des »weiblichen Lebenszusammenhangs«:

1. Louisens Pflegeeifer ging sehr weit. Sie sorgte so eifrig für das Wohlbefinden ihres langsam genesenden Patienten, daß die Folgen eines Tages nicht zu übersehen waren – bei ihr. (Über Louise *Gleich* und Ferdinand *Raimund*, in: *Fischer-Fabian*, S. 71)

2. Hegel drücken in dieser Zeit aber auch noch andere Sorgen. Sein Vermögen ist aufgezehrt und sein Professoren-Gehalt lächerlich niedrig. [...] Zudem hat er der Frau seines Hauswirts ein Kind gemacht. (Über N.N. und G.W.F. *Hegel*, in: *Koesters*, S. 129)

3. Fest davon überzeugt, das Geheimnis der Welt ergründet zu haben, verläßt er Dresden. Zurück bleibt eine Kammerzofe, der er ein Kind gemacht hat. (Über N.N. und Arthur *Schopenhauer*, in: *Koesters*, S. 189)

4. Sie hoffte auf Heirat, doch ihr Freund steuerte einen anderen Kurs, er hieß Freundschaft. Für ihn gab es keine andere Möglichkeit. [...] Zunächst jedoch geriet das Verhältnis in eine Krise. Im Sommer 1840 verließ Elise die Hansestadt, sie war schwanger. (Über Elise *Lensing* und Friedrich *Hebbel*, in: *Matthiesen*, S. 43)

111

5. Und als ob dieses bürgerliche Elend nicht genug sei, wurde auch das eheliche Verhältnis, vermutlich Anfang der sechziger Jahre, durch einen menschlichen Konflikt gestört. Allen sozialistischen Führern um 1900 war bekannt, daß Marx der Vater Frederick Demuths, Helene Demuths Sohn, war. (Über Helene *Demuth*, Haushälterin der Familie *Marx*, und Karl *Marx*, in: *Blumenberg*, S. 115)

Vier verschiedene Biographen schildern »Vorfälle« im Leben großer Dichter und Denker, die zugleich auch Vorfälle, besser gesagt: Katastrophen, im Leben fast unbekannt gebliebener Frauen waren, von denen wir in zwei Fällen nicht einmal den Namen kennen. Es handelt sich um Variationen **eines** Grundmusters: Eine Haushälterin, Kammerzofe oder sonstwie dienende und versorgende Frau, immer aber eine Frau in abhängiger Stellung, bekommt ein Kind von dem jeweiligen berühmten Mann. Von Heirat ist keine Rede. Was das im 19. Jahrhundert für die betroffene Frau gesellschaftlich, ökonomisch und daher oft auch gesundheitlich bedeutete, brauche ich hier nicht auszumalen.

Die Biographen zeigen aber keine Spur von Mitgefühl, Einfühlung in das Schicksal der Frau. Zwar ist von »Sorgen«, »Krise«, »Elend« und »menschlichem Konflikt« durchaus die Rede, jedoch hat nur *Hegel* »Sorgen«, nicht die Frau ohne Namen, die das Kind erwartet. Im Falle *Hebbel* gerät »das Verhältnis« in eine Krise, nicht Elise *Lensing*. Im Falle *Marx* belasten das »Elend« und der »menschliche Konflikt« nicht Helene *Demuth*, sondern die Familie bzw. die Ehe.

Weiter fällt an diesen fünf Texten auf, daß die Hauptbteiligten in keinem Fall **beide** als aktiv beteiligt geschildert werden. Über *Hegel* und *Schopenhauer* heißt es stereotyp: *Er machte ihr ein Kind.* (Wenn es eheliche Kinder gewesen wären, so hätten wir wohl zu lesen bekommen: *Sie schenkte ihm ein Kind*.) Im Falle *Raimund* war, so will der »launige« Text uns glauben machen, der Vater überhaupt nicht beteiligt, nur die Mutter ist aktiv geworden. Im Falle *Hebbel* und *Marx* war anscheinend niemand aktiv beteiligt; es kommen jedenfalls keine Handlungsverben vor: *Elise war schwanger; Marx war der Vater Frederick Demuths,* heißt es lediglich.

Zwei der Frauen werden mit Vornamen genannt, Louise und Elise, eine mit vollem Namen, Helene *Demuth*. Die beiden namenlosen Frauen werden eingeführt als *Frau seines Hauswirts* bzw. *eine Kammerfrau.* Ihnen wird nicht nur kein Name zugebilligt, sondern auch keinerlei aktive Beteiligung. In beiden und nur in diesen Fällen heißt es, »er machte ihr ein Kind«. Das mag, bei einer so kleinen Auswahl, Zufall sein. Nicht unplausibel scheint mir aber auch die Interpretation, daß dort, wo sowieso bloß eine so unerhebliche Person wie eine Kammerzofe oder die Frau eines Hauswirts betroffen war, das »Kavaliersdelikt« dem jeweiligen Kavalier auch ruhig als Tat zugeschrieben werden kann. In den anderen Fällen, wo die beteiligte Frau auch sonst ein »biographischer Faktor« ist, besteht eher die Neigung, die Tat, da peinlich, entweder ganz der Frau zur Last zu legen (Fall *Raimund*) oder zu mystifizieren, sie sozusagen mittels der Sprache aus der Welt zu schaffen *(Hebbel, Marx).*

Natürlich wäre es lohnend, diese Texte noch viel feiner zu analysieren. Ich habe sie aber, wie gesagt, nur vorgestellt, um den Begriff ›Empathie‹ einführend zu illustrieren. Es dürfte klar sein – auch ohne linguistische Analyse –, welche der beiden Hauptpersonen des »Vorfalls« dem jeweiligen Autor am Herzen lag und welche ihm herzlich egal war. Die Frage ist aber, welche sprachlichen Mittel diesen Eindruck hervorrufen. Um diese Mittel klar herauszupräparieren, d. h. um sie von anderen Einflußfaktoren getrennt halten zu können, brauchen wir eigentlich Texte, die sachlich noch enger zusammengehören als die soeben diskutierten. Es müßten Texte sein, die nicht verschiedene, sondern ein und denselben Sachverhalt schildern und darüber hinaus lexikalisch und syntaktisch möglichst übereinstimmen sollten bis auf diejenigen Elemente, in denen sich die Empathie manifestiert. Ich habe tatsächlich zwei solche Texte gefunden. Doch bevor ich diese beiden Texte vorstelle und analysiere, möchte ich den Stand der Forschung zum Thema ›Syntax und Empathie‹ referieren.

3 Die Theorie von *Kuno* und *Kaburaki* 1975 über Empathie-Phänomene in der Syntax

Was ich hier als »Empathie« einzukreisen versuche, hat zweifellos starke Ähnlichkeit mit dem, was die Literaturwissenschaft ›Perspektive‹ bzw. ›point-of-view‹ nennt. Meist wird unterschieden zwischen einer »auktorialen« Perspektive der allwissenden Überschau und einer »personalen«, die in eine der Personen der Handlung verlegt ist. Ein häufig eingesetztes Kunstmittel der personalen Perspektive ist z. B. die sogenannte erlebte Rede, auch »style indirect libre« genannt. Die wissenschaftliche Diskussion um diese Begriffe hat eine lange Tradition und füllt ganze Bibliotheken.

Verglichen mit diesem Forschungseifer kann der bisher seitens der Linguistik geleistete Beitrag noch nicht einmal als »Scherflein der armen Witwe« eingestuft werden, denn **diese** Witwe, die Linguistik, ist ja eigentlich nicht arm und hat trotzdem kaum mehr als ein Scherflein beigesteuert. Aus dem Jahre 1974 gibt es ein wichtiges Buch von *Cantrall* mit dem Titel *Viewpoint, Reflexives and the Nature of Noun Phrases;* ein Jahr später erschien die Arbeit von *Kuno* und *Kaburaki* über *Empathy and Syntax*. Viel mehr Einschlägiges gibt es m. W. nicht.

1976 hat *Kuno* die Hauptergebnisse aus *Empathy and Syntax* in dem Aufsatz »Subject, Theme and the Speaker's Empathy – A Reexamination of Relativization Phenomena« zusammengefaßt. Er schreibt dort (S. 431):

> I use the term »empathy« to characterize the speaker's identification, in varying degrees, with a participant in an event. For example, observe the following sentences:
> 3–1a. John hit Mary.
> 3–1b. John hit his wife.
> 3–1c. Mary's husband hit her.
> Assume that John's wife's name is Mary. In describing the event in which John hit Mary, the speaker can use any of the above three sentences (and the passive versions of 3–1a and 3–1c). 3–1b is a statement in which the speaker describes the event from John's side, and 3–1c from Mary's side. This can be seen from the fact that in 3–1b the speaker refers to Mary as *John's wife* (an expression which is John-centered), while in 3–1c he refers to John as *Mary's husband* (an expression which is Mary-centered). I say that in 3–1b the speaker is expressing his »empathy« with John, while in 3–1c, he is expressing his empathy with Mary. On the other hand, in 3–1a, the speaker is taking a more neutral position, and is describing the event rather objectively.

(Wenn wir *Kunos* Theorie auf seine eigene Syntax anwenden, stellen wir übrigens fest, daß sie »John-centered« ist, denn statt mit

Assume that John's wife's name is Mary hätte er seine Explikation natürlich auch mit *Assume that Mary's husband's name is John* beginnen können. Daß in dem Beispielsatz wieder eine Frau von ihrem Mann geschlagen wird, entspricht beliebter linguistischer Tradition, wie Ruth *Römer* schon 1973 nachgewiesen hat.)

Kuno nennt also den Ausdruck *John's wife* »John-centered«. Er erläutert diesen Begriff nicht, weshalb ich das, im Hinblick auf die angekündigte Textanalyse, hier nachhole:

Relationale Nomina wie *Schwester, Bruder, Mutter, Vater, Tochter, Sohn, Frau* (im Sinne von ›wife‹), *Mann* (im Sinne von ›husband‹) fungieren als ›heads‹ in Nominalphrasen, deren ›center‹ ein Lexem bildet, das zu dem ›head‹ in der *haben*-Relation steht:

meine Schwester	– Zentrum: ich
Ottos Tante	– Zentrum: Otto
Frau seines Hauswirts	– Zentrum: sein Hauswirt
sein Hauswirt	– Zentrum: er

Kunos Beobachtungen und Setzungen stimmen übrigens genau mit der feministischen Sprachkritik überein. Diese weist bekanntlich darauf hin, daß Frauen in der Regel als »Anhängsel« von Männern beschrieben werden. In *John's wife* ist, wie *Kuno* sagt, *John* das Zentrum. Demnach ist *wife* die Peripherie, um im Bild zu bleiben – oder, anders ausgedrückt: das Anhängsel.

Die Interaktion zwischen Empathie und Syntax regelt sich laut *Kuno* 1976 nach folgenden vier Prinzipien:

1. The Ban of Conflicting Empathy Foci
2. The Surface Structure Empathy Hierarchy
3. The Speech-Act-Participant Hierarchy
4. The Topic Empathy Hierarchy

Prinzip 1, »The Ban of Conflicting Empathy Foci«, besagt folgendes:

A single sentence cannot contain two or more conflicting foci of the speaker's empathy:
*Then, Mary$_1$'s husband$_2$ hit his$_2$ wife$_1$.
In the subject position the speaker has shown his empathy with Mary by referring to her husband as *Mary's husband* (and not as, say, *John*). On the other hand, in the object position, the speaker has expressed his empathy with John by referring to Mary as *his wife* (and not as *Mary*). Thus, the sentence contains two con-

flicting foci of the speaker's empathy, and hence, the low acceptability of the sentence.

Dieses »Verbot konfligierender Empathiezentren«, wie man *Kunos* Prinzip übersetzen könnte, ist für **Analysen** gegebener Texte nur insofern relevant, als man in aller Regel feststellen kann, daß es strikt geachtet wird.

Das zweite Prinzip, »The Surface Structure Empathy Hierarchy«, lautet wie folgt:

It is easiest for the speaker to empathize with the referent of the subject; it is next easiest for him to empathize with the referent of the object. It is most difficult for him to empathize with the referent of the by-passive agentive.
Subject $\geq$ Object $\geq$ ... $\geq$ By-Agentive.

Kuno illustriert dieses Prinzip u. a. mit folgenden Beispielen:

3–7 a. John hit his wife.
3–7 b. ?? John's wife was hit by him.
The fact that 3–7 b is ungrammatical seems to be due to violation of both [principle 1 and 2]. Namely, the speaker, by referring to John's wife as *John's wife* (and not as, say, *Mary*) has shown that he is empathizing with John. On the other hand, by applying Passivization and thereby placing *John's wife* at the top position and *John* at the bottom position of the Empathy Hierarchy, the speaker has shown that he is empathizing with John's wife at the exclusion of John. Thus, the sentence contains two conflicting empathy foci, and hence, the unacceptability of the sentence.

Dieses Prinzip der »Empathie-Hierarchie der Oberflächenstruktur« ist für Textanalysen zentral. Wenn es zutrifft, brauchen wir Texte nur daraufhin zu untersuchen, auf welche Personen die Subjekte referieren, um das Empathiezentrum zu ermitteln. Außerdem besagt es, daß der Ausdruck der Empathie eine Sache der Oberflächensyntax und nicht irgendwelcher als zugrundeliegend angenommener Strukturen ist. Ein Aktivsatz und sein zugehöriges Passivtransformat mögen zwar auf denselben Sachverhalt referieren, aber die Perspektive, aus der dieser Sachverhalt geschildert wird, ist laut *Kuno* allein der Oberflächenstruktur zu entnehmen. Meine bisherigen Eindrücke bezüglich der Empathiestruktur von Texten bestätigen diese Ansicht.

Prinzip 2 gibt uns indirekt noch einen weiteren wichtigen Hinweis. Ein Sachverhalt kann zwar aus der Sicht einer/s der Beteiligten geschildert werden, das bedeutet aber nicht unbedingt, daß auch die Partei des jeweiligen Empathiezentrums ergriffen wird. Normalerweise ist das zwar der Fall, aber es gibt zahlreiche Gegenbeispiele. Die Empathie wäre dann sozusagen eine mißglückte oder bloß formale oder stilistisch bedingte oder gar zum Zweck der Verfälschung oder Täuschung fingierte.

Das im zweiten Kapitel zuerst aufgeführte Beispiel ist eine gute Illustration dieser wichtigen Einschränkung. *Louise* ist zwar nach den *Kuno*schen Regeln das Empathiezentrum, denn *sie* ist Subjekt und *ihr langsam genesender Patient* ist »*ihr*-zentriert«. Aber die unvoreingenommene Betrachtung hatte ergeben, daß von wirklicher, glaubwürdiger und somit gelungener Einfühlung des Autors schwerlich die Rede sein kann.

Das dritte Prinzip, »The Speech-Act-Participant Hierarchy«, besagt folgendes:

> It is easiest for the speaker to empathize with himself (i.e., to express his own point of view); it is next easiest for him to express his empathy with the hearer; it is most difficult to empathize with the third party, at the exclusion of the hearer or himself.
> Speaker ≤ Hearer ≤ Third Person.

Kuno illustriert dieses »Prinzip der Empathiehierarchie der Sprechaktteilnehmer« u. a. mit folgendem Satz:

> 3–10. ?? John was hit by me.

Sein Kommentar dazu lautet:

> 3–10 is of dubious degree of grammaticality because the speaker is saying that he is not empathizing with himself (i. e., he is not expressing his own point of view). It is for this reason that passive sentences of the pattern of 3–10 can be used only in technical writing or in journalistic reporting style, in which the speaker is allowed to take a detached view of himself.

Das vierte und letzte Prinzip ist »The Topic Empathy Hierarchy«:

> It is easier for a speaker to empathize with an object (e.g., person) that he has been talking about than with an object that he has just introduced into discourse for the first time:
> Discourse-anaphoric < Dicourse-nonanaphoric.
> 3–12 a. John encountered an eight-foot-tall girl on the street.

3–12 b. ?? An eight-foot-tall girl encountered John on the street.

The pattern *x encountered y* requires that the speaker's empathy be placed on the referent of *x*: This is because the speaker could have said *y encountered x* if he were empathizing with the referent of *y*. The low degree of grammaticality of 3–12 b shows that it is difficult to empathize with the referent of an indefinite NP at the exclusion of an anaphoric NP.

Das Prinzip der Topic-Empathiehierarchie ist insofern interessant für Textanalysen, als es für bestimmte Verben Präferenzen hinsichtlich des Empathiezentrums festlegt. Zu diesen Verben zählt *Kuno encounter, meet* ›treffen‹ und *marry* ›heiraten‹, also die echt reziproken Verben, sowie *receive from* ›bekommen von‹ und *hear from* ›erfahren von‹, also solche Verben, die laut *Fillmore* den Kasusrahmen ›Experiencer – Agentive – Object‹ haben und den Experiencer zum Oberflächensubjekt wählen. – Obwohl *Kuno* seine Behauptungen nicht näher begründet, wirken sie auf mich plausibel. Sie bestätigen Eindrücke, die auch ich beim Umgang mit verschiedenen Texten über die Empathiestruktur dieser Verbklassen gewonnen habe. Um seine Behauptungen zu überprüfen, müßte allerdings eine größere Anzahl von Textanalysen durchgeführt werden.

Soweit also, in groben Zügen, die Theorie von *Kuno* und *Kaburaki* über die Zusammenhänge zwischen Syntax und Empathie. Eine tragende Voraussetzung dieser Theorie, die sie allerdings nicht explizit machen, scheint mir *Kunos* Analyse der Pronominalisierungsregularitäten in der indirekten Rede zu sein. Manche dieser Regularitäten, so *Kuno*, können nur erklärt werden, wenn man Aussagen dritter Personen auf Ich- oder Du-Aussagen zurückführt. Am überzeugendsten läßt sich das allerdings anhand von englischem Beispielmaterial demonstrieren. Die englische Reflexivpronominalisierung funktioniert bekanntlich anders als die deutsche. Man vergleiche:

1. Mary said to John that physicists like himself were a godsend.
   Mary sagte zu John, Physiker wie er wären ein Gottesgeschenk.
2. Mary heard from John that physicists like himself were a godsend.
   ... Physiker wie er ...

3. Mary said about John that physicists like him/*himself were
   a godsend.
   ... Physiker wie er ...
   (Beispiele aus *Kuno* (1975: 314 f.).)

Kuno führt diese Pronominalisierungsdaten, die sich **nicht** mit
Hilfe der *Ross*'schen *Command*-Regel (vgl. *Ross* 1970: 229 f.) erklären lassen, auf folgendes Prinzip zurück: »In direct speech, *NP
like myself/yourself* is grammatical, but *NP like himself-/herself* is
not« (*Kuno* 1975: 315).

 Formuliert in direkter Rede, enthalten die Beispiele (1) bis (3) folgende Nominalphrasen:

1. ... physicists like yourself   ⇒ himself
2. ... physicists like myself   ⇒ himself
3. ... physicist like him   ⇎ himself

Das Prinzip der Zurückführung auf Verhältnisse in der direkten
Rede läßt sich m. E. mit Gewinn auf andere Bereiche, vornehmlich
den der definiten Beschreibungen, ausdehnen und dann für Empa-
thie-Untersuchungen nutzbar machen. Nehmen wir einmal an,
Anna sei meine Freundin, Frau Müller ihre Mutter und die beiden
hätten miteinander gesprochen. Ich kann sagen:

4. Anna hat mit ihrer Mutter gesprochen.
5. Anna hat mit Frau Müller gesprochen.

Anna selbst wird von ihrer Mutter kaum als von »Frau Müller« reden. Sie wird, beispielsweise, kaum sagen: »Ich habe mit Frau
Müller gesprochen.« Wenn ich mit Anna spreche, bin ich, da sie
meine Freundin ist, zur Empathie geradezu verpflichtet und darf
nicht sagen: »Hast du mit Frau Müller gesprochen?« Wenn ich Satz
4. äußere, beschreibe ich das Ereignis eher aus Annas Sicht, ver-
setze mich in **ihre** Beziehungsstrukturen. Wenn ich 5. äußere, tue
ich das nicht, sondern ich beziehe mich eher auf meine eigene, weniger enge Beziehung zu Annas Mutter, oder auf die Beziehung einer Gesprächspartnerin, für die Annas Mutter eventuell auch nur
»Frau Müller« ist.

 Ein Beispiel aus einem biographischen Text soll das Gesagte noch
einmal aus einer anderen Perspektive beleuchten:

 Der Sohn ist tief gekränkt. Nach einem weiteren Streit mit der
 Mutter – diesmal geht es wieder um ihren Hausfreund –, verläßt

er sie endgültig. Obgleich *die Frau* noch 24 Jahre lebt, wird er ihr nicht mehr begegnen. (*Koesters,* S. 186; Hervorhebung von mir.)

Es handelt sich um Johanna *Schopenhauer* und ihren Sohn Arthur – besser gesagt: um Arthur *Schopenhauer* und seine Mutter Johanna *Schopenhauer,* denn die Probe stammt aus einem Text über Arthur *Schopenhauer.* Wenn der Autor im letzten Satz auf die Mutter mit *die Frau* referiert, so wirkt das auf uns mehr als kühl und distanziert, ja fast abschätzig. Es kann als Beweis der Einfühlung in Arthur *Schopenhauer* interpretiert werden, der möglicherweise 24 Jahre lang von seiner Mutter nur noch als von »der Frau« gesprochen hat. **Oder** es ist einfach die Perspektive des Autors. Wäre die Beziehung zwischen Mutter und Sohn nicht gestört gewesen, so hätten wir jedenfalls eher mit der Formulierung *Obgleich seine Mutter noch 24 Jahre lebt…* rechnen können, weil ein Biograph sich normalerweise weitgehend in seinen Helden einfühlt.

4 Analyse zweier Texte über die Widerstandskämpferin Hilde *Coppi* im Hinblick auf ihre Empathiestruktur

Es folgt nun die bereits angekündigte Feinanalyse zweier Texte über ein und dieselbe Person und ein und denselben Sachverhalt, die sich nur in ihrer Oberflächenstruktur unterscheiden und deren Unterschiede sich am besten als Unterschiede hinsichtlich des Grades an Empathie mit der Hauptperson, Hilde *Coppi,* interpretieren lassen.

Beide Texte haben also dasselbe »Thema«. Insofern sind sie auch gute Demonstrationsobjekte für den Unterschied zwischen Thema und Empathiezentrum – zwei Begriffe, die eng zusammengehören, aber doch unterscheidbar sind und unterschieden werden müssen.

Zunächst also die Texte. Ich nenne sie »Text A« und »Text B«.

A: *Hilde Coppi*
Mit ihrem Mann, Hans Coppi, wegen Zugehörigkeit zu einer sozialistischen Widerstandsgruppe im September 1942 verhaftet. Im Gefängnis wird der Sohn Fritz geboren; einen Monat darauf wird der Vater, acht Monate später, am 5. August im Alter von 34 Jahren, die Mutter hingerichtet.

B: Hilde Coppi wurde wegen Zugehörigkeit zu einer sozialistischen Widerstandsgruppe im September 1942 zusammen mit ihrem Mann verhaftet. Sie gebar im Gefängnis ihren Sohn Fritz. Einen Monat darauf wurde ihr Mann, acht Monate später, am 5. August 1943, sie selbst im Alter von 34 Jahren hingerichtet. (In Wirklichkeit hieß der Sohn auch Hans. Um die Beschreibung nicht unnötig zu komplizieren, habe ich ihn hier Fritz genannt.)

Zur Geschichte der Texte: Der erste erschien 1954 in dem Sammelband *Du hast mich heimgesucht bei Nacht. Abschiedsbriefe und Aufzeichnungen des Widerstandes 1933 bis 1945*, herausgegeben von Helmut *Gollwitzer*, Käthe *Kuhn* und Reinhold *Schneider*. Der zweite erschien 28 Jahre später, im September 1982, in dem Sammelband *Liebe Mutter, liebe Tochter. Frauenbriefe aus drei Jahrhunderten*, herausgegeben von Jutta *Radel*. Als Quelle für das Kapitel »Abschiedsbriefe deutscher Widerstandskämpferinnen« gibt Jutta *Radel* die Sammlung von 1954 an.

Es ist offensichtlich, daß Text B eine redigierte Version des Textes A ist. Warum aber wurde Text A redigiert und warum gerade so und nicht anders? Ich habe die Herausgeberin nicht extra gefragt, weil ich meine, daß der Grund für die Redaktion aus der Art der Redaktion und aus dem neuen Kontext, in den der alte Text gestellt werden sollte, direkt erschließbar ist. *Du hast mich heimgesucht bei Nacht* ist eine Dokumentensammlung über den Widerstand, genauer: über Männer des Widerstands – unter den 69 Personen sind nur 6 Frauen versammelt worden. *Liebe Mutter, liebe Tochter* ist dagegen ein Buch über Mütter und Töchter, auch Mütter und Töchter von Widerstandskämpferinnen.

Wir haben oben an dem Beispiel »Hast du mit Frau Müller gesprochen?« gesehen, daß es ein sozialer Verstoß ist, wenn ich einer Freundin gegenüber ihre Mutter als »Frau Müller« bezeichne. Der Ausdruck der Empathie wird also auch sehr streng durch die Beziehung geregelt, die **angesprochene** Personen zu den besprochenen Personen haben. Wer ist nun angesprochen bei dem Buch über den Widerstand, wer bei dem Buch über Mütter und Töchter? Es ist anzunehmen, daß das Widerstandsbuch sich (trotz seiner Zurückhaltung in bezug auf Widerstandskämpfer**innen**) an beide Geschlechter richtet, das Mütter-Töchter-Buch dagegen in erster Linie an Frauen, und zwar nicht nur an Frauen im allgemeinen, sondern vor allem an politisch sensibilisierte Frauen, Angehörige oder »Sympathisantinnen« der Frauenbewegung. Ohne die Frauenbewegung gäbe es nämlich solche Sammlungen wie die von Jutta *Radel* überhaupt nicht. Es ist dies ja auch durchaus nicht das einzige Buch dieser Art – gerade in den letzten Jahren sind sehr viele Sammlungen mit Frauenbriefen erschienen (z. B. *Böttger, Behrens, Sperr*). In den fünfziger und sechziger Jahren gab es dafür kein Publikum und daher auch keine solchen Veröffentlichungen.

Ganz gleichgültig, wie es um die Empathie der Herausgeberin selbst in bezug auf Hilde *Coppi* bestellt sein mag – sie **mußte** mit bestimmten Empathie-**Erwartungen** ihres Publikums rechnen und auf diese Rücksicht nehmen. Und einem für die Belange von Frauen sensibilisierten Publikum sind Texte wie A einfach nicht zuzumuten, so »unschuldig« und »gutwillig« dieser auch verfaßt worden sein mag. Ein Satz wie *Im Gefängnis wird der Sohn Fritz geboren,* der die Hauptperson nicht einmal **erwähnt,** verträgt sich nicht mit den Stilanforderungen der »Zielgruppe« dieses Buches.

Diese Erwartungen der Zielgruppe also sind es, da besteht für mich kein Zweifel, die die Herausgeberin zur Redaktion veranlaßt und die Art und Weise der syntaktischen Veränderungen diktiert haben. Möglicherweise gehört Jutta *Radel* selbst zu dieser Zielgruppe – aber das kann offenbleiben. Es spielt für die Analyse keine Rolle, ob zum Ausdruck gebrachte Empathie »echt« oder nur »gespielt« ist. Der individualpsychologische Begriff der Empathie, den *Kuno* und *Kaburaki* noch allein am Sprecher festmachen, wird durch diese Betrachtungsweise entpsychologisiert und im Kontext der Normen für soziale Interaktion verankert. Der **Ausdruck** meiner Empathie kann von meinen Sozialpartnern erwartet, ja sogar eingeklagt werden, wenn er ausbleibt. Bei Todesfällen z. B. habe ich mein »Beileid« zumindest zu »bezeugen«; Unterlassung wird als sozialer Verstoß gewertet und geahndet. Ob ich tatsächlich mitleide, können soziale Konventionen nicht regeln – per definitionem nicht.

So gesehen gewinnt die eingangs erwähnte Problemstellung der Literaturwissenschaftlerin noch an Brisanz. Ihre Empörung müßte sich nicht nur gegen die Autoren jener Zeitungsberichte, sondern mit noch größerer Vehemenz gegen die Zielgruppe solcher Texte richten – letztlich eigentlich gegen eine Gesellschaft, in der sich keine sozialen Konventionen herausgebildet haben, die das eklatante Fehlen von Empathiebezeugungen für Frauen sanktionieren.

Die Autoren handeln in voller Übereinstimmung mit ihrer Zielgruppe, sonst würden sie sich nämlich hüten, so zu schreiben.

Wenden wir uns lieber ab von diesem für unsere Gesellschaft so beschämenden Befund und kehren wir zu den beiden Texten zurück, wo wir – wenigstens einmal – das Gegenteil der sonst gültigen Empathiebezeugungsnormen nachweisen können.

Die Struktur von A entspricht der Textsorte »amtliches Protokoll«. Auf das Stichwort *Hilde Coppi* folgen, wie bei der Erfassung einer gerichtsnotorisch gewordenen Person, »relevante Informationen«, teilweise im Telegrammstil. Der einleitende Satz ist z. B. unvollständig; es fehlt sowohl das Subjekt als auch das finite Verb.

Text B dagegen hat die Form einer knappen Erzählung. *Hilde Coppi* fungiert nicht als Stichwort, als ein Punkt unter vielen auf einer Liste, sondern ist in den Text, als Subjekt des ersten Satzes, eingegliedert. Der gesamte Text könnte z. B. in einem Brief vorkommen, in dem einer Freundin oder einem Freund über das Schicksal Hilde Coppis berichtet wird. Hilde Coppi könnte dabei ohne weiteres eine Freundin, Nachbarin oder sonstwie gute Bekannte der Schreibenden sein. Eine mögliche Umgebung von Text B wäre etwa: »Du hast mich gebeten, Dir von unserer lieben Nachbarin, der Hilde Coppi, zu erzählen. Es fällt mir noch heute schwer, davon zu sprechen, also mache ich es kurz: Hilde Coppi wurde wegen Zugehörigkeit zu einer sozialistischen Widerstandsgruppe...«

Ein solcher Vorspann wäre mit Text A **nicht** kompatibel.

Text A informiert uns darüber, daß Hilde Coppis Mann Hans Coppi hieß. Jutta *Radel* hat diese Information gestrichen. Dafür erfahren wir bei ihr explizit das Todesjahr, 1943, das wir bei Text A erschließen müssen. Daß der Mann von Hilde Coppi ebenfalls Coppi hieß, hätten wir uns wohl denken können. Die Nennung des Vornamens hätte, informationstechnisch gesehen, durchaus gereicht. Die zweite Nennung des Nachnamens ist so redundant wie in Text B die Jahreszahl 1943. Es ist aber nun mal nicht üblich zu sagen »Hilde Coppi mit ihrem Mann Hans«. Üblich ist dergleichen nur bei Frauen und Kindern: »Ronald Reagan mit seiner Frau Nancy«, »Hilde Coppi und ihr Sohn Fritz«.

Was die Benennung und Beschreibung der drei Personen betrifft, so kann man in Text A zwei Perspektiven identifizieren, wohingegen Text B die einmal gewählte Perspektive beibehält. Stellen wir uns einmal ein Familienfoto vor. Es zeigt Hilde Coppi, Hans

Coppi und Fritz Coppi. Wenn wir die Personen jemandem beschreiben wollen, können wir ganz verschiedene Perspektiven wählen. Z. B. können wir sagen: »Das ist Hans Coppi, das ist seine Frau und das sein Sohn.« Oder: »Das ist Fritz Coppi, das ist seine Mutter und das sein Vater.« Diese möglichen Perspektiven wurden weder in Text A noch in Text B gewählt. Nehmen wir Hilde Coppis Perspektive ein, so sagen wir: »Das ist Hilde Coppi, das ist ihr Mann und das ihr Sohn.« Dies ist die Perspektive von Text B. Für Hilde Coppi finden wir die Bezeichnungen *Hilde Coppi, sie* und *sie selbst*, für Hans Coppi zweimal *ihr Mann*, für den Sohn *ihr Sohn Fritz*. Aber auch in Text A ist diese Perspektive realisiert: Auf Hilde Coppi wird referiert mit *Hilde Coppi*, auf Hans Coppi mit *ihr Mann, Hans Coppi*.

Neben den genannten »Innenperspektiven« (aus der Sicht der beteiligten bzw. abgebildeten Personen) sind auch noch Außenperspektiven denkbar, z. B. »Das ist Hilde Coppi, das Hans Coppi und das Fritz Coppi.« Oder: »Das ist die Mutter, das der Vater und das der Sohn.« Letztere Möglichkeit wählt Text A als zweite Perspektive. Entscheidend bei dieser Interpretation ist der Gebrauch des bestimmten Artikels. *Seine Mutter* und *sein Vater* hätte die Perspektive auf den Sohn verlagert, aber es heißt *der Sohn, der Vater, die Mutter* – »neutrale« Außenperspektive.

Wie oft werden die drei Personen erwähnt?

A: Hilde Coppi 3 × : *Hilde Coppi, ihren* Mann, *die Mutter*
    Hans Coppi 3 × : *Hans Coppi, ihrem Mann, der Vater*
    Fritz Coppi 2 × : *der Sohn   Fritz*
B: Hilde Coppi 6 × : *Hilde Coppi, ihrem* Mann, *sie, ihren*
                              Sohn *Fritz, ihr* Mann, *sie selbst*
    Hans Coppi 2 × : *ihrem Mann, ihr Mann*
    Fritz Coppi 2 × : *ihren Sohn   Fritz*

In Text A ist Hans Coppi sprachlich noch »präsenter« als Hilde Coppi. Auf ihn entfallen drei Nominalphrasen, auf Hilde Coppi nur zwei, die dritte Erwähnung geschieht mittels des Possessivdeterminans in *ihrem Mann*.

In Text B entfallen auf Hilde Coppi drei Nominalphrasen und drei Possessivdeterminantien, auf Hans Coppi zwei Nominalphrasen und auf Fritz Coppi ebenfalls zwei.

Das Kernstück der Redaktion in B ist natürlich der in einen Aktivsatz verwandelte Passivsatz aus A. Diese Veränderung rückt die

Hauptperson aus der »syntaktischen Versenkung« in A ins syntaktische Zentrum, somit auch ins Empathiezentrum, wie *Kuno* und *Kaburaki* lehren. A wertet die Information, daß »sie« »ihren« Sohn gebar, als redundant, »recoverable«, erschließbar – und deshalb tilgbar.

Bezogen auf die Erzeugung von Passivsätzen bereits in der Basiskomponente, wie Chomskys *Extended Standard Theory* sie vorsieht, können wir sogar sagen, daß in Text A die Information, daß es Hilde Coppi war, die diesen Sohn gebar, von Anfang an nicht vorhanden ist. Der Sohn wird geboren, basta. So wie er ist, wird dieser Satz generiert. Es braucht keine Agensphrase getilgt zu werden, weil gar keine erzeugt wurde.

Im letzten Satz erfahren wir dann allerdings, daß Hilde Coppi »die Mutter« war, vorher jedoch schon, daß Hans Coppi »der Vater« war. Diesbezüglich ist nun wiederum Text B weniger explizit. Für die Vaterschaft von Hans Coppi ergibt das sprachliche Material nur eine Wahrscheinlichkeit von 50 Prozent – weil nämlich das Possessivdeterminans *ihren* in *ihren* Sohn ambig ist und sich sowohl auf *Hilde Coppi* allein zurückbeziehen kann als auch auf *Hilde und Hans Coppi* (im Engl. hätten wir entsprechend *her* oder *their son*).

Im letzten Satz heißt es in A *die Mutter*, in B *sie selbst*. Das *selbst* hat hier die Funktion, nach einem Exkurs zu einem Neben-Empathiezentrum die Rückkehr zum Haupt-Empathiezentrum anzuzeigen.

Plank hat in »Zur Affinität von *selbst* und *auch*« (1979) drei Hauptfunktionen von *selbst* ermittelt. Ich möchte sie einmal anhand der folgenden Sätze verdeutlichen:

Der Chef kocht selbst gerne.   (≈ auch)
Selbst der Chef kocht gerne.   (≈ sogar)
Der Chef kocht gerne selbst.   (≈ (höchst)persönlich)

Das *selbst* in Text B läßt sich in keine der von *Plank* aufgestellten Kategorien einordnen. Wir finden dieses *selbst* Nr. 4 (ich nenne es das *selbst* der Rückkehr zum Empathiezentrum) in Umgebungen folgender Art:

Er fuhr mit dem Bus, sie selbst ging zu Fuß.

In Chalkidike ... verliebt er sich in die Tochter seines Vorarbeiters. Eleni ist fünfzehn, er selber etwas über zwanzig. (*Grieser* 1980: 115)

Diese Vorkommen von *selbst* können weder mit *sogar* noch mit *auch* noch mit *(höchst)persönlich* oder *eigenhändig* paraphrasiert werden, genausowenig wie das *selbst* in Text B.

Dieses Ergebnis zeigt, daß eine Analyse unter dem Gesichtspunkt der Empathiestruktur nebenbei auch noch neue Einsichten über Grammatikausschnitte vermitteln kann, die schon als gründlich erforscht gegolten haben.

Damit bin ich am Ende meiner Analyse angekommen. Ich möchte nun die wichtigsten Ergebnisse zusammenfassen.

1. Bei der Rezeption von Texten aller Art haben wir oft den unabweisbaren Eindruck, daß die Autoren sich in manche der beschriebenen Personen mehr einfühlen als in andere. Ein Konflikt im Zuge der Rezeption entsteht genau dann, wenn auf der Empfängerseite eine andere Empathieverteilung erwartet wird, als der Autor sie vorgenommen hat. Typisch für diese Art von Konflikt sind z.B. manche Texte von Männern über Männer und Frauen, die heute von vielen Frauen anders beurteilt werden, als es noch bis vor kurzem der Fall war.

2. Anders als die Literaturwissenschaft (Stichwort ›Perspektive‹ oder ›point-of-view‹) hat sich die Linguistik mit Empathiephänomenen bisher kaum auseinandergesetzt. Eine Ausnahme stellen die Arbeiten von *Cantrall* 1974 sowie von *Kuno* und *Kaburaki* 1975 dar.

3. *Kuno* und *Kaburaki* 1975 haben eine Sprecher-zentrierte Theorie über Syntax und Empathie entwickelt. Diese Theorie geht aus von bestimmten Sachverhaltsstrukturen und deren diversen Versprachlichungsmöglichkeiten. Der Sprecher kann eine der am Sachverhalt beteiligten Personen als Empathiezentrum wählen und die anderen Personen diesem Zentrum zuordnen. Die Empathiestruktur manifestiert sich in der Art der Beschreibungen sowie in den drei Hierarchien

Subjekt – Objekt – Passiv-Agens
Sprecher – Hörer – besprochene Person
Topic – Nicht-Topic

4. Diese Theorie von *Kuno* und *Kaburaki* habe ich anhand zweier Texte, die sich nicht inhaltlich, sondern nur syntaktisch unterscheiden, überprüft. Bei der Anwendung der Theorie stellte sich heraus, daß sie insofern ergänzt werden muß, als der

Sprecher den Ausdruck seiner Empathie gemäß den Erwartungen der Angesprochenen zu regulieren hat. Diese Erwartungen mögen zwar individuell verschieden sein, sind aber im wesentlichen doch stark gesellschaftlich bedingt und historischer Entwicklung unterworfen. Die beiden analysierten Texte können als Beweis dafür aufgefaßt werden, daß Empathie für bestimmte Personen und Personenkreise genau dann zum Ausdruck gebracht wird, wenn diese Personen den **Angesprochenen** nahestehen oder sonstwie wichtig und interessant sind. Das Verhältnis des »Sprechers« zu den beschriebenen Personen ist demgegenüber zweitrangig.

Weiter hat die Textanalyse ergeben:

a) Es gibt Textsorten, die mehr Empathie verlangen als andere. Amtliche Protokolle und private Briefe weisen diesbezüglich große Unterschiede auf. Wenn ein Kurztext theoretisch auch als Teil eines freundschaftlichen Briefes fungieren kann, so ist er schon dadurch als empathiehaltig ausgewiesen.

b) Das einmal gewählte Empathiezentrum kann innerhalb eines auch kurzen Textes wechseln oder sonstwie aufgegeben werden, etwa zugunsten einer »neutralen Außenperspektive«. Die neutrale Außenperspektive ist diagnostizierbar am Gebrauch symmetrischer Bezeichnungen wie *Mary and John* oder *Hilde, Hans und Fritz Coppi* oder *die Mutter, der Vater, der Sohn*.

c) Nach dem Exkurs zu einem Neben-Empathiezentrum kann zum Haupt-Empathiezentrum zurückgekehrt werden. Dies kann mit besonderen sprachlichen Mitteln angezeigt werden, z. B. mit der Partikel *selbst*.

d) Die Häufigkeit der Nennung einer bestimmten Person, sei es in unabhängiger oder abhängiger Konstruktion, korreliert mit ihrem Rang innerhalb der Empathiehierarchie. Die Häufigkeit wiederum ist abhängig von der Wahl bestimmter syntaktischer Strukturen. Im Aktivsatz z. B. muß das Agens genannt werden, während es im Passivsatz fehlen kann.

5. Für Empathie-Analysen allgemein gilt das Prinzip der Zurückführung auf die Verhältnisse in der direkten Rede: Empathie mit einer der beschriebenen Personen liegt dann vor, wenn für sie selbst und die anderen Personen diejenigen Bezeichnungen gewählt werden, die diese Person selbst gewählt hätte.

Ich glaube, daß linguistische Analysen der Empathiestruktur von Texten sinnvoll die bisher von der Literaturwissenschaft zum Thema ›Perspektive‹ geleistete Arbeit ergänzen können. Wenn das hier in Ansätzen vorgeführte Analyse-Instrumentarium weiter entwickelt wird, besitzen wir damit eine gute und interessante Methode, Texte neu zu betrachten, neu einzuordnen und neu zu beurteilen.

1982

Feminismus und Frauenbewegung
Versuch einer Begriffsklärung

Die Begriffe ›Frauenbewegung‹ und ›Feminismus‹ hängen zusammen – aber wie? Handelt es sich um zwei Bezeichnungen für ein und dieselbe Sache, wie bei dem Wortpaar *Korrektur* und *Berichtigung*? Ist demnach vielleicht das Wort *Feminismus* nur eine praktische Erfindung, um das Reden über das, was mit der Frauenbewegung zusammenhängt, ein bißchen zu vereinfachen? *Frauenbewegte Frau* oder *Anhängerin der Frauenbewegung* sind lange, komplizierte Ausdrücke – viel schneller spricht sich *Feministin*. Auch ist es nützlich, ein Wort wie *feministisch* zu haben, denn *frauenbewegt* wirkt nicht in allen Kombinationen überzeugend: *Frauenbewegte Theologie*? Da grinsen ja die Gegner noch breiter als über *Feministische Theologie*.

Oder verweisen die Begriffe ›Feminismus‹ und ›Frauenbewegung‹ auf zwei verschiedene (wenn auch verwandte) »Sachen«?

Feministische Publikationen (oder soll ich sagen: Publikationen der/zur Frauenbewegung?) kümmern sich nicht um diese anscheinend unerhebliche Frage einer Sprachwissenschaftlerin und Feministin. Sie haben wahrhaftig auch dringlichere Probleme zu lösen. Trotzdem – mich beschäftigt diese Frage, seit ich 1981 gebeten wurde, einen Sammelband zum Thema Feminismus herauszugeben (vgl. *Pusch* 1983). Wie konnte ich auch eine solche Aufgabe übernehmen, ohne den Unterschied zwischen Feminismus und Frauenbewegung zu kennen, ja ohne zu wissen, ob es überhaupt einen gibt?

Meine erste Reaktion auf die selbstgestellte »Frage nach dem kleinen Unterschied« fiel ziemlich schlicht und kindlich aus. Unter Feminismus stellte ich mir »eher etwas Theoretisches« vor, unter Frauenbewegung »eher etwas Praktisches, Konkretes«. Diese Reaktion ist darauf zurückzuführen, daß das Lateinische auch heute noch die Sprache der Wissenschaft/Theorie beliefert und *Feminismus* ein aus dem Lateinischen gebildetes Fremdwort ist. *Frauenbewegung* dagegen wirkt als einheimisches Wort vertrauter, näher, »praxis-näher«.

Der Griff zum Lexikon brachte auch keine Klarheit, sondern nur eine Überraschung, ein großes Staunen. Aber das Staunen ist ja oft der Anfang einer Klärung.

Der »Große Meyer«, derzeit das umfassendste enzyklopädische Lexikon in deutscher Sprache, bringt folgende Definition:

> *Feminismus* (lat.),
> das Auftreten weibl. Eigenschaften bei einem männl. Tier oder beim Mann.

In *Wahrigs* Großem Deutschen Wörterbuch heißt es:

> *Feminismus:* weibisches Wesen beim Mann
> (bes. Homosexuellen)
> *feministisch:* auf Feminismus beruhend, weibisch

Das *Duden*-Fremdwörterbuch meldet:

> *Feminismus:* das Vorhandensein oder die Ausbildung weiblicher Geschlechtsmerkmale beim Mann oder bei männlichen Tieren.

Diese Definitionen stammen aus den Jahren 1973 *(Meyer)* und 1974 *(Wahrig, Duden)* – und die Lexikographen sind sich einig wie selten. Offenbar verstehen wir aber inzwischen, nur zehn bzw. neun Jahre später, alle etwas ganz anderes unter Feminismus, als uns hier weisgemacht werden soll. Es ist fast unglaublich und doch symptomatisch, daß ›Feminismus‹, ein gesellschaftspolitischer Schlüsselbegriff der Gegenwart, noch vor so kurzer Zeit dem herrschenden Wissenskanon so fremd war, daß er dem enzyklopädisch-lexikographischen Zugriff einfach entgehen konnte.

Es ist (nicht nur für Linguist/inn/en) sehr aufschlußreich, die Geschichte der Wörter *Frauenbewegung, Frauenemanzipation, Frauenfrage, Feminismus* und *Feminist/in* in deutschen und ausländischen Wörterbüchern und Enzyklopädien zu verfolgen.

Hier nur eine kurze Zusammenfassung für die Wörter *Feminismus* und *Feminist/in* (ich danke Helmut *Walther* von der Gesellschaft für deutsche Sprache, Wiesbaden, für wertvolle Auskünfte):

Alexandre *Dumas* d. J. soll 1872 in seiner Schrift *L'homme-femme* das Wort *féministe* (nach dem lat. *femina*) gebildet haben. Andere Quellen verweisen auf den Frühsozialisten Charles *Fourier* (1772–1837) als Urheber des Begriffs ›féminisme‹. 1899 finden sich die Personenbezeichnungen *die/der Feministe* – also noch nicht eingedeutscht – in *Looffs Allgemeinem Fremdwörterbuch*. 1902 veröffentlichte Hedwig *Dohm* ihre Streitschrift *Die Antifemini-*

sten. 1912 finden wir erstmals *Feminismus* sowohl in *Koenigs Großem Wörterbuch der deutschen Sprache* als auch in *Genius' Neuem
Großen Fremdwörterbuch,* definiert als »Streben nach Gleichstellung des weiblichen mit dem männlichen Geschlecht«. *Genius*
nennt außerdem *der Feminist:* ›Anhänger dieser Richtung‹. *Die
Feministin* gab es 1912 also noch nicht. 1918, nach dem verlorenen
Krieg, veröffentlichte Eduard *Engel* ein »Verdeutschungswörterbuch« mit dem bezeichnenden Titel *Entwelschung.* Darin wird
vorgeschlagen, das »neue Modewort« *Feminismus* durch *Weibse-
rei, Geweibse, Verweibung, Weiblerei, Weiblingstum, Weiberwirt-
schaft* oder *Weiberherrschaft* zu »entwelschen«.

Verfolgen wir die Geschichte des Wortes *Feminismus* im Recht-
schreibungs-*Duden*, so erschließt sich uns ein bemerkenswertes
Kapitel der deutschen Lexikographie. Ich zitiere aus dem Gutachten der Gesellschaft für deutsche Sprache (H. *Walther*):

»Im Duden (Rechtschreibung) findet sich *Feminismus* erst 1929
(10. Aufl.), und zwar gleich mit der Angabe der *beiden* Bedeutungen, der politisch-gesellschaftlichen und – wenigstens mit einem
Anflug – der biologisch-medizinischen: ›Frauenemanzipation; Betonung des Weiblichen‹. So bis 1932 (3. Neudruck der 10. Aufl.);
1934 aber durfte es die Frauenbewegung und damit die ›Frauenemanzipation‹ nicht mehr geben. Jetzt lautet der Eintrag: ›über-
starke Betonung des Weiblichen; Vorherrschaft unmännlicher
Anschauungen‹. So bis... nein, nicht nur bis zum letzten
Drittes-Reich-Duden (1942; Normalschriftausgabe der 12. Aufl.),
sondern bis 1958 (14. Aufl.). Und auch in der folgenden Ausgabe
(1961, 15. Aufl.) gab es noch kein Zurück zur ›Frauenemanzipation‹, sondern: ›Verweiblichung bei Männern; Überbetonung des
Weiblichen‹. Dieser Zustand hielt an bis 1973 (17. Aufl.), und erst
1980 (18. Aufl.) lesen wir die uns heute befriedigenden Erklärun-
gen: ›Richtung der Frauenbewegung, die ein neues Selbstverständ-
nis der Frau und die Aufhebung der traditionellen Rollenverteilung anstrebt; Med., Zool.: Ausbildung weibl. Merkmale bei
männl. Wesen; Verweiblichung‹.« Soweit das Gutachten.

Zwar ging 1945 die Naziherrschaft zu Ende, nicht aber ihr massi-
ver Antifeminismus. Der blieb uns erhalten bis heute – warum
hätte man diese willkommene Errungenschaft auch gleich mit
aufgeben sollen?

Die Geschichte des Wortes *Feminismus* in den deutschen Wörterbüchern und Enzyklopädien von 1933 bis heute ist nur **ein** Beweis

für das ungebrochene Fortleben faschistischer Grundsätze – dafür aber einer, der an Deutlichkeit kaum zu übertreffen ist.

Im Gegensatz zu den Lexika weiß der Volksmund gut Bescheid über den Feminismus – und vor allem über Feministinnen. Auch herrscht ein feines Empfinden für den Unterschied zwischen Frauenbewegung und Feminismus. Nach weit verbreiteter Auffassung setzt sich die Frauenbewegung für die Gleichberechtigung ein, und das ist ganz in Ordnung so, es liegt da ja auch noch allerhand im argen. Feministinnen aber kämpfen für die Weiberherrschaft, und das ist unerträglich; diesem hysterischen Terror muß schleunigst ein Ende gesetzt werden. Ein am 28. Sept. 1982 veröffentlichter Leserbrief an die *Neue Westfälische* artikuliert diese Überzeugung recht deutlich:

> Ich war stets für die Frauenrechtlerinnen, die eine echte Gleichberechtigung der Frauen erkämpfen wollen. Aber ich habe etwas gegen die Sorte von Frauen, die sich Feministinnen nennen. Erstere sind m. E. ein positiver, letztere ein negativer Faktor unserer ohnedies schon kranken Industriegesellschaft. [...] keine ehrliche Frau kann bestreiten, daß Frauen emotioneller als Männer sind. Deshalb verneine ich die Behauptung der Feministinnen, die ja noch mehr als nur Gleichberechtigung der Frauen wollen, sondern schlicht auf die Herrschaft der Frauen hinarbeiten, daß sie eine friedlichere Welt als die Männer schaffen würden.

So einfach ist das. – Wenn der Briefschreiber die Feministinnen deshalb ablehnt, weil sie »auf die Herrschaft der Frauen hinarbeiten«, so wiederholt er damit einen weit verbreiteten Denkfehler, der für Frauen nicht ohne bittere Ironie ist. Man stellt sich nämlich vor, diese Herrschaft müsse (mit umgekehrtem Vorzeichen) genauso aussehen wie das, was wir alle täglich vor Augen haben: die Männerherrschaft. Diese ist, in der Tat, die Herrschaft der Männer über die Frauen. Wenn die Feministinnen sich und alle Frauen aus dieser Herrschaft befreien wollen, bedeutet das nicht, daß sie damit automatisch den Spieß umdrehen. Es bedeutet »lediglich«, daß wir die Herrschaft über uns selbst, Autonomie, Selbstbestimmung anstreben – also letztlich durchaus so etwas wie die allseits bereitwillig befürwortete Gleichberechtigung insofern, als **wir** Männern das Recht auf Selbstbestimmung niemals genommen haben. In dem hier umschriebenen Sinne wird auch ›Demokratie‹, einer unserer »heiligsten« Begriffe, verstanden: Herrschaft des Volkes – über sich selbst. Nicht Herrschaft des einen Volkes über ein anderes.

Die Befragung der drei Informationsquellen – feministische Literatur, Lexika und Volksmund – ergibt also folgendes:

Die feministische Literatur ignoriert die Frage. Die meisten Lexika verstehen unter Feminismus etwas **völlig** anderes als wir und scheiden damit als Informanten aus. Der Volksmund diagnostiziert einen deutlichen Unterschied zwischen Frauenbewegung und Feminismus/Feministinnen, da aber Feministinnen sich gewöhnlich als Mitglieder der Frauenbewegung verstehen, ist diese Unterscheidung unakzeptabel – eine Verzerrung zum Zweck der Diffamierung. Diese Verzerrung schlägt sich übrigens sogar im *Duden*-Fremdwörterbuch nieder. Über *Feministin* heißt es da, gleich nach der Information, daß Feminismus das Vorhandensein weibl. Geschlechtsmerkmale beim Mann sei:

Feministin, die: (oft abwertend) [junge] Frau, die [in einer Organisation] für die soziale Gleichstellung der Frau in der Gesellschaft eintritt und die traditionelle Rollenverteilung zwischen Mann und Frau bekämpft.

Interessant bei den Recherchen ist – und das hilft vielleicht weiter – daß die Unklarheiten ausschließlich den Begriff ›Feminismus‹ betreffen, nicht den der Frauenbewegung. Wie gesagt fristete das Wort *Feminismus* (in seiner heute gebräuchlichsten Verwendung) in deutschen Wörterbüchern seit dem Erstbeleg 1912 immer nur ein Kümmerdasein und wurde schließlich von den Nazis ausradiert. Demgegenüber ist der Begriff ›Frauenbewegung‹ schon sehr alt, vielleicht nicht ganz so alt wie diese Bewegung selbst (ca. 200 Jahre), aber doch wesentlich älter als ›Feminismus‹ und daher auch viel besser im gesellschaftlichen Bewußtsein verankert.

Die Frauenbewegung wird bekanntlich in zwei Phasen eingeteilt. Die erste Phase umfaßt in Deutschland etwa die Zeit von 1848 bis 1933 und wird »ältere« oder »erste Frauenbewegung« genannt. Die zweite Phase beginnt Ende der sechziger Jahre und heißt »Neue Frauenbewegung«. Zwischen beiden Phasen gibt es viele Gemeinsamkeiten und erhebliche Unterschiede. Ein Unterschied, der m. W. bisher nicht thematisiert wurde, ist eben der, daß erst seit und mit der **Neuen** Frauenbewegung der Feminismus (was immer das nun sein mag) international präsent und in aller Munde ist.

Es liegt daher nahe anzunehmen, daß »Feminismus« mit dem in Verbindung zu bringen ist, was die Neue Frauenbewegung von der ersten unterscheidet.

Die Neue Frauenbewegung bescheinigt sich selbst eine starke »Theorielastigkeit«, die frau der ersten Frauenbewegung nicht nachsagen kann. Deren Schwerpunkt lag eindeutig im Praktischen, vor allem in der Organisation. Es wurden Vereine und Verbände gegründet in einem Ausmaß, das der Neuen Frauenbewegung durchaus wesensfremd ist. Erst in jüngster Zeit mehren sich die Stimmen, die darauf hinweisen, daß der Zeitpunkt für eine straffere Organisation, ja überhaupt für Organisation, erneut gekommen ist.

Theoriebildung also als Spezifikum und Schwerpunkt der Neuen Frauenbewegung. Und die Theorie, die sie allmählich herausbildet, durchaus unter ständigem Rückgriff auf Ideen, Programme, Theoriefragmente der ersten Frauenbewegung, ist – der Feminismus. Natürlich.

Feminismus ist die Theorie der Frauenbewegung. – Dieser Satz, wenn er schließlich dasteht, wirkt ganz simpel und einleuchtend, fast wie eine Platitüde. Jedoch wird es uns, wie ich gezeigt habe, keineswegs leicht gemacht, zu dieser dann so platt und selbstverständlich klingenden Aussage hinzufinden.

Ähnlich wie *Sozialismus* sowohl die Lehre als auch die Bewegung des Sozialismus bezeichnet, kann *Feminismus* sowohl die Theorie/Lehre der Frauenbewegung bezeichnen als auch die Bewegung selbst. Aber die Umkehrung gilt nicht: *Frauenbewegung* bezeichnet nicht die Theorie der Frauenbewegung, logisch. – Kein Wunder, wenn frau sich in diesem Kuddelmuddel nicht gleich zurechtfindet.

1982

»Sie sah zu ihm auf wie zu einem Gott«
Das DUDEN-Bedeutungswörterbuch als Trivialroman*

1 Einleitung

Bis vor kurzem hätte ich auch nicht geglaubt, daß ein Wörterbuch so spannend sein kann wie ein Krimi und so tief aufwühlend wie ein Roman von Konsalik. Ja, Konsalik ist vielleicht der passendste Vergleich für die Kombination von Lesevergnügen und unaufdringlicher Lebenshilfe, die das DUDEN-Bedeutungswörterbuch[1], ganz nebenbei und sozusagen kostenlos, liefert. Denn um Aufklärung über das Leben als solches geht es uns ja eigentlich nicht, wenn wir es konsultieren, sondern um Aufklärung über Wortbedeutungen. Aber die in spannender Unterhaltung verpackte Lebenshilfe bekommen wir trotzdem, ob wir sie nun wollen oder nicht.

Bisher habe ich mir nur das erste der 26 Kapitel, *A* von *Aal* bis *Axt*, einverleibt. Es nimmt mit 86 von insgesamt 805 Seiten zwar nur ein Neuntel des Wörterbuch-Romans oder Roman-Wörterbuchs ein – aber seine Stoffülle ist schon so immens, so überwältigend, daß ich danach erst mal innehalten mußte, um zur Besinnung zu kommen.

Ich denke mir, daß ich das komplexe Geschehen und vor allem die mitreißenden Charaktere erst dann voll und ganz werde verstehen können, wenn ich mir vor dem Weiterlesen eine vorläufige Analyse erarbeite. Möge sie auch anderen Leser-inne-n des Werks eine sinnige Hilfe sein!

---

* Ich widme den Aufsatz Ruth *Römer,* die schon 1973 nachgewiesen hat, daß linguistische Beispielsätze nicht nur grammatische Regeln illustrieren, sondern oft auch bemerkenswerte Aufschlüsse über die Mentalität der Beispielproduzenten (das Maskulinum ist intendiert) erlauben. Vgl. auch *Trömel-Plötz* 1980 und die Anmerkung 9 auf S. 41 f. dieses Bandes.

2 Die Personen der Handlung

2.1 *Die Hauptpersonen*

Der Roman handelt von fünf Personen – von drei Männern und zwei Frauen. Die Männer werden im einleitenden Kapitel *A* rund 920mal erwähnt, die Frauen insgesamt etwa 180mal. Die Männer siegen mithin fünf zu eins – mit dieser Verteilung zeigt der Roman ein feines Empfinden für die Rangordnung im wirklichen Leben.

Die drei Männer heißen Klaus, Ulrich und Ludwig. Das erfahren wir aber erst nach bereits weit vorgerückter Lektüre. Bis die Namen preisgegeben werden, werden alle drei unterschiedslos nur »er« genannt. Dieser geniale Kunstgriff macht das Lesen zunächst verwirrend, aber je länger wir uns auf das schillernde Spiel mit den Identitäten einlassen, um so reizvoller wird es auch.

Zu Beginn des Romans erfahren wir über »Ihn«, daß er sich in der Sonne *aalte*, *abartig* veranlagt ist, plötzlich nach links *abgebogen* ist, die Ausführung des Plans *abgebogen* hat, den Revolver *abdrückte* und seinen Fehltritt *abbüßte*, indem er zwei Jahre *abbrummte*.[2] Ein schönes Früchtchen, dieser abartige Mensch, denken wir doch da. Aber was lesen wir dann über ihn? »Er ist streng, *aber* gerecht.« Außerdem: »Man *achtet* ihn wegen seiner Zuverlässigkeit.« »Sein Handeln zeugt von innerem *Adel*.«

Völlig klar: Der abartige Mensch muß ein anderer »Er« sein als der mit dem inneren Adel.

Und dann gibt es da noch einen sympathischen Durchschnittsmann, liebevoll in allen Einzelheiten seines Seins, Webens und Strebens gezeichnet. Vermutlich war er es, der plötzlich nach links *abgebogen* ist, denn solche eher unwesentlichen Tätigkeiten sind kennzeichnend für ihn: Es wird alles, aber auch alles über ihn zu Protokoll gegeben, ob er nun mitten im Satz *abbricht*, die Karten an der *Abendkasse* kauft, mit dem nächsten Zug *abfährt*, seinen Fahrschein *abfährt*, das ganze Dorf nach Eiern *abgrast*, einen Ast vom Baum *abhaut*, seinen Körper frühzeitig *abhärtet*, *abgelegte* Schuhe trägt, alle Geschäfte *abläuft* oder sich vergeblich damit *abmüht*, sein Auto zu reparieren. Er ist es, über den leider gesagt werden muß: »Was ihm an Begabung *abgeht*, ersetzt er durch Fleiß«, und es wundert uns dann auch nicht mehr, daß er einen *ab-*

gekämpften Eindruck macht und vergeblich gegen den Schlaf *ankämpft*.

Dieser Mann, Zentrum des Romans und Angelpunkt aller Beziehungen, heißt Ulrich. Wir erfahren es eher nebenbei in dem Satz: »Als sie Ulrichs *ansichtig* wurde, errötete sie.« Unser Durchschnittsmann hat nämlich eine kleine Durchschnittsfrau, für die er sich abrackert und die ihn dafür anhimmelt. Während er mit Vollgas *abbraust*, *braust* sie die Kinder in der Wanne *ab*. Sie *steckt* ihm eine Schleife oder eine Blume *an*, dafür *steckt* er ihr einen Ring *an*. Er ist ein *anständiger* Mensch, und sie spricht ein *anständiges* Englisch. Er läuft *am* schnellsten, wenn sie *am* Putzen ist. Sie *heftet* den Ärmel an das Kleid *an*, währenddessen *heftet* er das Schild mit Reißnägeln an die Tür *an*. Ihn haben sie bei der Firma *angenommen*, sie dagegen hat sich der kranken Kinder *angenommen*. Er hat den Teppich *ausgerollt*; sie hat den Teig rund *ausgerollt*. – Ja, die beiden sind ein Herz und eine Seele und ergänzen sich phantastisch. Christine heißt diese prachtvolle Frau an Ulrichs Seite. Wir erfahren es in dem schönen Satz: »Christine steht in der Küche und *wäscht auf*.«

Ulrich ist zweifellos ein Mann, mit dem sich jeder, aber auch jeder Leser identifizieren kann. Die Leser*in* natürlich nicht so ohne weiteres – aber auch sie wird gewiß das Allgemein-Menschliche in Ulrich erspüren. (Apropos Leserin: In seiner Funktion als Wörterbuch enthält der Roman natürlich auch Information zum Wort *Leser*. Wir erfahren, daß es ein maskulines Wort ist. Eine *Leserin* ist nicht vorgesehen. Vielleicht ist dies der Schlüssel zur Struktur des Romans???)

Unserem Durchschnittshelden Ulrich sind neben seiner Frau Christine noch zwei weitere Personen zugeordnet: Eben jener abartige Mensch, von dem schon die Rede war, und eine Art väterlicher Freund (der mit dem inneren Adel) namens Klaus (»Klaus ist *an* einem Sonntag geboren« – er ist eben ein Strahlemann von Geburt). Die Beziehung zwischen Ulrich und seinem edlen und hilfreichen Freunde Klaus spiegelt sich in folgenden Sätzen, die unmittelbar das Herz anrühren:

a) Klaus und Ulrich:
   Er *hielt* ihn von unüberlegten Handlungen *ab*.
   Er wollte ihn nicht dem Verdacht *aussetzen*.
   Er hat sich lobend über ihn *ausgesprochen*.

Er hat ihn mit seinem Bericht im Innersten *aufgerührt*.

Er hat seinem Freund eine Leiter *ausgeliehen*.

Er *suchte* für seinen Freund ein gutes Buch *aus*.

b) Ulrich und Klaus:

Er machte seine Zustimmung von einer Entscheidung seines Freundes *abhängig*.

Er *sprach* ihn um Hilfe *an*.

Er hat sich seinem Freund *anvertraut*.

Er *lieh* sich von seinem Freund ein Fahrrad *aus*.

Er *hing* ihm treu *an*.

Eigentlich müßte es unserem Ulrich mit seiner Mittelmäßigkeit, seinem Schutzengel Klaus und seinem liebenden Weib Christine ganz famos gehen – wenn, ja wenn da nicht der abartige Mensch und Brutalo Ludwig wäre (»Ludwig war kein *Asket* und Kostverächter«, o nein!). Ludwigs kriminelle Energie scheint unerschöpflich. Körperverletzung betreibt er als mondäne Sportart. Was tut er nicht alles dem armen Ulrich, seinem bevorzugten Opfer, an:

Er hat ihm mit dem Schwert ein Ohr *abgehauen*.

Er hat ihm drei Zähne *ausgeschlagen*.

Er hat ihn grob *angefahren*.

Er *pöbelte* ihn auf der Straße *an*.

Er *stellte* sich drohend vor ihm *auf*.

Er *nutzte* seine Schwächen rücksichtslos *aus*.

Aber auch Klaus der Große bleibt von diesem miesen Verbrecher nicht ungeschoren. Ludwig hat ihm eine große Summe Geldes *abgepreßt*. Klaus reagiert wie immer gentlemanlike: Ludwigs Verhalten *mutete* ihn lediglich höchst merkwürdig *an*, und er hat halt seine *Ansicht* über ihn geändert.

Daß Ludwig, der Erzschurke, »kein Kostverächter« ist, haben wir schon erfahren. Natürlich versuchte er schon als unreifer Knabe, Christine zu belästigen, aber: das Mädchen ließ ihn *abblitzen*; sie hat den aufdringlichen Burschen *abfahren* lassen; er hat sich bei ihr eine kräftige *Abfuhr* geholt, jawoll! Er hat bei ihr nichts *aufstecken* können. Aber der Ludwig läßt ja nicht so schnell locker: »Er nahm sich vor, ein Verhältnis mit ihr *anzuspinnen*« und »versuchte auf der Straße, mit ihr *anzubändeln*«, aber sie beachtete ihn gar nicht, und das »ist ihm übel *aufgestoßen*«. Ludwig schäumt:

»Er hat mich bei ihr *ausgeknockt*«, womit er zweifellos unseren Ulrich meint. »Er wollte mich bei ihr *ausstechen*!«

Später erfahren wir noch über Ludwig, daß er eine Frau mit dem Auto *angefahren* hat und *angeschuldigt* wird, die Frau ermordet zu haben.

Was für ein Finsterling!

Und was für eine Lichtgestalt ist dagegen Klaus, das Sonntagskind! Nicht nur daß er ständig die schützenden starken Arme über Ulrich, das sprichwörtliche Mittelmaß, ausbreitet. Das macht nur einen ganz geringen Bruchteil seines segensreichen Tuns aus. Ansonsten dürfen wir ihm bei folgenden geistigen und körperlichen Heldentaten zusehen:

Er hat das Examen mit Auszeichnung *absolviert*.

Er zeigt eine *akrobatische* Beherrschung seines Körpers.

Seine Seele vermag das *All* zu umfassen.

Er war *allseits* beliebt.

Er ist ein international *anerkannter* Wissenschaftler.

Er ist gegen den Weltmeister *angetreten*.

Er machte sich zum *Anwalt* der Armen.

Er ist sogar zum nationalen Märtyrer *arriviert*.

Sie haben sich an seinen Worten *aufgerichtet*.

Er *bäumte* sich gegen die Ungerechtigkeit *auf*.

Große Wirkung *ging* von ihm *aus*.

Es ist nicht *auszudenken*, was ohne seine Hilfe passiert wäre.

Unendliche Kraft *strömte* von ihm *aus*.

Wir sehen, in diesem Sittengemälde der heutigen Zeit ist alles richtig an seinem Platz, und Mann und Frau füllen ihren Platz aus, wie es sich gehört. Die Grundaspekte der Conditio humana – höchste Tugend, Mittelmaß und abgründige Verderbtheit – sind übersichtlich verteilt auf die drei männlichen Hauptpersonen. Weit entfernt ist dieses Werk von neumodischen Mätzchen wie Verweiblichung des Mannes und Vermännlichung der Frau. Der Mann leistet das Seine nach Maßgabe seiner Kräfte, seien sie nun gottähnlich, durchschnittlich oder kriminell. Die Frau leistet das Ihre nach ihren Kräften, und da sie bekanntlich keine besonderen Kräfte besitzt, leistet Christinchen auch nichts Besonderes:

1. SIE KÜMMERT SICH UM DIE KINDER:
   Sie *gibt* sich viel mit Kindern *ab*.

Das Kind war ihr *Abgott*.
Sie mußte den kleinen Jungen *abhalten*.
Sie *seifte* die Kinder in der Wanne *ab*.
Sie hat das Baby täglich *ausgefahren*.

2. SIE MACHT SO DIES UND DAS IM HAUSHALT:
Sie *kehrte* den Schmutz von der Treppe *ab*.
Sie hat den Kühlschrank *abgetaut*.
Sie näht sehr *akkurat*.
Sie kniete auf dem Boden und *las* alle Perlen *auf*.
Sie *nähte* einen Knopf *an* den Rock.

3. SIE KÜMMERT SICH UM IHR ÄUSSERES, MIT WECHSELNDEM
ERFOLG:
Sie ist immer *adrett* gekleidet.
Sie *steckte* ihr blondes Haar flach um ihren Kopf herum *auf*.
Sie hat sich heute abend *angemalt*.
Sie ist in diesen drei Wochen stark *abgemagert*.
Sie ist auffallend *gealtert*.
Sie *stülpte* vor dem Spiegel ihre Lippen *auf*.
Sie *schnürte* ihr Mieder *auf*.
Sie ist ziemlich *auseinandergegangen*.

4. SIE HAT GEFÜHLE, VOR ALLEM ÄNGSTLICHE:
In ihrem Gesicht *malte* sich Verlegenheit *ab*.
Die Angst *preßte* ihr den Atem *ab*.
Eine Laune hat sie *angewandelt*.
Sie *stampfte* zornig mit dem Fuß *auf*.
Der Gram *frißt* ihr das Herz *ab*.
Mit großer *Angst* erwartete sie seine Rückkehr.
Diese Vorstellung *ängstigte* sie.
Sie blickte sich *ängstlich* in dem dunklen Raum um.
Sie war schon immer sehr *ängstlich*.
Sie war *ängstlich* darauf bedacht, keinen Fehler zu machen.

5. SIE IST EIN WESEN UND HAT EIN WESEN:
Sie ist ein *ätherisches* Wesen.
Sie hat ein *ausgeglichenes* Wesen.

6. SIE IST KULTURELL INTERESSIERT. WARUM AUCH NICHT?
Sie geht viel ins Konzert. Warum *auch* nicht?
Sie stand voller *Andacht* vor dem Gemälde.
Sie hat lange nach den Karten für diese Vorstellung *angestanden*.

7. UND WAS SIE SONST NOCH SO MACHT:
   Auf diese Nachricht hin kam sie sofort *angereist*.
   Sie hat die Tasten der Schreibmaschine kräftig *angeschlagen*.
   Sie fuhr *anstelle* ihrer Schwester mit.
   Sie folgte einer plötzlichen *Ahnung* und reiste ab.
   Eine *Ahnung* wehte sie an.
   Ein Geräusch ließ sie *aufhorchen*.
   Sie *faßte* das Tuch vorsichtig *an*.
   Ein Vertreter hat ihr die Ware *angedreht*.
   Sie *kleidete* sich *aus*.
   Sie *übt* keinen Beruf *aus*.

8. IHRE GRÖSSTE UND SCHÖNSTE LEISTUNG: SIE KÜMMERT SICH UM
   »IHN«:
   Sie *betet* ihren Mann *an*.
   Sie *sah* zu ihm *auf* wie zu einem Gott.
   Sie hat ihn *angedichtet*.
   Sie hat ihn schon immer *angehimmelt*.
   Sie *sah* ihn *an* und lächelte.
   Sie nahm besonderen *Anteil* an ihm und seinem Schicksal.
   Sie fühlte in ihrem Herzen Sympathie für ihn *aufkeimen*.
   Sie pflegte ihn *aufopfernd*.
   Sie *harrte* bis zu seinem Tode bei ihm *aus*.

9. IHRE ANDEREN DREI LEISTUNGEN SIND AUCH RECHT NETT, ABER
   NICHT SO WICHTIG:
   Sie hat bei der Prüfung gut *abgeschnitten*.
   Sie ist mit *Abstand* die Beste in ihrer Klasse.
   Sie spielt *ausgezeichnet* Geige.

Soweit Christine, Urbild der deutschen Haus- und Ehefrau. Aber
Christine ist nicht die einzige Frau in dieser Familiensaga. Es geistert noch eine andere herum und treibt Schindluder mit den Männern. Zuerst *regte* sich das ganze Dorf über ihren Lebenswandel
auf, weil sie Ludwig *abgeknutscht* hat und sich von ihm *aushalten*
läßt, dem seinerseits das hübsche Mädchen als *Aushängeschild*
dient. Dann hat sie sich einen reichen Mann *geangelt*, nämlich
Klausimausi, und macht ihm fortan das Leben zur Hölle:

   Sie hat es nur auf sein Geld *abgesehen*.
   Sie hat ihm geholfen, sein Vermögen *aufzubrauchen*.
   Sie versuchte, die Mitarbeiter gegen ihn *aufzubringen*.
   Sie verlangte von ihm die *Aufgabe* seiner Stellung.

Sie verdient alles *andere* als Lob.
Sie ist ein *Ausbund* aller Schlechtigkeit.
Sie ist eine *Ausgeburt* von Faulheit und Borniertheit.

Dieses Weib ist so gräßlich, daß Klaus, wie immer gentlemanlike, uns ihren Namen verschweigt. Wir wollen ihn auch gar nicht wissen. Vergessen wir am besten diese Ausgeburt!

Zwischen Christine und der Ausgeburt gibt es – natürlich – keinerlei Verbindung. Die Männer haben vielfältigen Umgang miteinander, im Guten wie im Bösen, wie wir gesehen haben. Die Frau aber kennt nur die Beziehung zum Manne oder zum Kinde oder zu beiden. »Er zeigte ihr einige *Ansichten* von Berlin«, heißt es. »Sie zeigte ihr einige Ansichten von Berlin« – undenkbar, sowas kommt nicht vor. Die Frauen sehen und hören nichts voneinander. Und das ist gut so. Wir haben ja in den letzten zehn Jahren zur Genüge erlebt, wohin diese Frauenklüngelei unsere Gesellschaft führt.

2.2 Die Nebenpersonen

Der Roman ist überreich an Nebenpersonen. Da sind zunächst die engsten Angehörigen der Protagonisten: Eltern, Geschwister, Kinder. Über Christines Eltern erfahren wir, daß sie ihnen die Einwilligung zur Heirat schließlich *abgetrotzt* hat, daß sie dem Vater die Ausbildung zur Schauspielerin *abschmeichelte* und daß er seine Tochter einmal *ausführte*. Über Ulrichs Eltern hören wir:

Die Mutter bereitete das Frühstück, der Vater *aber* lag noch im Bett.
Die Mutter *hörte* ihn die Vokabeln *ab*.
Die Mutter *füllte* ihm *auf*.
Er ist finanziell von den Eltern *abhängig*.

Nicht nur Christine und Ulrich, auch ihre Eltern erfreuen sich also eines gesunden deutschen Familienlebens.

Neben diesen engsten Familienangehörigen gibt eine unübersehbare Schar von Männern aller Schattierungen und Berufssparten dem Roman ein durch und durch mannhaftes Gepräge. Vom *Abdecker* bis zum *Avantgardisten*, vom *Abenteurer* bis zum *Autor*, vom *Abgeordneten* bis zum *Ausländer* erhält jeder einzelne seinen kleinen Auftritt und wird liebevoll skizziert – in 80 Extra-Kapitelchen, überschrieben mit *Agitator, der – Angestellte, der – Arbeiter, der –* und so weiter.

Vielleicht stimmt die Zahl 80 auch nicht ganz genau; vielleicht habe ich in der Überfülle des Angebots den einen oder anderen Mann übersehen. Nicht entgangen sind meinem kritischen Auge jedoch die beiden Frauen

    Abiturientin, die –   *– Ärztin, die,*

die die Einheitlichkeit des Bildes doch ganz empfindlich stören. Ich schlage vor, diese beiden weiblichen Störfaktoren schleunigst auszumerzen, spätestens bei der nächsten Auflage. Es genügt schließlich, daß wir in der kruden Realität auch schon mal *der* Abgeordneten, *der* Angestellten, *der* Ansagerin, *der* Akademikerin usw. begegnen – aber in der Welt der Literatur wollen wir uns doch einfach entspannen und von solchen wildgewordenen Emanzen nichts hören und nichts sehen.

»Unentbehrlich für die Erweiterung des Wortschatzes« will der Wörterbuch-Roman sein, so steht's obendrauf. Auf **solche** Erweiterung aber verzichten wir gern. Also bitte fort mit der Abiturientin und der Ärztin!

Außer den in Einzelkapiteln vorgestellten *A*-Männern wimmelt es in dem ersten Kapitel dieses Romans noch von unzähligen anderen Männern, von A bis Z. Immer wieder treten der Chef, der Lehrer und der Schüler auf, auch Militär, Polizei, Politiker und Sportler sind reich vertreten. Frauen halten sich auch hier wohltuend im Hintergrund: An Berufen finden wir neben der bereits übel vermerkten *Ärztin* nur noch die *Amme* (Extra-Eintrag) sowie

die Sängerin:	Die Sängerin *fiel* gegen die Sänger stark *ab*.
die Schauspielerin:	Die Schauspielerin ist zur Diva *avanciert*.
	Die *Attitüden* und Gebärden der Schauspielerin sind gekünstelt.
die Tänzerin:	eine *abgetakelte* Tänzerin
die Sekretärin:	Ärgerlich *winkte* er der eintretenden Sekretärin *ab*.
	Am Abend *schwärmt* das Heer der Verkäuferinnen und Sekretärinnen *aus*.
die Verkäuferin:	Die Verkäuferin hat *ausgelernt*.
die Zeitungsfrau:	Die Zeitungsfrau *abfangen / abpassen*.

Schön, wie plastisch der Roman die Tatsache herausarbeitet, daß Frauen im Beruf untüchtig sind. Als Sekretärin, Verkäuferin oder Zeitungsfrau mögen sie gerade noch durchgehen. Ihr wahrer Beruf aber ist und bleibt der der Gattin, Hausfrau und Mutter.

Neben den berufstätigen Frauen treten überflüssigerweise noch auf: eine *attraktive* Frau, ein *adliges* Fräulein, ein *affiges*, ein *altkluges* und ein *aufgedonnertes* Mädchen, ein *altes* Mütterchen, eine *angeheiratete* Tante und eine *aparte* Dame. Banale oder regelrecht unsympathische Personen! Wie sagt doch Ulrich zu Klaus: »Ich bin von der dicken, schwitzenden Frau *abgerückt*.« Meine Empfehlung an die Wörterbuchredaktion: Rücken auch Sie in der nächsten Auflage entschlossen ab von so fragwürdigem »weiblichen Zierat«. **Uns** genügt vollauf die Gattin, Hausfrau und Mutter.

3 Schlußbemerkung

Ach, es wäre noch so vieles zu sagen über dieses packende Werk – aber ich will jetzt aufhören. Ich hoffe, daß diese kleine Einführung viele Menschen motiviert, den Roman zu lesen. Es erwartet sie ein Leseabenteuer ganz eigener und seltener Art, das kann ich versprechen.

Abschließend noch ein Wort zu der unangebrachten Bescheidenheit der Redaktion. Im Vorwort schreiben sie, sie hätten den *Grund*wortschatz des Deutschen in seinen *Grund*bedeutungen darstellen wollen. Viel viel mehr gelingt ihnen: Sie vermitteln einen tiefen, unvergeßlichen Einblick in die *Seele* des Deutschen, in seinen *Grund*empfindungs- und *Grund*gedankenschatz. Wir dürfen mit ihrer Hilfe bis auf den Grund dieses Abgrunds sehen – und wir erblicken: Mief, Spiessigkeit, Männlichkeitswahn, Pennälermentalität, Obrigkeits- und Schubladendenken. Und eine geradezu abgründige Frauenverachtung. Dies vor allem.

1983

Anmerkungen

1 DUDEN Bedeutungswörterbuch/DUDEN Band 10/. Bearbeitet von Paul Grebe, Rudolf Köster, Wolfgang Müller und weiteren Mitarbeitern der Dudenredaktion. Mannheim 1970: Bibliographisches Institut.
2 Hier und im folgenden sind diejenigen Wörter kursiv gesetzt, unter deren Grundform das jeweilige Zitat im DUDEN-Bedeutungswörterbuch zu finden ist.

Glossen

Die Glossen erscheinen seit Februar 1982 monatlich in der feministischen Zeitschrift *Courage*; die Serie wird fortgesetzt.

Die *Courage*-Redaktion hat, mit meinem Einverständnis, an manchen der Original-Glossen Änderungen vorgenommen. Manche dieser Änderungen habe ich hier wieder rückgängig gemacht, anderes habe ich für den Wiederabdruck leicht geändert. Außerdem habe ich jetzt die Glossen inhaltlich grob geordnet, wobei allerdings die inhaltliche Ordnung der chronologischen ziemlich entspricht: Während der ersten fünfzehn Monate habe ich hauptsächlich grammatische Aspekte aufgegriffen; danach geht es mehr um Fragen des Wortinhalts und des Stils.

Die aufmerksame Leserin wird feststellen, daß ich in den Glossen hin und wieder Material aus den Aufsätzen benutze – aber ich glaube, die Überschneidungen halten sich in Grenzen. Ich habe sie nicht durch Streichungen beseitigt, weil die Glossen, kurz und zugespitzt wie sie sind, besser als die Aufsätze für bestimmte Unterrichts- und Einstiegszwecke benutzt werden können.

Von Türkinnen Deutsch lernen!
Über Aufwendiges und Notwendiges

»Dörner im Auge« – so titelte der *Spiegel* (Nr. 49 vom 30. 11. 81, S. 62–64) seinen Artikel über die Türkin und diplomierte Wirtschaftswissenschaftlerin Elçin Kürsat, die soeben vom SPD-Bezirk Hannover in den Bezirksvorstand gewählt worden war. Sie kann also noch nicht mal richtig Deutsch – damit wir's gleich wissen. Und damit wir's noch genauer wissen und tüchtig lachen können, ist im Text folgender Kürsat-Ausspruch über die Situation ihrer Landsleute nachzulesen: »Die resignieren sich und bleiben Dörner im Auge.« Wie komisch wohl das Türkisch dieses anonymen *Spiegel*schreibers klingen mag? Falls es überhaupt erklingt.

Die Überschrift des Kürsat-Artikels in der *Zeit* (Nr. 50 vom 4. 12. 81, S. 63) lautet schlicht: »Ich war gar nicht geplant.« Das liest sich ja fast so, als ob diese Türkin doch richtig Deutsch könnte. Die Autorin des Artikels, Margrit Gerste, berichtet sachlich und mit Sympathie über Elçin Kürsat, über ihr Engagement gerade für türkische Frauen. Aber einige Überheblichkeiten kann auch sie sich nicht verkneifen. Sie zitiert Kürsat: »Meine Wahl ist ein erster Schritt zum gemeinsamen Handeln. Die Genossinnen und Genossen (so aufwendig nennt sie sie dauernd) haben begriffen, daß Lösungen gefunden werden müssen.«

Margrit Gerste aber hat anscheinend (noch) nicht begriffen, daß Formulierungen wie *Genossinnen und Genossen* nicht »aufwendig« sind, sondern bitter notwendig. Und zwar »dauernd«, ja!

Warum notwendig? Es gibt viele Gründe, über die innerhalb der Neuen Frauenbewegung schon viel gesagt und geschrieben worden ist. Die beiden wichtigsten Gründe sind:

Wenn statt *Genossinnen und Genossen*, wie derzeit weitgehend noch üblich, nur *Genossen* gesagt wird, bleibt unklar, ob Frauen überhaupt gemeint sind. Aus langer Erfahrung, die sich täglich bestätigt, wissen wir allerdings, daß wir in ca. 90% der Fälle **nicht** gemeint sind, wenn von ›Arbeitern‹, ›Politikern‹, ›Musikern‹, ›Entwicklungshelfern‹, ›Autoren‹ etc. etc. die Rede ist. Ich empfehle Margrit Gerste, sich die Ausgabe der *Zeit*, in der ihr Artikel abgedruckt ist, einmal genau daraufhin anzusehen.

Sie wird sich wundern. (Sogar ›Touristen‹ sind dort ausschließlich männlichen Geschlechts! (Vgl. S. 51))

Eine Faustregel, wie Frauenfeindlichkeit zu entlarven ist, lautet: »Eine Aussage, die bei einer Übertragung auf Männer komisch, bizarr oder beleidigend wirken würde, ist frauenfeindlich« – zitiert nach Sigrid Löffler, in derselben Ausgabe der *Zeit*, S. 57(!!).

Margrit Gerste soll mal versuchen, ihre Kollegen konsequent als ›Kolleginnen‹ anzusprechen. Mann würde es natürlich als »komisch, bizarr oder beleidigend« empfinden (s. o.).
Kommentar überflüssig.

Elçin Kürsat hat sich ihr Deutsch selbst beigebracht, wie wir hören. Ob sie wohl so differenziert und korrekt sprechen würde, wenn sie einem von Deutschen erteilten Unterricht ausgesetzt gewesen wäre? **Ich** jedenfalls habe es anders gelernt und erst spät begriffen, **wie** frauenfeindlich viele naiv und gutgläubig befolgte Regeln der deutschen Sprache sind.

Februar 1982

Die Menstruation ist bei jedem
ein bißchen anders

Frau gerät immer mal wieder in Badezimmer, Örtchen oder wie ihr es nun nennen wollt, in denen sie nichts Vernünftiges zu lesen findet. Vielleicht gehört ihr auch zu jenen Unverdrossenen, die sich in derartigen Notfällen dann eben mit vergleichsweise dürftigem Lesefutter begnügen – was so in Reichweite ist, Zahnpastatuben, Cremedöschen, Deodorants. Ich jedenfalls hatte neulich Gelegenheit, eingehend eine o. b.-Schachtel zu studieren. Der Schachtelaufdruck gab wenig her, aber es fand sich innendrin noch ein kleines feines Faltblättchen, eng mit Aufklärendem bedruckt. Ich las also, mäßig unterhalten, bis ich auf folgende Information stieß: »Die Menstruation ist bei jedem ein bißchen anders.«

Mag ja sein, daß die Menstruation bei *jeder Frau* oder, kurz, bei *jeder* anders ist und daß wir deshalb dankbar sein dürfen, daß die Firma o. b. ein so hochdifferenziertes Tampon-Angebot für uns parat hat, von »minimal« bis »spezial« oder was. Aber es wollte mir nicht einleuchten, wieso sie bei *jedem* anders sein soll. Bei *jedem Menschen* vielleicht? Haut ja wohl auch kaum hin.

Ich schrieb also der wissenschaftlichen Abteilung der Firma und bat um weitere Aufklärung – in dem Faltblättchen hatte nämlich auch gestanden, sie würden sich aller etwa noch offengebliebenen Fragen liebevoll annehmen. Es verstrichen vier Wochen, dann erreichte mich eine zerknautschte Geschenkpackung mit 40 o. b. (Typ: »normal«) und einem freundlichen Begleitschreiben. Man habe sich über meine Anteilnahme an ihrem Unternehmen sehr gefreut. Und was nun jenes *bei jedem* betreffe – möglicherweise habe die Verfasserin, ja es sei eine Verfasserin gewesen, da an Mädchen gedacht? Bei jedem Mädchen anders, vielleicht? Dennoch, man wolle meine Einlassungen gerne bedenken und die nächste Auflage des Faltblättchens abändern.

Trickreich, wirklich! – Nun habe ich all die düsteren Warnungen vor Killertampons im besonderen und Tampons im allgemeinen verinnerlicht – und kaufe trotzdem hin und wieder eine Schachtel o. b., um festzustellen, ob die Menstruation noch immer *bei jedem* oder vielleicht schon, äußerst sprachsensibel, *bei jeder (Frau)* anders ist.

(Nachtrag 1983: Das Faltblättchen wurde Ende 1982 abgeändert.)

März 1982

Zur Sache, Schätzchen!

Das Schätzchen, von dem hier die Rede sein soll, ist unser lieber deutscher Wort-Schatz. Dieser sogenannte Schatz enthält, wie wir wissen, allerlei wertlosen Plunder, besonders in der Abteilung ›Personenbezeichnungen‹. Viele Frauen sind deshalb der Meinung, das Schätzchen gehöre auf den Müll, weg damit! So weit möchte ich eigentlich nicht gehen. Immerhin enthält es doch auch sehr schöne, brauchbare Wörter, zum Beispiel *Frau*, *Schwester*, *Geschwister*, *Tochter*, *Mutter*, *Kind*, *Scheißkerl*, *Macker*, *Leberwurst*, *gesund*, *warm*, *liebhaben* und noch ein paar andere.

Ärgerlich wird es allerdings, wenn wir vertrauensvoll in den Schatz hineingreifen – und irgendeinen Mist hervorziehen. Solches passiert zum Beispiel, wenn wir eine präzise Vorstellung haben und das Wort, welches der Schatz für unsere Vorstellung bereithält, halb richtig und halb falsch ist. Und ein anderes Wort nicht vorhanden ist.

Neulich – ich lese grade Karin Hausens klugen Aufsatz »Women's History in den Vereinigten Staaten« – kommt meine Freundin Erika Hausen zu Besuch. »Du, ich lese grade einen Artikel von deiner Namensvetterin«, will ich sie munter begrüßen. Daß Karin und Erika Hausen keine ›Namensvettern‹ sind und auch nicht so genannt werden dürfen, ist ja klar. Aber auch die ›Namensvetterin‹ bleibt mir, gerade noch rechtzeitig, im Halse stecken. *Namenscousine* sage ich also. Später rede ich mit meiner Mutter über dies eigenartige Sprachproblem. Sie sage schon immer *Namensbase*, berichtet sie gelassen. Aber *Base* riecht mir zu streng nach Deutschtümelei. *Cousine* ist mir vertrauter, angenehmer, obwohl es genauso aus *Cousin* abgeleitet ist wie meine mißliche Eigenschöpfung *Vetterin* aus *Vetter*.

Im Herkunftswörterbuch (Der Große Duden, Band 7) steht unter *Namensvetter*: »Einer, der den gleichen Namen trägt (18. Jh.)«. *Eine, die* den gleichen Namen trägt, ist also nicht vorgesehen. In der deutschen Sprache gibt es kein Wort für sie – wir müssen es erfinden. Ich persönlich finde, nach meiner Odyssee (schon wieder so ein männlich geprägtes Wort!), inzwischen *Namensschwester* gut. (Übrigens: Der norwegische Wortschatz ist besser bestückt.

Dort gibt es die *navnesøster* ›Namensschwester‹ neben dem *navnebror* ›Namensbruder‹.)

Die Linguistik (sagen wir doch gleich: die Linguisten (männlich)) spricht/sprechen in derartigen Fällen von »lexikalischen Lücken« in der Sprache. Das Bild ›Lücke‹ suggeriert mehreres:

a) Eine Lücke, z.B. eine Zahnlücke, ist etwas relativ Harmloses. Das umgebende Ganze hat noch hinreichend festen Zusammenhalt. Wenn mir aber sämtliche Zähne des Oberkiefers fehlen, wäre es lächerlich, von einer Lücke zu sprechen.

b) Eine Lücke »entsteht«, sie »passiert«, niemand ist so recht für ihr Entstehen verantwortlich. Sie ist auch etwas eher Zufälliges, Unsystematisches. Es gibt z.B. Zifferblätter mit zwölf und Zifferblätter mit nur vier Ziffern: 3, 6, 9 und 12. Das vierziffrige Zifferblatt enthält keine »Lücken«, sondern es wurden acht Ziffern »ausgespart«, »weggelassen«. Eine »Aussparung«, »Ausklammerung« ist im Gegensatz zur Lücke etwas Beabsichtigtes.

Männer haben Frauen jahrtausendelang weitgehend aus dem öffentlichen Leben ausgeklammert – die Folge für den Wort»schatz« ist, daß eigenständige Bezeichnungen für Frauen einfach fehlen, und zwar ebenso systematisch fehlen wie die Ausklammerung systematisch war. Wörter wie *Student*, *Arzt*, *Pastor*, *Richter*, *Professor*, *Meister*, *Geselle* bezeichneten über einen langen Zeitraum ausschließlich: Männer. »Sprachnot« entstand erst, als seit Anfang dieses Jahrhunderts immer mehr Frauen dieselben Funktionen wie Männer übernahmen. Seitdem haben wir plötzlich »Studenten« und »weibliche Studenten« und so fort. Darüber hinaus wird uns eingeredet, Wörter wie *Arzt* seien »geschlechtsneutral«, könnten sich auf Frauen genauso beziehen wie auf Männer. Aber wenn ich dann erzähle »Unser Hausarzt hat neulich meinen Onkel geheiratet« – will es niemand begreifen. Lieber doch auf den Müll mit diesen Männerlumpen, die wir neuerdings anziehen dürfen, die aber nicht für uns geschneidert wurden und die uns deshalb entweder zu eng oder zu weit sind?

Heute ist uns die »Kauffrau« einigermaßen geläufig, aber die »Staatsfrau« noch lange nicht, trotz Golda Meir, Indira Gandhi, Margaret Thatcher, Vigdis Finnbogadottir und anderen. Und die »Stammhalterin« gibt es (als Möglichkeit) erst seit 1978, seit bei der Eheschließung auch der Name der Frau zum Familiennamen werden kann.

Gut, solche »Lücken« bzw. Aussparungen wie die lange fehlende

›Stammhalterin‹ oder ›Doktormutter‹ lassen sich historisch erklären. Es gibt eben (leider) erst seit kurzem Frauen, auf die diese Bezeichnungen anwendbar sind. Welche Erklärung aber gibt es für die fehlenden ›Namensschwestern‹? Namensschwestern gab es doch schon immer genauso viele wie Namensvettern.

Der deutsche Wort»schatz« dient, das läßt sich breit belegen, hervorragend männlichen Interessen. Wer ihn »gemacht« hat, diese Frage kann dabei ruhig offenbleiben. Frauen jedenfalls, soweit sie für diesen »Schatz« mitverantwortlich sind, haben sich selbst und ihre Interessen **nicht** wahrgenommen. Dieses Strickmuster ist uns ja auch aus anderen Bereichen als dem der Sprache hinreichend geläufig.

Halten wir also fest: Der deutsche Wortschatz eignet sich zum Ausdruck weiblicher Interessen und Sehweisen etwa so gut wie ein Rasierapparat zur weiblichen Körperpflege. Mag man uns den Apparat auch noch so sehr als »geschlechtsneutral« und für Frauen und Männer gleichermaßen entworfen und geeignet anempfehlen – es wird kaum Situationen geben, wo sich dieses Instrument für uns als praktisch erweist. Vielmehr sind wir genötigt, immer mehr **eigene** Instrumente für **unseren** Bedarf zu entwickeln.

Oder, um ein anderes Bild aufzugreifen: Es geht nicht darum, irgendwelche »Lücken« auszufüllen, sondern darum, die sinnlos mümmelnde untere Zahnreihe endlich durch eine obere zu einem ordentlichen Eß- und Sprechwerkzeug zu ergänzen.

Mai 1982

Herr und Hund

Meistens raunt Ben Witter in der *Zeit* eher Unverständliches, aber
am 12. 2. 82 wurde er ganz deutlich:

> Der Hund ist herrenlos, sagte die Frau.
> Ich pfiff, und sie trottete hinter mir her.

Da kaum anzunehmen ist, daß Witter mit »sie« den Hund meint –
wo bliebe dann auch der »Witz«, nicht wahr – dürfen wir folgern:
Frauen sind wie Hunde, auf Anpfiff willenlos gehorchend und hin-
ter dem »Herrn« hertrottend (und sei es auch Herrchen Witter).

Nein, das wird hier kein Gewitter auf Herrn Witter! Wie sagte
doch die große Dorothea Christina Erxleben, Deutschlands erste
promovierte Ärztin, schon vor über 200 Jahren:

> Ihr Gewäsche wird mich niemals verleiten, ihnen zu antworten
> und dadurch die edle Zeit zu verderben, mich selbst aber in Ge-
> fahr zu setzen, ihnen gleich zu werden.

Genau! Halten wir einfach fest, daß Tiere sowieso die besseren
Menschen sind: Sie machen wenigstens keine Herrenwitze im
Zweireiher, unsere Vierbeiner/innen.

Ich erinnere mich an einen Vorfall vor vielen Jahren, Studenten-
heim, Vollversammlung, Rechenschaftsbericht unseres Fahrradre-
ferenten. Er ist Portugiese, und er meldet folgendes, in vorwurfs-
vollem Ton: »Es stehen immer noch viele herren- und damenlose
Fahrräder im Schuppen rum!« Herzliches Gelächter allerseits über
den amüsanten Sprachschnitzer. Unser Portugiese war über einen
der vielen Stolpersteine der Männersprache Deutsch gefallen. Zu
»Herr« gehört »Dame«, so hatte er gerechnet. Aber so einseitig
sind ja unsere »Herren« nicht. Zu »Herren« gehören neben den
»Damen« auch noch »Frauen« und »Herrinnen«:

Herr
- Dame: *Sehr geehrte Damen und Herren!*
  Herrentoilette – Damentoilette
- Frau: *Herr Witter – Frau Pusch*
- Herrin: *Die Hausherrin – der Hausherr*

(Über diesen Stolperstein kam übrigens auch Dame Rechenberg
aus Goslar zu Fall. Ihr habt vielleicht von ihr gehört; sie wurde ja in

der Männerpresse ständig lächerlich gemacht. Spott und Kritik gingen aber an die falsche Adresse. Anzugreifen ist nicht diese Frau, sondern die deutsche Sprache als patriarchalisch organisiertes Verwirr-System.)

Mit dem *herr-* in *herrenlos* (oder auch *Herrenrasse*) hat es nun noch seine ganz eigene Bewandtnis. Es ist das nämliche *Herr*, das auch in *Herrgott* vorkommt und bekanntlich rein gar nichts neben sich duldet, schon gar nichts Weibliches. Eher noch wird es hinnehmen, als ›abstrakt‹, ›allumfassend‹ und ›allgültig‹ analysiert zu werden. Dieses *Herr*, so hören wir, ist eben einfach ›geschlechtsneutral‹. Es bedeutet ›Besitzer, Herrscher, Gebieter‹. Na, ›Herr‹ eben bedeutet es! Ein herrenloser Hund ist ein Hund ohne Herrn, egal welchen Geschlechts, ob Frauchen oder Herrchen. Kapiert? Und die Herrenrasse? Dito!

Herrenlos – welch tiefes, schönes Wort! Es bedeutet also ›frei‹, ›autonom‹, ›ohne Besitzer‹. Bevor die Herren sie in Besitz nahmen, zähmten, domestizierten, waren alle Tiere »herrenlos«, d. h. frei, in niemannes Besitz, unter niemannes Herrschaft. Erst die Herrenperspektive mit ihren verherrenden Folgen beschert uns auch den »herrenlosen Hund« als ein per se bedauernswertes, herumstreunendes, struppiges Wesen. Der richtige Hund hingegen, komplett mit Herrchen (egal ob weiblich oder männlich, s. o.) – was macht er zur Freude seines Herrn? Egal ob Weibchen oder Männchen, er macht: Männchen.

»Herr und Hund«, so nannte Thomas Mann (!) seine Erzählung. An der Herrenperspektive bleibt von vornherein nicht der geringste Zweifel. Die beiden anderen berühmten Erzählungen über Hunde stammen von Frauen: »Krambambuli« von Marie von Ebner-Eschenbach und »Flush« von Virginia Woolf. Ob es nur ein Zufall ist, daß die beiden Frauen den Hund im Titel »herrenlos« auftreten lassen und ihn beim Namen nennen?

April 1982

Wir Männschen

Wir Frauen bestreiten ja nicht, daß Männer Menschen sind. Es sind bekanntlich die Männer, die sich damit schwertun, daß auch Frauen Menschen sind.

»Ein Mensch ohne Frau ist eigentlich kein Mensch«, heißt es im Talmud. Frauen, die bloß einen Mann aufweisen können (das reicht anscheinend nicht zur Menschwerdung), werden aus der Klasse der Menschen hinausdefiniert.

Ein Mensch, so heißt das vielgelesene Buch mit »heiteren Versen« von Eugen Roth. Im Klappentext der -zigten Auflage steht zu lesen: »Eugen Roth hat den Menschen an seinen Achillesfersen gezeichnet, den verhinderten Don Juan ebenso wie Friederich, den argen Wüterich.« Die Verse seien »hundert kleine Spiegelein, aus denen wir herausgucken, du und ich, der Nachbar und der Vetter«. »Finden wir uns nicht auf irgendeiner Seite selbst wieder?« »Wir alle, wir Menschen, sind jeweils skizziert, wenn Eugen Roth beginnt: Ein Mensch...«

Ich, eine Frau, weder Nachbar noch Vetter, weder Don Juan noch arger Wüterich, finde mich da auf **keiner** Seite wieder. Ich finde sowohl in den Illustrationen als auch in den »heiteren Versen« nur Männer. »Ein Mensch...« – ist immer ein Mann.

Damit schließt sich der Kreis brüderlicher Männschlichkeit vom ehrwürdigen Talmud zur heiteren Gegenwart.

Als vor etwa zehn Jahren einige Frauen anfingen, *frau* statt *man* zu sagen, fanden andere das chauvinistisch, »unmenschlich«, ja männermordend. Wenn *man* schon abgeschafft werden soll, hieß es, dann ersetzt es doch besser durch *mensch*.

Aber ist *mensch* wirklich »menschlicher«, umfassender, als *frau* oder *man*? Immer wieder lesen und hören wir Frauen, daß *er*, der Mensch, männlichen Geschlechts sein muß. Andernfalls nämlich ergeben die meisten offiziellen Aussagen über »den Menschen« keinen Sinn. Und das Substantiv *Mensch* ist, genau wie *man*, abgeleitet von dem Wort *Mann* (genauer: von althochdeutsch *mannisco* ›männlich‹ über *mennisco*, *mennisc* zu *mensch*). *Frau* ist von der Wortgeschichte her tatsächlich viel besser geeignet, für **beide** Geschlechter zu stehen. Im Germanischen gab es den Stamm *frau-*

(›hochgestellte Person‹) mit den wahlweisen Endungen *-jo* für die Frau und *-ja* für den Mann.

Ob wir Frauen, Fraujo oder Frauja, so sinnige Sprachsitten nicht vollends wiederbeleben sollten? Immerhin – *frau* für *man* war schon ein vielversprechender erster Schritt.

(Dank an Adi Prasser für den Hinweis auf Eugen Roth)

Juni 1982

Damenwahl

Es gibt Damenschuhe und Herrenschuhe, Damenunterwäsche und Herrenunterwäsche. Es gibt im Eiskunstlauf die Kür der Damen und die Kür der Herren, im Skisport die Abfahrtsläufe der Damen und die der Herren.

Bei Tanzveranstaltungen gibt es hin und wieder Damenwahl. Die »Herrenwahl«, das Gegenstück der Damenwahl, findet zwar laufend statt, aber sie hat offiziell keinen Namen, keinen Platz im deutschen Wörterbuch. Wie kommt das?

Die Sprache arbeitet eben nach dem Ökonomieprinzip, erklären (männliche) Sprachwissenschaftler. Das Selbstverständliche, die Norm, wird nicht extra benannt. Wie praktisch! Deshalb also hieß früher die Schule, auf die mein Bruder ging, »Gymnasium« – und meine: »Mädchengymnasium«.

Es gibt da allerdings auch ein paar Bereiche, die ganz in die Zuständigkeit der Dame fallen, z. B. Parfüm, Handtaschen, Torte und Schokolade. Sind diese Produkte ausnahmsweise mal für Herren gedacht, so wird das sprachlich angezeigt: Herrenparfüm, Herrenhandtaschen, Herrentorte und Herrenschokolade. Die Produkte für uns Normalverbraucherinnen heißen dagegen nicht Damentorte oder so, sondern schlicht und praktisch: Torte. Weiß ja eh jeder (!), wer das Zeug frißt. Auch Udo Jürgens weiß ein Lied davon zu singen: »Aber bitte mit Sahne«, so schmachten bei ihm die dicken Damen im Café nach ihrer Torte.

Nun gut. 1975 hatten wir das Jahr der Frau. Wir wußten es auch ohne diesen Hinweis, daß alle anderen Jahre in erster Linie Jahre des Mannes sind. Das Jahr des Kindes, das Jahr der Behinderten – lauter erstaunlich unbekümmerte Eingeständnisse der *Herr*schenden, wem die andern Jahre rechtens gehören. Ich warte noch auf das Jahr der Gastarbeiter und der Alten, Pardon: Senioren. Jahre für Gastarbeiterinnen und Seniorinnen wird's wohl nicht geben – Frauen sind ja immer mitgemeint.

Die bloße Existenz des neuen Wortes »Frauenforschung« beweist, daß »Forschung« bisher nicht Forschung von und für Menschen war, sondern von und für Männer: Männerforschung.

Es war ein genialer Schachzug der Männer, Männerforschung einfach »Forschung« zu nennen, Männerjustiz einfach »Justiz«,

Männerpolitik einfach »Politik«, Männerpresse einfach »Presse«. Und gedeckt durch diesen Sprachbetrug, lamentieren sie nun ständig, wir seien so »separatistisch« mit unserem neuen Frauenkram! Gegen solche zynischen Verdrehungen hilft vor allem eins: Das Männliche überall namhaft machen! Es gibt keine Forschung, Justiz, Presse usw., die diese unseparatistischen Namen verdient. Und solange der männliche Separatismus sich nicht ändert, müssen wenigstens wir Frauen auf begriffliche Sauberkeit achten und die Dinge bei ihrem richtigen Namen nennen.

Übrigens: Bei den Mißwahlen wird eine Miß gewählt, bei den Bundestagswahlen der (Männer-)Bundestag. Die sprach- und damenbewußte Dame wählt folglich bei Damenwahl eine Dame.

Juli 1982

Malwinen oder Falkland-Inseln?

Zuerst (1527) hießen sie Islas San Antón, die Spanier hatten sie so genannt. 1600 kam der holländische Kapitän Sebald und taufte sie – wie wohl? Sebaldinen! 1690 kamen die Briten und nannten sie, nach einem Zahlmeister der Navy, Falkland Islands. 1764 kamen die Franzosen und tauften sie wieder um in Malouines. 1820 besetzten die Argentinier die Inselgruppe, für sie »Islas Malvinas«. 1833 kamen wieder die Briten und nahmen die Inseln, für sie noch immer »Falkland Islands«, erneut in Besitz.

Die Ureinwohner/innen, Robben und Pinguine, haben sich bis jetzt zu den diversen Besetzungs- und Benennungsaktionen ihnen gleichermaßen fremder und unerwünschter Herren nicht geäußert. Sie blieben einfach sprachlos.

Als meine Mutter geboren wurde, damals auch noch sprachlos, bekam sie den Nachnamen Gärtner, nach ihrem Vater (mit diesem Namen hatte mein Großvater zuvor schon den Namen meiner Großmutter gelöscht). Später kam mein Vater, und meine Mutter hieß fortan Pusch. Inzwischen heißt sie Wulff, nach ihrem zweiten Ehemann. Daß meine Schwester mit mir verwandt ist, ist auch nicht mehr am Namen zu erkennen. Sie heißt jetzt Seibolt.

Es leuchtet ein, daß sprachlose Wesen, wie Pinguine, Robben oder Säuglinge, nicht gefragt werden können, wie sie denn am liebsten heißen wollen. Weniger einleuchtend, ist, daß Gesetz und/oder Brauchtum mit erwachsenen Frauen so verfahren als wären sie Robben, Pinguine oder Säuglinge. Oder eine Inselgruppe im Südatlantik, die je nach Herrschaftsanspruch verschieden benannt wird.

Wir, die wir in dem Konflikt zwischen England und Argentinien Außenstehende waren, hörten in den Nachrichten mal »Falkland-Inseln«, mal »Malwinen«. Letzteres allerdings viel seltener, denn Argentinien ist weit weg und hat eine Militär-Diktatur, England ist nah, EG- und NATO-Partner und das »Mutterland der Demokratie«.

Bei meiner Mutter und meiner Schwester dagegen kommen keine verwirrenden Doppelbenennungen vor, alles ist »herr«lich geregelt. Auch ich, weit entfernt, irgendwelche Besitzansprüche mittels Benennung anzumelden, schreibe brav an »Frau Wulff« und

»Frau Seibolt«. Im Telefonbuch stehen sie beide nicht, nur ihre Ehemänner.

Namen sind Schall und Rauch? Namen sind vor allem: Besitzanspruch oder Besitznachweis. Ob die Herren eine Inselgruppe oder eine Frau als ihren Besitz reklamieren – das damit einhergehende (Um-)Benennungsverfahren ist dasselbe und wird höllisch ernstgenommen. In Großbritannien ist es ein Politikum, wie jene Inselgruppe genannt wird. »Malwinen« – ausgeschlossen, Hochverrat! Aber niemand – außer ein paar wildgewordenen Emanzen – nimmt an der offiziellen Bezeichnung »United Kingdom« Anstoß. Nicht einmal die Queen. (»God save the King« allerdings wagen sie ihr denn doch nicht ins Gesicht zu singen.)

Die Schwestern in den USA sind uns ja in vielem voraus. Als Nachnamen wählen sie sich neuerdings weibliche Vornamen – weil **alle** Nachnamen, auch die unserer Vorfahr**innen**, unbrauchbar sind, denn es sind Namen, die diese Frauen von ihren Männern »übernehmen« mußten.

Julia Stanley, bekannte feministische Linguistin, nennt sich heute Julia Penelope. Noch unbestätigt sind Gerüchte, wonach sie mit dem Faltboot zu den Malwinen oder Falkland-Inseln unterwegs ist, um Port Stanley in Port Penelope umzutaufen.

August 1982

Das liebe Gott

»Vater unser, der du bist im Himmel« – so haben wir alle gelernt, uns Gott vorzustellen: als gütigen, manchmal auch zornig-strafenden Vater, zu Gericht sitzend droben auf dem Himmelsthron, mit Rauschebart womöglich. Weiblich oder mütterlich wirkt er nicht gerade. Er hat ein (uneheliches) Kind, ebenfalls männlich, namens Jesus.

Feministinnen haben auch vor **dieser** Männerbastion nicht haltgemacht und respektlose Sprüche geprägt wie: »When God created man she was only joking (Als Gott den Mann erschuf, hat sie sich bloß einen Scherz erlaubt).« Die Kraftmeierin legt los: »Meine Göttin noch mal!«, und die Frau ohne Knete bittet vertrauensvoll: »Liebe Göttin, schenk mir doch ein *Emma*-Abo!« (Ein *Courage*-Abo hat sie anscheinend schon bekommen, göttinseidank!) Und die feministische Pastorin verabschiedet die verdutzte Gemeinde mit den Worten: »Gott segne dich und behüte dich, sie lasse ihr Angesicht leuchten über dir und gebe dir Frieden.«

Es reicht, wenn wir die Männerherrschaft auf der Erde haben, denken diese Frauen. Nicht auch noch im Himmel. Dort, ab sofort: Frauenpower.

Andere sind gemäßigter und gesellen Gottvater eine Mutter zu: »Vater und Mutter unser im Himmel.« Ob wir uns Gott als Elternpaar oder als zweigeschlechtig oder als geschlechtslos vorstellen, ist unser Bier.

Die alten Germaninnen (Männer sind selbstverständlich immer mitgemeint), vom Christentum noch ungeschoren, hatten eine sehr sympathische und, von heute aus betrachtet, äußerst fortschrittliche Gottesvorstellung. Das germanische Wort *guda*, Vorläufer des Wortes *Gott*, war sächlich. Es bezeichnete ein »göttliches Wesen«, weder weiblich noch männlich. »Liebes Gott«, mögen unsere Vorfahrinnen gebetet haben, »mach daß es ein Mädchen wird!«

September 1982

Mitgliederinnen

Vor drei Jahren hörte ich das Wort zum erstenmal – von einem (männlichen) Sprachwissenschaftler. Ich dachte, ich hätte mich verhört. Er aber, aktives Mitglied einer stark profeministischen Berliner Männergruppe, schien nie etwas anderes gehört zu haben als – *Mitgliederinnen*. Die Berliner Szene! An mein Provinz-Ohr dringen die neusten Creationen eben relativ spät.

Ich redete auf ihn ein, später auch auf die vielen Frauen, die immer wieder von irgendwelchen »Mitgliederinnen« sprachen. »*DAS Mitglied*«, dozierte ich, »ist doch eine der wenigen nun wirklich geschlechtsneutralen Personenbezeichnungen, die wir haben! Ihr nennt doch Mädchen auch nicht *Kinderinnen* und reserviert *Kinder* für Jungen!«

Meine Gesprächspartnerinnen waren wenig beeindruckt und sagten weiter *Mitgliederinnen*. Andere wieder meinten: »*Mitgliederinnen*? Auch nicht besser als *Mitglieder*! Wir können es nicht mehr hören, das Wort *Glied*! Und wieso überhaupt ›mit Glied‹??! Wir Frauen sind ›ohne Glied‹, und darauf sind wir stolz!«

Mitglied also als Bezeichnung für das männliche Geschlecht, *Ohneglied* für das weibliche? – Diese Idee hat sich, soweit ich informiert bin, nicht durchsetzen können. Zu negativ das ganze Wort. Sollen wir uns etwa auch noch selbst definieren als diejenigen, denen etwas fehlt? Noch dazu sowas? Nein danke!

Also auf ins Positive! Was hat das weibliche Geschlecht dem »Glied« entgegenzusetzen? – Das Wort war schnell gefunden: *Mitklit* von *Klit* wie *Klitoris*. (Und für den Herrn macht sich dann vielleicht *Ohneklit* ganz bezaubernd?)

Na schön. Manche mögen's eben klar und deutlich.

Doch die meisten von uns sind ja mit ihrem weiblichen Schamgefühl geschlagen. Im Büro, in der Schule, im Betrieb, in der Uni will das kühne Wort *Mitklitoris* uns einfach nicht so selbstverständlich von den Lippen. Manche lösen das Problem vielleicht mittels der Kurzform *Mitklit*, die von »den anderen« garantiert als »Mitglied« gehört wird. Uralte weibliche Taktik: das Kühne so tun, daß es möglichst niemand merkt und wir ungeschoren davonkommen.

Eine Bekannte schrieb mir neulich, sie sage seit einiger Zeit nur noch *Mitfrau*: »Der Verein ›Frauen und Kultur‹ hat schon 37 zahlende Mitfrauen.« Auch nicht schlecht!

Ich finde es eindrucksvoll, wie bunt es zur Zeit in der deutschen Sprache zugeht. Wo es früher nur ein einziges Wort gab – *Mitglied/er* –, hab' ich jetzt die Auswahl zwischen

Mitglied(er)in / Mitgliederinnen
Mitklit, Mitklitoris
Ohneglied
Mitfrau
Mitglied/er

Und doch finde ich auch etwas Bedenkliches an dieser munteren Wortschöpferei. Ihr **Anlaß** scheint mir eine übertriebene Konzentration auf das männliche Glied zu sein. Haben wir das nötig, frage ich mich bestürzt. Harmlose Wörter wie *Gliederung*, *Gliedmaßen*, *gliedern*, *eingliedern* – fällt uns etwa auch dazu nur der Penis ein, so daß weitere sprachliche Säuberungsaktionen angeraten sind? Wir sagen ja den Männern nach, **sie** dächten immer nur an »das eine«. Weibliche Wortschöpfungen wie *Ohneglied* und *Mitklitoris* legen den Verdacht nahe, daß auch Frauen noch entschieden zu oft daran denken.

Diese besorgten Zeilen schreibt euch eine, die zur Zeit in der Möse wohnt – so heißt nämlich der Ortsteil des Dorfes Niedermehnen, wohin ich mich zurückgezogen habe. Die männliche Dorfbevölkerung hat bisher keine Umbenennung in Richtung »Glied« oder »Pimmel« oder was weiß ich verlangt. Und die Frauen finden auch nichts dabei, in der Möse zu wohnen. Für sie alle ist das eben seit Jahrhunderten einfach ein Ortsteil und kein Geschlechtsteil.

Ich gestehe, daß ich diese souveräne Gelassenheit noch nicht erreicht habe. Aber ich finde sie nachahmenswert.

Oktober 1982

Das vibrierende Weib

Die deutsche Sprache ist uns manchmal zu eng, manchmal zu weit – richtig passen tut sie selten. Sie ist ja auch nicht von/für uns gemacht.

Für erwachsene weibliche Personen gibt es gleich drei Bezeichnungen: *Frau*, *Dame* und *Weib* – für erwachsene männliche Personen hingegen nur zwei: *Mann* und *Herr*. Die Entsprechung für *Weib* fehlt bei den Herren. Sollen wir uns nun freuen über diese reichere Auswahl? Kaum – erstens ist *Weib* veraltet: **wenn** es benutzt wird, dann höchstens als Schimpfwort (»altes Weib«, »Klatschweib«, »Weibergeschwätz«). Zweitens ist es sächlich, und wir finden nun mal feminine Bezeichnungen netter für uns, weshalb wir auch *das Fräulein* abgeschafft haben (*das Mädchen* ist ein Fall, mit dem wir uns bald beschäftigen sollten/werden).

Obwohl nun das Substantiv *Weib* nicht mehr wie früher durch sämtliche Texte geistert, die von Frauen handeln, führen wir die Silbe *weib* doch beständig im Munde: *weiblich* und *Weiblichkeit* sind vermutlich neben *Frau* die in der Neuen Frauenbewegung hierzulande am häufigsten benutzten Wörter. Wir haben nämlich keine anderen. Die Ableitungsreihe für *Mann* heißt, schlicht und logisch: *männlich*, *Männlichkeit*. Für *Frau* dagegen heißt sie, kompliziert und unlogisch: *weiblich*, *Weiblichkeit*. *Fraulich* und *Fraulichkeit* können wir nicht verwenden, weil ihre Bedeutung zu eng ist und von vielen noch dazu als negativ empfunden wird. Wohingegen *weiblich* und *Weiblichkeit* wertfrei sind, im Gegensatz zu *Weib*. Findet ihr noch einigermaßen durch? Die Verwirrung stifte nicht etwa ich, sondern sie ist System. Die deutsche Sprache als Frauen-Verwirr-System.

Schlägt frau die Wörterbücher auf, um sich über den Ursprung der Verwirrung aufzuklären, so wird sie dies Ziel nicht erreichen, aber sie kann erstaunliche Entdeckungen machen. (Mach dir ein paar vergnügte Stunden – schlag nach unter *Weib*!) Was die Herren da wieder an Überraschungen für uns parat haben, ist schon einzig. Es ist nämlich bis heute nicht geklärt, auf welche Wurzel das Wort zurückgeht. Deshalb sind der »wissenschaftlichen« Spekulation Tor und Tür geöffnet. Und die sieht, etwa im Fall des Duden-Herkunftswörterbuchs, so aus: Vielleicht gehen *Weib* und *vibrieren* auf dieselbe Wurzel zurück (olala!). Das *Wei* von *Weib* steckt auch in dem Wort *Weide*, wo es soviel wie »sich drehen, winden« bedeutet.

Und nun die zwingende Schlußfolgerung, Originalton Duden: »›Weib‹ würde demnach eigtl. ›die sich hin und her bewegende, geschäftige (Haus)frau‹ bedeuten.«

Merke, oh Weib: **Wenn** frau sich schon bewegt, dann bitte nur im Hause und als Hausfrau.

November 1982

Gegrüßet seist du, Josef!

Die schöne Weihnachtszeit ist da und lädt uns ein, mal wieder über Maria und Josef nachzudenken. Sie waren ja in vieler Hinsicht ein denkwürdiges Paar. Wenn wir sie mit anderen berühmten Paaren vergleichen, z. B. mit Adam und Eva, Hänsel und Gretel, Caesar und Cleopatra, Dante und Beatrice, Abaelard und Héloise, Tristan und Isolde, Herodes und Mariamne, Hermann und Dorothea, Romeo und Julia – so steht dieses Paar, Maria und Josef, vollends einzigartig da: Wird doch diese Maria, obwohl bloß eine Frau, immer an erster Stelle genannt! *Josef und Maria*, das klänge uns so verquer in den Ohren wie *Isolde und Tristan* oder *Gretel und Hänsel* oder wie *quer und kreuz* statt *kreuz und quer*.

Es gibt viele Möglichkeiten, eine Rangordnung zu symbolisieren. In der bildenden Kunst z. B. geschieht es mittels der Größe und der Gruppierung im Vorder- bzw. Hintergrund. Die Hauptperson steht in der Regel im Vordergrund und ist größer dargestellt als die Nebenfiguren.

In der Sprache ist die *Reihenfolge* **das** Mittel, um die Rangordnung auszudrücken: Die Hauptperson oder Hauptsache wird an erster Stelle genannt, alle weiteren haben sich auf den darauffolgenden Plätzen zu arrangieren: *Vater, Sohn und Heiliger Geist. CDU/CSU.* Die Regierung *Schmidt/Genscher* bzw. *Kohl/Genscher. Er, sie, es. Vater und Sohn. Mutter und Kind. Bruder und Schwester. Mann und Frau. Herr und Frau Müller.* Du sollst *deinen Vater und deine Mutter* ehren.

Dies ist der graue Alltag und die graue Wirklichkeit: Die Frau an seiner Seite und auf ihrem, dem zweiten Platz, wo die Nebensachen eben hingehören. Damit der graue Alltag uns Zweitrangigen ein bißchen vergoldet werde, gibt es die Formen der Höflichkeit und die sogenannte Ritterlichkeit. »Ladies first« heißt es dann, und mann läßt uns den Vortritt. Die Festreden beginnen mit »Sehr geehrte Damen und Herren« – aber das Fest endet mit »Wein, Weib und Gesang«.

Und drittens gibt es, neben dem grauen Alltag und dessen gelegentlicher Verunklarung durch das Ladies-first-Gerede, drittens gibt es auch noch Wunder. Eine Frau wird Königin oder sogar

Muttergottes. (Päpstin? Nicht doch!) Frau und zweitrangig hin oder her, es hilft nix, sie muß auf den ersten Platz, der Mann auf den zweiten: Queen Victoria und Prinz Albert, Queen Elizabeth und Prinz Philip, Königin Beatrix und Prinz Claus.

Gegrüßet seist du, Maria! Aber du auch, Josef.

Dezember 1982

Die Zukunft ist weiblich?

Ein Professor der Psychologie schickte mir neulich folgenden Kommentar zu meinen »Aktivitäten in Sachen Sprache und Geschlecht«: Gegen diesen ausgesprochenen Feminismus und die von ihm propagierte Umwandlung der Sprache habe er doch einiges einzuwenden. Und außerdem heiße es immerhin *die* Sonne und *der* Mond. Das Hauptgestirn sei also im Deutschen – im Gegensatz zu den meisten anderen Sprachen – ein Femininum. Was doch wohl dafür spreche, daß das Weibliche durchaus nicht zweitrangig sei.

Viele Männer argumentieren so kindlich bis verworren, wie es dieser Professor tut. Unsere liebe Frau Sonne, Spenderin der Wärme, des Lichtes, ja des Lebens, sie ist weiblich – also gib dich schon endlich zufrieden, zänkisches Weib! Meist werden noch andere holde Weiblichkeiten mit angeführt: Mutter Erde, Mutter Natur, die Liebe, die Treue, die Freiheit, die Gerechtigkeit, die Weisheit, die Klugheit, die Stärke, die Kraft, die Kühnheit, die Kunst, die Musik, die Malerei und die Literatur. In den romanischen Sprachen ist sogar das Leben selbst weiblich: *La vie, la vita, la vida*.

Und die Dummheit? Die Schwäche? Die Falschheit? Die Verderbtheit? Die Niedertracht und die Heimtücke? Die Sünde, die Sucht und die Krankheit? Die Bosheit und die Gemeinheit? Klar, die sind auch alle weiblich, typisch weiblich sogar! Die Frau ist nun mal ein schillerndes, widersprüchliches, unergründliches Wesen.

Was nun den Mann betrifft – männlich sind der Mut, der Verstand, der Geist, der Genius (deutsch leider *das Genie*), der Kampf – und der Tod. Der Staat ist Vater Staat, und der Krieg ist der Vater aller Dinge. Und die Polizei? Sie ist nur aus Versehen weiblich. Das sehen wir schon daran, daß sie unser Freund und Helfer ist, nicht unsere Freundin etwa. Oder gar Helferin.

Wenn gilt »Die Zukunft ist weiblich«, so muß auch gelten »Die Vergangenheit und die Gegenwart sind weiblich«. Wollen wir das wirklich? **Diese** Gegenwart und **jene** Vergangenheit sollen auch noch weiblich sein?!

Es ist – natürlich – alles nicht ganz so simpel. Die Sprache, ebenfalls weiblich(?), ist viel zu kompliziert und komplex für so schlichte Zuschreibungen und Erklärungsversuche.

Die Menschen sind **nicht** herumgegangen und haben die »weiblichen« Dinge und Begriffe wie *Nadel* und *Liebe* mit einem Femininum belegt und die »männlichen« wie *Speer* und *Kampf* mit einem Maskulinum. Diese These vertrat die Sprachwissenschaft zwar noch im 19. Jahrhundert, aber sie ist inzwischen widerlegt, seit wir wissen, daß »der primitive Mensch«, der solcherart naiv benennend herumspaziert sein soll, nur in unserer überheblichen Einbildung existiert. Unhaltbar ist diese These auch, weil sie nicht erklärt, warum der »naiv personifizierende Mensch« Sprachen ausgebildet hat, die überhaupt kein grammatisches Geschlecht haben (z. B. Chinesisch, Türkisch, Mongolisch, Finnisch, Ungarisch).

Tatsache ist, daß in denjenigen Sprachen, die grammatisches Geschlecht haben, Frauen meist mit femininen und Männer mit maskulinen Wörtern bezeichnet werden. Tatsache ist weiterhin, daß die Genera (Geschlechter) auf den (gewaltigen!) »Rest«wortschatz **beliebig** verteilt sind und dort nichts, aber auch rein gar nichts, mit »weiblich« oder »männlich« im biologischen oder mythologischen oder irgendeinem sonstwie »einleuchtenden« Sinn zu tun haben. Im Deutschen ist der Tod »männlich«, im Französischen und Italienischen »weiblich«: *la mort, la morte*. Im Deutschen ist die Liebe »weiblich«, im Französischen und Italienischen ist sie »männlich«. Im Deutschen und Italienischen ist der Tisch »männlich«, im Französischen »weiblich«. Im Deutschen ist das Messer »sächlich«, im Französischen und Italienischen »männlich«.

Tatsache ist schließlich, daß wir alle (einschließlich jenes Psycho-Profs) dazu neigen, bei der Personifikation von Gegenständen und abstrakten Begriffen uns erstmal an das grammatische Geschlecht zu halten. Der Staat wird zu »Vater Staat«, weil es zufällig *der* Staat heißt (und auch sonst nicht ganz unpassend scheint!). In Cocteaus Film »Orphée« tritt der Tod als Frau auf, weil es im Französischen *la mort* heißt. Wir Deutschen hingegen kennen den »Gevatter Tod«, den Sensen*mann*. Und wir kennen Frau Sonne, die für den Hl. Franziskus, »natürlich«, Bruder Sonne war.

Übersetzen wir mal »Die Zukunft ist weiblich« ins Französische und Italienische: »Le futur est masculin.« – »Il futuro è maschile.« Klingt toll, nicht? Fast so schön wie: »Die Atombombe ist weiblich, und der Frieden ist männlich.«

Februar 1982

Der Richtige

Wann hat schon mal eine von uns 6 Richtige im Lotto angekreuzt?!
Ich kenne keine einzige. Anders bei den Wahlen – da haben wir es
seit Bestehen der Bundesrepublik insgesamt auf stolze 6 Richtige
gebracht: Adenauer, Erhard, Kiesinger, Brandt, Schmidt und
Kohl. Bei Kohl mußten wir noch nicht mal ein Kreuzchen machen
und bekamen trotzdem den Richtigen.

Sonst immer diese enttäuschende und langweilige Warterei auf
»den Richtigen«, der dereinst kommen soll und doch nie in Sicht ist
– hier, in der Politik, ist dafür gesorgt, daß wir weder warten noch
wählen müssen, sondern auf jeden Fall einen abkriegen, und zwar
den Richtigen. Weil in der Politik *der* Richtige eben automatisch
das Richtige ist für uns. *Die* Richtige dagegen – wie das schon
klingt! Genauso paradox wie *die Staatsfrau*, *die Regierungsfrau-
schaft* oder *der Schwangere*.

Deshalb brauchen wir uns auch um den 6. März gar keine Gedanken zu machen. Ob gewählt wird oder nicht, ob wir rot, grün,
braun, schwarz, tiefschwarz oder gar nicht wählen – *der* Richtige
ist uns auf jeden Fall gewiß. Er fällt uns in den Schoß, ob wir ihn da
haben wollen oder nicht.

Wer die Wahl hat, hat die Qual. Und die Wahl hat in unserem Lande, gerne Vaterland genannt, der Wähler. Nur er muß sich mit der
Frage abquälen, welche der diversen Männerriegen seine Interessen am besten vertritt. Uns Frauen bleibt alle Qual erspart, in diesem unserem Lande.

Unserem?

März 1983

Dieter Lattmensch

Im Jahre 1980 haben meine Kolleginnen Guentherodt, Hellinger, Trömel-Plötz und ich in der Fachzeitschrift *Linguistische Berichte* »Richtlinien zur Vermeidung sexistischen Sprachgebrauchs« veröffentlicht. Vergleichbare Richtlinien gibt es in den USA schon seit über zehn Jahren. Große Verlage und Berufsorganisationen lehnen z. B. den Abdruck von Manuskripten ab, wenn sie nicht den Richtlinien entsprechend formuliert sind.

Auch in der Bundesrepublik gibt es große Organisationen, die sich von Berufs wegen mit Sprache befassen. Eine von ihnen ist der Verband deutscher Schriftsteller (*sic*). Bundesvorsitzender dieses Verbandes von 1969–73 war Dieter Lattmann. 1968 war er Präsident der Bundesvereinigung deutscher Schriftstellerverbände. Von 1972–80 war er Mitglied des Bundestags (SPD).

Am 13. Februar 1983 sendete der Hessische Rundfunk einen 10-Minuten-Kommentar von Dieter Lattmann über unsere Richtlinien. O-Ton Lattmann:

> Als Mann von heute, verunsichert durch Feminismus, wie es sich gehört, habe ich hinreichend begriffen: Will ich meinem Geschlecht nicht auch noch mißbräuchlich in der Sprache frönen, muß ich vor allem auf die Endungen achten. [. . .] Ein solches Programm schüchtert Leute wie mich nur noch zusätzlich ein. Weiß ich doch ohnehin nicht, wie ich es bei der Wortwahl richten soll, um nicht ständig als Chauvi dazustehen. [. . .] Mit subjektiver Erfahrung hat jene Generalverdammnis für mich ohnehin kaum etwas zu tun, denn, wie so viele meinesgleichen, wurde ich von Kindesbeinen an über die Schule bis ins Private und zum Teil selbst im Beruf eher von zugreifender Weiblichkeit als von entschiedenen Männern geprägt. (Armer Dieter – selbst im Beruf?!)
> Nun hat, genau besehen, ein solches Programm auch seine Tükken: wenn nämlich . . . die ›Männer des 20. Juli‹ durch die ›Frauen und Männer‹ ersetzt werden, hapert es mit der Geschichte. [. . .] Andererseits bleibt es wohl allzu vordergründig verstanden, wollten die Linguistinnen ernstlich . . . die ›Woche der Brüderlichkeit‹ durch die ›Woche der Menschlichkeit‹ aus-

tauschen, denn mit dem biblischen Bruder ist seit alters wie auch mit Jungfrau und Mutter etwas umfassender Menschliches gemeint. (Na gut – einigen wir uns also auf ›Woche der Mütterlichkeit‹?)

Die Sprache ist in Bewegung. Sie korrigiert das Antiquierte und weiß sich selber Rat. Diesen Prozeß gilt es zu fördern. Aber nicht ihm durch neue Restriktion Gewalt anzutun. (Immer diese gewalttätigen Frauen!)

Stellt sich doch uns Dieter hin – und blamiert sich öffentlich bis auf die Knochen. Weibliches Mitleid regte sich in mir, und ich schrieb ihm einen langen Brief voll kostenloser Nachhilfe. Wies ihn z. B. darauf hin, daß wir die schöne Formulierung ›Die Frauen und Männer des 20. Juli‹ seinem Genossen Helmut Schmidt verdanken, bei dem es anscheinend weniger mit der Geschichte hapert als beim Genossen Lattmann. Und so weiter und so fort.

Dieter zeigte sich erkenntlich mit zwei Sätzen auf einer Postkarte: »Da Sie sich die Mühe gemacht und mir ziemlich ausführlich … geschrieben haben, möchte ich mich wenigstens dafür bedanken. Vielleicht bin ich kein guter ›Gegner‹, weil in der Regel lieber ein Mensch, als nur ein Mann.«

Mai 1983

Eine halbe Sekretärin

In der *Zeit* vom 27. Mai 83 (S. 34) schreibt Joachim Dyck, Professor für Neuere deutsche Literaturwissenschaft an der Universität Oldenburg:

> Die meisten Kollegen, die jetzt die 50 überschritten haben, wurden auf Lehrstühle berufen, die »ausgestattet« sind: eine Sekretärin (mindestens eine halbe), eine wissenschaftliche Hilfskraft, einen Assistenten zur persönlichen Verfügung.

Von dem Wort *ausgestattet* distanziert sich der Professor, indem er es in Gänsefüßchen setzt. Er bedient sich zwar der gängigen Ausdrucksweise, gibt aber gleichzeitig zu verstehen, daß er sie nicht recht passend findet. Warum, das erfahren wir nicht. Meine Vermutung: Der Professor weiß auch, daß eine Ausstattung normalerweise aus Dingen, Ausstattungs*stücken*, besteht. Ein Zimmer wird mit Möbeln ausgestattet. Hier aber wird ein Möbelstück mit Menschen ausgestattet: mit einer Sekretärin, einer Hilfskraft, einem Assistenten. Und das findet der Professor vielleicht auch etwas unfreundlich diesen Menschen gegenüber, selbst wenn mit ihnen kein x-beliebiger Stuhl, sondern ein Lehrstuhl ausgestattet wird.

So weit, so feinfühlig. Schließlich darf mensch von einem Literaturprofessor auch eine gewisse Sprachsensibilität erwarten – dafür wird er ja bezahlt.

Die halbe Sekretärin dagegen bekommt von ihm keine distanzierenden Gänsefüßchen, mit denen sie sich über ihre Totalverstümmelung oder Zersägung (oder wie soll ich mir diese arme halbierte Frau vorstellen?) hinwegtrösten könnte. Halbe Sekretärinnen findet der Professor völlig normal. Kein Grund, das Sprachsensibelchen hervorzukehren. Und daß die Kollegen drei Unter-Menschen *zu ihrer persönlichen Verfügung* haben, findet er auch nicht gänsefüßchenreif.

Nur ein kurzer Satz – aber er hat es in sich! *Die Kollegen*, *der Assistent* treten als Maskulina auf. Nun wissen wir aber, daß der Professor auch Kolleg*innen* hat, wenn auch nur ganz wenige, und daß es auch ein paar Uni-Assistent*innen* gibt. Ob ihr Kollege sie einfach übersehen hat oder ob sie sich »mitgemeint« fühlen sollen, das verrät der Satz nicht. An anderer Stelle des Textes wird es noch rätselhafter. Da heißt es über Hochschullehrer, sie hätten »Probleme mit Frau oder Freund«. Darf der Hochschullehrer heutzutage statt Frau auch schon mal einen Freund haben? Oder bezieht sich das *oder Freund* auf die Hochschullehrer*in*, von der man ja weiß, daß sie es nicht zu einem Ehemann bringt, höchstens zu einem Freund?

Da fruchtloses Grübeln ungesund ist, halten wir uns lieber an die weniger dunklen Stellen des Textes. Sonnenklar ist jedenfalls, daß die *Sekretärinnen*, ob halbiert oder unversehrt, eine geschlossene weibliche Gesellschaft bilden. In diesen Kreis der Halbierbaren verirrt sich kein Mann.

Ein Lied aus uralten Zeiten, das geht mir nicht aus dem Sinn:

> Seht ihr die Mondin stehen?
> Sie ist nur halb zu sehen
> Und ist doch rund und schön.

Juli 1983

Frauen und Lesben?

Seit einiger Zeit gibt es an einigen deutschen Universitäten »Frauen- und Lesbenreferate«. Die Uni Oldenburg hat damit angefangen, sagten mir stolz die Frauen des dortigen Referats. Die sonst übliche Bezeichnung »Frauenreferat« hätte ihnen nicht zugesagt, weil sie die vielen mitarbeitenden und anzusprechenden Lesben unsichtbar läßt.

Viele Frauen an der Uni sind Lesben, und obwohl es »natürlich« keine Statistik gibt, weiß jede frauenbewegte Unifrau, daß Lesben sowohl in den Frauenreferaten als auch allgemein unter Studentinnen und Dozentinnen prozentual weit stärker vertreten sind als in der weiblichen Gesamtbevölkerung. Auch ich finde es daher sehr wichtig, daß lesbe sprachlich endlich sichtbar wird entsprechend ihrem Rang.

Also alles prima mit der Erweiterung des »Frauenreferats« zum »Frauen- und Lesbenreferat«? Ich finde nein!

Frauen und Lesben – das ist, bedeutungsmäßig, eine total absurde Konstruktion, ähnlich wie *Südfrüchte und Apfelsinen*, denn Lesben **sind** bekanntlich Frauen und Apfelsinen **sind** Südfrüchte. Wenn die Konstruktion nur absurd wäre, könnte es ja noch angehen – absurd kann ja sehr schön und witzig und erfrischend sein. Aber diese Konstruktion ist nicht nur absurd, sie ist gefährlich.

Im Dritten Reich machten die Nazis aus Deutschen plötzlich »Deutsche und Juden« (»Deutsche, wehrt euch gegen die Juden!«). Einige Deutsche waren nun »sprachlich sichtbar« als *Juden*, abgesetzt von den anderen Deutschen, als ob sie nicht dazugehörten. Und einige Frauen sind jetzt sprachlich sichtbar als *Lesben*, abgesetzt von den anderen Frauen, als ob sie keine wären.

Der Mensch und seine Frau – **wie** lange kämpfen wir schon gegen diese unverschämte sprachliche Ausgrenzung des weiblichen Geschlechts. Und nun unterläuft uns fast dasselbe – noch dazu in bester Absicht!

Was ist also zu tun? Erstens müssen wir die Bezeichnung *Frauen- und Lesbenreferat* schleunigst wieder abschaffen (Frauen sind auch nur Menschen, und Irren ist menschlich!). Zweitens müssen wir eine neue Formulierung finden, die das richtige Gewollte nicht in derart falscher, weil diskriminierender Weise zum Ausdruck bringt.

Ich finde z. B. *Feministisches Referat* eine passable Lösung. Feministinnen sind sowieso als Lesben verschrien – diesen Umstand könnten wir uns positiv zunutze machen. *Schwesternreferat* fänd ich aus ähnlichen Gründen auch nicht schlecht. Oder vielleicht *Frauenfreundinnenreferat*? Dem sprachlich bereits bestens eingebürgerten *Frauenfeind* träte positiv die *Frauenfreundin* gegenüber – noch dazu schön doppelsinnig oder breitbandsinnig, so breit wie das Spektrum weiblicher Empfindungen. Ob die Frauenfreundin sich als Freundin im zärtlichsten oder im bloß politischen Sinne verstehen will, bleibt ihr überlassen.

Wißt ihr noch andere, bessere Vorschläge? Und was meint ihr überhaupt zu dem Problem? Eure Meinung würde mich sehr interessieren.

Nachschrift

Irgendwo habe ich gelesen, daß es in Dänemark seinerzeit mit der Aussonderung der jüdischen Bevölkerung durch die Nazis nicht geklappt hat, weil der dänische König ostentativ den Judenstern trug. Nach diesem Vorbild wäre es **auch** eine Lösung, die Frauenreferate einfach *Lesbenreferate* zu nennen.

September 1983

Scham und Schande

»Sitz nicht so da, man kann ja deine ganze Schande sehen!« – Eine Schweizerin erzählte mir, daß kleine und auch größere Mädchen in der Schweiz noch heute so angeherrscht werden. Die Schriftstellerin Marlene Stenten berichtet, in ihrer Familiensprache hätte »das« *Baba Stink* geheißen.

Und welches Wort gab es in meiner Familie »da«für? Gar keins. Es gab nur die schamvoll umschreibenden Ortsangaben. Die neuen Jeans waren vielleicht »im Schritt« zu eng, und »zwischen den Beinen«, »unterrum« oder »da unten« hatten wir uns sauberzuhalten. Auf der anderen Seite sollten wir uns »die Nase« putzen und nicht etwa »in der Gesichtsmitte«. Schlaue und beängstigende Folgerung schon früh, bevor wir es dann endgültig erfuhren: »Zwischen den Beinen«, da war etwas Widerliches, zu widerlich, um es auch nur auszusprechen.

Dann kam der Biologieunterricht. Die äußeren Geschlechtsteile der Frau (also unsere) hießen: *Scham* (aha!) – mit folgenden *Schamteilen*: *Schamhaar*, *Schamhügel*, große *Schamlippen*, kleine *Schamlippen*. Für den Mann hörte das Schämen schon beim Schamhaar auf. Der Rest hieß nicht etwa *Schamstengel* und *Schambeutel*, sondern *Glied* und *Hoden*.

Der nächste Lernschritt war, daß das Besitzen einer »Scham« fast automatisch die »Schande« nach sich zog, wenn wir nicht höllisch aufpaßten, denn junge Mädchen konnten »geschändet« werden von »Sittenstrolchen« oder »entehrt« von ehrbaren Männern. Und unsere »Ehre« hing paradoxerweise direkt mit unserer »Scham« zusammen.

Eine schwierige Sprache, schwer zu begreifen. Da gab es einerseits den Film »Susi und Strolch« mit einem ganz süßen Strolch, anderseits die Sittenstrolche. Und wenn die Sittenstrolche uns »mißbrauchten«, dann waren **wir** geschändet, nicht sie. Und die ehrbaren Männer »entehrten« **uns** durch selbigen Mißbrauch, nicht sich selbst. Anscheinend waren wir mitsamt unserer »Scham« ein Genußmittel wie Alkohol oder Nikotin. Nur daß der Alkoholmißbrauch die Mißbrauchenden selbst in Schimpf und Schande brachte, doch nicht den Alkohol!

Eine Sprache von Verrückten, geeignet, selbst die Vernünftigste

verrückt zu machen. Es wird Zeit, daß wir die Sprach- und Macht-
haber nicht mehr alleine werkeln lassen. Venus steigt auf den Ve-
nushügel und lächelt mit ihren süßen Venuslippen: »*Scham* – wat is
dat denn? Ach so, Sie meinen *Charme*!«

April 1983

Wir leben im Matriarchat!

In den Industrienationen hat die Gebärfreudigkeit der Frauen letzthin erschreckend nachgelassen. Während noch bei unseren Groß- und Urgroßmüttern 10–20 Kinder keine Seltenheit waren, ziehen die meisten von uns die Null-Lösung vor. Wo aber nichts hervorgebracht wird, kann auch nichts wachsen! Und vom Wachstum hängt schließlich unser aller Wohlergehen ab.

Da also die Frauen sich so schnöde ihrer Gebärpflicht entziehen, hat die Industrie selbst diese Aufgabe übernommen. Die Industrie ist, anders als unsere wahllos drauflosgebärenden Großmütter, auf Effektivität bedacht. Sie produziert grundsätzlich nichts Unrentables – also keine Söhne, denn die können ja nun mal nichts aus sich selbst hervorbringen, diese Wachstums-Flops. Die Industrie gebiert nur Töchter, streng parthenogenetisch, denn diese Methode verursacht den geringsten Aufwand. Die Töchter heißen Tochtergesellschaften. Wenn eine Firma oder Gesellschaft oder ein Konzern eine solche Tochter geboren hat, darf sie sich Muttergesellschaft, Mutterfirma oder Mutterkonzern nennen. Bringt die Tochtergesellschaft wieder eine Tochter hervor, wird die Tochter-Tochter auch wohl Enkelin genannt. Die Firma Icmesa in Seveso ist z. B. eine Enkelin der Hoffmann-La Roche. Nun mag die Hoffmann-La Roche zwar zahllose Enkelinnen haben, deshalb ist sie aber noch lange keine Oma-Gesellschaft. Knackig wie sie ist, produziert sie noch laufend eigene Töchter – Urbild einer vitalen Mutter in den allerbesten Jahren und Umständen. Wir müssen also unterscheiden zwischen altmodischen Müttern, die noch Töchter **und** Söhne gebären und Gefahr laufen, irgendwann auch mal Oma zu werden, und jenen ewigjungen Müttern, denen die Zukunft gehört, weil sie sich auf das Wesentliche konzentrieren.

Da suchen wir immer nach Spuren des Matriarchats in der grauen Vorzeit – und haben es direkt vor unserer Nase! Ein Matriarchat von geradezu utopischer Kühnheit und Konsequenz. Kein männliches Wesen ward jemals gesehen in diesem vor Gebärlust vibrierenden Mütter-Töchter-Clan. Nicht mal bei Hochzeiten (auch Fusionen genannt) – und was sind das doch für gewaltige Mammutti-Hochzeiten!

Ja, die Industrie, diese hocheffiziente Supermutter, ist mindestens so schlau wie eine Krebsgeschwulst. Die bringt nämlich auch nur Tochtergeschwülste hervor, denn nur die garantieren weiteres Wachstum. Von einer Sohngeschwulst ist mir noch nie etwas zu Ohren gekommen.

Juni 1983

Ich bestätige hiermit die Empfängnis
Ihres geschätzten Kindes

Der Mann ist aktiv, er ist derjenige, der Neues schafft. Die Frau ist passiv, sie ist die Empfängliche und Empfangende.

Woher mann das so genau weiß? Na! Betrachten wir doch mal denjenigen Vorgang, der als der schöpferische schlechthin gilt: die Erschaffung des Menschen. Die beiden ersten Menschen erschuf Gott (ob *die* oder *der* oder *das* Gott, lassen wir hier mal offen). Alle weiteren Menschen erschuf der Mann. Wer es nicht glauben will, die hat zu viel Medizin studiert und zu wenig die Bibel und »unsere« »Mutter«sprache. Diese beiden wirklich ehr- und vertrauenswürdigen Quellen lassen keinen Zweifel daran, daß der Mann der *Erzeuger* der Kinder ist – auf Neudeutsch: ihr Produzent. Er *erzeugt* sie mittels seines *männlichen Samens. Samen* braucht Nähr- oder *Mutterboden*, damit daraus etwas entstehen kann. Wenn für den männlichen Samen gerade keine *Gebärmutter* zur Hand ist, genügt auch eine Nährlösung und ein Brutkasten, und nach neun Monaten ist das Kind fertig.

Doch nicht? Da fehlt noch was? Die weibliche Eizelle etwa? Ja dann ist aber doch der männliche Same gar kein richtiger Same, denn aus richtigem Samen entsteht das Neue, es muß nur noch ein bißchen ernährt werden.

Der männliche Same ist auch kein richtiger Same. Er heißt nur so. Und damit wir Frauen komplett vernebelt würden, wurde früher nicht nur die männliche Keimzelle, die ohne die weibliche gar nichts bringt, »Samen« genannt, sondern auch die gesamte Nachkommenschaft. Zum Beispiel »Abrahams Samen«.

Kommen wir vom Samen zur Empfängnis. Wer empfängt was? *Sie* empfängt ein Kind von *ihm*. Üblicherweise muß ich ja, wenn ich etwas empfange, etwa ein Paket, einen Brief, eine Radio- oder Fernsehsendung, das Empfangene nicht selbst herstellen. Wär ja auch noch schöner! Vielmehr kriege ich es fix und fertig geliefert. Nicht so, wenn ich ein Kind empfange. Da empfange ich nichts außer dem männlichen »Samen«, der mit echtem Samen etwa soviel Ähnlichkeit hat wie ein falscher Hase mit einem richtigen. Den »Rest« darf ich selbst erledigen.

Wer jetzt noch daran zweifelt, daß der Mann aktiv und schöpferisch ist und die Frau passiv und empfangend, die ist eben selbst schuld.

Juli 1983

Bettnässen und Busengrapschen

»Das funktionelle Bettnässen stellt eine (beibehaltene oder wieder aufgenommene) Verhaltensstörung dar, die im allgemeinen auf eine falsche Erziehung, auf mangelndes Anpassungsvermögen, seelische Unausgeglichenheit oder eine neurotische Erkrankung des Kindes zurückzuführen ist« (Meyers Enzyklopädisches Lexikon).

Das nenne ich eine klare ernste Sprache, nüchtern und sachlich, kurz: dem Leiden angemessen. Zum besseren Einprägen nochmal die Kernbegriffe: *Verhaltensstörung*, *falsch*, *mangelndes Vermögen*, *unausgeglichen*, *neurotisch*, *Erkrankung*.

Obwohl der Säugling beständig ins Bett macht, hat er zwei Jahre Schonfrist. Erst wenn er es dann immer noch tut, wird er »Bettnässer« geschimpft und so energisch therapiert, daß die Störung normalerweise bald abklingt. Erwachsene Bettnässer sind äußerst selten, heißt es.

Wie wir wissen, nässen Säuglinge nicht nur Bett und Windel, sondern sie grapschen auch nach Mamas Busen. Auch dies wird während der Schonfrist nicht als krankhaft definiert. Spätestens im Alter von zwei Jahren jedoch sollte den Kleinen das Busengrapschen wie das Bettnässen abgewöhnt sein. Bei Mädchen gelingt in der Regel beides problemlos, während Knaben sich fast durchweg als gestört erweisen und es hinsichtlich des Busengrapschens oft bis ins Greisenalter bleiben.

In den letzten Wochen ist diese peinliche männliche Geschlechtskrankheit durch den Fall eines einschlägig gestörten grünen Abgeordneten Gegenstand öffentlicher Debatten geworden. Allerdings läßt die Debatte vorerst noch den nötigen Ernst vermissen. So nennt beispielsweise *Emma* den Gestörten humorig »den grünen Busenfreund«. Würde wohl *Emma* einen armen Bettnässer »feuchtfröhlich« nennen oder ähnlich? Und *Courage* spricht von einem »Grapschtick«. Würde *Courage* wohl das Bettnässen als »Pinkelmarotte« verharmlosen?

Daß die Gestörten selbst ihre Störung verniedlichen würden, war dagegen zu erwarten (sie verwenden das von Bettnässern her bekannte Bagatellisierungsvokabular wie »Aufbauschen«, »Nichtigkeit«, »Sehnsucht nach Wärme« und so weiter).

Halten wir fest: Unsere Männer sind verhaltensgestört. Wir müssen diese Krankheit endlich ernst nehmen. Denn die Erfahrung lehrt: Wer Busen grapscht, der macht auch ins Bett (Alte Ammenweisheit).

Oktober 1983

Stramme Leistung

»Sie trägt keinen BH, und sie kann es sich leisten«, hieß es neulich in der *Funk-Uhr* über Joan Collins, die in der TV-Serie »Denver-Clan« die Alexis Carrington spielt. Wie schön für Joan Collins, daß sie sich das, was sie tut, auch leisten kann. Das fachmännische Urteil stammt übrigens von einer Frau, Frances Schoenberger, die allerdings mit keinem Sterbenswörtchen verrät, **wieso** die Collins sich das leisten kann.

Ist ja auch nicht nötig, weil sowieso alle wissen, was gemeint ist. Der Busen der Collins wird halt einer von der zulässigen Sorte sein. Kein Hängebusen, wie er an unsereiner peinlich herunterbaumelt. Und auch kein Winzbusen, den frau mittels eines ausgestopften Büstenhalters zu einer ordentlichen Büste erst aufdonnern muß.

Warum heißt das Ding eigentlich »Büstenhalter« (in der Schule, noch fern von der Pubertät und dem Ernst des Lebens, nannten wir es verächtlich »Busenschoner«)? Unter einer Büste stelle ich mir eher Beethoven in Gips auf dem Klavier vor. Und warum wird der Büstenhalter zu »BH« abgekürzt? Hosenträger heißen doch auch nicht »HT«. Sagen wir vielleicht: »Unser BH (Buchhalter) hat mir neulich einen KH (Kerzenhalter) geschenkt«? Was ist der Unterschied zwischen einem Büsten- und einem Buchhalter, daß der eine abgekürzt wird und der andere nicht?

Nun, der Büstenhalter **ist** eben intim, und der Buchhalter **wird** höchstens mal intim. Ein Buchhalter und ein Kerzenhalter können sich sehen lassen, ein Büstenhalter eben nicht. Deswegen wird er zum BH versachlicht, verunkenntlicht, entschärft oder was. Damit wir es uns leisten können, darüber zu sprechen, was wir uns leisten können.

November 1983

Angehübscht

In Nordrhein-Westfalen hat es sich ausgehübscht. Justizministerin Inge Donnepp tritt im Dezember zurück, und dann gibt es keine Frau mehr in der NRW-Regierung.

Die Frauen in Nordrhein-Westfalen, die nun wieder von einer ausgewogenen Männerriege regiert werden, wurden von Ministerpräsident Rau und dem SPD-Fraktionsvorsitzenden Denzer getröstet, »die nächstes Jahr zu bildende Mannschaft für den Wahlkampf werde gleich mit mehreren Frauen angehübscht sein«. So wörtlich in der *Neuen Westfälischen* vom 5. 10. 83.

Gleich mit mehreren – Donnerwetter! Die unscheinbare deutsche Sprachpartikel *gleich* (klein, aber oho!) hat u. a. die Funktion, die Überschreitung einer Grenze, eines Maßes (oft die Erfüllung eines Übersolls) anzuzeigen:

Wenn man ihm den kleinen Finger gibt, nimmt er gleich die ganze Hand.

Sie sollte zwei Sätze streichen und strich gleich die ganze Seite.

Ohne das *gleich* klängen diese Sätze viel weniger »maßlos«.

Die »gleich mehreren Frauen« sind ja auch ein maßloses Entgegenkommen!

Und erst das *angehübscht!* Zunächst einmal impliziert diese raffinierte Kreation, daß die Mannschaft jetzt nicht hübsch ist. Denn genauso wenig wie eine dicke Soße noch angedickt werden kann, kann eine hübsche Mannschaft noch angehübscht werden. Eine Mannschaft darf auch gar nicht hübsch sein, weil ein Mann nicht hübsch sein darf, ein Politiker schon gar nicht. Ein Mann ist höchstens »gutaussehend«, bei »schön« wird es problematisch, und »hübsch« ist nur was für Frauen, Kinder und Gegenstände.

Ob wohl diese unhübsche Mannschaft schon dadurch »angehübscht« wird, daß überhaupt Frauen darin vorkommen sollen? Oder müssen die Frauen auch noch selber hübsch sein? Eine Soße wird mit Mehl angedickt, aber das Mehl selber ist nicht »dick«. Trotzdem glaube ich, daß die Trostspender an hübsche Frauen gedacht haben. Maßlos wie sie sind in ihrem Entgegenkommen, finden sie sicher jede Frau, eben weil sie eine Frau ist, hübsch.

Das *an-* in dem *angehübscht* hat es mir angetan! Ein *an*gefressenes Blatt ist noch ziemlich intakt, ein *an*gelesenes Buch noch lange nicht ausgelesen. Und eine wenn auch angehübschte Mannschaft bleibt im Kern, wie und was sie sein soll: eine Mann-schaft.

Dezember 1983

Postfrische Brüder

Das Briefmarkensammeln ist, ähnlich wie das Sammeln von Münzen, ein ausgesprochen männliches Hobby. Frauen finden es anscheinend sinnvoller, sich um die Zähnchen der lieben Kleinen zu kümmern als um die Zähnchen von Briefmarken. Dabei haben Frauen das Briefmarkensammeln im vorigen Jahrhundert erfunden. Allerdings sammelten sie, ihrer weiblich-oberflächlichen Natur entsprechend, die bunten Bildchen weder systematisch noch als interessante Geldanlage, sondern aus Freude am Dekorativen – etwa um damit lustig die Wände des Salons oder des Kinderzimmers zu bekleben.

Bald darauf aber nahm der Mann die Sache in die Hand, begründete die zähnchenzählende »Wissenschaft« Philatelie, und prompt wurde die Briefmarke zur »Aktie des kleinen Mannes«.

Spätestens seit Hitler, Himmler und Konsorten wissen wir: Der »kleine Mann« ist oft alles andere als harmlos. Und sein scheinbar so friedlich-besinnlicher, auf uns Frauen oft kindisch wirkender Kult mit »seiner Aktie«, der Briefmarke, ist auch überhaupt nicht harmlos.

Seltenheit, nicht mehr Schönheit, ist schon lange absoluter Trumpf in der Philatelie. Die paar erhaltenen Briefstücke aus Auschwitz, Treblinka und anderen Konzentrationslagern (am liebsten mit Zensurvermerk!) erzielen auf Auktionen höchste Preise.

Sehr selten ist auch »Katastrophenpost« – eins der exklusivsten Sammelgebiete. Welche Freude für den Sammler, wenn er ein Stück aus Postsäcken abgestürzter Flugzeuge, untergegangener Schiffe und verunglückter Eisenbahnen ergattert. Auch Kriege, Taifune, Hochwasser- und Erdbebenkatastrophen »liefern« beliebte und vor allem wertvolle Sammelobjekte. Katastrophenpost aus Euroshima, so es sie denn geben wird, wird mit Sicherheit *der* Hit bei unseren amerikanischen Freunden.

Wir mögen das alles pervers finden – aber uns fehlt eben der Durchblick! Pervers ist höchstens das, was manche so über ehrenwerte Briefmarkensammler denken. Da schreibt ein Leser an die Zeitschrift *Phila-Report* im Okt. 83 unter der Überschrift »Briefmarken und Sex«:

»Darf ich Ihnen mal meine Briefmarkensammlung zeigen, junge Frau?« Kein Ausdruck wird so häufig mißverstanden wie dieser: Die meisten meinen, er deute auf irgend etwas, während er in Wahrheit nur auf Philatelie deutet. Dennoch ähneln sich Frauen und Briefmarken mehr, als man gemeinhin glaubt: Die ungestempelten Exemplare sind oft begehrter und beschädigte Exemplare sind wertlos. Einen wesentlichen Unterschied allerdings gibt es – zum Glück: Frauen sind keine Briefmarken.«

Frauen *können* ja auch keine Briefmarken sein, du Schlaumeier – weil nämlich Briefmarken Männer sind, genauer gesagt: Brüder!

»Anhand der Katalogisierungen können Sie außerdem feststellen, daß sich langfristig gestempelte Wohlfahrtsmarken im Preis besser entwickeln als ihre postfrischen Brüder.«

So die *Siegerpost*, »Deutschlands Briefmarkenzeitschrift mit der höchsten Auflage«, Heft 307, 1983, S. 35.

Januar 1984

Explosion einer geschundenen Seele

In der Serie »Verbrechen in Deutschland« der *Welt am Sonntag* berichtete Alex Baum am 13. 11. 1983 unter dem Titel »Einer 26jährigen Pädagogin war ihre Karriere wichtiger als ihre Familie« über den »Tod einer emanzipierten Frau«. Die emanzipierte Frau, Roswitha Dengler, starb in der Nacht vom 9. zum 10. Januar 1983. Die Gerichtsmedizin stellte fest,

> daß Roswitha Dengler an zentraler Lähmung infolge Gewalteinwirkung am Hals (Würgen) verstorben sei.

Der Ehemann, Ulrich Dengler, sagt,

> es sei zu einer Tätlichkeit gekommen, in deren Verlauf er seine Frau weggeschubst habe. Dabei sei sie zu Boden gefallen, und er habe feststellen müssen, daß sie tot sei.

Weiter lesen wir in dem Bericht:

> Ulrich Dengler legte seine tote Frau ins Bad und verschloß es, damit sein Sohn Florian von der Sache nichts erfahre. Am folgenden Morgen frühstückten die beiden gemeinsam, und am Nachmittag, als Florian schlief, brachte er die unbekleidete tote Frau in den Keller und verstaute sie in Müllsäcken.

Wir erfahren nicht, wie dem zartfühlenden Mordspapa das Frühstück schmeckte, warum er die Tote nackt auszog und was das »verstaute sie in Müllsäcken« zu bedeuten hat. Wie »verstaut« man eine Tote in Müllsäcken (damit sie in den Kofferraum paßt, wo die Polizei sie schließlich fand)? Mich packt Grauen, Entsetzen ... Von einem Beil, einer Säge ist nirgends die Rede, aber von einer Explosion:

> In der Nacht explodierte die geschundene Seele dieses Mannes. Bei einem Streit kam seine Frau ums Leben.

»Geschunden« war die Seele dieses Mannes, so lesen wir, weil er

> sein Lebensideal darin sah, für seine Frau und seinen Sohn zu sorgen. Er opferte sich für die Seinen – bis er zum Pantoffelhelden wurde.

... er wusch Geschirr, wusch die Wäsche (auch die seiner Frau), plättete, nähte, wischte Staub und putzte die Treppe. Er hatte einen 20-Stunden-Tag.

Seine Frau aber dankte es ihm nicht, daß er auch ihre Wäsche wusch, sondern wollte einen Vertrag unterschreiben, der

ihr ein Doktorat zusicherte und sie zu einer Ganztagsstelle als wissenschaftliche Hilfskraft an der Universität verpflichtete. Ulrich Dengler war maßlos enttäuscht – – –

– – – und so kam es denn, wie es kommen mußte: Seine Seele explodierte, und infolge dieser Gewalteinwirkung an ihrem Hals verstarb seine emanzipierte Frau.

Es ist klar, daß allein die Frau an dieser Explosion schuld ist, deren Folgen ihr armer Mann jetzt auslöffeln muß. Aber

Er kann wahrscheinlich mit milden Richtern rechnen. Sein Anwalt ... über seinen Mandanten: »Ein bemitleidenswerter Mann, der Held einer modernen Version der griechischen Tragödie vom unschuldig Schuldigwerden.«

(Dank an Ulrike Hofmann für den Hinweis auf diesen Zeitungsartikel.)

Februar 1984

Zeichenerklärung

*   bedeutet: Der Ausdruck, vor dem das Zeichen steht, ist ungrammatisch. Zum Beispiel:
> * *Wo sein die Bahnhof?*

?   bedeutet: Der Ausdruck, vor dem das Fragezeichen steht, ist seltsam, abweichend, »nicht ganz normal«. Zum Beispiel:
> ? *Du hast so schöne blonde Augen!*

⇒, ⇏ bedeutet: »wird zu« bzw. »wird nicht zu«.
Der Doppelpfeil symbolisiert (Transformations-)Beziehungen zwischen Ausdrücken. Zum Beispiel:
> *als sie ankam* ⇒ *bei ihrer Ankunft*
>   ⇏ *bei seiner Ankunft*

Bibliographie

Bartsch, Miša. 1982. *Sprachwandel unter dem Einfluß der Frauenbewegung*. Unveröff. Magisterarbeit. Universität Konstanz.

Baudouin de Courtenay, Jan. 1929. »Einfluss der Sprache auf Weltanschauung und Stimmung.« *Prace Filologiczne* 14, 185–255.

Baumann, Peter und Ortwin Fink. 1979 (1976). *Wie tierlieb sind die Deutschen?* Frankfurt/M. Fischer TB 3013.

Behrens, Katja. Hg. 1981. *Frauenbriefe der Romantik*. Frankfurt/M. Insel TB 545.

Benz, Ute. 1982. *Sexistische Inhalte in einem Französischlehrbuch*. Unveröff. Magisterarbeit. Universität Konstanz.

Berger, Brigitte und Peter L. Berger. 1974. *Individuum & Co. Soziologie beginnt beim Nachbarn*. Stuttgart. Übs. Monika Plessner. (= *Sociology. A Biographical Approach*. London 1972).

Berger, Peter L. und Thomas Luckmann. 1966. *The social construction of reality*. New York. Deutsch: *Die gesellschaftliche Konstruktion der Wirklichkeit. Eine Theorie der Wissenssoziologie*. Frankfurt/M. 1969. Fischer TB 6623. 1980.

Berthold, Luise. 1958. »Ein unausrottbarer Sprachgebrauch?«. *Mädchenbildung und Frauenschaffen* 1958/8.

Berthold, Luise. 1964 (1981). »Sprachliche Glossen zur Gleichberechtigung«. *Der Sprachdienst* 1981/1, 3–5.

Berthold, Luise. 1983. »Weiblichkeitswahn und Männlichkeitswahn«. *Der Sprachdienst* 1982/5–6, 79–80.

Beuys, Barbara. 1980. *Familienleben in Deutschland. Neue Bilder aus der Vergangenheit*. Reinbek bei Hamburg.

Binnick, Robert I., Alice Davison, Georgia M. Green und Jerry L. Morgan. Hg. 1969. *Papers from the fifth regional meeting of the Chicago Linguistic Society, April 18–19, 1969*. Chicago.

Blumenberg, Werner. 1962. *Karl Marx in Selbstzeugnissen und Bilddokumenten*. Reinbek bei Hamburg. Rowohlts Monographien 76.

Böttger, Fritz. Hg. 1979 (1977). *Frauen im Aufbruch. Frauenbriefe aus dem Vormärz und der Revolution von 1848*. Darmstadt, Neuwied.

Borst, Arno. 1979 (1973). *Lebensformen im Mittelalter*. Frankfurt, Berlin, Wien. Ullstein TB 34004.

Brantenberg, Gerd. 1980. *Die Töchter Egalias. Ein Roman über den Kampf der Geschlechter*. Berlin. Übs. Elke Radicke. (= *Egalias døtre*. Oslo 1977).

Brehmer, Ilse. Hg. 1981. *Sexismus in der Schule*. Weinheim, Basel.

Brehmer, Ilse. 1983. »Was ist feministische Pädagogik?« in: Pusch. Hg. 1983. S. 367–376.

Brinkmann, Hennig. ²1971. *Die deutsche Sprache. Gestalt und Leistung.* Düsseldorf.

Buttorf, Douglas und Edmund L. Epstein. Hg. 1978. *Women's language and style. Studies in contemporary language* 1. Department of English, University of Akron, Ohio.

Cantrall, William. 1974. *Viewpoint, reflexives, and the nature of noun phrases.* Den Haag.

Carstensen, Broder. 1978. »Wörter des Jahres 1977«. *Der Sprachdienst* 1978/1, 1–8.

Carstensen, Broder. 1979. »Wörter des Jahres 1978«. *Der Sprachdienst* 1979/2, 17–24.

Carstensen, Broder. 1980. »Wörter des Jahres 1979«. *Der Sprachdienst* 1980/2, 17–23.

Carstensen, Broder. 1981. »Wörter des Jahres 1980«. *Der Sprachdienst* 1981/2, 17–31.

Carstensen, Broder. 1982. »Wörter des Jahres 1981«. *Der Sprachdienst* 1982/1–2, 1–16.

Cooper, William E. und John Robert Ross. 1975. »World order«, in: Grossman, San und Vance. Hg. 1975. S. 63–111.

Dingeldein, Heinrich J. und Hans Friebertshäuser. 1983. »Luise Berthold zum Gedenken«. *Der Sprachdienst* 1983/11–12, 172.

Duden Bedeutungswörterbuch (Duden Bd. 10). Bearbeitet von Paul Grebe, Rudolf Köster, Wolfgang Müller und weiteren Mitarbeitern der Dudenredaktion. Mannheim 1970.

Duden Fremdwörterbuch (Duden Bd. 5). 3., völlig neu bearbeitete und erweiterte Auflage. Mannheim 1974.

Durkheim, Emile. 1897. *Le suicide.* Deutsch: *Der Selbstmord.* Neuwied 1970.

Elias, Norbert. ²1969. *Über den Prozeß der Zivilisation. Soziogenetische und psychogenetische Untersuchungen.* Zweiter Band: *Wandlungen der Gesellschaft. Entwurf zu einer Theorie der Zivilisation.* Bern.

Engel, Eduard. 1918. *Entwelschung. Verdeutschungswörterbuch für Amt, Schule, Haus, Leben.* Leipzig.

Fischer-Fabian, S. 1981. *Ein Hauch von Seligkeit. Die Frauen großer Dichter.* München, Zürich. Knaur TB 793.

Förster, Uwe. 1978 a. »Wortzuwachs und Stilempfinden im Deutsch der siebziger Jahre«. *Der Sprachdienst* 1978/5, 65–69.

Förster, Uwe. 1978 b. »Wortzuwachs und Stilempfinden im Deutsch der siebziger Jahre (Fortsetzung)«. *Der Sprachdienst* 1978/6, 84–88.

Frauenjahrbuch '76. München 1976. Frauenoffensive.

Friday, Nancy. 1979. *Wie meine Mutter*. Übs. Ute Seesslen. Frankfurt/M. (= *My mother my self*. New York 1977.)

Fromm, Erich. 1973. *The anatomy of human destructiveness*. New York.

Genius, Adolf. ²1912. *Neues großes Fremdwörterbuch*. Regensburg.

Götze, Alfred. 1918. *Wege des Geistes in der Sprache* (= *Volksbücher zur Deutschkunde* 1). Leipzig.

Goffman, Erving. 1967. *Stigma. Über Techniken der Bewältigung beschädigter Identität*. Übs. Frigga Haug. Frankfurt/M. (= *Stigma. Notes on the management of spoiled identity*. Englewood Cliffs, N.J. 1963).

Gollwitzer, Helmut, Käthe Kuhn und Reinhold Schneider. Hg. 1954. *Du hast mich heimgesucht bei Nacht. Abschiedsbriefe und Aufzeichnungen des Widerstands 1933–1945*. München, Hamburg. Siebenstern TB 9.

Goop, Margrit. 1982. *Sprachkritik in der Frauenbewegung am Beispiel der Zeitschrift ›Courage‹, 1981*. Unveröff. Lizentiatsarbeit. Universität Basel.

Grieser, Dietmar. 1980 (1978). *Piroschka, Sorbas & Co. Schicksale der Weltliteratur*. Frankfurt/M. Fischer TB 2214.

Grossman, Robin E., L. James San und Timothy J. Vance. Hg. 1975. *Papers from the parasession on functionalism, April 17, 1975*. Chicago Linguistic Society. Chicago.

Guentherodt, Ingrid. 1980. »Behördliche Sprachregelungen gegen und für eine sprachliche Gleichbehandlung von Frauen und Männern«. *Linguistische Berichte* 69, 22–36.

Guentherodt, Ingrid, Marlis Hellinger, Luise F. Pusch und Senta Trömel-Plötz. 1981. »Richtlinien zur Vermeidung sexistischen Sprachgebrauchs«. *Linguistische Berichte* 71, 1–7.

Günthner, Susanne. 1982. *Praktizierte feministische Sprachkritik – am Beispiel dreier Verständigungstexte*. Unveröff. Zulassungsarbeit zur wiss. Prüfung in Germanistik für das Lehramt an Gymnasien. Universität Konstanz.

Harweg, Roland. 1973. »Involvierende und evolvierende Prädikatbildung«. *Linguistische Berichte* 25, 39–46.

Hellinger, Marlis. 1980 a. »Zum Gebrauch weiblicher Berufsbezeichnungen im Deutschen. Variabilität als Ausdruck außersprachlicher Machtstrukturen«. *Linguistische Berichte* 69, 37–58.

Hellinger, Marlis. 1980 b. »›For men must work, and women must weep‹: sexism in English language textbooks used in German schools«. *Women's studies international quarterly* 3.2/3, 267–275.

Henzen, Walter. 1965. *Deutsche Wortbildung*. Dritte, durchgesehene und ergänzte Auflage. Tübingen.

Heuser, Magdalene. Hg. 1982. *Frauen – Sprache – Literatur. Fachwissenschaftliche Forschungsansätze und didaktische Modelle und Erfahrungs-*

berichte für den Deutschunterricht (= *Informationen zur Sprach- und Literaturdidaktik* 38). Paderborn, München, Wien, Zürich.

Hiatt, Mary P. 1976. »The sexology of style«. *Language and style* 9.2, 98–107.

Hoffmann, Ulrich. 1979. *Sprache und Emanzipation. Zur Begrifflichkeit der feministischen Bewegung.* Frankfurt/M., New York.

Jacobs, Roderick A. und Peter S. Rosenbaum. Hg. 1970. *Readings in English transformational grammar.* Waltham, Mass., Toronto, London.

Kalverkämper, Hartwig. 1979. »Die Frauen und die Sprache«. *Linguistische Berichte* 62, 55–71.

Key, Mary Ritchie. 1975. *Male/Female Language.* Metuchen, N.J.

Koenigs Großes Wörterbuch der Deutschen Sprache. Bearb. und hg. von Theodor Voigt und Richard Zoozmann. Berlin 1912.

Koesters, Paul-Heinz. 1982. *Deutschland deine Denker. Geschichten von Philosophen und Ideen, die unsere Welt bewegen.* München. Goldmann-STERN-Bücher 11 509.

Kohut, Heinz. 1973. *Narzißmus. Eine Theorie der psychoanalytischen Behandlung narzißtischer Persönlichkeitsstörungen.* Frankfurt/M.

Kramarae, Cheris. 1981. *Women and men speaking. Frameworks for analysis.* Rowley, Mass.

Kuno, Susumo. 1975. »Three perspectives in the functional approach to syntax«, in: Grossman, San und Vance. Hg. 1975. S. 276–336.

Kuno, Susumo. 1976. »Subject, theme, and the speaker's empathy. A reexamination of relativization phenomena«, in: Li. Hg. 1976. S. 417–444.

Kuno, Susumo und E. Kaburaki. 1975. *Empathy and syntax*, in: *Formal Linguistics.* Report No. NSF-30. Department of Linguistics. Harvard University.

Lahnstein, Peter. 1977 (1970). *Report einer »guten alten Zeit«. Zeugnisse und Berichte 1750–1805*. München. dtv 1290.

Laing, Ronald D. 1961. *The self and others.* London.

Lakoff, George und Mark Johnson. 1979. *Toward an experiential philosophy. The case from literal metaphor.* Vervielfältigt. 55 S. University of California, Berkeley.

Lakoff, George und Mark Johnson. 1980. *Metaphors we live by.* Chicago.

Lakoff, Robin. 1973. »Language and women's place«. *Language in society* 2, 45–80.

Lakoff, Robin. 1975. *Language and women's place.* New York.

Lewis, David. 1969. *Convention. A philosophical study.* Cambridge, Mass.

Li, Charles N. Hg. 1976. *Subject and Topic.* New York.

Looff, Friedrich Wilhelm. 1899. *Allgemeines Fremdwörterbuch*. Langensalza.

Ljungerud, Ivar. 1973. »Bemerkungen zur Movierung in der deutschen Gegenwartssprache. Eine positivistische Skizze«, in: *Linguistische Studien* 3 (= *Sprache der Gegenwart* 23). S. 145–162. Düsseldorf.

Luckmann, Thomas. 1979. »Soziologie der Sprache«, in: René König. Hg. 1979. *Handbuch der empirischen Sozialforschung*. Bd. 13: *Sprache, Künste*. S. 1–116. Stuttgart. dtv wiss. Reihe 4248.

Lunde, Katrin und Luise F. Pusch (in Vorbereitung): *Gerd Brantenbergs ›Egalias døtre – Die Töchter Egalias‹. Eine kontrastive feministisch-linguistische Analyse Norwegisch : Deutsch.*

Matthiesen, Hayo. 1970. *Friedrich Hebbel in Selbstzeugnissen und Bilddokumenten*. Reinbek bei Hamburg. Rowohlts Monographien 160.

McConnell-Ginet, Sally, Ruth Borker und Nelly Furmann. Hg. 1980. *Women and language in literature and society*. New York.

Mead, George Herbert. 1934. *Mind, self, and society*. Chicago.

Meyers enzyklopädisches Lexikon in 25 Bänden. Bd. 8: Enz-Fiz. Mannheim 1973.

Miller, Alice. 1979. *Das Drama des begabten Kindes und die Suche nach dem wahren Selbst*. Frankfurt/M.

Miller, Casey und Kate Swift. 1976. *Words and women. New language in new times*. New York.

Miller, Casey und Kate Swift. 1980. *The handbook of non-sexist writing. For writers, editors, and speakers*. New York.

Moulton, Jane, George Robinson und Christina Elias. 1978. »Sex bias in language use. ›Neutral‹ pronouns that aren't«. *American Psychologist* 33.11, 1032–1036.

Müller, Gerhard und Helmut Walther. 1983. »Momentaufnahmen. Beobachtungen zum sprachlichen Geschehen 1982«. *Der Sprachdienst* 1983/1–2, 1–24.

Mulch, Roland. 1981. »Das Hessen-Nassauische Volkswörterbuch. Luise Berthold 90 Jahre«. *Der Sprachdienst* 1981/1, 1f.

Nilsen, Alleen Pace et al. 1977. *Sexism and language*. Urbana, Illinois.

Nohr, Karin et al. 1983. »Rollenstereotypisierung im Grammatikunterricht. Analyse moderner deutscher Schulgrammatiken und Sprachbücher und Empfehlungen für den Umgang mit ihnen im Grammatikunterricht«. Referat bei der 5. Jahrestagung der Deutschen Gesellschaft für Sprachwissenschaft in Passau, März 1983.

Opitz, Claudia. Hg. 1984. *Weiblichkeit oder Feminismus? Beiträge zur interdisziplinären Frauentagung Konstanz 1983*. Weingarten.

Plank, Frans. 1979. »Zur Affinität von *selbst* und *auch*«, in: Weydt. Hg. 1979. S. 265–284.

Postal, Paul M. 1969. »Anaphoric islands«, in: Binnick, Davison, Green und Morgan. Hg. 1969. S. 205–239.

Pusch, Luise F. 1978. »Die sprachliche Darstellung von Ausdruckshandlungen oder Brauchen wir eine Etholinguistik?« Unveröff. Ms. 20 S.

Pusch, Luise F. Hg. 1983. *Feminismus. Inspektion der Herrenkultur. Ein Handbuch*. Frankfurt/M. edition suhrkamp 1192.

Radel, Jutta, Hg. 1982. *Liebe Mutter – Liebe Tochter. Frauenbriefe aus drei Jahrhunderten*. Frankfurt/M., Berlin, Wien. Ullstein TB 20230.

Römer, Ruth. 1973. »Grammatiken, fast lustig zu lesen«. *Linguistische Berichte* 28, 71–79.

Ross, John Robert. 1970. »On declarative sentences«, in: Jacobs und Rosenbaum. Hg. 1970. S. 222–277.

Sarges, Heidrun. 1983. »Frauen und Mathematik – Mädchen und Mathematikunterricht«, in: Pusch. Hg. 1983. S. 340–366.

Saussure, Ferdinand de. 1916. *Cours de le linguistique générale*. Lausanne. – Benutzte Ausgabe: *Grundfragen der allgemeinen Sprachwissenschaft*. Hg. v. Charles Bally und Albert Sechehaye. Unter Mitwirkung von Albert Riedlinger übs. v. Hermann Lommel. Berlin [2]1967.

Schulz, Muriel R. 1975. »The semantic derogation of women«, in: Thorne und Henley. Hg. 1975. S. 64–75.

Schulz, Muriel R. 1978. »A style of one's own«, in: Buttorf und Epstein. Hg. 1978. S. 75–83.

Sollwedel, Inge. 1970. »Das neue Frauenbild in den Lesebüchern«. *Informationen für die Frau* 19, 6–8.

Spender, Dale. 1980. *Man made language*. London. Boston, Henley.

Sperr, Monika. Hg. 1981. *Liebe Mutter, liebe Tochter. Frauenbriefe von heute*. München.

Spitz, René. 1965. *The first year of life. A psychoanalytical study of normal and deviant development of object relations*. New York.

Staiger, Emil. [8]1968. *Grundbegriffe der Poetik*. Zürich.

Stanley, Julia P. 1977. »Gender-marking in American English: Usage and reference«, in: Nilsen et al. 1977. S. 43–74.

Stefan, Verena. 1975. *Häutungen. Autobiographische Aufzeichnungen, Gedichte, Träume, Analysen*. München.

Thorne, Barrie und Nancy Henley. Hg. 1975. *Language and sex. Difference and dominance*. Rowley, Mass.

Trömel-Plötz, Senta. 1978. »Linguistik und Frauensprache«. *Linguistische Berichte* 57, 49–68.

Trömel-Plötz, Senta. 1979. *Frauensprache in unserer Welt der Männer*. Konstanz.

Trömel-Plötz, Senta. 1980. »Sprache, Geschlecht und Macht«. *Linguistische Berichte* 69, 1–14.

Trömel-Plötz, Senta. 1982. *Frauensprache – Sprache der Veränderung.* Frankfurt/M. Fischer TB 3725.

Trömel-Plötz, Senta. Hg. (im Druck): *Gewalt durch Sprache. Die Vergewaltigung von Frauen in Gesprächen.* Frankfurt/M.

Wahrig, Gerhard. 1974. *Großes deutsches Wörterbuch.* Rheda.

Watzlawick, Paul. 1967. *Pragmatics of human communication. A study of interactional patterns, pathologies, and paradoxes.* New York.

Wellmann, Hans. 1975. *Deutsche Wortbildung. Typen und Tendenzen in der Gegenwartssprache.* Zweiter Hauptteil: *Das Substantiv.* Düsseldorf.

Werner, Fritjof. 1983. *Gesprächsverhalten von Frauen und Männern.* Frankfurt/M., Bern.

Weydt. Harald. Hg. 1979. *Die Partikeln der deutschen Sprache.* Berlin, New York.

Wienold, Götz. 1967. *Genus und Semantik.* Meisenheim.

Wilmanns, W. ²1899. *Deutsche Grammatik.* Bd. II: *Wortbildung.* Straßburg.

Yaguello, Marina. 1978. *Les mots et les femmes. Essai d'approche sociolinguistique de la condition féminine.* Paris.

Zumbühl, Ursula. 1981. »Unterricht in Englisch und Sexismus«. *Linguistische Berichte* 76, 90–103.

Nachweise

Der Mensch ist ein Gewohnheitstier, doch weiter kommt man ohne ihr. *Eine Antwort auf Kalverkämpers Kritik an Trömel-Plötz' Artikel über »Linguistik und Frauensprache«* erschien 1979 in *Linguistische Berichte* 63, 84–102, und wurde leicht überarbeitet.

Der Piloterich. Ein Beitrag der außerirdischen Linguistik ist eine bearbeitete und gekürzte Fassung des Artikels »Die männliche Gruppe als referenzsemantische Grundeinheit«, der 1980 in *Linguistische Arbeiten und Berichte, FU Berlin* 15, 178–181, erschien.

Das Deutsche als Männersprache. Diagnose und Therapievorschläge erschien 1980 im Sonderheft »Sprache, Geschlecht und Macht I« der *Linguistischen Berichte* 69, hg. von Senta Trömel-Plötz und mir, S. 59–74. Nachdruck in *Heuser* 1982. Eine auf zwei Drittel gekürzte Fassung erschien im Mai 1981 in der *Basler Zeitung (Magazin)*. Der Artikel wurde für diesen Band leicht überarbeitet.

»Eine männliche Seefrau! Der blödeste Ausdruck seit Wibschengedenken«. Über Gerd Brantenbergs »Die Töchter Egalias« erschien 1981 als Rezension, ohne Titel, im Sonderheft »Sprache, Geschlecht und Macht II« der *Linguistischen Berichte* 71, hg. von Senta Trömel-Plötz und mir, S. 74–79. Geringfügige Änderungen für diesen Band.

Frauen entpatrifizieren die Sprache. Feminisierungstendenzen im heutigen Deutsch. Eine auf die Hälfte gekürzte Fassung erschien am 26. 6. 1982 im *Magazin* der *Basler Zeitung*, S. 6–7, unter dem Titel »Eine Wasserfrau ist kein Wassermann. Frauen entpatrifizieren die deutsche Sprache«.

Weibliches Schicksal aus männlicher Sicht. Über Syntax und Empathie. Eine auf zwei Drittel, d. h. um die technisch-linguistische Argumentation gekürzte Fassung erschien am 11. 5. 1983 im *Magazin* der *Basler Zeitung*, S. 6–7, unter demselben Titel.

Feminismus und Frauenbewegung. Versuch einer Begriffsklärung. Bearbeitete und gekürzte Fassung eines Aufsatzes, der unter demselben Titel als Einleitung des Sammelbandes *Feminismus. Inspektion der Herrenkultur* (*Pusch* 1983) erschien.

»Sie sah zu ihm auf wie zu einem Gott« – *Das DUDEN-Bedeutungswör-terbuch als Trivialroman* erschien zuerst in *Der Sprachdienst* 1983/9–10, S. 135–142. Nachdruck in *Opitz* 1984.

Die Glossen erscheinen seit Februar 1982 monatlich in der Zeitschrift *Courage*.

Feminismus
Inspektion der Herrenkultur
Ein Handbuch
Herausgegeben von Luise F. Pusch

edition suhrkamp 1192
554 Seiten

Was ist Feminismus? Feminismus ist eine Frage: gestellt von den falschen Personen (Frauen) an die falschen Adressen (Politik, Militär, Wissenschaft usw.) zu jeder unpassenden Gelegenheit. Die Frage lautet: Was haben *wir* davon? Sie zerstört die Fundamente des Patriarchats.

Das Handbuch versammelt Aufsätze feministischer Wissenschaftlerinnen über ihre Arbeitsgebiete und deren von Männern verantwortete Defizite.

Mit Beiträgen von Cheryl Benard, Cheryl Benard/Edit Schlaffer, Ilse Brehmer, Marliese Dobberthien, Christiane Erlemann, Esther Fischer-Homberger, Heide Göttner-Abendroth, Marlies Gummert, Magdalene Heuser, Petra Karin Kelly, Berta Lösel-Wieland-Engelmann, Renate Möhrmann, Judith Offenbach, Luise F. Pusch, Janet Radcliffe Richards, Eva Rieger, Rosemarie Rübsamen, Heidrun Sarges, Herrad Schenk, Christiane Schmerl, Hannelore Schröder, Dorothee Sölle, Senta Trömel-Plötz, Ulrike Stelzl, Marianne Wex.

edition suhrkamp. Neue Folge

Neue Historische Bibliothek
Hg. von Hans-Ulrich Wehler